Academic Freedom in a Plural World

Academic Freedom in a Plural World

Global Critical Perspectives

Edited by
Nandini Ramanujam and Frédéric Mégret

CEU PRESS

Central European University Press
Budapest–Vienna–New York

Published in 2024 by
Central European University Press

Nádor utca 9, H-1051 Budapest, Hungary
Tel: +36-1-327-3138 or 327-3000
E-mail: ceupress@press.ceu.edu
Website: www.ceupress.com

ISBN 978-963-386-653-5 (hardcover)
ISBN 978-963-386-654-2 (ebook)

Library of Congress Cataloging-in-Publication Data

Names: Mégret, Frédéric, editor. | Ramanujam, Nandini, editor.
Title: Academic freedom in a plural world : global critical perspectives / Edited by Nandini Ramanujam and Frédéric Mégret.
Description: Budapest ; New York : Central European University Press, [2024] | Includes bibliographical references and index.
Identifiers: LCCN 2024032696 (print) | LCCN 2024032697 (ebook) | ISBN 9789633866535 (hardback) | ISBN 9789633866542 (adobe pdf)
Subjects: LCSH: Academic freedom--History. | Democracy and education. | Education and globalization. | BISAC: EDUCATION / Comparative
Classification: LCC LC72 .A44 2024 (print) | LCC LC72 (ebook) | DDC 378.1/213--dc23/eng/20240808
LC record available at https://lccn.loc.gov/2024032696
LC ebook record available at https://lccn.loc.gov/2024032697

Contents

Acknowledgments

The authors' are grateful to the International Institute of Education's (IIE) Vartan Gregorian Fund for its generous support to this book project. We thank all the at-risk scholars hosted by our center who have served as an inspiration for this project. Our continued engagement with the Scholars at Risk Network, IIE's Scholar Rescue Fund, and the New University in Exile Consortium has served as an impetus to frame the discourse and practice of academic freedom in a global context.

McGill University and the Faculty of Law have lent us unequivocal support throughout this project. Our sincere gratitude to Dr. Vishakha Wijenayake and Nicolas Kamran for their steadfast support from its conception until the end.

Chapter 1

Introduction

Nandini Ramanujam and Frédéric Mégret

Academic freedom may seem like it has never been so intensely challenged. The concept appears at times as if it is ill-loved, ill-understood, and ill-protected. Academic freedom is not only violated but is also increasingly contested. There is no doubt that considerable pressures have come to bear on universities that vie to reshape their function. In that respect, pressures on academic freedom must also be seen as part of a broader crisis of universities. Over the past decade alone, the rise and ubiquity of digital media; profound changes in global academic flows; rankings; competition over students; and social networks have all contributed to a profound transformation not only of universities but also of discourses about universities.

At the same time, the discourse about academic freedom has a life of its own. The sense of academic freedom being "under siege" may be exaggerated for political ends. Moreover, why and how academic freedom is under threat is not always clearly understood. The range of threats against academic freedom is typically broader and diverse than various sectoral or national approaches suggest. Understanding this is a first step to exploring how academic freedom's importance might be reassessed in more complex and nuanced terms than has sometimes been the case.

The inspiration for this book came at a time when the authors—the codirectors of McGill University's Centre for Human Rights and Legal Pluralism—were made to be particularly alert to the precariousness of academic freedom. The Centre for Human Rights and Legal Pluralism, which hosted a series of events that eventually gave rise to this book, has long been involved in the Scholars at Risk program, providing refuge to a number of academics no longer capable of engaging in their work in their universities and sometimes fleeing their country. We are mindful of the extraordinary risks that academics with independent views can face. At the same time, the Centre has over the years hosted events involving contentious issues that led it to experience first-hand the sensitivity of questions of academic freedom.

It can seem at times as if academic freedom is a topic about which everything has been said already and yet its contours remain blurry and, perhaps more importantly, contested. It has certainly spun a considerable literature of a historical, political scientific, philosophical, moral, sociological, and legal nature.[1] Rather than a work of normative or political theory, this book has sought to engage in an analysis of the diversity of threats to academic freedom as they emerge and in their context. The point is of course not to be exhaustive but to think critically about a number of emblematic situations or incidents where claims about academic freedom being curtailed have precipitated ongoing efforts to refine it. The intuition is that academic freedom lives and is sustained through a variety of practices and that only by erring fairly close to those practices can one discern its contours.

In other words, the idea is to produce a better understanding of academic freedom, paradoxically, through a careful understanding of challenges to it. Instead of the exercise of endless theoretical refinement of definitions, it may be that it is when we see academic freedom being violated, threatened, or reneged upon that we produce better conceptualizations of its core meaning. But we also want to caution against a vision of academic freedom as being merely and constantly attacked. We will also use the term "challenged" here to reflect the fact that some violations of academic freedom are also quite explicitly attempts to contest and shift its definition and are, therefore, not always best understood as violations. Moreover, in addition to the negative dimensions of various assaults on academic freedom, it bears emphasizing that it is also, in perhaps less spectacular ways, constantly upheld, supported, and promoted.

1 One book published in 2000 and devoted only to surveying the field of existing writings already gives an indication of how relatively vast that literature was at the time; see Stephen H. Aby and James Kuhn, *Academic Freedom: A Guide to the Literature* (New York: Bloomsbury, 2000). The literature has arguably grown significantly since then.

The Present Moment

Although the book has no strict temporal framework, it attempts to capture the particular moment within which it was conceived. The point is not that threats to academic freedom are anything new. Indeed, much can be gained from examining some of the current instances under the light of previous episodes, for example, the Cold War. In fact, several of the chapters go back in time to understand some of the origins of academic freedom and the legacies we have to reckon with. One is reminded that academic freedom is, as a specific institutional principle, not that old and that its protection was long legally uncertain and ad hoc. Many universities were in fact not historically devoted to the unadulterated pursuit of free inquiry but, more often than not, dedicated to shaping a dominant orthodoxy and training students in its mannerisms. It is generally the rise of modern universities in the nineteenth century, notably the Humboldtian model of higher education, that is credited with entrenching the principle in the West.

Even then, however, the rise of academic freedom as a defining principle of scholarly pursuit was a slow one. It would also be wrong to think that the ushering in of modernity dealt a death blow to obscurantist or authoritarian forces dedicated to suppressing academic freedom. Protections of academic freedom in some countries or universities are of recent vintage and some are clearly wanting. While there has been considerable improvement in the degree of academic freedom enjoyed in previously authoritarian systems,[2] academic freedom is in essence a reversible progress. Globally, it has witnessed some notable "ups" and "downs" (with arguably an identifiable decline since the 2010s).[3] It is thus important to pay attention to the notion's historicity if only to understand it as correlated with broader developments in society.[4]

The changing fortunes of academic freedom are related to general social developments, but they are not reducible to them and must be seen as also significantly predicated on changes within the confines of the university.

2 See, e.g., Peter D. Eckel, *Governing Universities in Post-Soviet Countries: From a Common Start, 1991–2021* (Cambridge: Cambridge University Press, 2023); Maia Chankseliani, *What Happened to the Soviet University?* (Oxford: Oxford University Press, 2022).

3 Lars Lott, "Academic Freedom Growth and Decline Episodes," *Higher Education* (December 18, 2023).

4 Niclas Berggren and Christian Bjørnskov, "Political Institutions and Academic Freedom: Evidence from across the World," *Public Choice* 190 (2022): 205–228.

Throughout the twentieth century, at least some academics moved out of the ivory tower and into the political fray. As universities' power of influence over "young minds" and the connection between theoretical ideas and political praxis became clearer, questions have been asked about the political power that universities inevitably wield. Note the irony that in continuing such trends, academics have heeded the call for universities to be "relevant" and produce research that has a "high impact," even as outside actors may not always approve of the results. Nonetheless, it is fair to say that the intensity of questions about academic freedom has reached a fever pitch as a result of a combination of unusual forces.

The editors sensed, as others have,[5] that there is something in the current moment, and the particular maelstrom of challenges it triggers, that is at least specific if not unique. In this collection, the emphasis is certainly on the post–Cold War era but more specifically a postglobalization era inaugurated by 9/11 and marked by anxieties about climate change, an unanticipated return of populism, increased political polarizations, the COVID pandemic, the fear of radicalization, a global immigration crisis, the ubiquity of surveillance technology, or the rise of artificial intelligence. To these broad phenomena must be added a range of challenges specific to universities and institutions of higher learning, including their continued global attractiveness for students but also budgetary crises, politicization, "neoliberalization," "wokeness," remote learning, and so on. It is in the crucible of these different forces that academic freedom is being not only attacked or entrenched but also, perhaps most significantly, transformed.

Between Universalism and Fragmentation

Like many of today's debates, the question of academic freedom has become a global one, as a growing literature testifies.[6] The very notion of academic

5 Henry Reichman, *The Future of Academic Freedom* (Baltimore: Johns Hopkins University Press, 2019).

6 Risa L. Lieberwitz, "Higher Education and Academic Freedom: The Challenges of International and Comparative Research," *Bilgi Ekonomisi ve Yönetimi Dergisi* 3 (2008): 15–24; Niclas Berggren and Christian Bjørnskov, "Political Institutions and Academic Freedom: Evidence from across the World," IFN Working Paper No. 1388, Research Institute of Industrial Economics; Philip G. Altbach, "Academic Freedom: International Realities and Challenges," in *Tradition and Transition* (Leiden: Brill, 2007), 49–66; Simon Marginson, "Academic Freedom: A Global Comparative Approach," *Frontiers of Education in China* 9 (2014): 24–41.

freedom is the product of the academic circulation of ideas and certain conceptions of universities that have not always been evident but have gradually, through imposition, replication, or influence, spread across the world. One thing that testifies to that universalism is the actual historical spread of ideas of academic freedom from Germany to France, from Europe to the Far East, from metropolitan capitals to colonial possessions, and so on. One should not underestimate the degree to which academic freedom is a function of the slow effect of academic socialization and underpinned, ultimately, by the particular mores of discourse and respect of a transnational *république des lettres*. As Sophie Bisping emphasizes in her chapter in this collection, even the most local recent flareups around the question of academic freedom often have deep roots in a global question about the limits of academic speech.[7]

The debate itself, however, has tended to arise in quite national siloes, a reminder that universities have often been deeply involved in state-building projects and often coincide with particular national approaches to higher education. A considerable part of the discourse on academic freedom long emerged principally from the scholarly anglosphere or was devoted to specific countries only,[8] with relatively few comparative studies,[9] notably includ-

7 Bisping, "Academic Freedom and Social Justice in Quebec," this volume.

8 Michiel Horn, *Academic Freedom in Canada: A History* (Toronto: University of Toronto Press, 1998); Carolyn Evans and Adrienne Stone, *Open Minds: Academic Freedom and Freedom of Speech of Australia* (Melbourne: Black, 2021); Olivier Beaud, *Le savoir en danger: menaces sur la liberté académique* (Paris: Presses Universitaires de France, 2021); Terhi Nokkala and Agneta Bladh, "Institutional Autonomy and Academic Freedom in the Nordic Context: Similarities and Differences," *Higher Education Policy* 27 (2014): 1–21; Ernest Van den Haag, "Academic Freedom in the United States," *Law & Contemporary Problems* 28 (1963): 515; Arthur Schlesinger, "Academic Freedom: The Development of Academic Freedom in the United States," *Journal of Higher Education* 27 (June 1956): 338–350.

9 Margrit Seckelmann et al., eds., *Academic Freedom under Pressure? A Comparative Perspective* (Cham: Springer, 2021); Nokkala and Bladh, "Institutional Autonomy and Academic Freedom in the Nordic Context"; Valentina Moscon, "Academic Freedom, Copyright, and Access to Scholarly Works: A Comparative Perspective," in *Balancing Copyright Law in the Digital Age*, ed. Roberto Caso and Federica Giovanella (Berlin: Springer, 2015), 99–135; Ann Martin-Sardesai et al., "Government Research Evaluations and Academic Freedom: A UK and Australian Comparison," *Higher Education Research & Development* 36 (2017): 372–385; Marginson, "Academic Freedom"; Terence Karran, "Academic Freedom in Europe: A Preliminary Comparative Analysis," *Higher Education Policy* 20 (2007): 289–313; Ruchi Saini, "A Comparative Analysis of Academic Freedom within Higher Education Institutions (HEIs) in India and the USA," *Journal of Comparative and International Higher Education* 12 (2020): 37–44; Pio Ciprotti, "Comparative Insights in Matters of Academic Freedom," *Persona & Derecho* 6 (1979): 411; Rosamunde F. J. Becker, "Academic Freedom in England and Germany: A Comparative Perspective," *World Studies in Education* 7 (2006): 5–24.

ing the Global South.[10] This can give the dominant debate a strangely provincial and hegemonic outlook, even as a variety of global and transnational efforts are underway to protect academic freedom.

Nonetheless, for all the global spread of ideas about academic freedom, it remains crucial to understand their genesis and the challenges they raise against the background of local, national, and regional trajectories. Academic freedom is widely employed as a term, but it does point to a variety of cultural, social, and legal realities often closely connected to the particular histories of universities.[11] For example, in his chapter in this collection, Liviu Mattei emphasizes the specificity of the crisis of academic freedom in Europe as shown in the plight of Central European University or Turkish universities.[12] Zhidong Hao, in turn, highlights the extent to which academic freedom has deep roots in China even as the notion has Westernized and even as Chinese regimes' commitment to it has fluctuated.[13] Kwadwo Appiagyei-Atua insists on the extent to which Africa has long had its own tradition of academic inquiry until the slave trade and colonization.[14]

Identifying Key Challenges

In addition to this geographic fragmentation of attention, the diversity of focus is reinforced by the fact that different observers are more sensitive to some functional aspects of the threat to academic freedom than others. Some commentators have been concerned with threats from outside universities, while others have underlined the importance of threats from within; some are concerned with public threats, while others emphasize the importance of private ones; and some worry about academic freedom as it impacts teaching, while others are concerned about its impact on research. Part of the challenge of promoting academic freedom, it turns out, is that it requires

10 Zhidong Hao and Peter Zabielskis, eds., *Academic Freedom under Siege: Higher Education in East Asia, the U.S. and Australia* (Cham: Springer Nature, 2020).

11 Philip G. Altbach, "Academic Freedom: International Challenges and African Realities," *Journal of Higher Education in Africa / Revue de l'enseignement Supérieur En Afrique* 3 (2005): 17–34.

12 Matei, "The Crisis of Academic Freedom at the Beginning of the 21st Century: Europe in a Plural World," this volume.

13 Hao, "How Structure, Culture, and the Individual Together Constrain and Enable Academic Freedom in China: A Historical Perspective," this volume.

14 Appiagyei-Atua, "Coloniality and Diversity of Academic Freedom: The African Context," this volume.

academic institutions to simultaneously deal with quite different attempts to circumscribe it. As editors, we gathered a range of authors to think about three quite different challenges to academic freedom that mix the old and the new, not always in predictable or even legible ways.

First, a continued pattern of interferences by states, both traditional authoritarian and new populists or nationalists, along with monitoring of universities, requirements of advance notification of events including international participants, discriminatory denials of visas, and invasive radicalization prevention programs. In other words, even as other concerns may dominate the Western academic agenda, old-style, top-down interference by states has hardly disappeared in our era and is in fact very much alive, even as it may take new forms. This type of interference sometimes translates into physical and psychological threats to academics, but also attempts to control the curriculum and political attacks on universities. It is based on the broader suppression of dissent, the fear that universities will become a hotbed of contestation, and draws on anxieties, real or pretextual, about immigration, terrorism, foreign interference, or loosely labeled "extremism," for example.

Attempts to control university research by governments can manifest themselves in subtle and less subtle ways, underscoring the dependency of many universities on funding by governments. The state often uses public coffers as a lever to exercise control over academic institutions, sometimes threatening or effectively defunding entire departments that are deemed inimical. As Andrey Shcherbovich, himself the victim of an academic purge in Russia, points out in his chapter for this collection, states will not hesitate to dissolve entire departments that they see as inimical to their agendas.[15] Universities are sometimes enlisted to address problems—illegal immigration or radicalization come to mind—that are far broader and that they are ill-equipped to deal with without endangering their core mission.[16]

15 Shcherbovich, "Academic Freedoms in Modern Russia: 'Dawn' and 'Dusk' of the Higher School of Economics," this volume.

16 Joanna Gilmore, "Teaching Terrorism: The Impact of the Counter-Terrorism and Security Act 2015 on Academic Freedom," *Law Teacher* 51 (2017): 515–524; Tara McCormack, "Academic Freedom in an Age of Terror?" in *Why Academic Freedom Matters: A Response to Current Challenges*, ed. Cheryl Hudson and Joanna Williams (Essex: Civitas, 2016), 146; Emily Danvers, "Prevent/ing Critical Thinking? The Pedagogical Impacts of Prevent in UK Higher Education," *Teaching in Higher Education* 28 (2023): 1264–1279.

Even mere pressures to ensure that universities "serve" society or seemingly innocuous measures such as student evaluation can be deployed to stifle free research and superimpose demands on scholars that divert them from the pursuit of knowledge for knowledge's sake or at least according to their own agenda. To the extent that these demands (for example, to express only "correct" or "patriotic" views) are internalized by scholars, they may involve a broad subjugation of academic agendas to political priorities. In conflict situations, the life and security of academics and the ability of universities to function may come under threat and attack by both state and nonstate armed groups. Academic freedom can fizzle not so much through direct attacks but through the chilling consequences of a climate of fear in which one never really knows if one is crossing the line.

Moreover, state legislation has been instrumentalized to restrict the institutional autonomy of universities and to potentially label individual academics and academic institutions as threats to national security. It targets criticism of governments but also sensitive topics such as occupied or contested areas. It has taken an increasingly high-tech form with the rise of the surveillance state, notably through the monitoring of academics on social media. Crucially, it has come from both the political right and the political left. This pattern of interference manifests itself in transnational ways too, as when foreign students are enlisted by their state of nationality against the host institution and country.[17] In their chapter, for example, Teng Biao and Catherine Malanga suggest that there is a deep connection between the suppression of academic freedom in China and abroad through a variety of techniques.[18]

Second, challenges to the universities and the professorate have begun to manifest themselves from within the classroom as a result of demands by students for content and pedagogy more reflective of society's diversity. The significance of academic freedom has been problematized in light of efforts to decolonize universities; fight antisemitism, Islamophobia, and racism;

---

17 Sophie McNeill, *They Don't Understand the Fear We Have: How China's Long Reach of Repression Undermines Academic Freedom at Australia's Universities* (New York: Human Rights Watch, 2021); Subcommittee on Africa, Global Health, Global Human Rights, and International Organizations of the Committee on Foreign Affairs House of Representatives, *Is Academic Freedom Threatened by China's Influence on U.S. Universities?* (CreateSpace, 2015).

18 Biao and Malanga, "China's Rising Threats to Global Academic Freedom: Spectrum, Impacts, and Response," this volume.

challenge the suppression of indigenous voices; as well as demand sensitivity in the treatment of controversial topics. The fear is sometimes that "safe spaces" and "freedom *from* speech" will hamper academic freedom, but it is worth noticing that such fears can themselves be magnified or unjustly portray demands for sensitivity to justify further curtailments of academic speech.[19]

Conservative groups have also been active in seeking to control what is said in the classroom and at events, often in defiance of the focus on diversity. It is sometimes argued by conservatives that the problem of academic freedom has been exactly reversed: the problem is not that unorthodox views in the university are being punished from outside, but that a stifling academic climate of conformism has outsiders insist on far greater diversity.[20] Ironically, the idea of academic debate having to tiptoe around the fragilities of the "vulnerable student" is a product of late modern developments in academia itself, and notably the idea that all knowledge is power and so both relative and potentially violent, so that academia should be constantly trying to minimize the harm it causes through knowledge.[21] Yet concerns about universities becoming "cuddled" sites of dogmatic political correctness often profoundly ignore the day-to-day reality of campus life. Ill-thought-out measures to "protect" academic freedom can be inspired by agendas that in reality seek to curtail it, as Jean-François Gaudreault-DesBiens hints in his chapter.[22]

The politicization of campuses is not new, but, in a context of increased polarization, it may lead to self-censorship, cancelation of controversial events, and monitoring by political groups seeking to discredit instructors, raising concerns that certain views will be considered taboo. The digitalization of the classroom and the role of social media have contributed to breaking down the walls of the university in ways that render it much more open, but also more vulnerable to tensions within society. Some universities have also long been affiliated with particular religious denominations rais-

19 John Palfrey, *Safe Spaces, Brave Spaces: Diversity and Free Expression in Education* (Cambridge: MIT Press, 2017).

20 Joanna Williams, *Academic Freedom in an Age of Conformity: Confronting the Fear of Knowledge* (Cham: Springer, 2016).

21 Stuart Waiton, "Examining the Idea of the 'Vulnerable Student' to Assess the Implications for Academic Freedom," *Societies* 11 (September 2021): 88.

22 Gaudreault-DesBiens, "The Political Cosmetology of Academic Freedom," this volume.

ing concerns about the ability to discuss certain controversial topics,[23] but the problem now seems to affect a much broader range of institutions. As Isaac Kamola puts in his chapter for this collection, "dark money" has influenced the agenda of several state legislatures in the United States, banning the teaching of critical race theory or other "divisive concepts," notably after the Black Lives Matter movement.[24]

Third, a range of more diffuse forces have arguably constrained academic freedom. These include the continued effects of corporatization of universities, private funding, and employment precarity in North America and beyond. Austerity measures amidst budget crises, combined with global rankings competition and the need to attract international students and onerous research evaluation requirements, generate considerable pressure for research to align with institutional expectations of deliverables as well as corporate sponsors' priorities. The turn to universities themselves to more managerial models, as emphasized by Chavan Kissoon and Terence Karran in their chapter in this collection, has led to a technology creep in the UK education system that can reduce academics' autonomy and erode academic freedom.[25]

Donor threats to pull out of funding initiatives if certain academics are not removed or events canceled point to the long-term dynamics of fundraising and for-profit research in a context where the increasingly corporatized culture of higher education institutions can make them ill-placed to mount a vigorous defense of academic freedom. As Hani Morgan shows in his chapter in this collection, even something as banal as industry funding of research can lead to limitations in publication and, by ricochet, have effects on research design, notably as a result of the threat of lawsuits.[26] Kristen Lyons in her chapter also warns of the risks associated with the alignment of universities with the corporate sector, especially when it comes to the mining

23 James Jeffrey Tillman, *Academic Freedom in Church-Related Colleges and Universities: A Theological and Educational Analysis* (PhD dissertation, Baylor University, 1991); Douglas A. Knight, "Academic Freedom and the Plight of German Theological Studies," *Religion* 32 (April 2002): 107–112.

24 Kamola, "Academic Freedom and Dark Money Donors: The Cases of Wisconsin, North Carolina, and Florida," this volume.

25 Kissoon and Karran, "Academic Freedom: Swimming against the Technological Tide," this volume.

26 Morgan, "Restricting Academic Freedom at Universities: How Corporations Contribute to the Problem," this volume.

and fossil fuel industries, and the attendant effect on research agendas and the curriculum in terms of meaningfully responding to the climate crisis.[27]

This raises questions about the extent to which academic research agendas are being alternatively hindered or coopted by special private interests and what can be done to better insulate the university from the resulting pressures. The mere precarization of academic work, although it may not be primarily targeted at curtailing academic freedom, can easily have that effect given how it deprives junior scholars of the protections of tenure. Finally, new technologies are not always exactly helping either, in a context in which the links that bind academics to each other and to students are frayed. As Katarzyna Kaczmarska and Corinne Lennox point out in their chapter for this collection, for example, the move to online learning that has been precipitated in part by the pandemic, while offering opportunities for students, also increases the risks of digitalized surveillance and authoritarian reach.[28]

To Define or Not to Define?

The book's span as an edited collection is too broad to offer a single definition of academic freedom, and we as editors were wary of imposing a one-size-fits-all definition (in the best tradition of academic freedom!), lest this preempts unorthodox understandings of what the term entails. Starting from a definition seemed less useful than arriving at elements of one tentatively and over the entire arc of the book. Our readers will be the judges of the extent to which our various contributors ultimately converge or diverge in how they interpret academic freedom. But our endeavor is certainly part of a collective effort to refine an understanding of academic freedom as, broadly, the right of academics to pursue knowledge free of outside interference and the many permutations around that theme as they emerge from actual defenses of the principle when it is perceived as threatened or challenged. This is not exclusive of thinking about how academic freedom can be made to incorporate other values and academic pursuits, nor does it exclude wariness with some of the uses or intonations of academic freedom as it is actually practiced.

---

27 Lyons, "Mining and Fossil-Fuel Entanglements with the University in an Era of Climate Change: Impacts for Academic Freedom and Climate (In)action," this volume.

28 Kaczmarska and Lennox, "Academic Freedom in Online Learning," this volume.

The basic foundation of academic freedom has long been that the pursuit of knowledge is best guaranteed within universities as part of an unhindered exercise in which even outrageous or scandalous views can be aired. This includes the freedom to both engage in research and teach free of interference. Academic freedom has sometimes been extended to extracurricular activities as well since it would otherwise be quite easy to sanction academics for their activities outside of university. Evidently, academic freedom has a cost, including occasionally sustaining research or pronouncements that, despite the strictures of tenure, turn out (but often with the benefit of hindsight) to have been wrongheaded or problematic.

Nonetheless, the suggestion that the definition of academic freedom is axiomatic and uncontested should be resisted. Academic freedom presents the paradox of being broadly protected and central to academic life, yet to be constantly confronted with not only threats but also actual challenges to its definition. It will not always be clear, moreover, that academic freedom is being violated given the roundabout ways in which various actors seek to constrain it. Many attacks on academic freedom will pass as efforts to uphold it. Vague accusations, for example, that universities do not "represent" society or have become politically oriented can be used to manipulate their composition based on criteria other than academic merit.

Academic freedom can be invoked in coded ways and at counterpurpose to justify greater control of universities; it can sometimes appear as little more than a reflex invocation disconnected from its origin; and it suffers from ambiguities long associated with the notion of freedom. It is discussed by various constituencies in ways that are sometimes ill-thought-out and create false dichotomies. The solicitousness of groups purporting to be preoccupied with academic freedom when they are mostly concerned with pushing a particular political agenda, one often inimical to the goals of the university unless it agrees with their politics, should be taken with wariness.[29] At the same time, criticism of how issues of academic freedom are treated on campuses cannot be rejected outright simply because it comes from persons whose political views one disagrees with.

29 Joan Wallach Scott, *Knowledge, Power, and Academic Freedom* (New York: Columbia University Press, 2019).

The attack from the left on decolonial or antiracist grounds has also proved difficult to respond to, perhaps because it claims some of the very liberal values on which academic freedom itself has been based, even as it reframes them powerfully. For some, academic freedom is a privilege that allows academics to wield political bully pulpits at best, or say things that are false or hurtful at worst, a sort of license for the benefit of a cuddled elite. The standard answer is that academic freedom can occasionally be used in this way, but it is important to note that it also comes with constraints, notably those imposed by the onerous requirements of publication, obtaining research funding, or promotion. Academic freedom is not a license to engage in abusive or reprehensible behavior, and it does not free those to whom it applies from civility and the demands of moral behavior. What academic freedom is is an insistence that the pursuit of knowledge in universities should be governed by strictly academic criteria and that this will ultimately be for the greater good.

One concern is that this is a case of too little, too late. The classic defense of academic freedom has been to double down on its liberal tenets.[30] Still questions have long arisen about academic freedom being abused or providing shelter for discriminatory, inflammatory, or hateful views. Whether it is Holocaust denial or blatantly racist,[31] antisemitic,[32] or anti-Palestinian[33] views, especially when professed extra muros, the concern may be that academic freedom provides cover for views that are unfathomable. This will be especially the case when the normal gatekeeping of academia seems to have malfunctioned and scholars manage to air views in ways that fall significantly below the standards of serious scholarship.[34] As Tamara Thermitus puts it in her chapter in this collection, it is sometimes difficult to disentan-

30 See, e.g., Jonathan Rauch, *Kindly Inquisitors: The New Attacks on Free Thought* (Chicago: University of Chicago Press, 2013).

31 Michael Bérubé and Jennifer Ruth, *It's Not Free Speech: Race, Democracy, and the Future of Academic Freedom* (Baltimore: Johns Hopkins University Press, 2022).

32 Cary Nelson, *Hate Speech and Academic Freedom: The Antisemitic Assault on Basic Principles* (Boston: Academic Studies Press, 2024).

33 Malaka Shwaikh and Rebecca Ruth Gould, "The Palestine Exception to Academic Freedom: Intertwined Stories from the Frontlines of UK-Based Palestine Activism," *Biography* 42 (2019): 752–773.

34 Kristian Skrede Gleditsch, "Houston, We Have a Problem: Enhancing Academic Freedom and Transparency in Publishing through Post-Publication Debate," *Political Studies Review* 19 (2021): 428–434.

gle invocations of academic freedom in the public debate from a strong sense of "white" privilege.[35]

Even there, there will be those who argue that freedom should prevail given the sheer difficulties in a liberal society of drawing the line between use and abuse and the relative exceptionality of the latter.[36] Moreover, there will be concerns that too often restrictions to academic freedom have affected not only those who arguably abused it but also minority opinions scorned by the powers that be.[37] Finally, the risk is that one will invite unwanted meddling from the authorities or private actors keen on denouncing or remodeling academic standards for their own agendas of reining in academia's freedom.[38] One of the questions in this context is, beyond broad debates about academic freedom, the need to parse out carefully who gets to invoke it and with what success.[39]

Still, as several contributors point out, the debate in practice need never be as dire or clichéd as opposing "academic freedom" to diversity. Sophie Bisping suggests, for example, that academic freedom concerns from academics and demands for social justice from the student body (although, no doubt, both can share the concerns of the other) can be reconciled and should not be simply pitted against each other.[40] In very much the same spirit, Angela Campbell invites us to think less in terms of irreducible rights and more in terms of "relationships" that are affected by actual incidents on campus.[41]

---

35 Thermitus, "Freedom for All: Academic Freedom in a Pluralistic Society," this volume.

36 Stanley Fish, "Holocaust Denial and Academic Freedom," *Valparaiso University Law Review* 35 (2000–2001): 499–524.

37 Matthew Abraham, "The Question of Palestine and the Subversion of Academic Freedom: Depaul's Denial of Tenure to Norman G. Finkelstein," *Arab Studies Quarterly* 33 (2011): 179–203.

38 Hugh Willmott, "Commercialising Higher Education in the UK: The State, Industry and Peer Review," *Studies in Higher Education* 28 (2003): 129–41; Caitlin Cassidy, "Ministers Will No Longer Approve Australian Research Council Grants under Bid to Stop 'Political Interference,'" *The Guardian*, November 29, 2023, www.theguardian.com/australia-news/2023/nov/29/political-interference-australian-research-council-grants-stopped.

39 Johnny Eric Williams, "The Academic Freedom Double Standard: 'Freedom' for Courtiers, Suppression for Critical Scholars," *Journal of Academic Freedom* 9 (2018): 1–10.

40 Bisping, "Academic Freedom and Social Justice in Quebec," this volume.

41 Campbell, "The Simultaneous, Crucial Pursuit of Academic Freedom and Equity, Diversity, and Inclusion through a Relational Approach," this volume.

Universities and Their Environment

One approach might be that whether academic freedom is protected or not depends largely on whether a university operates in a liberal system. The claim is that liberal societies may better rise to the challenge of protecting universities from illiberal reach, although even there, there is considerable room for improvement. There is certainly some truth to the empirical claim of a correlation between liberalism, both at home and globally, and the ability of academic freedom to thrive. This is not altogether surprising given the close proximity of the ethos of academic freedom, democracy, and human rights.[42]

However, it also needs to be pointed out that threats to academic freedom in our era largely transcend the liberal-authoritarian political divide. Although the tactics may differ, the registers also borrow from each other, and authoritarian tendencies emerge in so-called liberal states, even as liberal tendencies are visible in authoritarian ones. As Vincent Wong shows in his contribution to this collection, there is by now "a transnational blueprint for academic unfreedom" that goes from US anticritical race theory campaigns, to suppression of scholarship critical of China's repression of the Xinjiang Uyghur, to Israeli suppression of research on the occupation of Palestinian territories.[43] The reassertion of liberal orthodoxy, in this context, as several contributors to this collection point out, does not do justice to liberalism's own occluded potential for oppression[44] or the challenge of understanding actual, situated challenges to academic freedom.[45]

Another connection that has increasingly been made in this context is between the protection of academic freedom and human rights. It also stands to reason that support for academic freedom is broadly conducive to human rights and vice versa. Independent universities can act as vital checks against a culture of government meddling more generally. They help nurture challenging and even unorthodox ideas that are part of a healthy democratic

---

42 Julia C. Lerch, David John Frank, and Evan Schofer, "The Social Foundations of Academic Freedom: Heterogeneous Institutions in World Society, 1960 to 2022," *American Sociological Review* 89 (2024): 88–125.

43 Wong, "Nationalist Backlash to Anti-racist Education: A Transnational Blueprint for Academic Unfreedom," this volume.

44 Thermitus, "Freedom for All: Academic Freedom in a Pluralistic Society," this volume.

45 Wong, "Nationalist Backlash to Anti-racist Education."

culture. This has driven an insistence that academic freedom, like human rights, is a universal value, even though it stands to be implemented differently in different contexts.[46] Certainly, the protection of academic freedom in practice often needs and relies on, even as it is distinct from, broader rights protections embedded in liberal societies such as the freedoms of opinion, expression, and association. The US Supreme Court, for example, has occasionally stepped in, developing its own form of First Amendment–infused academic freedom jurisprudence.[47] Sejal Parmar makes the point in this collection that academic freedom has increasingly appeared in international human rights instruments, even as its status there is sometimes a little uncertain.[48]

At the same time, as Vincent Wong points out also in this collection, the language of liberalism can at times obscure rather than shed light on the multifaceted reality of encroachments on academic freedom.[49] Equating academic freedom and human rights claims to the freedom of expression tends to limit and trivialize the specificity of the former. It can lead to an overemphasis on a few incidents of speakers being denied the ability to speak on campuses at the expense of attention to the constant threat of erosion of academic standards by governmental or corporate interference, or by scholars themselves.[50] As Angela Campbell points out, pitting the rights claims

46 William G. Tierney and Michael Lanford, "The Question of Academic Freedom: Universal Right or Relative Term," *Frontiers of Education in China* 9 (2014): 4–23.

47 William W. Van Alstyne, "Academic Freedom and the First Amendment in the Supreme Court of the United States: An Unhurried Historical Review," *Law & Contemporary Problems* 53 (1990): 79; Lawrence Rosenthal, "Does the First Amendment Protect Academic Freedom?" *Journal of College and University Law* 46 (2021): 223; David M. Rabban, "A Functional Analysis of Individual and Institutional Academic Freedom under the First Amendment," *Law & Contemporary Problems* 53 (1990): 227; Julie H. Margetta, "Taking Academic Freedom Back to the Future: Refining the Special Concern of the First Amendment," *Loyola Journal of Public International Law* 7 (2005): 1; Neal H. Hutchens and Jeffrey C. Sun, "The Tenuous Legal Status of First Amendment Protection for Individual Academic Freedom," *Journal of the Professoriate* 7 (2013): 1–25; Richard H. Hiers, "Academic Freedom in Public Colleges and Universities: O Say, Does That Star-Spangled First Amendment Banner yet Wave," *Wayne Law Review* 40 (1993): 1; Judith Areen, "Government as Educator: A New Understanding of First Amendment Protection of Academic Freedom and Governance," *Georgetown Law Journal* 97 (2008): 945; Vikram David Amar and Alan E. Brownstein, "A Close-Up, Modern Look at First Amendment Academic Freedom Rights of Public College Students and Faculty," *Minnesota Law Review* 101 (2016): 1943; Tierney and Lanford, "The Question of Academic Freedom."

48 Parmar, "Beyond the Periphery? Academic Freedom as a Matter of Human Rights," this volume.

49 Wong, "Nationalist Backlash to Anti-racist Education."

50 Farhana Sultana, "The False Equivalence of Academic Freedom and Free Speech: Defending Academic Integrity in the Age of White Supremacy, Colonial Nostalgia, and Anti-intellectualism," *ACME: An In-*

of academics over the rights claims of others in terms of nondiscrimination can quickly degenerate into a fruitless exercise of recrimination.[51] This suggests that a more modest, pragmatic, and even instrumental understanding of academic freedom may ultimately serve the concept better than insistence on some grand human rights narrative.[52]

Instead of seeing academic freedom as an individual right, then, it may be more helpful to understand it as a right that can be used or reinterpreted by members belonging to certain groups or communities and that pertains in fact to those groups and communities as such. Like diplomatic immunities, for example, academic freedom is a privilege meant not for the personal benefit of scholars (even though, de facto, they may stand to benefit in some cases from being entitled to it) but for the benefit of scholarly inquiry, which is not the same thing. Indeed, many formulations of academic freedom specifically emphasize the need for research to be conducted for the common good, which means not for the individual good of researchers but for donors or outside groups. This can also allow for cross-constituency alliances united by a shared interest in the promotion of academic freedom, even as they agree about little else: left and right, professors and students, public and private sector, and so on.

Academic Freedom as a Claim to Autonomous Governance

At its heart, the claim of academic freedom is a claim of independence of the academic milieu, one foregrounding the importance of its self-regulation. Contra Soviet intimations that science should serve socialist revolution and even five-year plans,[53] or Conservative hostility in the United

ternational Journal for Critical Geographies 17 (2018): 228–257.

51 Campbell, "The Simultaneous, Crucial Pursuit of Academic Freedom and Equity, Diversity, and Inclusion through a Relational Approach."

52 See, e.g., Stanley Fish, *Versions of Academic Freedom: From Professionalism to Revolution* (Chicago: University of Chicago Press, 2014).

53 *Academic Freedom under the Soviet Regime: A Symposium of Refugee Scholars and Scientists Who Have Escaped from the USSR, on the Subject, "Academic Freedom in the Soviet Union as a Threat to the Theory and Practice of Bolshevik Doctrine"; Conference at Carnegie Endowment for International Peace Building United Nations Plaza, New York, April 3–4, 1954* (Institute for the Study of the History and Culture of the USSR, 1954); Jiří Pelikán, *Civil and Academic Freedom in the USSR and Eastern Europe* (Nottingham: Spokesman Books, 1975).

States to universities becoming unmoored from the priorities of donors[54] all the way to McCarthyism,[55] it suggests that there is an institutional but also societal interest in universities being managed by themselves. As Jacob Levy points out in his chapter for this collection, academic freedom is better understood as a form of "associational freedom," almost guild-like, quite distinct from the freedom of speech and regulated by its own internal criteria of "excellence."[56] Sijbolt Noorda, one of the *éminences grises* of the Magna Carta Universitatum, also emphasizes the close links between academic freedom and university autonomy in his own chapter.[57]

One great vulnerability in this context, no doubt, is the fact that universities need to be independent of some of the very constituencies (the state, donors) on which they are de facto dependent. Maintaining that independence suggests that protecting academic freedom is as much the work of making sure that it is not violated in individual cases, as it is the task of thinking in terms of broad institutional determinants. The rise of professors' associations (perhaps most notably the American Association of University Professors, AAUP), for example, is one manifestation of how academic freedom has been fought for and protected by its most direct beneficiaries. The crucial role of academics in denouncing attacks on academic freedom, even when they target fellow scholars they fundamentally disagree with, bears underlining.[58] The rise of indicators to measure academic freedom by evaluating universities' independence through their regulatory environment may also go some way toward elucidating patterns of decline or corrosion.[59]

---

54 William F. Buckley, *God and Man at Yale: The Superstitions of "Academic Freedom"* (New York: Simon and Schuster, 2012).

55 Andrew Feffer, *Bad Faith: Teachers, Liberalism, and the Origins of McCarthyism* (New York: Fordham University Press, 2019); David R. Holmes, *Stalking the Academic Communist: Intellectual Freedom and the Firing of Alex Novikoff* (Burlington: University of Vermont, 1989); Charles Howard McCormick, *This Nest of Vipers: McCarthyism and Higher Education in the Mundel Affair, 1951–52* (Champaign: University of Illinois Press, 1989); Ellen Schrecker, *No Ivory Tower: McCarthyism and the Universities* (Oxford: Oxford University Press, 1986); Jimee Dee Kille, *Academic Freedom Imperiled: The McCarthy Era at the University of Nevada* (Las Vegas: University of Nevada Press, 2004).

56 Levy, "Academic Freedom as Freedom of Complex Association," this volume.

57 Noorda, "Academic Freedom and University Autonomy: An Agenda for Professional Public Engagement," this volume.

58 Robyn Bartel, "Academic Freedom and an Invitation to Promote Its Advancement," *Geographical Research* 57 (2019): 359–367.

59 Terence Karran, Klaus Beiter, and Kwadwo Appiagyei-Atua, "Measuring Academic Freedom in Europe: A Criterion Referenced Approach," *Policy Reviews in Higher Education* 1 (2017): 209–239; Janika Span-

Initiatives such as Scholars at Risk programs can also, in addition to providing a much-needed escape route for imperiled academics, manifest a more profound sort of transnational academic solidarity.[60]

Questions such as tenure or discipline can become flashpoints in the ongoing debate about scholarly freedom, as has the right division of labor between university administrators and collegial governance by faculty members. By the same token, the need to diversify universities in an age when their indebtedness to problematic patterns of capital accumulation, including through slavery or colonialism, has become increasingly clear may call into question the traditional criteria of what counts as scholarly achievement. "Merit" or "excellence" can be just as coded as the emphasis on diversity, equity, and inclusion (DEI initiatives, as they are known). What seems less helpful, as Jean-François Gaudreault-DesBiens points out in his chapter, is extensive reporting obligations imposed on universities to ensure that they protect academic freedom.[61]

One revealing challenge to university governance of academic freedom is the tendency to ask institutions of higher learning that they "take sides" in a range of social or geopolitical issues that they are ill-suited to take sides on, on which their members may have a range of positions, and which it was never the university's vocation to decide on qua institution. The temptation for social actors, especially those connected to universities, to use the legitimacy of universities to make political statements is a strong one especially given the tendency to frame positions in hypermoral terms and the way in which universities and their communities may be impacted by outside events, making neutrality very challenging.[62] But it is also likely to lead to backlash, possibly at the cost of making parts of the student and scholarly bodies with different views feel, in turn, unwelcome.[63] Invariably, it seems to

---

nagel and Katrin Kinzelbach, "The Academic Freedom Index and Its Indicators: Introduction to New Global Time-Series V-Dem Data," *Quality & Quantity* 57 (October 2023): 3969–3989.

60 Kudus Oluwatoyin Adebayo, "The State of Academic (Un)freedom and Scholar Rescue Programmes: A Contemporary and Critical Overview," *Third World Quarterly* 43 (2022): 1817–1836.

61 Gaudreault-DesBiens, "The Cosmetology of Academic Freedom."

62 Adrienne Lu, "Should College Administrators Take Political Positions?" *Chronicle of Higher Education*, December 2, 2022, www.chronicle.com/article/the-apolitical-university.

63 The debate was particularly apparent in the wake of Brexit, Black Lives Matter, or the war between Israel and Hamas following the attacks of October 7, with a majority of commentators expressing a guarded call for neutrality. See Stephen M. Walt, "Universities Shouldn't Ever Take Sides in a War," *Foreign Policy*, February 6, 2024, https://foreignpolicy.com/2023/10/31/universities-israel-palestine-hamas-gaza-

have led universities down a path of constantly readjusting their communication and satisfying no one.

Ultimately, it is academics themselves who are on the front line of defending academic freedom (again, not for their own sake but for what academic freedom permits). One worrying trend in that context is that the erosion of academic freedom is also a result of the tendency of some academics to back off from defending it when it is threatened.[64] Increasingly, the task involves properly defending academic freedom to constituencies beyond and even within universities that may not be that familiar with its origins and rationale. Such work is crucial to dispel any feeling that academic freedom is a form of artificial privilege and to convince various groups that they too stand to benefit from it in the long term, even evidently as it may lead to certain views being aired that they disagree with strongly.

Conclusion: Promoting Rather Than Protecting?

Academic freedom is quite dependent on institutional and even judicial protections that may not always be readily available. Both the law and human rights guarantees have a role to play in ensuring that it is not gradually marginalized. But it is also worth noting that its integrity is uniquely dependent on universities themselves, including their higher administration and governance, which in some cases may be coopted or influenced by the powers that be, creating a particularly delicate interface between the community of scholars and its broader social environment (this is particularly the

---

war-take-sides/; Robert P. George, "Universities Shouldn't Be Ideological Churches," *The Atlantic*, June 15, 2023, www.theatlantic.com/ideas/archive/2023/06/university-statements-political-issues-abortion-princeton/674590/; Matthew Reisz, "Be Honest and Take Sides on Big Issues, Universities Told," *Times Higher Education*, March 18, 2021, www.timeshighereducation.com/news/be-honest-and-take-sides-big-issues-universities-told; Daniel Diermeier, "Principled Neutrality," *Inside Higher Ed*, May 4, 2022, www.insidehighered.com/views/2022/05/05/academic-leaders-shouldnt-take-political-stances-opinion.

64 Bill Durodie, "Securitising Education to Prevent Terrorism or Losing Direction?" *British Journal of Educational Studies* 64 (2016): 21–35; Stuart Waiton, "Academic Freedom and Freedom of Speech: The Assault of Vulnerability," in *Teaching and Learning Practices for Academic Freedom*, vol. 34, ed. Enakshi Sengupta and Patrick Blessinger, Innovations in Higher Education Teaching and Learning (Bradford: Emerald, 2020), 71–92.

case when those politically responsible for higher education turn out to be its political enemies).[65]

This suggests the importance of nurturing rather than just protecting academic freedom, a constant drive to create conditions that are hospitable to its flourishing rather than a defensive violations-based focus. In that respect, the genre of defending academic freedom has expanded notably in the past decades, including a number of sui generis global and bottom-up efforts in the best tradition of academic self-regulation, such as the Magna Carta Universitatum (signed by more than 1,000 universities around the world). In addition, a range of international organizations, such as UNESCO or the Council of Europe, have become more active in promoting and upholding academic freedom. These efforts point to the collective nature of protecting academic freedom in the sense that attacks on it in some contexts inevitably reverberate across universities because they attack the very idea of independent academic institutions.

The challenge seems to be, at any rate, to defend anew and in the evolving terms of society's debates, the justification of academic freedom for generations and constituencies that bring a new range of concerns to the table.[66] It is also the challenge of developing positions that resist the test of time and, crucially, that one is ready to live with even as they are associated with a range of often opposing political views.[67] In that respect, mere nostalgia for an earlier, more genteel era of supposed collegial liberal exchange is a distraction: if ever that era existed (and there is reason to think that it did not or only as a result of the enduring power of particular elites), it is long gone. Academic freedom may be vulnerable to evolutions in and of society, but to want to address the challenges it poses merely by changing society is clearly a

65 Michael Ian Cohen, "Education Populism? A Corpus-Driven Analysis of Betsy Devos's Education Policy Discourse," *Education Policy Analysis Archives* 29 (2021): n16; Joanne Barkan, "The Miseducation of Betsy Devos," *Dissent* 64 (2017): 141–146.

66 See, e.g., for subtle treatment of both sides of this argument, Vinay Harpalani, "'Safe Spaces' and the Educational Benefits of Diversity," *Duke Journal of Constitutional Law & Public Policy* 13 (2018): 117–166; Michele Moody-Adams, "Is There a 'Safe Space' for Academic Freedom?" in *Academic Freedom*, ed. Jennifer Lackey (Oxford: Oxford University Press, 2018), 36. On safe space vs. academic freedom as a false binary, see S. Ha DiMuzio, "Safe Space vs. Free Speech: Unpacking a Higher Education Curriculum Controversy," *Journal of Curriculum and Pedagogy* 20 (2023): 368–392.

67 Lexi Lonas, "'No Credibility': Critics Cry Foul as Colleges Press for Free Speech amid Israel-Hamas Conflict," *The Hill*, October 20, 2023, https://thehill.com/homenews/education/4265290-no-credibility-critics-foul-colleges-free-speech-israel-hamas-conflict/.

distraction in a context in which the social reality and environment of universities has fundamentally changed.

Perhaps what has struck us the most in pursuing this project is the extent to which academic freedom is ill-protected, in the end, by stereotypical oppositions between, for example, liberal and authoritarian cultures. Of course, these capture something, but today's debates in academia are far more complex and require far more creativity than, for example, a mere defense of either untrammeled free speech or a singular focus on equity and diversity. Rather, many of our contributors are interested in thinking through not only new ways of reconciling opposites but also ways of doing so that are informed by local circumstances, attention to history and place, as well as the thickness of institutional projects. This suggests a healthy space for pluralism in how we go about addressing these no doubt pressing problems.

PART I

Imagining, Defending, Conceptualizing Academic Freedom

Chapter 2

Academic Freedom as Freedom of Complex Association

Jacob T. Levy[1]

Introduction

In this essay, I aim to not only restate but also redescribe the core of academic freedom as a practice and a value (and it is both). I do not aim at normative novelty, but I do think that the redescription can shed new light on a variety of current disputes. The core traditional value of academic freedom is under serious threat around the world, and the responses to that threat are sometimes muddled by confusion about both what the value is and how it is justified; in the essay's final section, I will try to resolve some of those confusions.

Academic Freedom Is Not Freedom of Speech

Academic freedom resembles, but is importantly distinct from, liberal democratic freedom of speech and freedom of expression, and we should begin by distinguishing the former from the latter. To take the simplest, and yet a powerful and important, example of the difference to begin with: freedom of speech includes in general the freedom to lie. I say "in general" advisedly;

1 Thanks to Alec Crisman and Shal Marriott for research assistance.

there are limits ranging from prohibitions on commercial fraud to restrictions on defamation to, in some jurisdictions, restrictions on denying particular historical facts such as the existence of the Holocaust. But the exceptions are narrow and pretty well defined. Liberal democracies have struggled in recent years to understand how to manage rising tides of deliberate misinformation on topics ranging from public health to election integrity precisely because a general respect for free speech *does* include the freedom to lie, and because our reasons for distrusting states as adjudicators of speech very much do include a distrust of how impartially, reliably, or fairly they would judge truth. And so, to choose a few examples, an astrologist who lies about the relationship between humanity and the stars, a celebrity or politician who employs a ghostwriter and then lies about the authorship of the resulting book, and an online commentator who lies about sources for quotations and factual claims, are all protected by freedom of speech.

Matters are quite otherwise on campus. Employing a ghostwriter and passing the work off as one's own is an expellable offense for students and a fireable offense for even tenured professors. The same is true for misrepresentations of what was found in an experiment, an archive, or a text, or indeed misrepresentations about whether the experiment ever happened, or the archive was ever consulted. In an astronomy classroom, neither an instructor who begins to teach astrology nor a student who submits a paper relying on horoscopes as a research method will find any protection in academic freedom.

There is thus a close connection between universities and the pursuit of truth that is not replicated in the broader social sphere. There is a limited analogy to be drawn here between the professional ethics of a university and the professional ethics of the practice of law, between the university and a courtroom. Liberal democratic freedom of speech protects neither the perjurer who lies under oath nor the lawyer who puts a witness on the stand knowing that they intend to commit perjury; those actions do too much damage to the truth-seeking character of the legal enterprise.

I think there is promise in analogies between university norms and the ethical codes of the other learned professions, a point to which I will return. But this analogy in particular runs out quickly; we don't characterize the courtroom as being constituted *by a special kind of freedom*. The university, like the courtroom, restricts many activities that harm the truth-seeking enterprise and yet *is* constituted by a special kind of freedom. So, if academic freedom is not simple freedom of speech, what is it?

Academic Freedom Is an Associational Freedom

Academic freedom is not, in the first instance, an individual right at all. It is, rather, an associational right, more like the corporate *libertas ecclesiae* of medieval disputes between the Catholic Church and political rulers than like the modern Protestant-style freedom of individual conscience that is protected in many constitutional democracies. It is the freedom of the scholarly association to engage in the core functions of discovering, teaching, and preserving knowledge—the functions, paradigmatically, of the laboratory, the classroom, and the library—according to scholarly disciplines, norms, and practices, without external rules of dogma or ideology. The conclusions of research and inquiry must be reached according to the scholarly rules that govern that kind of research and inquiry; they must not be dictated in advance. No particular conclusion—Christian orthodoxy or scientific racism or Lamarckianism or Bolshevism or McCarthyist anti-Communism or astrology or what have you—is ruled out ab initio. But those conclusions must be generated from within the association, through scholarly inquiry; they must not be externally imposed.

Similarly, teaching must proceed according to internal scholarly standards, not externally imposed orthodoxies. While I will for the most part omit further discussion of libraries, the principles are similar in kind; the acquisition and preservation of accumulated knowledge proceeds according to a kind of scholarly evaluation of importance, not according to agreement with particular doctrines.

There are four distinctive things to note about this associational freedom.

The first is that is in large part a jurisdictional claim. As *libertas ecclesiae* was the liberty *of the church*, so is academic freedom the liberty *of* the university or other scholarly association. When an external actor—in the modern world, most typically a state—dictates the content of research or teaching, academic freedom simply *is* violated, regardless of the particular content at issue. It doesn't matter whether the state purports to protect intellectual freedom or diversity against on-campus orthodoxy and hegemony. It doesn't even matter whether the view the state promotes is true and the idea that has become campus orthodoxy is false. The practice of academic freedom may be justified by—overall, in the long term—*serving* the promotion of truth and informed debate. But that is not the same as allowing recourse to "truth" or "debate" as excuses for external interference. Research and teaching lie within the academic jurisdiction of the university, as theology and the occupancy of ministerial roles lie within the jurisdiction of the church. This much is definitional; it is not a *justification* for academic freedom so defined. But it is worth stating explicitly at a time when off-campus actors sometimes do claim that their interference in research and teaching *promotes* academic freedom, indeed protecting it against universities themselves.[2]

The second is that academic freedom necessarily makes constant reference to the scholarly norms internal to the scholarly association. For a shorthand we might call those norms something like "truth-seeking," but that is only a shorthand. In order to stress the particular character of the truth-seeking enterprise, we might say something like "scientific method," but that is misleading with respect not only to the medieval university that nonetheless had academic freedom,[3] but also with respect to, for example, humanistic disciplines whose search for truth might be better understood as interpretive. We can see the practice of academic freedom in place across changes in time and changes in discipline as to *what counts* as the internal scholarly norms. We can ask of a medieval faculty of theology or a modern department of biology whether it was or is protected by academic freedom, despite the tremendous difference in intellectual content as to what is being protected.

The third, which follows, is that since universities are constitutively pluralistic in their intellectual approaches—even in their earliest years, the mode of inquiry in a faculty of theology was not just like that in a faculty of law—academic freedom will necessarily be a *nested* associational freedom. It encompasses not only the liberty of the university against (most typically) the state and (sometimes) nonstate actors ranging from churches to donors, but also the self-governing freedom of each internal scholarly association, each faculty or school or disciplinary department. I have elsewhere discussed

2 An Act Respecting Academic Freedom in the University Sector, 2022, vol. 21, www2.publicationsduquebec.gouv.qc.ca/dynamicSearch/telecharge.php?type=5&file=2022C21A.PDF; United States, Executive Order 13864: Improving Free Inquiry, Transparency, and Accountability at Colleges and Universities, 2019.

3 Hastings Rashdall, *The Universities of Europe in the Middle Ages* (Cambridge: Cambridge University Press, 2010 [1895]).

a general category of *complex associations*, associations that are rightful bearers of freedom of association but that generate internal ecosystems of further association.[4] The university is a complex association par excellence. Indeed, this is built into the language itself. A *universitas* is an encompassing association, in some relevant sense a *universal* association.[5] A *collegium*, a college made up of colleagues, is a smaller, thicker, and more particular association that simultaneously partakes in the broader community of the *universitas*. These concepts from civil law did not only refer to academic institutions: a medieval city might be a *universitas*, and the trade and mercantile guilds within it, *collegia*. But it is to academic institutions that these generic legal categories stuck as names. The university is a universal association encompassing the collegial colleges—and faculties and departments and centers and institutes—within it.

The fourth is that, notwithstanding the corporate and associational character of academic freedom, it will often be individual scholars—researchers, teachers, students—whose academic freedom is violated and who must try to vindicate the right. In the simplest case, if the state mandates one conclusion or prohibits another in teaching or in scholarly inquiry, it will often be an individual teacher or researcher whose work is impaired. It is the individual researcher who might be prohibited from publishing results or conducting experiments, who might be disciplined or denied renewed employment or fired. It is the individual teacher who will be punished for assigning prohibited material. This is true and real, and yet does not change the associational character of the right—because academic freedom is *not* impaired when those same consequences fall on the individual teacher or researcher for violation of the relevant scholarly norms. Being fired for research fraud, being denied renewed employment for switching one's research and teaching entirely away from the scholarly unit's area, being prevented from publishing results by peer reviewers who judge the research to fail the scholarly stan-

4 Jacob T. Levy, *Rationalism, Pluralism, and Freedom* (Oxford: Oxford University Press, 2015).

5 While this is an extension by analogy, not part of the etymology, it's also worth thinking about *universities* rather than only *a university* as universal. From the medieval origins of the European university onward, it has been an important feature of universities that they recognized each other as peer institutions, for example, by treating each other's degrees as valid, not requiring separate examination before recognizing a graduate of another university as qualified to teach (*jus ubique docendi*). The norms of academic freedom have themselves, imperfectly but genuinely, become part of what is now a global system of mutual recognition.

dards of evidence and argument: none of these are violations of academic freedom. When the individual suffers adverse consequences (a) from the scholarly community or association (b) for scholarly reasons, this is the *exercise* of scholarly self-government, not the violation of it.

Both (a) and (b) are required, which is why academic freedom is not *completely* a collective jurisdictional right. A university or department may not mandate the results of inquiry any more than a state may. The self-governing scholarly association sets what Michael Oakeshott described as the *adverbial conditions* of scholarly activities.[6] In order to reach a conclusion, you must use these evidentiary standards, these rules of logic and evidence, these tests of validity. The self-governing association that instead mandates a dogma does violate the academic freedom of the individual scholar—whether that be the researcher pursuing original inquiry, the teacher whose syllabus is forcibly truncated, or the student whose paper is penalized for reaching a disfavored conclusion. However, the freedom that is violated is not the open-ended individual freedom of speech or expression. It is the freedom relative to the scholarly association, the freedom to be judged within the scholarly enterprise *only* according to the internally appropriate adverbial rules of scholarly inquiry, argument, and conduct. It is the freedom of members of the scholarly association—researchers, teachers, students—to be free to pursue that association's scholarly mission according to its scholarly rules, and to be immune from being judged as scholars according to nonscholarly norms such as conformity to an orthodoxy. In an important sense the individual who presents a claim of having their academic freedom violated is seeking to vindicate the relevant *self-governing scholarly community's* norms against outsiders, or else is standing on those norms against even the community's own local authorities.

To put it another way, the university's jurisdictional autonomy over research and teaching is far-reaching against outside actors but is strictly limited to its own members. In the university's assessment of them—the grades and honors a student receives, the evaluation of an instructor's teaching, the assessment of research, the assignment of benefits or penalties for academic employees—it must limit itself to the quality of inquiry, *not* to the

6 Michael Oakeshott, "The Rule of Law," in *On History and Other Essays* (Indianapolis: Liberty Fund, 1999 [1983]).

orthodoxy of the conclusion reached. Neither may it corrupt those evaluations with consideration of nonscholarly matters such as the person's religious or political views. The associational autonomy of the communities of inquiry is justified by their being *communities of inquiry*, however great the interdisciplinary or intermethodological differences might be about what "inquiry" means. And, as always, jurisdictional rules precede consideration of the substantive merits of a particular case. The state lacks jurisdiction over the conclusions of research. So does the university; so does the disciplinary department! The student, instructor, or researcher who has followed the locally appropriate rules of inquiry and argument may not be subject to institutional disadvantage because of the unpopular conclusion they reached.

It is not always or only individuals whose academic freedom is prima facie violated in this way. When right-wing governments from Hungary to Florida prohibit whole disciplines or scholarly methodologies—gender studies, critical race theory—then the attack on the relevant scholarly community itself sits right on the surface. In extreme cases, a whole department or faculty might be shuttered, or a whole university driven out of the country. My point is not to deny this, but rather to emphasize that even in the very common case when an individual scholar is the prima facie victim of a violation, it is still a violation of a *corporate and associational* freedom.

So: academic freedom is mostly jurisdictional, but it includes a substantive commitment to each scholarly association's local rules of scholarly inquiry. It is institutionally committed to truth-seeking, but the rejection of dogmatism means that in no particular case may the truth or falseness of a conclusion be appealed to as a reason to override it. It is corporate and associational but frequently looks like an individual freedom, and sometimes even an individual freedom against the scholarly association itself. And it is the peculiar associational freedom of a *complex* association, a freedom whose subject is not only the university as a whole but also—indeed, much of the time, *primarily*—the constituent associations within it. I think that this is a description of the norms and practices; it is not intended to be reformist or novel. But when it is spelled out explicitly we see that the norms and practices are somewhat complicated, and we can see the kinds of errors people fall into when they pick out just one or another piece of the whole.

Questions of Application

The arguments developed so far yield some results that are prima facie surprising, though they are consonant with the actual practices of academic freedom. To highlight the counterintuitiveness of the results, I will first juxtapose two kinds of cases that have often been in the news in recent years.

1. When a controversial speaker from outside the university tries to speak on campus and is met with protests, the speaker's academic freedom is not violated—even if the speaker is a scholarly expert rather than a professional provocateur, and even if the speech in question is actually disrupted or prevented.
2. When a member of the university, including a student or a non-tenure-track, nonunionized, contingently employed instructor, speaks *off* campus, including on highly controversial matters outside their scholarly expertise, including on social media or to intellectually disreputable media, they *are* still protected by academic freedom.

It's perfectly reasonable to find this surprising. An interrupted scholarly lecture seems to be squarely within the core of a university's concern. An uninformed and inflammatory tweet that incites public outrage does not. And yet these are the conclusions demanded by the arguments presented here.

Academic freedom is associational; the nonmember visiting speaker is not a member of the association. In disputes about visiting speakers, everything turns on the questions of whether they are invited and hosted, and if so, by whom. From the perspective of the association, the finest scholar in the world is nothing but a trespasser if they arrive on campus uninvited and help themselves to a lectern and a microphone. This is stylized, of course; different universities have different norms about the openness of their campus as property and as space. At a university whose campus space is generally open to the public, general free speech rights might well come into play if an off-campus speaker (or, say, pamphleteer) is prevented from offering their views on campus grounds. But that right is not, as we have seen, academic freedom.

Academic freedom is indeed at stake when an off-campus speaker is invited and hosted by a unit of the university, by one of the various nested associations whether a student club or an academic department. However, the academic freedom at issue *is that of the sponsoring organization*. It is the associational freedom of the club or department. The speakers themselves are not members of the academic community at issue, and they are, at worst, guests who have been treated impolitely.

This distinction matters, I think, in two ways. One is that it helps us to stop making the speakers themselves the stars of the show. This is helpful insofar as there is now a kind of professional circuit of provocateurs whose traveling road show depends precisely on their ability to antagonize student protestors into protesting them. Universities have been unwitting and unwilling partners in the creation of this circuit. They provide both the stage and the foils of the show, allowing the starring martyrs to "cancel culture" to rise to greater and greater celebrity. It is the general *openness* to visiting speakers in vast numbers—being invited and hosted by the whole array of university associations—that makes possible the media narrative of universities as being ideological cloisters hostile to free debate. No one ever gets "canceled" when they try to present controversial ideas to a condominium association or a bowling league or a community theater group, because neither of those associations has any general practice of hosting speakers at all. Churches might occasionally do so, but everyone expects that a speaker at a church will be speaking within the boundaries of the church's own mission. The practice of having visiting speakers at universities, while decidedly secondary to the core research and teaching activities of university members, is a very common adjunct to those activities, because it is very common for the university's associations to want to host them for the benefit of students and the broader community, as because of the intellectual benefits of scholarly exchange. This is all valuable, but it has made universities vulnerable to this kind of hostile parasitism of people building their celebrity by trying to speak at universities and getting protested. It's hard to know how to extricate universities from this unhappy trend, but at a minimum, those within the academy should refrain from contributing to it. And that means decentering the visiting speaker in our debates.

But the distinction also matters in focusing attention where it belongs: on the academic freedom of the organization or institution that invited the speaker in the first place. Protesting an invited speaker is a normal part of on-campus debate and disagreement. But actually preventing their speech is an attack *on other members of the academic community*, on the club or department that invited them. And while those of us who care about the academic community should not want to contribute to the celebrity martyrdom of outsiders taking advantage of that community, we also should not minimize the wrong done to the other scholars in such an attack. Focusing normative attention on the speaker has also been an easy way to excuse disruptions: the speaker's own objectionable speech or conduct elsewhere, their status as being hateful or deceptive, becomes all the argument one needs to shut them down. But the protestors' fellow scholars are the people whose academic freedom is actually being infringed, and the sins of the speaker are a distraction from that fact.

Here, by the way, is where I would return to the analogy of professional ethics that I mentioned at the beginning of the essay. In this set of disputes, those who disrupt an event like this sometimes help themselves to the language of civil disobedience. Perhaps they commit a formal wrong in preventing someone they consider a spreader of hateful lies from speaking (so this line of argument runs). But they do so conscientiously in the pursuit of justice or truth, just as civil disobedients might commit trespass or violate traffic regulations or parade restrictions when they use the force of their assembled bodies to prevent or protest injustice in the democratic public sphere. That is an analogy that appeals to a politically heroic ideal.

But if we think of the university, not like a democratic state but as a space constituted by a professional ethic, and if we think of respecting our colleagues' (including students') academic freedom as a core piece of that ethic, things look rather different. Lawyers are often involved in cases that excite their genuine commitment to justice. And yet "my client's cause is truly, importantly just" is no excuse at all for withholding documents that are due in discovery, for suborning perjury or bribing a witness or threatening a juror. Nor is "my client's cause is truly unjust" an excuse for violating attorney–client privilege. So too for the priest violating the sanctity of confession, or the doctor violating the rules of informed consent. The conscience of the professional is no excuse at all for violating the rules that constitute their office, and the lawyer facing disbarment is rightly regarded very differently from the civil disobedient. To disrupt a lecture or research presentation, or for that matter to disrupt a classroom or laboratory, seems to me of that kind. A visiting speaker might be a very bad scholar indeed; some of the celebrity provocateurs on the lecture circuit certainly are. But to violate the academic freedom of our colleagues whose department, center, student association, and so on invited them is a violation of the shared scholarly enterprise itself.

I would, in general, distinguish speakers who were invited by a unit of the university—from a student club to a department or research institute—to share their *ideas* from categories of prominent guests given a speaking platform as a deliberate honor for them as *persons*. The important cases of the latter are recipients of honorary degrees and speakers at university graduation and convocation ceremonies. (These are often but not always the same.) The space for a reasonable, collegial protest of such honorees is wider than it is for visiting speakers hosted by peers exercising their associational academic freedom. It is not just that there is no right to an honorary degree; to that extent, they resemble ordinary outside speakers, who also do not have a right to be there. It is that honoring is different from hearing out; and that the captive audience of graduating students awaiting their degrees is different from the voluntary audience of an ordinary speaker. This does not mean that actually disrupting a graduation event is respectful; it surely disrespects one's fellow students. But it does mean that protesting before the fact the decision to honor someone one regards as dishonorable is thoroughly appropriate. Here, too, popular discourse about campus life gets things backward. There is an annual public commentary on how shameful it is for university students to object to this or that graduation speaker or honorary degree recipient because it shows that they do not appreciate freedom of speech and open debate. But the famous speakers at issue usually do not lack opportunities to express themselves. The protests object to the honor, to which the (usually very familiar) expressed ideas are secondary; and to the decidedly non–debate-like experience of being a captive audience at the moment when the students' degrees should be the center of attention.

Now consider the speech of the member of the university association, outside their area of academic expertise. This is the category of expression that is referred to in the American Association of University Professors principles as "extramural utterances," and it's the source of constant confusion in public debate. The confusion is understandable at first glance. When the professor of engineering writes an uninformed post on social media about race and IQ, when the graduate student in Chinese history makes an inflammatory comment about the Israel–Palestine dispute on cable news, when the adjunct instructor in psychology engages in vaccine misinformation or promotes conspiracy theories about sex trafficking, maybe that is protected by freedom of speech, but what does it have to do with scholarship? If academic freedom is the practice of a truth-seeking community that prioritizes the expert use of the tools of inquiry appropriate to each field of study, why should talking through one's hat outside the classroom or the laboratory be protected?

The answer lies in academic freedom's status as jurisdictional, and in remembering what it *means* to be protected by it. Extramural expression is outside the evaluation of the scholar as a scholar (as always, meaning either students or academic staff) and, accordingly, fundamentally outside the jurisdiction of the academic association. The examples listed above left unstated what the scholar in question was to be protected *from*; the answer is, adverse *academic* consequences. The student may not be failed in a class or expelled from a degree program or denied an academic award. The member of the academic staff may not be denied tenure or have it revoked, or be denied a sabbatical or pay raise to which they would be entitled on academic merit. This, it should be emphasized, is not some marginal fact about academic freedom, some problem that arose recently in the era of social media and cable news. It was central to the articulation of the value in the late nineteenth and early twentieth centuries, when politicians, donors, and other powerful actors tried to demand that university professors be fired or not hired because they were, for example, communists or atheists. The eventual practice of academic freedom rightly developed a two-pronged response. If they reached communist or atheist conclusions as part of their research within their area of expertise (political economy or political philosophy or metaphysics), then that was a protected scholarly outcome. And if their communism or atheism lay outside their scholarly work, then it was irrelevant to it.

Insofar as academic freedom involves a rejection of dogmatism and enforced orthodoxy about conclusions, it is in general best for universities to refrain even from expressing disagreement with the controversial extramural speech of one of their academic members, though they frequently do so in the panicked heat of the moment. Overwhelmingly often, the best practice would be for the institution to say nothing more than this in its corporate voice:

> As is true for all members of our scholarly community in their public commentary and social media engagement, this scholar's comments solely represent his or her own views. As is true for all members of our scholarly community, this scholar's ability to express those views is protected both by freedom of speech and in a different way by principles of academic freedom, which forbid the university from acting to punish academic staff or students for the content of their extramural expressed opinions. The university as an institution does not normally take positions on matters of social and political controversy, in order to best protect the freedom of its members to pursue inquiry that supports or opposes such positions. Accordingly, the university does not normally comment, whether in support or in opposition, on the expressed opinions of its professors or students.

And on the principle that those in positions of power should not create the perception appearance that they are threatening to misuse it, at least those university officials in a direct line of authority above the scholar—the student's professors and advisors; the professor's chair or dean, the university's provost or president—should not say much more than that in their *individual* capacity, either. There are plausible exceptions to these norms, but these are the right baseline norms, and they are too often forgotten.

Conclusion: Safe Spaces

I conclude with one final counterintuitive implication of understanding academic freedom as the nested freedom of a complex association. One popular off-campus indictment of university students is that they are afraid to confront debate and disagreement, and wish to be coddled inside a so-called safe space. This line of criticism, too, is almost completely backward; the freedom of a complex association to a substantial degree just *is* the existence of a nested community of safe spaces.

The basic unit of academic freedom is a community of inquiry, most paradigmatically a disciplinary department but it can be anything from a student club to a multidisciplinary research institute. Within *any one* of those, scholars have the ability to work together, exploring ideas and knowledge within parameters that are, locally and for the moment, taken for granted.

Building knowledge together requires building on a shared body of (locally and for the moment) agreed-upon understandings and findings, and using (locally and for the moment) accepted methods of inquiry, standards of evidence, and kinds of argument. On a complex university campus, physicists—whether in a laboratory or in a classroom—don't have to *constantly* reply to a philosopher challenging their knowledge of epistemology. Neither do the political scientists find their work interrupted by the physicist telling them that it is not a *real* science, or the historians by the economist complaining that their work lacks microfoundations, or the literary humanists by the social scientist complaining that their scholarship is too subjective to be replicable. There are, to be sure, interdisciplinary moments when those challenges are explored and debated. But those are the exceptions to a baseline rule that each intellectual community is free to go about its business, studying according to methods, tools, and agreed-upon prior knowledge that is taken for granted. (This will be familiar to readers of Kuhn as the practice of "normal science.")

Mutatis mutandis the same is true for everything from an interdisciplinary center to a student club. An interdisciplinary center for gender studies does not spend all day, every day replying to the campus conservative who repetitively insists that feminism is the real sexism in modern society. A student Christian fellowship gets on with the shared exploration of a shared faith, not subject to endless interruption from the argumentative atheist. And so on, and so on. Likewise, within each of these associations, the status of the scholars as rightful members of the scholarly community is taken for granted. Literature professors do not have to convince economists or physicists that they are real scholars who should be allowed on campus. Students from marginalized communities, meeting in their affinity groups, likewise do not have to respond to constant challenges to the legitimacy of their presence.

When some of those communities meet and blend, that does not change the basic pattern; it establishes a new locally appropriate set of subjects, questions, methods, and so on. None of the university spaces ever becomes a Hyde Park soapbox; each is always a safe space for those who want to engage in locally appropriate exploration, examination, or study. Indeed, I think this is much of *why* universities cultivate and subsidize their internal ecosystems of student clubs and associations. The university as a complex association is founded on an appreciation of a plurality of communities of inquiry, each pursuing their own *internal* studies, discussions, and debates; and it makes sense that the younger scholarly members of the community would self-organize in ways that mirror the self-organization of disciplines, centers, faculties, and so on. And when they do, they seek safe spaces, where new questions can be asked and debated, building on shared assumptions and secure in the knowledge that their status as members of the scholarly community isn't one of the topics locally up for debate.

The implication is counterintuitive in different ways for different readers. To the on-campus reader sympathetic to protected associations and safe spaces, it brings an unwelcome limitation; my safe space ends where your associational freedom begins. The appeal to shared assumptions is always local and provisional, and the university *as a whole* cannot mirror the safety of the association without turning those assumptions into dogma. There is no right to intrude into *other* parts of the university—other departments, other clubs' events—and to insist that one's own locally shared assumptions and conversational boundaries be recognized and enforced in them.

But to the unsympathetic off-campus critic, the implication is even more surprising and even more unwelcome. The students seeking their safe spaces are not acting contrary to the spirit of academic freedom. They are carrying it on, and carrying it out.

CHAPTER 3

Academic Freedom and University Autonomy

An Agenda for Professional Public Engagement

SIJBOLT NOORDA

INTRODUCTION

Interest in academic freedom and university autonomy seems to come and go in waves. After phases of relative rest and silence, these concepts can gain new relevance. We are currently experiencing such a revival in many parts of the world, which is a solid justification for delving deeper into some aspects that often remain underexposed.

While in most discussions of academic freedom individual rights and individual security predominate, this chapter focuses on institutional autonomy and freedom in and of the academic community. This is not about abstract notions or concepts but about academic freedom, independence, and autonomy as core living values in contemporary universities.

We may begin with the essence of a university: What is a university? A basic definition would be an institution of adult education and scholarly research. The learning part is the core task of every university. It is conducted by students, mostly young adults and some older, who are supported and inspired by their teachers and tutors, as well as by their peers. It is their aim to acquire knowledge, skills, and competencies in one or several academic and/or professional fields, culminating with a certification or degree. The result is an academic professional's access pass to the job market inside and outside of academia.

Depending on the profile of the university, the research part is equally or less pronounced. It is mainly carried out by qualified senior researchers together with a good number of junior researchers and PhD students, preferably with many students involved in one role or another from their undergraduate years on.

All of this is done with the further motive of developing scientific knowledge as well as educating new generations of academic professionals, not just out of self-interest but as a service to society and a contribution to the public good.

For a university to be able to meet these ambitions and tasks, it naturally needs several favorable framework conditions (in terms of material provisions and scholarly competencies and the like). Yet to be able to fulfill its tasks properly, a university needs more; it needs a considerable degree of freedom: the freedom to think and teach, to plan and prioritize, to collaborate with colleagues at home and around the world, all in the interest of how we can best serve present and future societies and more generally sustainable human life on our planet. In other words, the freedom of the academy rests on its function; it is a crucial requirement and prerequisite for its performance.

In this sense, this chapter is about the freedom of the university and its members and how it is best used.

Definitions

Before addressing some key current challenges that universities and their members face in maintaining and using their freedom and independence, it should be clear how these concepts of freedom and independence are used in the present context. Quite often, explanations of freedom and independence refer either to their different lexical meanings (e.g., freedom refers to the ability to do something, while liberty is permission to do something; or positive freedom is the ability to do something, while negative freedom is the lack of restrictions) or to the comparative use of freedom in a legal context (e.g., comparing academic freedom with freedom of expression or discussing the relationship between freedoms and rights or obligations and responsibilities). However, since words acquire their meaning through their usage, one should look beyond lexical or legal meanings for context and usage.

A very common setting for statements about freedom is that of the individual. A common version defines freedom as a situation or ability in which one can do whatever one wants. There are no obstacles, only a maximum range of options for the individual.[1] Still, some philosophers have seen good reason to qualify such statements, either emphasizing that ability should imply capacity (one has the opportunity and means to do whatever one pleases) or adding that the statement is not about no matter what but about things of value to the individual concerned and/or to others as well.[2] Such qualifiers point to two much-discussed problems: unlimited freedom for one individual easily violates unlimited freedom for other individuals; declaring someone free without enabling that individual to realize their freedom is little more than offering an empty shell.

However, the individual is not the only point of reference for freedom in common parlance. One can also speak of societies characterized by various degrees of freedom. Either in terms of their autonomy as a nation (as opposed to nations that are ruled or occupied by others: a free society governs itself) and/or in terms of the degree of freedom enjoyed by a society's citizens (a free society is one that allows individuals to live a life of freedom).

A third possible reference is made less frequently. This is about the independence of institutions in society and the freedom of professional associations and their members. In many societies, autonomous institutions (such as the judiciary) perform a crucial function, independent of individual citizens and political government. Even more commonly, professions such as medicine or art are defined as independent and free, meaning that those in these professions can exercise the decision-making powers that every true professional needs to deliver quality work, to serve their clients and the general public in the best possible way, free from outside interference.

1 See, e.g., "Freedom," *Oxford Advanced Learner's Dictionary*, www.oxfordlearnersdictionaries.com/definition/english/freedom.

2 See, e.g., Joel Feinberg, "Freedom and Liberty," in *The Shorter Routledge Encyclopedia of Philosophy*, ed. Edward Craig (London: Routledge, 2005), 294.

Professional freedom and independence in this sense imply that within their functional domain members of these groups or guilds are allowed to be autonomous: they set and follow their own rules, in the interest of the quality of their professional performance. As a corollary of these freedoms, professional institutions or guilds and their members have a responsibility to act in accordance with professional standards and to be accountable to their peers' forum for the quality of their work. Independent judges are bound by rules and criteria of professional quality and integrity.

As I see it, the academic profession belongs exactly in this category. The postwar German constitution contains the pointed statement "Kunst und Wissenschaft, Forschung und Lehre sind frei" ("Arts and Sciences, Research and Teaching Are Free"), which expresses the fundamental independence of these professions and the guild's members. This is a qualified freedom, within a specific, broadly defined professional domain with its own norms and rules.[3]

It is precisely this type of institutional and professional freedom and independence that characterizes the Magna Charta Universitatum's (MCU) principles and statements, both in its original version of 1988 and in its recent 2020 version.[4] The universities referred to by these statements are autonomous institutions (that enjoy independence, set their own norms and rules, and assume responsibility and accountability), and the members of these institutions (be they academics or students) enjoy academic freedom (which is fundamentally a qualified freedom that comes with responsibility).[5]

Two Relevant Domains

Guided by these preliminary explorations, the present chapter will explore some key issues of academic freedoms in two relevant domains: on the one hand, the university and its external positioning and interaction with and perception by society; on the other hand, the academic community itself with its own internal arrangements, values, and behaviors. The first is about

3 Germany, *Grundgesetz für die Bundesrepublik Deutschland*, Article 5.

4 MCU 2020. The 2020 version of the Magna Charta not only repeats and underlines the core principles of the 1988 original but adds a number of key commitments and responsibilities of universities, most of them in terms of public service.

5 My approach may be termed a *professional* understanding of academic freedom; see Matthew W. Finkin and Robert C. Post, *For the Common Good: Principles of American Freedom* (New Haven: Yale University Press, 2009), 9.

how the academy positions itself in society, how it interacts with other societal bodies or groups, and how it wants to be perceived. The second concerns shared values of the academy itself and in particular the relationship between the academy as a community and the freedoms of its members.

Before discussing these two domains it is crucial to consider the importance of the link between academia and society. Universities are not standalone institutions. They are meant to serve a greater purpose, such as the purpose of serving society and its sustainable development on our planet in a responsible manner. This implies knowing and deciding how to do this well, including selecting and designing appropriate programs of teaching, learning, and research, assuming that most if not all academics are fit and ready to contribute. Freedom and autonomy are prerequisites of the university in that they allow the university to shape its specific mission and strategies independently.[6] For the sake of clarity, I would like to add right away that these freedoms should not allow universities to betray their fundamental mission. It is not freedom in the sense of free-for-all. It is a freedom that allows independent institutions to carry out their professional task with the assumption that they agree on professional rules and adhere to their professional values.

In this chapter, I have chosen to focus on the role and mission of the university itself for two reasons. For one, how a university lives and uses its freedom is a comparatively underexposed topic, although one of paramount importance. Much more attention is usually paid to external actors and outside influences, and the role of authorities, funders, and legislators regarding autonomous universities, with the main message that they should grant, recognize, and protect the university's independence and not interfere in its core mission and decision-making. For another thing, in times of intense social changes and more than the usual political turbulence, universities as independent social institutions should not passively wait and see what will happen (to them) but rather actively define and protect their position in society, vis-à-vis authorities, funders, and legislators, both in terms of their autonomy and of their independent engagement in societal developments, wherever and whenever their position in society and their ability to contribute to its development and well-being is at stake.

6 See Frank H. T. Rhodes, "Universities and the Democratic Spirit," in *Higher Education and Democratic Culture: Citizenship, Human Rights and Civic Responsibility*, ed. Josef Huber and Ira Harkavy (Strasbourg: Council of Europe Publishing, 2007), 45.

University and Society

> Universities acknowledge that they have a responsibility to engage with and respond to the aspirations and challenges of the world and to the communities they serve, to benefit humanity and contribute to sustainability.

This is a core statement of the new 2020 edition of the MCU. It is not so much a new insight as it is one to be revisited, retested, and reapplied over time because it is such a contingent pursuit. It takes on different forms with changing circumstances since it fundamentally is a relational aspiration. Times are changing and with them the university and its mission.

There is general agreement that the university's raison d'être is to serve society, to prepare new generations for professional roles in society, to contribute to the development of culture and civilization, and to support innovation in the workplace, in technology or energy production and use. In academia we seem to have truly embraced this belief, knowing that our end users and beneficiaries are companies and communities, schools and start-ups, hospitals as well as hydrogen plants. We are confident that in the final analysis, all we do is done well from a societal perspective.

Chris Brink aptly describes this conviction with the metaphor of Adam Smith's invisible hand. If we do our academic profession well, it will eventually end up having beneficial effects, one way or another.[7] Although indeed a good number of examples can be given of quite late and often unintended beneficial effects and uses of scientific knowledge, this spontaneous, accidental "natural" causality is not enough. If the academy's mandate of engaging with society and creating a healthy impact in society is to fully develop and unfold its effects in good time and where they are needed, it must be based on a dedicated overall strategy and be designed in direct interaction with relevant partners in society.

However, society is a broad and rather frayed concept and phenomenon. Most of us have our own preferred society, the type of society or part of society we work for and are familiar with. Particularly in today's fragmented

7 Chris Brink, *The Soul of the University: Why Excellence Is Not Enough* (Bristol: Bristol University Press, 2018), 35–36.

societies where the common good is perceived very differently by different groups with different interests and concerns, it is very tempting to be choosy about the kind of society we envision and would like to work for.

At the same time our commitment to fairness, to public benefit, should prevent us from being picky, not allowing us to line up with those parties and institutions in society that seem to be our natural allies or our best-paying partners, rather than with those who would most likely benefit most from our involvement. Otherwise, universities run the risk of being viewed as elite institutions, not because of their high-quality performance, but because they are an integrated part of the establishment and with preference serve the interest of that establishment and its members.

So, if we want to serve society well, we should seriously ask ourselves "What society?" And to answer that question fairly we must base our judgment on sound analysis and avoid bias and prejudice. Consequently, university strategies and policies of engagement with society require serious reconnaissance work, to identify pressing needs and what the university could and should deliver to public benefit.

Two years ago, the Council of Europe[8] published a volume of articles on academic freedom, institutional autonomy, and the future of democracy. It offers a clear and instructive reflection of the interdependence between university and society in relation to fundamental values, in particular freedom and autonomy, with the ironic statement that academic freedom and institutional autonomy at universities do better in situations where they are least demanded. In open societies with a high degree of accepted diversity and respectful public debate and controversy, faculty and students as well as universities naturally benefit from this societal climate. In less permissive societies, dissident opinions and independent institutions are under constant attack.

In this context, the 1988 MCU and its fundamental principles of independence and freedom certainly remain of high relevance.[9] The third principle reads in full: "Freedom in research and teaching is the fundamental principle of university life, and government and universities, each as far as in

8 Sjur Bergan, Tony Gallagher, and Ira Harkavy, eds., *Academic Freedom, Institutional Autonomy and the Future of Democracy* (Strasbourg: Council of Europe Publishing, 2020).

9 For more on this point, see Sijbolt Noorda, "University Autonomy and Academic Freedom Revisited," in *Academic Freedom, Institutional Autonomy and the Future of Democracy*, ed. Sjur Bergan, Tony Gallagher, and Ira Harkavy (Strasbourg: Council of Europe Publishing, 2020), 199–211.

them lies, must ensure respect for this fundamental requirement. Rejecting intolerance and always open to dialogue, a university is an ideal meeting-ground for teachers capable of imparting their knowledge and well equipped to develop it by research and innovation and for students entitled, able and willing to enrich their minds with that knowledge."

This principle reflects a strong academic tradition of freedom in research and teaching and requires that it be promoted, respected, and protected by both universities and government. However, history teaches us that the social contract underlying higher education, which allows and protects its core values, is particularly vulnerable and easily damaged in situations of repression and heightened state control. Developments in several countries around the world in recent years clearly show how governments are violating university freedoms by invoking national emergencies and higher state interests.

At the same time, it has become clear that living and preserving the freedom, openness, and tolerance that should characterize university life is also a major challenge elsewhere. To get it right is not a matter of course, at home and abroad and in international cooperation. Within repressive regimes, it is not easy to live up to the commitment formulated in 2020 MCU ("universities are non-discriminatory spaces of tolerance and respect where diversity of perspectives flourishes and where inclusivity, anchored in principles of equity and fairness, prevails. They therefore commit themselves to advance equity and fairness in all aspects of academic life including admissions, hiring and promotion practices") by actually promoting and upholding this openness and tolerance. There is often a tension between the ideal of the university as a beacon and an example of this attitude and disposition on the one hand, and the contemporary trend of group exclusivity and bubble comfort, characteristic of many contemporary societies and their institutions on the other hand. It is a key challenge for independent institutions like the university how to avoid becoming just another partisan institution, nicely living in its own sphere, at the risk of being viewed by others as an establishment that is primarily serving its peers and partners of preference.

Universities should be *lighthouses* and role models for openness and tolerance, pointing the way for society. If universities do not practice the ideals of freedom and diversity within their walls, they not only limit the creative potential of their community of scholars and students, but also do not function as a good model to the outside world. This is about realizing a crucial willingness to create space for different opinions and positions, for debate and solid argument, both in the field of scholarship itself and regarding the societal context in which universities are integrated.

I would like to suggest that this lighthouse function is one of the key things public service universities should do. However, getting this right is by no means easy because of the risks of outside pressure, government intervention as well as internal disagreements or lack of support. In my own years as university president, I have often seen how strong our tendency to be with like-minded people is. Inviting colleagues with very different approaches often led to protests and accusations. "Why would you want to offer her/him a platform?" Our leaning toward the mainstream and the usual is very strong indeed. We all easily bend and bow toward the comfort of the known and supportive, just as easily as we stray away from the strange and challenging.

However, if we as universities are not able to embrace diversity and open ourselves to different views and traditions, we are certainly missing our calling. In positive terms, successful beacons are a tremendous asset and a major contribution to creating trust in universities as public institutions, and in education and research as reliable tools for the development of societies and the well-being of their citizens.

Similarly, John Sexton expresses what he sees as the duty of universities: "Universities are ... protected areas of thought and dialogue; but, precisely because they enjoy the benefit of protection and thus a special capacity to incubate ideas, they must mobilize outward from their protected position to become even greater forces than they now are for the advancement of thought and dialogue in society generally. ... They must stand as witnesses for their core values and act as a reproach to dogmatism and its consequences. They must extend their most salient internal activity—the meaningful testing of ideas—as a model for wider public discourse."[10]

A Kasbah or a Community?

No university can achieve this without a solid common value base. Without shared values, common norms, and criteria, it is simply impossible to get

10 John Sexton, *Standing for Reason: The University in a Dogmatic Age* (New Haven: Yale University Press, 2019), 16.

it right. These are the indispensable foundation stones of the institution's self-understanding.

Some of these values are fundamental and enable universities to be what they are meant to be. The most important of these are autonomy and academic freedom. Other values concern the operational functioning of a university and the quality of our work. This includes integrity and fairness. A third set of values I would call social values. It is about the responsiveness of the academy toward society and the social quality of our access strategies, the priorities in research, and the equity of outreach.

Values are important beliefs or ideals shared by members of a community or institution about what is good or bad, desirable, or not, given the nature and mission of the institution. They serve as rough guidelines for attitude, behavior, and engagement. In the case of a university, they define what kind of institution a university wants to be. They are fundamental principles of institutional self-understanding and positioning in society, they guide academic communities in their (inter)national relations, with whom they work in which way and to what purpose, and how to deal with cultural diversity, including different value priorities. Therefore, it is crucially important for every university community to identify, discuss, and agree on core values.

Such a shared basis of values cannot be taken for granted. It cannot and should not be equated with a mission statement of the institution's leadership. For it to truly be a value base and a trusted institutional compass, it must be deeply ingrained in the academic community that, again, is not self-evident.

The contemporary university is often more of a *kasbah* with a multitude of individual shopkeepers or a sports field for individual career competitions than a cooperative, collegial community with shared ideals and values, no matter how much robust institutional resilience and the protection of university autonomy and academic freedom require a strong community in which basic values are discussed and shared—not just solemnly remembered and recited at festive occasions, only to be activated in times of crisis and conflict.

It would be naïve and even unwise to turn a blind eye to reality and the positive aspects of individual ambition and competition in the university. They are an indispensable positive force in many ways. What is the issue then? It is about keeping the balance. If individual professional success is the only aspiration, the academy will not achieve its goals and will not be able to develop its full potential as a public institution with a social mission. What is needed is a common denominator and a strong awareness of the professional academic identity I mentioned earlier. Independent institutions like the university can only maintain their independence and play their role in society through the committed work of their members. Professional freedom and independence imply that members are allowed to be autonomous within their functional area: they should set and follow their own rules in the interest of the quality of their professional performance. As a corollary of these freedoms, however, professional institutions or guilds and all their members have a responsibility to act in accordance with professional standards and to be accountable to their peers' forum for the quality of their work.

The university development agenda should therefore not only include fair funding and opportunities for individual career development, but also the affirmation of professional academic identity and associated values and practices. The professional community is an essential pillar of the academy in this context, allowing the institution to maintain and corroborate its independent position based on shared values and collegial support.

In addition, the cooperative, collegial community is also decisive in terms of content. Of all the relevant issues, I shall mention only one. It is our long and very successful tradition of disciplinary teaching & learning and research. This tradition has given us great success, there is no doubt about that. Nevertheless, there are many good reasons for a serious rethink. This is not just the observation that new findings in science can very often be found in the no man's land between the disciplines or in the places where disciplines meet; nor just the observation that in many professions young graduates are expected to work in multidisciplinary teams and have the skills to do so successfully; rather, it is, above all, the observation that many of the central challenges of human life on this planet require multilateral thinking, complexity thinking, and interdisciplinary skills.

The 1988 MCU already stressed our responsibility for the future of our societies. It used lofty language to emphasize our responsibility to our ecosystem. "The future of mankind," it said, "depends on cultural, scientific and technical development," of which universities as centers of culture, knowledge, and research are key drivers. This is to be done through the education of younger generations, but it also requires broader service to society, a forward-looking perspective, in the interests of a broad development of societies, and the promotion of due respect for the natural environment.

At that time the far-reaching and structural consequences of such a future orientation were not yet seen. Like the urgent need to reorganize our teaching & learning and research across monodisciplinary boundaries and into new study and research configurations. If the university is to live up to its mission of serving future generations, it should not be afraid to adapt its structures and programs. Whether the issue is social cohesion or lack of it, sustainable economies and the way to get there, renewable energies and their price, ethics of the digital age, sustainable food and nutrition, or healthy aging—in all these cases we cannot make progress unless we collaborate, unless we do crossovers, unless we dare to be different. Some years ago, the first cohort of students from the new undergraduate program Future Planet Studies at the University of Amsterdam evaluated their experiences. A large majority liked what they learned, would do it again, and would recommend their peers to do the same. Their main criticism, however, was directed at their teachers. Not in terms of their academic quality or their pedagogical skills, but precisely because of their lack of interdisciplinary experience and attitude. The program was appreciated as interdisciplinary but the teachers themselves were deemed to be lagging.

That explains nicely what I mean. For universities to be successful in addressing today's great challenges, we—educators and researchers—must commit to rethinking and retraining. I have learned from those who have done so that this is not a pipe dream. It can be done, and it can be done well, through collaborative, collegial academic communities.

It is one of the key responsibilities of university leadership to build and protect such collaborative communities, along with the affirmation of professional academic identity and associated values and practices. Deans, provosts, and presidents—all have a crucial role to play as the enablers, facilitators, and protectors of the academic community and its commitment to diversity, openness, frankness, and integrity.[11] This is by no means a simple task, as it requires a mix of engagement and restraint; modesty because one should not will to be the only leading voice of the university, and courage because one should will to be the staunch defender of a space where many

11 On the university leader as guardian of a sacred space, see Sexton, *Standing for Reason*, 38–48.

voices can and actually do speak up. Yet, of the many important roles university leaders must play these days this may very well be the most important.

Conclusion

This chapter aimed to show that academic freedom and university autonomy are both a program and a multifaceted challenge that should be understood as a commitment agenda rather than a statement of privilege.

The contemporary university needs more than proclaiming and demanding these freedoms. Using them well requires a serious rethinking of traditional structures and practices. This will not be done through crisis meetings or mission statements. It will require nothing less than revitalizing the professional community aspect of the academy and the values associated with it and restoring the balance between individual career interests and the public role of a university. This is the path to shaping an agenda for professional public engagement.

Chapter 4

The Political Cosmetology of Academic Freedom

Jean-François Gaudreault-DesBiens

Introduction

Academic freedom is under threat in various parts of the world. Promoted by authoritarian governments, the rise of the concept of "illiberal democracy"—arguably an oxymoron—is consubstantial to a reduction of academic freedom—think of Hungary, Poland, and Turkey[1]—all this in a context where totalitarian states, such as Russia, China, or Iran, are becoming increasingly assertive in the promotion of an "alternative" model to the Western liberal one.

Needless to say that academic freedom, as this concept has been understood in liberal democracies for the past century or so, is at best a figment of the imagination in such states.[2] Even in one of its birthplaces—the United States—academic freedom is challenged by populist politicians who, under the guise of defending either a mythical national narrative or an equally mythical vision of American society, oversee legislative projects deliberately seeking to forbid the discussion of various topics or critical approaches, such

1 Vanessa Frangville et al., *La liberté académique: Enjeux et menaces* (Brussels: Éditions de l'Université de Bruxelles, 2021).

2 In all three countries, academic freedom is almost nonexistent, and even decreasing; see "Academic Freedom Index," https://academic-freedom-index.net/.

as Critical Race Theory. All this takes place in a context where some militant groups associated with the so-called woke left sometimes resort to strategies or practices that effectively hinder free speech in academic settings; this is what is now commonly referred to as the "cancel culture."

Canada is not immune to such dynamics. In 2018, the Government of Ontario implemented a policy targeted at "upholding free speech" in the province's universities and colleges. It was followed the next year by the Alberta government, and, in 2022, the Quebec National Assembly enacted the Act Respecting Academic Freedom in the University Sector (hereinafter designated as the "AAFUS").[3]

Although I will look at all these initiatives in this chapter, I will primarily focus on the Quebec legislation, as the context in which it was adopted reveals the influence of social variables that tend to play out more significantly in the United States and some European countries than in English-speaking Canada. As well, Quebec's critical position vis-à-vis some policy choices largely supported in English-speaking Canada might be relevant. I shall analyze the broader political context in which the Act arose and examine the legal regime it puts in place. I will then argue, in light of Ontario's experience, that the reporting obligations imposed upon universities in this legislation will likely be of limited effectiveness with a view to tangibly protecting academic freedom. Particularly in light of the fact that it pays lip service to a most important precondition of academic freedom, that is, institutional autonomy, I will argue that the Quebec legislation represents an expression of an increasingly widespread phenomenon that I call the "political cosmetology of academic freedom," which is far from being confined to Quebec.

Defending Academic Freedom: A New Political Interest

In August 2018, after a series of perceived speech-related incidents in Ontario universities, the provincial government issued a directive on freedom of expression in academia.[4] From January 1, 2019, any university (or

3 AAFUS, RLRQ, c. L-1.2.

4 Ontario Government, "Upholding Free Speech on Ontario's University and College Campuses," news release, August 30, 2018, https://news.ontario.ca/en/backgrounder/49950/upholding-free-speech-on-ontarios-university-and-college-campuses; Ontario Government, *Ontario Protects Free Speech on Cam-*

college) receiving public funding was required to have developed and made public its own free speech policy and to meet a minimum standard set by the government in doing so. Since then, university policies on the subject, applicable to teaching, administrative and support staff as well as to students and guests, must: (1) define freedom of expression by taking up the principles set out in the University of Chicago Statement on Principles of Free Expression; (2) ensure that the disciplinary regulations in force apply to student actions disrespecting the policy; (3) ensure that student associations comply with the policy through negative incentives such as nonfunding or withdrawal of institutional recognition; (4) use existing university complaint resolution mechanisms to resolve complaints based on a violation of the freedom of expression policy, with unresolved complaints to be referred to the Provincial Ombudsman; and (5) report annually to the Higher Education Quality Council of Ontario on the application of the policy, this council being responsible for monitoring the implementation of the government's directive at the university level and ensure compliance.[5] In the event of failure to file the required annual report or if the council finds that a university is not respecting its policy, the latter may see a portion of its government grant reduced.

In the summer of 2019, the Alberta government followed in the footsteps of its Ontario counterpart by issuing a similar directive, aimed at requiring the adoption by the board of each Alberta university of a policy on freedom of expression, also inspired by the University of Chicago Statement on Principles of Free Expression. Such a policy must at least incorporate the following parameters: (1) the exercise of freedom of expression in an academic context must not violate Canadian law; (2) the university must be recognized as a place where any idea or subject can be discussed and where each member of the community has the greatest possible latitude when it comes to expressing themselves, listening, questioning and learning; (3) members of the university community have the right to criticize and question the opinions expressed by other people on campus, without however being

puses Mandates Universities and Colleges to Introduce Free Speech Policy by January 1, 2019, August 20, 2018, accessed April 26, 2023, https://news.ontario.ca/en/release/49948/ontario-protects-free-speech-on-campuses.

5 O. Reg. 336/06: Higher Education Quality Council of Ontario under Higher Education Quality Council of Ontario Act 2005, S.O. 2005, c. 28, Sched. G, Art. 9.

able to obstruct the latter's exercise of their own freedom of expression; (4) the university should not attempt to shield students from ideas or opinions with which they disagree or find offensive and although mutual respect and civility should be valued, they do not justify in themselves the imposition of constraints on freedom of expression; (5) the university may regulate when, where and how freedom of expression is exercised to ensure that the ordinary course of its business is not interfered with; (6) the university may restrict forms of expression that violate the law, defame a person, constitute a threat or harassment or violate privacy or compromise the confidentiality of information; (7) the fact that ideas are perceived, even by a majority of people, as being offensive, reckless, immoral or misguided does not constitute a reason to prevent their discussion; (8) it is for individuals, not the university, to pass judgment on such ideas without seeking to prevent their expression but rather by contesting them openly and vigorously.[6] The Alberta government indicated that the conformity of the university policy adopted in response to its directive would be the subject of a meticulous examination by the responsible ministry without however mentioning, unlike its Ontario counterpart, specific sanctions in the event of noncompliance.

In February 2023, following the cancelation by the University of Lethbridge of a lecture that was to be given by a professor who had criticized the Black Lives Matter movement and spoken of possible benefits that may have resulted from the operation of residential schools,[7] the government of Alberta added to the obligations initially imposed on the province's universities that of submitting an annual report on conflicts involving academic freedom on campuses.[8]

Rather than opting for action by the executive power, through a directive, as the Ontario and Alberta governments had done before, the Quebec government preferred to draft a statute aimed at strengthening the guarantees of the exercise of freedom of expression on campuses, with of course all

---

6 Office of the Minister, Alberta Advanced Education, "Letter to Mr. Michael Phair, Chair, Board of Governors, University of Alberta," July 4, 2019, www.ualberta.ca/provost/media-library/FoE/letter-from-minister-nicolaides-free-speech.pdf.

7 Jason Herring, "In Reversal, University of Lethbridge Cancels Controversial Professor's Guest Lecture," *Calgary Herald*, January 30, 2023, https://calgaryherald.com/news/local-news/university-lethbridge-bar-controversial-prof-frances-widdowson-guest-lecutre-campus.

8 Alberta Government, "Strengthening Free Speech on Campus," February 3, 2023, www.alberta.ca/release.cfm?xID=86483F3395F5B-DB9F-3F72-8E60723CABE7A341.

the symbolism attached to the legislative process, especially in a jurisdiction where the law is partly anchored in the Romano-Germanic tradition. The AAFUS thus defines the "right to university academic freedom" as "the right of every person to engage freely and without doctrinal, ideological or moral constraint, such as institutional censorship, in an activity through which the person contributes to carrying out the mission of an educational institution," which includes the freedom "(1) to teach and discuss; (2) to research, create and publish; (3) to express their opinion about society and about an institution, including their respective institution, and about any doctrine, dogma or opinion; and (4) to freely take part in the activities of professional organizations or academic organizations."[9]

The AAFUS also requires universities to adopt a policy on academic freedom, specifying that it must provide for the establishment of a committee representative of the community, including students, leaders, and members of the staff. This committee is responsible, among other things, for monitoring the implementation of the policy and examining complaints relating to infringements of academic freedom, and, if applicable, for making recommendations concerning such complaints or about any other matter relating to university academic freedom.[10] The AAFUS expressly states that the policy can neither prevent the discussion of ideas or subjects likely to shock during activities contributing to the university's mission nor impose that such activities be preceded by a trigger warning.[11]

Each university must appoint a person responsible for the implementation of its policy. The minister responsible for the AAFUS is also given the power to have the necessary corrective measures taken by the person he or she designates if an institution fails to comply with the obligations to which it is subject. Last, an annual reporting obligation, specifying in particular the number of complaints handled and the measures taken in their regard, is imposed on each university.

Interestingly, all three provincial initiatives on the protection of academic freedom have paradoxically been characterized by a massive intrusion into universities' internal affairs. In the Quebec case, in addition to imposing upon them evaluation criteria for actions or activities located at the heart

9 AAFUS, s 3.
10 AAFUS, s 4.
11 AAFUS, s 4.

of their mission, they are required to put in place a process allowing for the implementation of such criteria and to establish a monitoring system for their decisions. All this is in a context where the principle of the autonomy of universities from the government is nowhere to be found in the statute's prescriptive provisions.[12]

The Context of the Three Provincial Initiatives

At the inception of the Ontario, Alberta, and Quebec academic freedom initiatives was a perception that this particular freedom, and more generally, free speech was under threat on campuses. It is not the purpose of this chapter to measure the magnitude of this threat, if any. However, it is worth noting, first, that governmental attempts at censoring academic speech still represent a marginal issue in Canada, as opposed to other countries such as the United States where several states are currently prohibiting the discussion of some topics, mostly pertaining to race or gender. Secondly, although some incidents have been reported in Canada involving academics having been stigmatized, and sometimes formally sanctioned by their university, for something they had said and that had offended students or other academic stakeholders, it would be an overstatement to say that there is a censorship pandemic in the country.

It is, rather, informal forms of censorship, irrespective of formal legal sanctions taken against "offenders," that have prompted some Canadian provincial governments to take a stance on academic freedom. And they have done so, in part at least, for political reasons, as incidents involving academic freedom can easily be turned into wedge issues. Indeed, although "culture wars" are not as salient in Canada as they are in its neighbor to the South, they exist nonetheless. For example, it has been argued that the Ontario government's decision to issue a directive on academic freedom served electoral goals linked to a conservative agenda:

> By bringing together two very different constituencies. On the one hand, there are those on the right who have chosen to weaponize free expression, pushing relentlessly and aggressively at the outer boundaries of

12 The AAFUS alludes to university autonomy, but only in its preamble, which has no prescriptive effect.

> speech and vilifying those who express concerns. ... How better to do that than to use the rhetoric of liberalism to attack one of the principal repositories of liberal, Enlightenment values—the university? The other constituency [the] Ford [government] is seeking to draw in are those who genuinely care about universities and have come to believe, from the high-profile media stories of campus free speech controversies, that campus free expression is endangered. This is a potentially larger constituency than his core right-wing base. Ford's campus free speech policy aims to unite these two very different groups against an unspecified university and university-educated "elite" that has betrayed its own liberal values.[13]

The motivations were arguably the same in Alberta.[14]

Using academic freedom as a wedge issue was possibly in the mind of the Quebec government's strategists as well, at least initially. To wit, the government's sudden interest in academic freedom was triggered by an event involving the "n-word" at the University of Ottawa, which is a bilingual university *in Ontario*, not Quebec. A lecturer had used that word in the context of a course that dealt with how various minority groups "resignify" demeaning words that were used against them by majority groups. In that case, the "n-word" was not used as an insult. However, several students objected to its use by the lecturer, arguing in essence that it should never be pronounced, particularly by a non-Black person, and this, irrespective of the context and intent of the use. The university's administration briefly suspended the lecturer, and the university's president by and large adopted the students' narrative, arguing that the reconciliation of the instructor's academic freedom and the students' right to dignity justified the university's action in that case.[15] A labor relation grievance was filed as a result by the lecturer's union, and the arbitral award is still awaited at the time of writing.

---

13 James L. Turk, "Universities, the Charter, Doug Ford, and Campus Free Speech," *Constitutional Forum* 29 (2020): 31, 35–36.

14 Canadian Press, "Post-secondary Schools Must Report on Free Speech Efforts on Campus, Minister Says," *Toronto Star*, February 3, 2023, accessed April 26, 2023, www.thestar.com/news/canada/2023/02/03/post-secondary-schools-must-report-on-free-speech-efforts-on-campus-minister-says.html.

15 Jacques Frémont, "Message du recteur Jacques Frémont au sujet d'un incident récent à la Faculté des Arts," October 19, 2020, www.uottawa.ca/notre-universite/medias/nouvelles/message-du-recteur-jacques-fremont-au-sujet-dun-incident-recent-faculte-arts.

It is beyond the purview of this chapter to analyze the substance of this case. Suffice it to say that it created a deep rift within the University of Ottawa community as to the meaning and limits of academic freedom and, more generally, freedom of expression. Over this particular dividing line was superimposed another one, not so clear-cut, but yet unmissable, that is, one between the views held by what seemed to be the majority of the English-speaking faculty, leaning toward the objecting students' views, and those held by what appeared to be a majority of the French-speaking faculty, more inclined toward a robust defense of academic freedom.[16] The same type of divide would be reproduced within Afro-descending communities, with French speakers being far from unanimous about the legitimacy of a blanket prohibition of the n-word while most of their English-speaking counterparts seemingly supported that prohibition.[17] Interestingly, this n-word incident and its treatment by the University of Ottawa made the headlines in Quebec's French-speaking press while being much less noticed in the rest of Canada. This probably explains why it caught the Quebec government's attention, which saw in it an opportunity to promote its political agenda of criticizing Canadian multiculturalism and its potential pitfalls.

It would be unfair, however, to reduce what led to the Quebec legislation on academic freedom solely to a political instrumentalization of this incident at the University of Ottawa. Although it is true that the government opportunistically used it to further what could be characterized as its "antiwoke" agenda, it nevertheless took the issue seriously enough to set up an independent commission responsible for inquiring about the state of academic freedom in the province. The creation of such a commission had previously been recommended by the province's chief scientist in a report on the university of the future published in 2020. In it, the chief scientist identified the protection of academic freedom against the influence of "extra-academic values" as one of the major challenges facing universities and called upon the provincial government to elaborate a "document" addressing the issue.[18] In

16 Pierre Anctil, "De message en communiqué, ou comment l'Université d'Ottawa trace les contours d'une crise," in *Libertés malmenées: Chronique d'une année trouble à l'Université d'Ottawa*, ed. Anne Gibert, Maxime Prévost, and Geneviève Tellier (Montréal: Leméac, 2022), 235–259.

17 See the analysis of one of Quebec's most famous novelists, incidentally of Haitian origin: Dany Laferrière, "Le poids d'un mot," www.academie-francaise.fr/le-poids-dun-mot.

18 Rémi Quirion, *L'Université québécoise du futur: Tendances, enjeux, pistes d'action et recommandations*, recommandation 3, (Québec: Gouvernement du Québec, 2021), https://cdn-contenu.quebec.ca/cdn-

that sense, it would indeed be a mistake to assimilate, without making all the appropriate caveats, the Quebec initiative to the purely political, in the partisan sense, instrumentalization of academic freedom by the Ontario and Alberta governments.

The independent commission set up by the Quebec government was composed of reputable academics, and headed by a former government minister with legal training. It held several audiences, conducted polls, and received briefs from various stakeholders such as universities, academics, unions, and human rights organizations. Its report noted that the legal regime concerning academic freedom in Quebec was formed of a patchwork of various provisions of collective agreements and university policies, that academic freedom was probably insufficiently protected in some universities, and that a general regime applicable to all universities would lift potential doubts as to the legal status and scope of academic freedom. It thus recommended the adoption of a law protecting that freedom, which led the way to the enactment of AAFUS.[19]

Top-Down Approaches as Paper Satisfactions?

Legal sociologists distinguish between the concrete (or instrumental) and symbolic effectiveness of legal norms.[20] Concrete effects are those that flow directly from the application of such norms, which may be desired or adverse,[21] and that can be observed by examining the behavior of the social

contenu/adm/min/education/publications-adm/rapport-reflexion-consultation/Rapport-universite-quebecoise-futur.pdf.

19 Commission scientifique et technique indépendante sur la reconnaissance de la liberté académique en milieu universitaire (A. Cloutier, chair), *Reconnaître, protéger et promouvoir la liberté universitaire* (Québec: Ministère de l'enseignement supérieur, 2021), https://cdn-contenu.quebec.ca/cdn-contenu/adm/min/education/publications-adm/enseignement-superieur/organismes-lies/Rapport-complet-Web.pdf?1639494244.

20 Valérie Demers, *Le contrôle des fumeurs: Une étude d'effectivité du droit* (Montréal: Éditions Thémis, 1996), 67–86.

21 An example of a potential adverse effect, at least from a provincial government standpoint, of the Quebec statute (and of the Ontario and Alberta directives) could be that these initiatives will possibly subject all universities in these provinces to the application of the Canadian Charter of Rights and Freedoms, at least when the implementation of such initiatives is concerned. Government action—executive in the cases of Ontario and Alberta, and legislative in the case of Quebec, which forces universities in these provinces to act within specific parameters to protect expressive freedoms in the academic context—in all likelihood makes that charter applicable to such universities, even when they are not private in the sense that they are not controlled by the government. Indeed, as LaForest J. stated in *Eldridge v. British*

actors targeted by them. At the opposite end stands the symbolic effects of legal norms, which designate the effects that these norms may have on representations, attitudes, opinions, and so on. For example, norms that enshrine broadly enunciated values, such as academic freedom, may have symbolic effects even if their actual concrete effects are unfathomable. Symbolic effects "take on meaning by symbolizing the public affirmation of social ideals and norms."[22] They may also help shift social representations or public opinion.[23] It is obviously reductionist to analyze the effectiveness, or lack thereof, of legal norms from such a dichotomic perspective, as if there were no gray areas between effectiveness and ineffectiveness.[24] Yet, the concrete vs. symbolic dichotomy is useful for the sake of making sense, albeit provisionally, of the impact of Quebec's AAFUS.[25]

As to the concrete effects of the AAFUS, it seems fair to predict that it will level the field between potential claimants grounding their claim in academic freedom, irrespective of whether or not they and their university are bound by a collective agreement. In so doing, the AAFUS will alleviate the burden placed on those evolving in universities without such agreements. Prior to the adoption of the AAFUS, such claimants had to demonstrate that academic freedom was indeed protected in their university; moreover, they had to map its scope. On this question, whenever the scope of conventional protections of academic freedom is narrower than what the AAFUS provides for, the latter will in all likelihood prevail. Being a public order stat-

---

Columbia (Attorney General), [1997] 3 SCR 624 at para 43: "In order for the Charter to apply to a private entity, it must be found to be implementing a specific government policy or program." As several authors have noted regarding the Ontario and Alberta directives, this type of governmental action, which imposes very specific guidelines on entities that are a priori private and the implementation of which is monitored by reporting obligations, is likely to trigger the application of the Canadian Charter; see Jamie Cameron, "Compelling Freedom on Campus: A Free Speech Paradox," *Constitutional Forum* 29 (2020): 5, 17; Turk, "Universities, the Charter, Doug Ford, and Campus Free Speech," 31, 42.

22 Lawrence M. Friedman, *The Legal System: A Social Science Perspective* (New York: Russell Sage Foundation, 1975), 265.

23 Demers, *Le contrôle des fumeurs*, 73.

24 Jean Carbonnier, *Flexible droit: Pour une sociologie du droit sans rigueur*, 8th ed. (Paris: Librairie générale de droit et de jurisprudence, 1995), 132–134. On the various "shades" of legal effectiveness, see also Yann Leroy, "La notion d'effectivité du droit," *Droit et Société* 79 (2011): 715–732.

25 I say "provisionally" because the effectiveness of legal norms can be examined over various periods of time, and it is not impossible that previously unnoticeable effects eventually surface a few years after the enactment of the norms examined. Legal effects can indeed be deferred, wilfully or not.

ute, it now supplements the infra-state legal orders where academic freedom is not formally protected.

The AAFUS thus establishes a minimal protective threshold for academic freedom. It is not irrelevant to observe, however, that the first so-called gain stemming from the AAFUS, that is, providing a normative foundation for academic freedom across Quebec, is more theoretical than anything. Indeed, the only university in the province whose professors do not work under a collective agreement is McGill. Yet, that university's policies formally protect academic freedom, and it is difficult to imagine a situation where a court would not take that into consideration when adjudicating a claim based on that freedom. From that perspective, the second "gain" allegedly brought about by the AAFUS, that is, a formal definition of academic freedom applicable across the province, is likely to be more useful.

The third innovation of the AAFUS resides in the obligation imposed upon universities to adopt policies concerning academic freedom, with a local committee monitoring their implementation. Since the AAFUS expressly specifies that the said policies cannot forbid addressing ideas or topics that may be deemed offensive, or to compel the use of trigger warnings, some academics may perhaps be reassured about the scope of the formal protection they now enjoy under the AAFUS.

The primary implementation mechanism envisaged in the AAFUS for monitoring universities' behavior pertaining to the protection of academic freedom lies in the imposition upon them of annual reporting obligations to the government. This focus on accountability is typical of the New Public Management approach, which has hugely influenced governmental policies on academia since the 1990s. Governmental policies adopting this approach tend to induce institutions to comply with social norms without formally directing them on what to do.[26]

This begs one crucial question: to what extent is such an approach susceptible to actually curbing the threats to academic freedom in university settings? If one reflects on this question from the perspective of the rights holders—in essence, those participating in the realization of the university's mission, mainly faculty, lecturers, and graduate students—the likeliest

26 Christine Musselin, "Vers un marché international de l'enseignement supérieur?" *Critique internationale* 39 (2008): 13–24.

answer is not much. Indeed, the reporting obligations essentially focus on "(1) the number of complaints processed and the time frame in which they were processed; (2) the measures applied, if any, and (3) any other information requested by the Minister concerning the implementation of this Act."[27]

Imagine a hypothetical situation where a professor engages in a certain discourse with students who, in turn, find it offensive. Suppose further that the professor invokes their academic freedom to shield this speech from possible complaints, especially considering the fact that the speech held to be offensive by students is perfectly legal. Next, imagine that a student files a complaint. Under the AAFUS, the process would look like this: (1) the committee or body responsible for reviewing the complaint would look into the student's complaint; (2) even if it found something wrong with the "manner" used by the professor in his speech and even if it was really offensive, insofar as it is legal, it is probable, even certain, that the complaint would be dismissed; (3) the university where this event allegedly took place would allude to the complaint in its annual report to the government and mention that it was internally resolved.

Yet, the plaintiff student would probably remain aggrieved or unsatisfied if nothing else is done—and I am not even talking about sanctioning the professor. It is thus open to wonder how the AAFUS can really facilitate the resolution of conflicts caused by the exercise of freedom of expression in a university context, at least if one attributes to the process envisaged the underlying mission of pacifying tense situations.

It seems very unlikely that the top-down solution envisaged in the AAFUS would equip universities to effectively resolve some types of speech-related crises. Think of an event that took place in 2023 at McGill Law School, that is, a conference involving Robert Wintemute of King's College that could not be held because the demonstration of trans activists protesting against the speaker had gone out of control. The activists opposed the views on gay marriage and conversion therapy of a group to which Wintemute is affiliated, which they deemed transphobic.[28] Wintemute's academic freedom and freedom of expression were indeed violated as a result of the in

27 AAFUS, s 8.

28 Daniel J. Rowe, "McGill Speaker's Talk Cancelled after Trans Activists Protest," *CTV News Montreal*, January 10, 2023, https://montreal.ctvnews.ca/mcgill-speaker-s-talk-cancelled-after-trans-activists-protest-1.6224317.

situ cancelation of the conference. Yet, McGill never canceled it in advance despite prior information that a demonstration would be held. By so doing, the university upheld academic freedom. It is only when serious security concerns arose as the demonstration unfolded, on the very premises of the conference, that the event was canceled.

Thus, we are not faced here with a situation where a "woke administration" preemptively caved in to potential protesters. What is to be noted for this chapter is that, in the kind of situation in which McGill found itself, the AAFUS does not provide any useful tool to effectively protect academic freedom, as it simply does not address that type of external threat. Rather, by imposing obligations solely on universities, it seems to envisage academic freedom as a zero-sum game between these universities qua institutions and the holders of that freedom. More precisely, it is as if threats to academic freedom could only come from actions taken or omissions made by university administrations.

However, it is trite to observe that a significant number of events nowadays associated with "cancel culture" are not caused by the cowardice of academic administrators (although some are). They are instead provoked by militants whose practices, sometimes bordering on illegality, raise reasonable concern about the safety of participants in the events targeted. Moreover, institutionally recognized student associations may also adopt policies or make decisions that are susceptible to abridging academic freedom or freedom of expression. The AAFUS is useless to both universities and academic freedom in such situations, as those who are substantively responsible for violating that freedom remain invisible through the prism of this piece of legislation.

My skepticism with regard to top-down approaches in the management or regulation of academic freedom is, in a way, reinforced by the nature of the follow-ups that have resulted from the implementation of Ontario's policy on freedom of expression in postsecondary institutions. Recall here that under the directive adopted by the Ontario government, the Higher Education Quality Council of Ontario has been collecting since 2019, as required by the governmental directive, information from institutions subject to the reporting obligation. The information collected under the directive is essentially the same as what the AAFUS contemplates.

Consulting the first four reports (2019–22) is quite telling. In its first report (2019), the Higher Education Quality Council of Ontario noted the ambiguity of the government's directive in the event of a conflict between freedom of expression, on the one hand, and aspirations related to civility and respect, on the other hand, noting that university policies adopted under the aegis of the directive are often ambiguous, whereas one should logically infer from the policies, which supposedly enshrine the principles put forward by the University of Chicago, that they will ensure the primacy of freedom of expression over the largely moral duties of civility and respect.[29] In the four reports it has published so far, the council has observed that Ontario colleges and universities have reported just a few events every year, which were all resolved internally. The 2020 report mentions that it is apparent that the methods of collecting information vary largely according to the school, with the uncertainties that may result from this when it comes to having a truly reliable inventory.[30] For 2021 and 2022, the COVID-19 pandemic, which has forced institutions to hold many events online rather than in person, may account for the still limited number of incidents.[31]

Yet, it is perhaps the 2021 report that is the most interesting, except for what it does not say rather than for what it says. That report covers a time interval during which high-profile incidents occurred, in particular, the one provoked at the University of Ottawa by the use of the "n-word," which I mentioned earlier. The report summarizes what happened during the period covered in two laconic sentences: "Four formal complaints were reported across the system during the 2020/21 reporting cycle. All of these were, to the involved institutions' knowledge and understanding, resolved internally."[32] In other words, during the period covered, it was business as

29 Higher Education Quality Council of Ontario, "Freedom of Speech on Campus: 2019 Annual Report to the Ontario Government," https://heqco.ca/wp-content/uploads/2020/01/HEQCO-2019-Free-Speech-Report-to-Government-REVISED-3.pdf.

30 Higher Education Quality Council of Ontario, "Freedom of Speech on Campus: 2020 Annual Report to the Ontario Government," https://heqco.ca/wp-content/uploads/2020/12/FINAL-HEQCO-Free-Speech-on-Campus-Annual-Report-to-Government-December-2020.pdf.

31 Higher Education Quality Council of Ontario, "Freedom of Speech on Campus: 2022 Annual Report to the Ontario Government," https://heqco.ca/wp-content/uploads/2022/12/HEQCO-2022-Free-Speech-on-Campus-Annual-Report-for-web-site-December-2022.pdf.

32 Higher Education Quality Council of Ontario, "Freedom of Speech on Campus: 2021 Annual Report to the Ontario Government," 3, https://heqco.ca/wp-content/uploads/2021/11/HEQCO-Free-Speech-on-Campus-Annual-Report-to-Government-November-2021.pdf.

usual. Yet, the n-word incident at the University of Ottawa created a deep rift within the university with, in addition to a labor grievance, an internal committee headed by a former Supreme Court justice,[33] ripple effects in the media and political arena, as well as books published in the wake of the controversy.[34]

Can anyone be surprised by the narrative provided by the Higher Education Quality Council of Ontario's 2021 report? Probably not, since the whole system put in place under the provincial directive relies on self-declaration, and seeks to obtain only a minimum of qualitative data on what actually happens on the ground. In this respect, reading the report submitted by the University of Ottawa to the council for that year is very instructive.[35] This report, which, we must assume, tells the truth, informs us that during the reporting period, the university did not receive any formal complaints concerning freedom of expression on its campus. More specifically, the university states that no formal complaint has been received about the application of its policy on freedom of expression with regard to: (1) events related to its curriculum or extra-curriculum; (2) instances where the university misapplied its policy; (3) cases that would have resulted in sanctions under this policy; (4) cases that could have been forwarded to the Provincial Ombudsman. In its previous report for 2020, the same university had reported four formal complaints, the first due to the comments of a professor who, on social media, had argued that members of a particular demographic group were racist, the second about posters put up on campus and perceived to be racist, the third because of another poster that questioned and denigrated psychology, psychiatry and psychotherapy as scientific disciplines, and, finally, the fourth because of the sexist nature of comments made by a male professor about menopause in women. Each of these complaints was handled internally and dismissed on the grounds that while the

33 Michel Bastarache (chair), *Report of the Committee on Academic Freedom* (Ottawa: University of Ottawa, 2021), www.uottawa.ca/about-us/sites/g/files/bhrskd336/files/2021-11/report_committee_academic_freedom_en_final_v9.pdf.

34 Rachad Antonius and Normand Baillargeon, eds., *Identité, "race," liberté d'expression: Perspectives critiques sur certains débats qui fracturent la gauche* (Québec: Presses de l'Université Laval, 2021); Gibert et al., *Libertés malmenées*.

35 University of Ottawa, "Freedom of Speech Annual Report Template (2021)," www2.uottawa.ca/about-us/sites/g/files/bhrskd336/files/2022-03/free_speech_annual_report_2021_-_university_of_ottawa_-_final.pdf.

controversial speeches could be considered offensive, they were not illegal and therefore did not violate the university's free speech policy.[36]

We can perhaps rejoice that freedom of expression (or, where applicable, academic freedom) prevailed in these cases. But is this result really attributable to the specific policy that the provincial directive had imposed upon universities to adopt? The fact is that such universities, with or without an academic freedom policy, could hardly sanction speech that is perfectly legal anyway, unless it also qualifies as harassment within the meaning of employment law, in which case it would then become illegal. In fact, analysis of the accountability mechanism put in place by the Ontario policy reveals that this accountability to a governmental body, insofar as it is largely formal, in no way makes it possible to take the measure of all the complexity of the dynamics that take place in the field and that intertwine formality and informality, as well as law, politics and the micromanagement of human relations.

The formal "victory" of a member of the teaching staff, if indeed one can speak of a "victory" because of the primacy—justified in many respects—of academic freedom, is in no way a guarantee of an actual pacification of social relations. In the absence of more targeted interventions rooted in the reality of the field, nothing can prevent the "winner" from continuing to be the object of informal pressure from their colleagues or other members of the university community encouraging them to change their teaching practices, or even to be stigmatized on social networks or elsewhere for having held an otherwise legitimate discourse in a university context. And if, by chance, they really made an honest mistake by speaking this way but apologized for it, this clumsiness could haunt them for a long time to come in a context where social actors seem less and less inclined to recognize in their interlocutors that they can sometimes wander without having acted with malice. In an increasingly polarized world, forgiveness is becoming a scarce resource.[37]

Formalist and bureaucratic approaches may therefore not be very effective in countering the informal dynamics of exclusion, stigmatization, or even harassment, which influence the concrete turn taken by conflicts arising

---

36 University of Ottawa, "Freedom of Speech Annual Report Template (2020)," www2.uottawa.ca/about-us/sites/g/files/bhrskd336/files/2022-03/university_of_ottawa_-_free_speech_annual_report_english_september_3_2020.pdf.

37 Rachida Azdouz, "Éloge de l'indulgence," *Vaste programme*, December 22, 2022, https://vasteprogramme.ca/2022/12/22/eloge-de-lindulgence/.

from the exercise of academic freedom or freedom of expression in a university context. This is a major stumbling block against macroscopic, somewhat overhanging initiatives aimed at protecting academic freedom, whether they take the legislative route or take the form of policies noncompliance with which can ultimately be sanctioned by the government exercising its spending power, that is, by cutting its funding to "delinquent universities."

A second pitfall stems from the very nature of the standards invoked in the context of contemporary debates on academic freedom. Although macroscopic government initiatives seek to define, directly or indirectly, academic freedom, the proposed definitions retain an element of indeterminacy. In fact, whether it concerns academic freedom or, more broadly, freedom of expression, or even the right to dignity, we must be aware that these rights and freedoms are by and large enunciated as legal *principles* rather than as legal rules strictly speaking, that is to say, norms whose meaning and scope are largely undetermined and whose actualization takes place in particular contexts.[38] Moreover, the reconciliation of competing rights and freedoms is an eminently casuistic exercise, where the relative weight of the principles in question—which is not "declared" in advance[39]—varies according to the circumstances.[40] These observations equally apply to the Quebec legislation that, while elevating the protection of academic freedom as a matter of public order, still has to be construed with other normative instruments of the provincial legal order. This includes the Charter of Human Rights and Freedoms that not only protects one's freedom of expression but also the "right to the safeguard of his dignity, honour and reputation" and the "right to full and equal recognition of his human rights and freedoms, without distinction, exclusion or preference based" on various prohibited grounds of discrimination.[41] In such a normative ecosystem, academic freedom is just a right among others, even if one grounds the protection of its expressive dimension on constitutional or quasi-constitutional instruments. It can thus

38 Chaim Perelman and Raymond Vander Elst, *Les notions à contenu variable en droit* (Brussels: Bruylant, 1984).

39 George P. Fletcher, "Two Modes of Legal Thought," *Yale Law Journal* 90 (1981): 978.

40 On the balancing of competing rights, see Jean-François Gaudreault-DesBiens, "Les hiérarchies passagères, ou de la contingence dans l'équilibrage entre droits fondamentaux," *Revue québécoise de droit constitutionnel* 4 (2012): 7.

41 Charter of Human Rights and Freedoms, RLRQ, c. C-12. Freedom of expression is protected at s 3, the right to dignity at s 4, and the right to equality at s 10.

be justifiably restricted in a free and democratic society on the basis of competing rights or other social interests. From this perspective, the air of absolutism conferred on the protection of academic freedom under the AAFUS must be relativized.

Conclusion

In this chapter, I have expressed some skepticism about the AAFUS' effectiveness with a view to tangibly protecting academic freedom "on the ground." Only time will tell if my skepticism was justified or not. Yet, for now, a question must be raised: could anything else, other than the AAFUS, have been done to better protect this freedom?

A first step could have been to elevate the juridical status of academic freedom by *explicitly* enshrining it, as well as the principle of institutional academic autonomy, in Quebec's Charter of Human Rights and Freedoms. As of now, it is only the expressive dimension of academic freedom that is arguably protected by the charter, under the guise of freedom of expression. That protection is thus merely derivative and implicit. Providing explicit, quasi-constitutional protection to academic freedom and institutional autonomy would have sent a stronger message than ordinary legislation, not only to the academic community but to the general public as well. Moreover, it would have reinforced the idea that academic freedom and institutional autonomy are consubstantial to democracy itself.[42] Furthermore, in all likelihood, litigation over academic freedom would have become more public and transparent, instead of being confined to the relative obscurity of labor grievances or administrative processes, as it currently is most of the time. Ultimately, the enshrinement of academic freedom in quasi-constitutional legislation could perhaps have served a pedagogical role by inducing citizens to take that freedom more seriously.

Notwithstanding that first step, a second one could have been to impose upon legally accredited student associations obligations to protect and promote academic freedom, as defined in the AAFUS, and freedom of expression, and to annually report to the government in this respect. Sanctions could have been imposed on associations failing to uphold such freedoms,

42 In practice, s 3 of AAFUS, which protects and defines academic freedom, could have been incorporated in the Charter of Human Rights and Freedoms as a new, autonomous freedom, but with the addition of university autonomy as a second prong of academic freedom so protected.

either by action or by omission. It must be noted that in Quebec, the Act Respecting the Accrediting and Financing of Students' Associations recognizes the right of individual students to belong to a student association and to participate in its activities and administration.[43] It also establishes a framework for the accreditation of such an association, which, once accredited, is regarded as the sole representative of the student community vis-à-vis the educational institution where it operates, with ensuing obligations imposed on the latter, such as the duty to provide some spaces and services to the association. In a nutshell, this Act creates between the educational institution and the accredited student association a legal relation akin to that existing between a union and an employer. Since the Act contains provisions specifying the (mostly procedural) conditions for obtaining the accreditation but also for revoking it, the protection and promotion of expressive freedoms within the student community and the university could have been incorporated as a duty imposed upon all accredited associations, with the potential revocation of their accreditation for failing to do so.[44] Such a legislative measure would convey the important message that students, as rights holders themselves, are also responsible for protecting and promoting expressive freedoms in universities. Admittedly, it would only impact accredited associations rather than the myriad of interest-based student associations that animate student life. A further limit to the effectiveness of such a measure might also be that many students, who nowadays tend to adopt a very expansive definition of "harm"[45] and who, on that basis, are increasingly inclined to report comments that they find offensive,[46] simply do not value expressive freedoms as much as their predecessors did. Should this hypothesis be

43 Act Respecting the Accrediting and Financing of Students' Associations, RLRQ, c. A-3.01.

44 Technically, the internal bylaws and regulations of a university may provide for sanctions on student associations that fail to respect them, but, again, the legal status of such bylaws and regulations cannot be compared to that of a public order statute.

45 Kate Hidalgo Bellows, "More Students Endorse an Expansive Definition of 'Harm.' Colleges Aren't So Sure," *Chronicle of Higher Education*, May 3, 2023, www.chronicle.com/article/more-students-endorse-an-expansive-definition-of-harm-colleges-arent-so-sure?sra=true&cid=gen_sign_in#:~:text=With%20this%20expanded%20definition%20comes,everyone%20is%20embracing%20this%20rhetoric.

46 Jessica Blake, "'Teaching on Eggshells': Students Report Professors' Offensive Comments," *Inside Higher Education*, July 21, 2023, www.insidehighered.com/news/students/free-speech/2023/07/21/students-likely-report-instructors-offensive-comments?utm_source=Inside+Higher+Ed&utm_campaign=a7ac1237a7-DNU_2021_COPY_02&utm_medium=email&utm_term=0_1fcbc04421-a7ac1237a7-236422286&mc_cid=a7ac1237a7&mc_eid=5caa7f21ba.

correct, it would point to a cultural-generational paradigm shift that the law would have a hard time capturing.

That being said, imposing duties to promote and protect expressive freedoms to both university administrations and student associations is the path that the UK Parliament has taken in May 2023, with the enactment of the Higher Education (Freedom of Speech) Act 2023, which amends the Higher Education and Research Act 2017 to insert various measures protecting academic freedom and freedom of expression in universities.[47]

In a nutshell, the new UK law requires universities to take measures to protect the freedom of expression of their staff, members, students, and potential guests, by ensuring that no individual or legal entity is prevented from using university premises because of objections relating to their ideas, beliefs, policies, or objectives.[48] Academic freedom is defined as the freedom of members of the academic staff to express themselves, within the limits of the law, to challenge accepted ideas and put forward new ideas as well as controversial or unpopular opinions, without fear of direct or indirect disciplinary sanctions.[49] The Act also requires universities to adopt a code of practice explaining how their values promote freedom of expression and specifying the procedures to be followed by members of staff and the student body when holding conferences, meetings, or other activities on university premises, the conduct expected of them during such activities and, finally, the criteria used to assess whether or not an activity may be held.[50] As mentioned, this Act places equivalent obligations on student bodies to those of universities.[51] Interestingly, it also creates a right of action against universities or student bodies that fail to comply with their legal obligations in relation to freedom of expression, when a complaint made by a person victim of a violation of that freedom has previously been upheld by the Office for Students. However, such an action can only be successful if that person demonstrates that they have suffered a pecuniary or nonpecuniary loss as a result of the violation.[52] Moreover, the Office for Students is made responsible for setting up a mechanism for investigat-

47 Higher Education (Freedom of Speech) Act 2023 (UK), 2023 c. 16, www.legislation.gov.uk/ukpga/2023/16/enacted.

48 Higher Education (Freedom of Speech) Act 2023, s 1 (A1 (1), (2), (3), (4)).

49 Higher Education (Freedom of Speech) Act 2023, s 1 (A1 (6) (7)).

50 Higher Education (Freedom of Speech) Act 2023, s 2 (A2).

51 Higher Education (Freedom of Speech) Act 2023, s 3 (A4, A5).

52 Higher Education (Freedom of Speech) Act 2023, s 4 (A7).

ing complaints based on alleged breaches, by action or omission, of provisions protecting freedom of expression and academic freedom, and is therefore empowered to examine and rule on such complaints.[53] This body is further allocated the task of ensuring that organizations comply with their legal obligations in terms of freedom of expression and academic freedom; failure to do so could even lead to the imposition of fines in the case of student associations.[54] The monitoring mandate of the Office for Students goes as far as encompassing potential violations of freedom of expression occurring in the context of activities organized by universities or student unions with overseas funding.[55] Finally, a kind of free speech ombudsman—the Director for Freedom of Speech and Academic Freedom—is created to oversee the performance of the Office for Students in discharging its duties toward the protection of expressive liberties in universities.[56]

The new UK law adopts a much more granular approach than Quebec's AAFUS. In this respect, and again time will tell, it could perhaps be more successful than the AAFUS in effectively curbing threats to freedom of expression in universities. However, the flip side is that it encroaches more significantly upon the universities' administrative autonomy than its Quebec counterpart. Moreover, what the effects of the new statutory tort created in the Act to remedy violations of expressive liberties on campuses will be is unknown. On the one hand, its breadth is such—for example, any visiting speaking engaged in lawful speech could potentially target a university where they have been deplatformed (this could theoretically include a flat earther who has managed to get an invitation ...)—that one may legitimately fear that this new tort could trigger an open season on universities. On the other hand, the requirement that proof of a pecuniary or nonpecuniary loss be made could severely reduce its concrete usefulness. These potential challenges to the implementation of this new statutory tort raise questions as to whether its creation is not first and foremost a mere symbolic exercise.

Irrespective of its level of granularity, any top-down legislative intervention regarding academic freedom is bound to face hurdles in its concrete implementation, which takes place in different academic, ideological,

53 Higher Education (Freedom of Speech) Act 2023, ss 5, 6, & 8.
54 Higher Education (Freedom of Speech) Act 2023, s 7 (69B).
55 Higher Education (Freedom of Speech) Act 2023, s 9 (69D, 69E).
56 Higher Education (Freedom of Speech) Act 2023, s 10.

and social contexts. As alluded to earlier, there are limits as to what laws can do when they try not only to grasp but to change deep cultural dynamics. In this respect, it is arguable that in several jurisdictions, particularly English-speaking ones, the combined action of some variables has created a new cultural dynamic that can only be superficially affected by formal legal intervention. One such variable lies in the rise of academic capitalism, with the culture of customer service (students, donors, etc.) that accompanies it, which may induce university administrations to cave in to the most frivolous claims for fear of not meeting the expectations or desires of these clienteles. Another one is the acute ideological polarization observable on many campuses, which, with the echo chambers it flourishes in, undermines the dialogical environment that is necessary to tackle difficult questions in a complex manner. When coupled with some form of radical identity politics, left and right, this deleterious impact can only be amplified.

Thus, beyond its symbolic function and occasional concrete effects,[57] the explicit consecration of academic freedom, particularly in its expressive dimension, by legislation or a governmental policy risks being of little help, from a normative point of view, in order to resolve the complex situations emerging on the ground. It therefore seems appropriate to meditate on these words of Jean Carbonnier:

> No sooner do we perceive the evil than we demand the remedy; and the law is, in appearance, the instantaneous remedy. Whether a scandal breaks out, an accident occurs, an inconvenience is discovered: the fault lies with the gaps in the legislation. Just make one more law. And we do it. It would take a lot of courage for a government to deny this paper satisfaction to its public opinion.[58]

The expression "paper satisfaction" is crucial here, as "paper satisfaction" goes beyond what we often call a "paper tiger." The latter refers to the enactment

57 See my observations in this chapter on the concrete effects, including positive ones, that the Quebec and UK legislations might bring about, as opposed to the "soft law" approach adopted by Ontario and Alberta.

58 Jean Carbonnier, *Essais sur les lois* (Paris: Défrénois, 1979), 276. Translation of: "Il faut donc se méfier des exercices de cosmétique législative ou politique, qui offrent un faux sentiment de sécurité aux titulaires de la liberté académique et qui répondent peut-être davantage à des objectifs politiciens qu'à un véritable engagement des pouvoirs publics à l'égard de l'objet de la loi ou de la politique."

of merely ineffective or inefficient laws—tigers with no claws, so to say—while the former seeks to grasp a political impulse that deliberately instrumentalizes legislation as an appropriate response to some *alleged* popular demand, irrespective of the effectiveness, efficiency, or even soundness of the law so enacted. Such a response fundamentally illustrates a cosmetic, and sometimes populist, approach to the elaboration of public policies.

We must therefore be wary of exercises in legislative or political cosmetics, which offer a false sense of security to holders of academic freedom and which perhaps respond more to political objectives than to a real commitment by the public authorities with regard to the purpose of the law or policy. Such legislative or political initiatives may sometimes be well-intentioned and sometimes stem from more cynical electoral calculations. In an interesting twist, such initiatives, as evidenced in Ontario, Alberta, and Quebec, seek to achieve their objectives not only by being silent on the vexing issue of the protection of university autonomy, but also by actively interfering in that autonomy by increasing universities' reporting obligations to governments, but to a much lesser extent than the UK's Higher Education (Freedom of Speech) Act 2023.

It is hard not to think, in that context, that these initiatives are part of a broader trend that the expression "cosmetology of academic freedom" decently captures in my view. My point is not to reduce the controversies that have surrounded academic freedom in the past few years to mere manifestations of a "moral panic." There certainly is evidence of such a panic, which is meticulously entertained by right-wing commentators,[59] but there are also genuine threats facing academic freedom, stemming both from the right and from the left, and this, everywhere on the planet. They need to be taken seriously, beyond purely formal and managerial satisfaction.

59 In the context of Quebec, see Francis Dupuis-Déri, *Panique à l'université: Rectitude politique, wokes et autres menaces imaginaires* (Montréal: Lux Éditeur, 2022).

CHAPTER 5

How Structure, Culture, and the Individual Together Constrain and Enable Academic Freedom in China

A Historical Perspective

ZHIDONG HAO

Academic freedom is under siege everywhere in the world.[1] But do different cultures share the concept of academic freedom? Is it a universal value? Does the Chinese society, which is largely authoritarian and dictatorial both historically and in contemporary times, appreciate it as other democratic societies do?

This chapter argues that the concept of academic freedom has deep historical roots in China even if it was not termed as such in ancient times. Structurally political regimes have viewed free thinking or academic freedom differently at different times based on their pragmatic needs. Culturally Chinese society has also had competing views on academic freedom throughout history and the concept has gained Western characteristics in modern

1 Zhidong Hao and Peter Zabielskis, eds., *Academic Freedom under Siege: Higher Education in East Asia, the U.S., and Australia* (Cham: Springer Nature, 2020).

times as China has begun to interact with the world since the nineteenth century. Individually some scholars have strived to be free, independent, and critical, bearing the consequences thereof, while others have assisted the rulers as scholar-officials in suppressing free thinking.

In this chapter, I first briefly summarize how classical sociologists view the importance of structural, cultural, and individual factors in constraining and enabling social behavior. Then I explain how academic freedom, or free thinking, has been viewed and practiced throughout history in China at these three different levels. We will see what roles these factors, together and in interaction, have played in a tug-of-war over academic freedom.

The Interaction between Structure, Culture, and the Individual

As Marx famously states, "Men make their history, but they do not make it just as they please; they do not make it under circumstances chosen by themselves, but under circumstances directly found, given, and transmitted from the past."[2] Here Marx is already talking about the three factors that influence human behavior: "men" here refers to individuals themselves, while "circumstances" refers to both structure and culture that individuals find themselves in and that they have to interact with. Arguably, all human behavior is a result of this interaction including, of course, academic freedom as a norm, value, and belief.[3] We will now examine how classical sociological theorists explain the role of these three factors in constraining and enabling human behavior and see what light they may shed on our understanding of the historical development of academic freedom in China.

Structure in Interaction with Culture and the Individual

By structure, I mean political and economic systems like democracy, totalitarianism, capitalism, and socialism (with Chinese characteristics) and

2 Karl Marx and Frederick Engels, *The Marx-Engels Reader*, ed. Robert C. Tucker, 2nd ed. (New York: W. W. Norton, 1978), 595.

3 Zhidong Hao, "Academic Freedom under Siege: What, Why, and What Is to Be Done," in *Academic Freedom under Siege: Higher Education in East Asia, the U.S., and Australia*, ed. Zhidong Hao and Peter Zabielskis (Cham: Springer Nature, 2020).

social relations like class. Sociologists have long emphasized how structure influences culture and the individual as Marx does above. Here are more examples.

When Marx says that it is people's social being that determines their consciousness, he is saying that it is a structure that influences culture. Ideology or consciousness is embedded in social relationships, and social circumstances condition people's perception of the world they live in.[4] Therefore, "the ruling ideas are nothing more than the ideal expression of the dominant material relationships."[5]

Likewise, Weber talks about social circumstances that define what class people belong to, that is, "a specific causal component of their life chances, [represented] exclusively by economic interests in the possession of goods and opportunities for income" and "under the conditions of the commodity or labor market."[6] Weber says that the individual bureaucrat "is only a single cog in an ever-moving mechanism [of bureaucracy] which prescribes to him an essentially fixed route of march."[7] That is indicative of the relationship between structure and the individual in other social, economic, and political mechanisms as well. It is a powerful statement of how strongly structure, whether it is class or bureaucracy, can influence the individual.

Durkheim observes that in the forced division of labor the individual "is no longer anything but an inert cog in the machinery, set in motion by an external force and always moving in the same direction and in the same way."[8] He is also talking about how powerful social circumstances are in determining what people can and cannot do.

In my discussion on the structural constraints on academic freedom in contemporary times, I listed the influences of government policies regarding tenure, freedom of speech, the composition of the board of trustees, shared governance, austerity measures, and the role of the court on such issues, both in democracies and authoritarianism.[9] In our edited book, we provide

4 Anthony Giddens, *Capitalism and Modern Social Theory: An Analysis of the Writings of Marx, Durkheim and Weber* (Cambridge: Cambridge University Press, 1971), 41–43.

5 Marx and Engels, *The Marx-Engels Reader*, 64.

6 Max Weber, *From Max Weber* (New York: Oxford University Press, 1946), 181.

7 Weber, *From Max Weber*, 228.

8 Emile Durkheim, *Emile Durkheim: Selected Writings*, ed. Anthony Giddens (Cambridge: Cambridge University Press, 1972), 178.

9 Hao, "Academic Freedom under Siege."

many examples of how structural factors like these have influenced both culture and individual behavior in academia.[10]

Culture in Interaction with Structure and the Individual

Probably the most famous argument for the importance of culture is Weber's work on the Protestant ethic and the spirit of capitalism, but Weber says also that he does not mean to "substitute for a one-sided materialistic an equally one-sided spiritualistic causal interpretation of culture and history."[11] In other words, he is saying that both structure and culture are important in influencing historical development. For Weber, the content of ideas is itself an independent variable of historical significance although both culture and structure are important and one cannot be replaced by the other in social analysis.[12]

Culture is equally important in Durkheim's analysis. For him, the *conscience collective*, or a strongly defined set of values and beliefs, gives a certain society its unity and individuality.[13] Individuals perform duties defined in law and in custom externally to themselves. Such norms, values, and beliefs have so much imperative and coercive power that they impose themselves on the individual.[14] Individuals have to bear consequences if they violate them.

Marx does not dispute the importance of culture either although he does emphasize the importance of structure. This is why Marx and Engels say that "consciousness can sometimes appear further advanced than the contemporary empirical relationships, so that in the struggles of a later epoch one can refer to earlier theoreticians as authorities."[15] Furthermore, "all collisions in history have their origin ... in the contradiction between the productive forces and the form of intercourse."[16] Examples of the latter may include

---

10 Hao and Zabielskis, *Academic Freedom under Siege*.

11 Max Weber, *The Protestant Ethic and the Spirit of Capitalism* (New York: Charles Scribner's Sons, 1958), 183.

12 Giddens, *Capitalism and Modern Social Theory*, 194.

13 Durkheim, *Selected Writings*, 243. See also Anthony Giddens, "Introduction: Durkheim's Writings in Sociology and Social Philosophy," in *Emile Durkheim: Selected Writings*, ed. Anthony Giddens (Cambridge: Cambridge University Press, 1972), 6.

14 Durkheim, *Selected Writings*, 63–64.

15 Karl Marx and Frederick Engels, *The German Ideology*, ed. C. J. Arthur (New York: International Publishers, 1947), 88.

16 Marx and Engels, *The German Ideology*, 89.

collisions of various classes, contradictions of consciousness, battles of ideas, political conflict, and so on. They believe in the understanding of the "totality" of historical development, that is, the "reciprocal" relationship between the forces of production and "the different theoretical products and forms of consciousness, religion, philosophy, ethics, etc."[17] In Giddens' words, for Marx, there is a link between class structure and ideology. While the former determines the latter, there is also a reciprocal relationship between the two.[18]

In my study on academic freedom under siege, I identified academic capitalism (commercialization and corporatization) in democracies and authoritarianism in semi- or nondemocracies, if not totalitarianism yet, like China.[19] Culture is an important force in influencing not only academics' but also policymakers' behavior. And its influence cannot be separated from the influence of structure and the efforts on the part of the individual.

The Individual in Relation to Structure and Culture

We have already mentioned Marx at the beginning of the chapter about individuals making history. Sociological theorists do indeed recognize the importance of the individual. For Marx and Engels, "circumstances make men just as much as men make circumstances."[20] "Men are producers of their conceptions, ideas, etc.—real, active men, as they are conditioned by a definite development of their productive forces and of the intercourse corresponding to these."[21]

These individuals who make history are active human beings and they surely include elites with their corresponding beliefs. Durkheim, for example, observes that "the autocratic ruler [in despotism] embodies in his person the moral dominance of the *conscience collective* and thus the repressive sanctions which are called into play for deviation from its dictates appear as political sanctions wielded by the autocrat."[22] As for ordinary individuals, they "imitate their superiors, ... and the causes which lead men to imi-

17 Marx and Engels, *The German Ideology*, 58.
18 Giddens, "Introduction: Durkheim's Writings," 209.
19 Hao, "Academic Freedom under Siege."
20 Marx and Engels, *The German Ideology*, 59.
21 Marx and Engels, *The German Ideology*, 47.
22 Giddens, "Introduction: Durkheim's Writings," 46–47.

tate, to obey each other, are already social."[23] While the role of the state is to liberate individuals, the latter need to form secondary groups to counterbalance the power of the former.[24] For Durkheim, the individual is "an active agent as well as a passive recipient of social influences."[25] This is the case when "the Catholic accepts his faith ready-made, without scrutiny, [while the] Protestant is far more the author of his faith."[26]

When Weber discusses traditional domination, charismatic domination, and legal domination, he is mainly talking about how political leaders exert power. And demagogues as political leaders are certainly moving history.[27]

For sociological theorists, "the individual acts upon the world at the same time as the world acts upon him," and individuals do play an active role as creators of social reality.[28] For Abbott, "individuals are central to history because it is they who are the prime reservoir of historical connection from past to present," which is what he calls the "historicity of individuals."[29] In other words, they are the embodiment of structure and culture, and all three factors are in constant interaction with one another. "Individuals and social entities are made dynamically through time, and moreover, their relation to one another at a moment (ecology) constitutes a mutual conversation."[30] As an important social force, these individuals are not only the elites but also ordinary persons, and other social entities are structures and cultures of all kinds.[31]

In my work on academic freedom, I discuss individual faculty members bringing lawsuits to the court to defend their rights, unionization in the United States, and international advocacy groups.[32] Clark summarizes the role of the individual in academe very well:

> When the faculty member feels that this sensitive right is infringed, he will run up the banners of academic freedom and inquiry, or he will fret

23 Giddens, "Introduction: Durkheim's Writings," 77.
24 Durkheim, *Selected Writings*, 197–202.
25 Giddens, *Capitalism and Modern Social Theory*, 71.
26 Durkheim, *Selected Writings*, 242.
27 Weber, *From Max Weber*, 78–79, 96, 103, 107.
28 Giddens, *Capitalism and Modern Social Theory*, 210–211.
29 Andrew Abbott, "The Historicality of Individuals," *Social Science History* 29 (2005): 3.
30 Andrew Abbott, *Processual Sociology* (Chicago: University of Chicago), xi, 1–2.
31 See Abbott on "atomic individuals": Abbott, *Processual Sociology*, 16.
32 Hao, "Academic Freedom under Siege."

> and become a festering sore in the body politic of the campus, or he will retreat to apathy and his country house, or he will make it known in other and greener pastures that he will listen to the siren call of a good offer.[33]

In other words, the individual may become an active member in defending academic freedom or a passive recipient in accepting his or her fate. Whatever the person does, the individual has a role to play, an important one at that.

Structurally How Political Regimes Approach Academic Freedom in China

Now we are able to go back to the main topic of the chapter and examine how structural, cultural, and individual factors have influenced academic freedom in China's history. We will see that these three factors may be equally important in affecting academic freedom.

How Political Regimes Approach Free Thinking in Ancient History

The nature of the political regime, more authoritarian or more democratic, is a structural issue, so the view of the regime is a structural level point of view, which either fosters or obstructs free academic thinking and debates. It is a major part of the social circumstances we mentioned earlier. Historically speaking, when the political control in China is fragmented and loose, free thinking is valued, and the academy thrives. But when China is politically unified and strong with centralized and dictatorial leadership, free thinking is stifled and the academy suffers. So structurally how academic freedom is approached depends on the nature and status of the political regime.

Probably the most well-known example of free thinking in Chinese history would be in China's Spring and Autumn Period (770–476 BCE) and the following Warring States Period (475–221 BCE) (春秋戰國時期) when One Hundred Schools of Thought Contended (百家爭鳴). In the former period, about 170 political entities or kingdoms in central China were in constant

33 Burton R. Clark, *On Higher Education: Selected Writings* (Baltimore: The Johns Hopkins University Press, 2008), 131.

wars with one another, with bigger ones swallowing smaller ones, and kings, dukes, and princes being killed one after another. Even in the latter period, there were still seven major states remaining to continue to fight for power.

In their attempt to survive in a brutal world, the kings and dukes relied on scholars to provide them with ideas to solve domestic and foreign relations problems. They wanted to attract more talents to help them. This was a time when literally close to a hundred schools of thought were born, including Confucianism, Daoism, Legalism, Maoism, and so on. Within each of those schools, there were various branches. These schools of thought focus on philosophy, politics, economy, education, and military affairs, and so on.[34]

But the severest suppression of free thinking came when in 221 BCE the state of Qin defeated the other six states and established a unified Chinese empire, which ended several hundred years of the Autumn and Spring and the Warring States Periods. The first emperor of China, Qin Shi Huang 秦始皇, followed ruthless despotism, the most symbolic events of which were "the burning of books and killing of Confucians" (焚書坑儒). Books of Confucian classics and other schools of thought were burned, except those kept by official scholars, those that supported despotism, and those on agriculture and divination. Over four hundred Confucian scholars were killed because they criticized the Qin regime for its cruel despotism and the emperor for his obstinance in pursuing his policies. And they cited previous kings who they thought he should follow instead (以古非今).[35]

How Political Regimes Approach Academic Freedom in Modern Times

Such a cycle of opening up and suppression of free thinking and academic autonomy has been repeated in the next two thousand years many times, and the past hundred years are no exception. The Republican era in mainland China between 1911 and 1949 resembled the Warring States Period in that the central government was not strong enough to control local governments or the various rebelling forces like the Chinese Communist Party (CCP).

34 Liu Zehua, *Zhongguo zhengzhi sixiang shi ji* (Beijing: Renmin chubanshe, 2008), 115–119.

35 Derk Bodde, "The State and Empire of Ch'in," in *The Cambridge History of China*, ed. Denis Twitchett and Michael Loewe (Cambridge: Cambridge University Press, 1986), 20; Zehua, *Zhongguo zhengzhi sixiang shi ji*, 14.

Political regimes and forces needed intellectuals to support them. As a result, the latter had a lot of maneuvering room and the academy flourished. Intellectuals freely debated the idea of "the people," "Chinese," and "democracy". Even the CCP, headed by Mao Zedong, was strategically advocating democracy against what they believed to be Chiang Kai-shek's dictatorship.

But like the history of two thousand years ago, once the CCP seized power in mainland China, it started a series of movements to suppress any thoughts that contradicted the CCP ideology and its own brand of Marxism, Leninism, and Mao Zedong Thoughts. Mao boasted that he was a contemporary version of the first emperor of China except that he was more powerful than Qin Shi Huang. He said that the first emperor killed only 468 Confucians, but he killed 46,000 scholars. He said that he was a hundred times more powerful.[36] Indeed, in the Anti-Rightist Movement in 1959, the CCP identified at least 500,000 intellectuals to persecute. Some were killed, and others were put into prison and labor camps. Many died in those tribulations.

History has repeated itself even in the most recent times. After Mao died in 1976, there was a period of opening up from Hua Guofeng to Deng Xiaoping until 1989. Democracy again became the catchphrase of the day. The CCP regime was contemplating what to do to prevent Maoist disasters from happening again, and it needed intellectuals' help in political and economic reforms. But Deng's suppression of the democratic movement in 1989 practically ended the opening up of free speech and academic freedom. Even if economic reforms continued under Jiang Zemin and Hu Jintao, political suppression steadily intensified and culminated in the Xi Jinping era of now.

In 2013, immediately after he came to power, Xi issued the order of "Seven No's." Academic freedom has become the regime's enemy. Intellectuals have largely not been able to discuss in college classrooms and write about and publish on issues concerning civil society, civil rights, universal values, legal independence, press freedom, the privileged capitalistic class, and the historical wrongdoings of the Party.[37] University authorities have installed surveillance cameras in the classroom, and student informants are to report any

36 Sun Yancheng, "Mao Zedong: Qin Shi Huang suan sha? Ta zhi keng le si bai liu shi ba ge ru," https://news.china.com/history/all/11025807/20150925/20463469_all.html.

37 Xi Chen, "Mingjing yuekan du jia quan wen kanfa Zhonggong 9 hao wenjian," *Molihua*, September 22, 2013, www.molihua.org/2013/08/9_7925.html.

deviant speech by the professor in class to the authorities, that is, anything that is deviant from the party line.

Indeed, quite a number of professors have gotten in trouble for free speech in class or online. Ilham Tohti of the Central Minzu (ethnicities and nationalities) University has been sentenced to life in prison for advocating in the classroom and on social media for the Uyghur minority's rights. So are a number of other Uyghur professors. More were fired because of their online and/or in-class speech criticizing the CCP and its state:

Yang Shaozheng of Guizhou University[38]
Shi Jiepeng of Beijing Normal University[39]
Wang Gang of Hebei Engineering University[40]
You Shengdong of Xiamen University[41]
Deng Xiangchao of Shangdong Jianzhu University[42]
Tan Song of Chongqing Normal University, and so on.[43]

There are more examples in a Scholars at Risk report and the list keeps growing. The difference between now and before is that dissenting intellectuals are not killed although they may be imprisoned or fired.[44]

In sum, the few examples we have shown in Chinese history indicate that at the structural level, political regimes may loosen up or crack down on academic free thinking depending on their pragmatic needs. When the state is divided or otherwise fragmented or at least in transition, there is more academic freedom because the political regime needs it. So they view academic freedom more favorably. When the state is unified, powerful, and strong,

38 Ling Yun, "Guizhou daxue jiaoshou Yang Shaozheng bei kaichu," *Epoch Times*, August 21, 2018, www.epochtimes.com/gb/18/8/16/n10644441.htm.

39 Shi Tao, "Wangluo yanlun 'yuyue hongxian,' Bei Shida jiepin jiaoshi," *Deutsche Welle*, 2017, www.dw.com.

40 Mingpo, "Jian weiquan weixin qun Hebei jiaoshou bei chao," *Mingpo Canada*, July 9, 2018, www.mingpaocanada.com/van/htm/News/20180709/tcad1_r.htm.

41 Mingpo, "Jian weiquan weixin qun Hebei jiaoshou bei chao."

42 Lin Ping, "Deng Xiangchao zai wangshang zhuanfa fengci Mao Zedong de wenzhang hou zaodao mao fen weigong bing bei xiaofang qiangzhi tuixiu," *Radio Free Asia*, January 10, 2017, www.rfa.org/mandarin/yataibaodao/zhengzhi/yl-01102017101853.html.

43 Luo Siling, "Chongqing jiaoshi duo nian diaocha tugai zhenxiang, shijiu da qian tu zao kaichu," *New York Times*, September 29, 2017, https://cn.nytimes.com/china/20170929/cc29-tansong/.

44 Scholars at Risk, *Free to Think 2018: Report of the Scholars at Risk Academic Freedom Monitoring Project* (New York: Scholars at Risk, 2018).

and it is more autocratic or dictatorial, as it is now, the rulers would think that academic freedom is a threat to their power so they view it unfavorably. They suppress academic freedom.

Culturally How Thinkers View Academic Freedom

Thoughts That Foster Academic Freedom

If there are two structural trends of fostering and suppressing academic free thinking respectively throughout Chinese history, the same is true with regard to cultural trends even within the same school of thought. Confucianism, for example, believes that degree holders had an obligation to speak out "when the government deviated from Confucian ideals."[45] With that came the movements of *qingyi* or "pure opinion," that is, scholars were free to criticize as they wanted, not in fear of retaliation by the political regime.[46]

Mencius, another great thinker of Confucianism, upholds the so-called *hao ran zhi qi* 浩然之氣, that is, the will and spirit that are on a grand scale, strong and upright. He believes that a *da zhang fu* 大丈夫, or a gentleman, "is not to be bewildered by wealth and honor, shaken by poverty and humbleness, or ready to bend before authority and force." This is the same as what Confucius was teaching, "The army can be deprived of its commander-in-chief, but a person cannot be deprived of his will and spirit."[47] Xun Zi, yet another thinker of Confucianism, believes that morality and justice are above anything else. One follows morality and justice rather than a king (從道不從君).[48]

Daoism, too, has fostered a free spirit in scholarly pursuit. Lao Zi, the major founder of Daoism, advocated *dao fa ziran* 道法自然, that is, man follows the laws of the Earth, the Earth follows the laws of Heaven, Heaven follows the laws of Dao, Dao follows the laws of Nature. So man follows the

45 Merle Goldman, *China's Intellectuals: Advise and Dissent* (Cambridge, MA: Harvard University Press, 1981), 3.

46 Merle Goldman, *Sowing the Seeds of Democracy in China* (Cambridge, MA: Harvard University Press, 1994), 5–7.

47 Zhidong Hao, *Intellectuals at a Crossroads: The Changing Politics of China's Knowledge Workers* (Albany: SUNY Press, 2003), 328.

48 Zehua, *Zhongguo zhengzhi sixiang shi ji*, 282–285.

laws of nature. Politically he advocates *wu wei er zhi*, or governing by doing nothing, meaning collecting less taxes, practicing less punishment, engaging in less military actions, and fostering frugality.[49] This encouraged the emergence of a group of scholars in Confucius's time, called *yinshi* or recluse, who were interested only in the interpretation of concepts rather than becoming officials as Confucianism would like them to. In the same spirit, Zhuang Zi, another founder of Daoism, said that he would not wish to be "harnessed" to an office, but would rather exist like a free pig in a muddy ditch.[50]

This free spirit in pursuing truth and justice while defying authorities has been handed down in the next two thousand years to scholars and intellectuals. It explains why some intellectuals have chosen a critical path in their scholarly and political pursuit as we will see in the next section. This tradition was later combined with the Western concept of academic freedom and became an important cultural trait in the Chinese academy.

In 1898, the Imperial University, the predecessor of Peking University, was established. It was "patterned after the University of Tokyo, which in turn had been influenced by both French and German academic patterns."[51] In 1916, Cai Yuanpei, the president of Peking University, adopted the principle of *sixiang ziyou, jianrong bingbao* 思想自由兼容並包 or freedom of thinking and accommodation of different points of view. The university would be a place "where different ideas and values of Orient and Occident, antiquity and modernity, could be studied objectively, debated freely, and selected discriminately."[52]

Cai Yuanpei made a connection between the traditional and the modern in terms of free-thinking spirit and academic freedom. (Cai himself is an example of the importance of the individual factor.) Even in contemporary authoritarian China, Peking University still claims to adhere to academic freedom as one of its major principles.[53] It is no wonder then that when university professors in Beijing were interviewed for a research project, they all

---

49 Zehua, *Zhongguo zhengzhi sixiang shi ji*, 333.

50 Hao, *Intellectuals at a Crossroads*, 35.

51 Ruth Hayhoe, *China's Universities, 1895–1995: A Century of Cultural Conflict* (New York: Garland, 1996), 18.

52 John Israel, *Lianda: A Chinese University in War and Revolution* (Stanford: Stanford University Press, 1998), 119, cited in Robert A. Rhoads et al., *China's Rising Research Universities: A New Era of Global Ambition* (Baltimore: The Johns Hopkins University Press), 67.

53 Hao, "Academic Freedom under Siege," 4.

wished they could have more academic freedom. They were concerned about the degree to which they could pursue a full range of scholarly interests and whether they could publish their studies in China. Professors were certainly concerned about the administration's practice of screening students with "radical thoughts" and "independent lifestyles."[54] As I discussed earlier, cultural intellectuals' longing for free thinking and publication is both traditional and contemporary.

Thoughts against Academic Freedom

But the more dominating thoughts may be the suppression of free thinking. Liu Zehua points out that most of the One Hundred Schools in the Autumn and Spring Period as well as in the Warring States Period are more likely to contend for the kings to adopt their plans of despotism.[55] Some strands of Confucianism, for example, advocated the hierarchical relationship between the kings and their subjects, father and son, and husband and wife, with the latter occupying lower status. They strategize for the rulers and ask the rulers to behave themselves. This contradicts the free-thinking strands we discussed earlier.

As a result of this thinking, many followed the Confucian teaching of *xiu shen, qijia, zhi, guo, ping tianxia* 修身齊家治國平天下, or perfect oneself, get one's family in order, guide or govern one's country in the right course, and bring peace to the world.[56] They thus become organic to political rulers, whoever they are. Shang Yang and Li Si (speaking of the individual factor) helped Qin in its ruthless government and political despotism such as the burning of books and the killing of Confucians. Legalism believes in the rule by law, agricultural and military strength, the total power of the ruler, and making use of human nature that pursue profit and advantage.[57]

Nowadays we see statism, following the ancient Legalist tradition, justify the one-party dictatorship or authoritarianism of the CCP. Statism believes that the state is the center, and the core goal of modernization is the state's

54 Rhoads et al., *China's Rising Research Universities*; Hao, "Academic Freedom under Siege," 5.

55 Zehua, *Zhongguo zhengzhi sixiang shi ji*, 119–120.

56 Hao, *Intellectuals at a Crossroads*, 378.

57 Zehua, *Zhongguo zhengzhi sixiang shi ji*, 120–124.

own prosperity and capacity. The state is not a tool for public good, but it is the public good.[58]

Statism does not say that it is against academic freedom. But by emphasizing the power of the state, it is in fact doing so. Accordingly, the role of the academy is to serve the state in whatever capacity the state needs. We will give examples of individuals who advocate statism in the following section. Suffice it to say that Chinese culture in contemporary times especially in the form of statism is largely hostile to academic freedom, as we have also demonstrated in the first section on structure. Indeed, culture and structure are closely related to one another and they work in tandem either for or against academic freedom. It's a perennial fight within and between structure and culture.

Individuals Choose to Go for or against Academic Freedom

At the individual level, academics or scholars assess the structural and cultural level points of view and come to their own conclusions on the issue and choose to practice academic freedom, facing consequences, or assisting the rulers in suppressing academic freedom. This section will discuss these vastly different individual points of view and practices.

Intellectuals for Free Thinking and Criticism

At the end of the Eastern Han dynasty (25–220), over three thousand scholars and students launched a movement criticizing government politics and policies and the conduct of the imperial households, eunuchs, and even the emperor. The movement was crushed by the government and two to three hundred scholars and sometimes their whole families were sentenced to death, exile, or imprisonment. This was the famous *danggu*, or "party cases," in 166–169. As scholars and students, they must have understood what political regimes and traditional cultures would like them to do. They apparently made a choice in favor of free thinking and criticism in the often competing requirements of both structure and culture.

58 Zhidong Hao, "What Kind of Nation-State Do They Want to Build: Chinese Intellectuals and Nationalism in Contemporary China," *2021 Spring Joint International Conference on the Evolution of Knowledge Geography and Current State of Knowledge Convergence*, April 22, 2021.

Another famous case concerned the critical movement of the Donglin Academy in the early 1600s of the Ming dynasty. Led by Gu Xiancheng, a deposed scholar-official who founded the academy in 1604, the Donglin scholars and students criticized the government officials for their corruption in their regular gatherings. They demanded open criticism and reform. Like the consequences of the "party cases" about 1,600 years earlier, many scholars and students in Donglin Academy and other academies in the country were either executed or jailed and their academies were destroyed. Cheng Ding, an early Qing scholar, wrote twenty-four books commemorating 120 such scholars.[59]

Similar persecutions happened again and again in China's history. Here is another example. In 1957 the so-called rightists played a critical role and were persecuted as I mentioned earlier. In the Xi Jinping era, many intellectuals continue to criticize government politics and policies. They are not executed like in the Qin or Ming dynasties or the Mao era, but the punishment is still harsh, quite in line with the ancient Legalist doctrines and practices. A few university professors are imprisoned for their criticism, like Iliam Tolhti and some others in Xinjiang, who are Uyghur intellectuals. They are accused of separatism although what they have done is nothing more than advocating for ethnic autonomy as promised by the constitution. I gave some examples above of professors who criticized the party's politics and policies and then lost their jobs. Three citizen journalists went to Wu Han to investigate the pandemic in 2020. One is now imprisoned (Zhang Zhan), another is strictly restricted in his activities (Chen Qiushi), and the third one still missing (Fang Bin).

As I mentioned earlier, either in ancient or contemporary times, intellectuals made a choice to exercise their right to criticize the government, understanding that the political structure and traditional culture have competing requirements for them. If some intellectuals believe in academic freedom and free thinking and choose to criticize the government, others choose to defend despotic practices and as such stifle academic freedom.

Intellectuals against Free Thinking and Criticism

The most famous or infamous scholar-officials or intellectuals in Chinese history who served a suppressive political regime should be Shang Yang

59 For this movement and the "part cases," see Hao, *Intellectuals at a Crossroads*, 28–29.

(?–338 BCE) and Li Si (284–208 BCE) of the kingdom and the later empire of Qin. Shang Yang led the reform of Qin, establishing land ownership, rewarding military achievement, setting up administrative regions, encouraging agriculture while suppressing commerce, and unifying the measurement systems. But he also banned lobbying and burned Confucian classics because Confucianism was not conducive to his ruthless policy of punishing anyone who was not engaged in agriculture and/or military expeditions. He also encouraged people to watch each other and inform the government of anyone who was not following the government policies. In addition, to rule effectively, the ruler had to keep the ruled ignorant according to his doctrines.[60] It seems that at least some of his policies regarding free thinking and speech are still implemented today. Shang Yang lost his life in political infighting: he was executed by hanging, drawing, and quartering, one of the harshest punishments in Chinese history.

When Li Si became the prime minister of the first emperor of Qin, he continued his predecessor Shang Yang's reforms including further administrative changes and clarifying the responsibilities of local officials, standardizing the language writing systems, and so on. But he also led the most extensive burning of books as well, that is, not only Confucian classics but other "unnecessary" books, too, as we discussed earlier.[61] And he assisted in the killing of Confucian scholars. Like Shang Yang, he also lost his life in political infighting: he was cut in two at the waist, another of the cruelest punishments in Chinese history similar to that received by Shang Yang.

Fast forward to 1957, many intellectuals were caught in the so-called Hundred Flowers Blossom movement and were encouraged to inform against others and criticize others for their deviant thoughts: anything different from the Chinese brand of Marxism-Leninism-Mao Zedong Thought and any criticism against the CCP would be viewed as deviant. Indeed, by that time, the CCP had already developed a cadre of intellectuals who would faithfully follow the party directives and engage in various forms of thought reform to bring others in line with the party. Any free thinking or academic freedom was out of the question.

60 Zehua, *Zhongguo zhengzhi sixiang shi ji*, 144–145, 156–157.

61 Bodde, "The State and Empire of Ch'in."

The same happened in the Xi Jinping era. Here are some examples of intellectuals advocating statism. It is true that they do not directly advocate the suppression of academic freedom, but that idea is embedded in statism, as we can see in what they say. And they echo what Shang Yang and Li Si did some two thousand years ago.

Wang Shaoguang 王紹光 and Hu Angang 胡鞍鋼 advocate that the state capability is its ability to absorb/assimilate, to control, to legitimize, and to coerce. For Wang Hui 汪暉, the state is the party, and the party-state represents the general interest of the people. Jiang Shigong 強世功 would say that one should just follow whatever the party says since there is no right and wrong in politics. For him, there is only violence and government between friends and foes. Zhang Weiwei 張維為 even says that violence is good 善, and the government is a necessary good, not a necessary evil. For Pan Wei (潘維), the CCP represents all people's interests. Han Yuhai (韓毓海) admires a party like the CCP for it has extreme power to expand and conquer worldwide, and a great ability to coordinate and mobilize various social forces inside 極強的擴張和征服能力，高度的整合與動員能力. When Zheng Yongnian 鄭永年 called for Hong Kong's "second return to China," and Tian Feilong 田飛龍 and Chen Duanhong 陳端洪 accused the social movement in Hong Kong of splitting China, they said that individual freedom and rights have to yield to the state authority and state interest.[62]

There are many other examples like these in contemporary China, examples of intellectuals who choose to be the think-tank of the CCP and its one-party dictatorship. They serve as the organic intellectuals of the government and as spokespersons of the government's suppressive policies. They are successors to Shang Yang and Li Si although they may not be as ruthless as these ancient figures were.

Conclusions

So how do structure, culture, and the individual collectively and reciprocally constrain and enable academic freedom in China, then? From the above historical and contemporary analysis, we can see that structurally political regimes view free thinking as a pragmatic matter. They encourage it if they

62 Hao, "What Kind of Nation-State Do They Want to Build."

need it, and they suppress it if they don't, especially when they think academic freedom threatens their rule. So their views on free thinking can be favorable or unfavorable depending on needs.

Culturally both traditional and contemporary thinking have components that favor academic freedom. But there are also cultural traits that are despotic and dictatorial. So there are at least two schools of thought on academic freedom, for and against. Individually there are scholars who believe in academic freedom. They practice academic freedom but have to face consequences if they venture into fields that are taboo, like the Seven Nos we mentioned earlier. But there are also scholars who believe in statism, assisting the rulers to suppress free thinking and publication. Again this is true in both traditional and contemporary China.

In today's China, because of the conflicts we discussed earlier, the trend against academic freedom is dominating at the structural, cultural, and individual levels. As such, the struggle for academic freedom is going to be an uphill battle. The battle will continue even when the Chinese regime changes into one that believes in universal values of human rights and democracy as it does now in liberal democracies. It promises to be a long arduous and perennial battle.

I hope my study will shed light not only on the Chinese case, but on cases in other countries as well in regard to the importance of structural, cultural, and individual factors in influencing academic freedom. In a nutshell, individuals are not just passive recipients of the structural and cultural status quo; they can be active agents in protecting academic freedom. It is the interaction, within and between, of the three factors that makes or breaks academic freedom.

CHAPTER 6

Beyond the Periphery?

Academic Freedom as a Matter of Human Rights

SEJAL PARMAR

INTRODUCTION

Long defended by the world's leading human rights advocacy organizations and championed by Scholars at Risk,[1] academic freedom has regularly been framed as a matter of human rights by scholars in recent years.[2] Yet, within a broad and burgeoning academic literature on the subject, there has been relatively little focused scholarly analysis of academic freedom from the perspective of international human rights law and the approaches of

1 Human Rights Watch, *Zimbabwe: Government Moves to Curb Academic Freedom* (New York: Human Rights Watch, 1990); Amnesty International, "South Korea: Six Researchers Arrested," www.amnesty.org/ar/documents/asa25/023/1991/en/. See also Scholars at Risk, "History," www.scholarsatrisk.org/about/#History.

2 See, e.g., Special Issue on Academic Freedom and Internationalisation, *International Journal of Human Rights* 26 (2022); Jennifer Wright et al., "Supporting Academic Freedom as a Human Right: Challenges and Solutions in Academic Publishing," *International Journal of Human Rights* 26 (2022): 1741; Antoon de Baets, "Academic Freedom between History and Human Rights in a Global Context," in *Third International Handbook of Globalisation, Education and Policy Research*, ed. Joseph Zajda (Cham: Springer, 2021), 923; Katrin Kinzelbach, *Researching Academic Freedom: Guidelines and Sample Case Studies* (Erlangen: FAU University Press, 2020); Klaus D. Beiter, Terence Karran, and Kwadwo Appiagyei-Atua, "Academic Freedom and Its Protection in the Law of European States: Measuring an International Human Right," *European Journal of Comparative Law and Governance* 3 (2016): 254.

UN human rights bodies. This arguably reflects the relatively limited attention historically paid by the UN human rights system, including the UN charter- and treaty-based bodies, to academic freedom as such as a thematic human rights issue despite the recognition of academic freedom as a prerequisite for the right to education by UN Committee on Economic, Social, and Cultural Rights ("CESR") in 1999.[3] This chapter takes stock of the attitudes and approaches of these UN human rights bodies toward considering academic freedom as such as an issue of international human rights law over recent years. It begins by identifying and unpacking factors informing a certain hesitancy toward understanding and addressing challenges to academic freedom as concerns of international human rights law, before identifying how this has given way to a more direct and receptive engagement with cases of specific threats to academic freedom as such and the phenomena, especially since 2015. The chapter suggests that academic freedom is moving from being a side-lined issue toward becoming a more mainstream one as a result of emerging concerns from UN human rights bodies and mechanisms. This trend, which is reflected in various ways through the outputs of UN human rights bodies and their development of international soft law norms in recent years, is likely to continue and should be welcomed because it strengthens the possibilities for more effective advocacy of academic freedom both through the UN system and before domestic policymakers.

In Peripheral Vision

The relationship between academic freedom and human rights has often appeared an unclear and uncertain one. This has partly been informed by normative and structural challenges concerning the foundation and formulation of academic freedom within the framework of international human rights law, as well as a sense that this international legal framework and the work of UN human rights bodies are of "marginal" importance to the pursuit of academic freedom and that they are too remote from its everyday challenges.[4] The present part identifies five reasons why academic freedom

3 Committee on Economic, Social and Cultural Rights, "General Comment No. 13 on the Right to Education (Article 13)," UN Doc E/C.12/1999/10 (1999), paras. 38–40.

4 David Kaye, "Report of the Special Rapporteur on the Promotion and Protection of the Right to Freedom of Opinion and Expression," UNGAOR, 75th Sess., UN Doc A/75/261 (2020), para. 57.

might have seemed to be on the peripheries of international human rights law and the interests of the UN human rights system for so long, and also why international human rights law has often hitherto played a limited role in the advocacy of academic freedom.

First, there is "no single, exclusive international human rights framework" for the protection of academic freedom or the connected principle of institutional autonomy.[5] Numerous treaty provisions across both core international human rights treaties, namely the International Covenants on Civil and Political Rights ("ICCPR") and the International Covenant on Economic, Social and Cultural Rights ("ICESCR"), serve to protect academic freedom in various ways, as demonstrated by the engagement of a number of UN human rights bodies and mechanisms on the subject, which will be discussed later. These provisions concern a panoply of rights, including most notably freedoms of opinion and expression and the right to education, in addition to the right to peaceful assembly and association, thought, conscience, and religion, and the right to scientific advancements.[6] While this range of provisions may reinforce a sense of the interdependence and indivisibility of the rights relevant to the context of academic freedom, these multiple underpinnings also deliver a sense of instability and fragmentation as to the legal basis of academic freedom, uncertainty about where it "belongs" within the international human rights framework, and also confusion as to its precise definition, meaning, rationale and scope.[7]

In the absence of an explicit treaty provision that would have provided academic freedom a clear legal basis, the most significant assertion of academic freedom by a UN human rights body to date remains the CESR's General Comment No. 13, the committee's authoritative interpretation of

5 Kaye, "Report of the Special Rapporteur," para. 5; Liviu Matei, "Is a Global Common Reference for Academic Freedom Desirable? Is It Possible?" *King's College London Presidential Series* III (2023): 5. Interestingly, however, Article 13 of the Charter of Fundamental Rights of the European Union, which became legally binding on the EU with the entry into force of the Treaty of Lisbon in December 2009, explicitly provides that "academic freedom shall be respected" and that "research shall be free of constraint."

6 Articles 17 (privacy), 18 (freedom of thought, conscience and religion), 19 (freedom of opinion and freedom of expression), and 21 (right to peaceful assembly and association) ICCPR. Articles 13 (right to education) and 15 (right to scientific advancements) ICESCR.

7 Beiter, Karran, and Appiagyei-Atua question whether academic freedom has a "home" in either or both the covenants; see Klaus D. Beiter, Terence Karran, and Kwadwo Appiagyei-Atua, "Yearning to Belong: Finding a 'Home' for the Right to Academic Freedom in the U.N. Human Rights Covenants," *Intercultural Human Rights Law Review* 11 (2016): 107.

Article 13 of the International Covenant on Economic, Social and Cultural Rights on the right to education, which was adopted in December 1999.[8] The text draws on UNESCO Recommendation concerning the Status of Higher Education Teaching Personnel, which was adopted in November 1997, to define academic freedom and institutional autonomy:

> 39. Members of the academic community, individually or collectively, are free to pursue, develop, and transmit knowledge and ideas, through research, teaching, study, discussion, documentation, production, creation, or writing. Academic freedom includes the liberty of individuals to express freely opinions about the institution or system in which they work, to fulfill their functions without discrimination or fear of repression by the State or any other actor, to participate in professional or representative academic bodies, and to enjoy all the internationally recognized human rights applicable to other individuals in the same jurisdiction ...
> 40. The enjoyment of academic freedom requires the autonomy of institutions of higher education. Autonomy is the degree of self-governance necessary for effective decision-making by institutions of higher education in relation to their academic work, standards, management, and related activities.

General Comment No. 13 still remains the key basis for human rights considerations of academic freedom, even though other highly relevant soft law instruments have subsequently been adopted, as discussed in the next part.

Second, although the protection of academic freedom may be rooted in a range of human rights, there are clearly collective and institutional dimensions to academic freedom—"the collective right of faculty to set the norms of academic debate, free from interference by administration, governing boards, or the state"[9]—as well as its accompanying principle of institutional autonomy, which sets it apart from traditionally individualistic notions of

8 On general comments of the CESCR, see Philip Alston, "The Committee on Economic, Social and Cultural Rights," in *The UN and Human Rights: A Critical Appraisal*, ed. Frédéric Mégret and Philip Alston (Oxford: Oxford University Press, 2020), 453.

9 Eva Cherniavsky, "Against the Common Sense: Academic Freedom as a Collective Right," *AAUP Journal of Academic Freedom* 12 (2021): 9.

human rights.[10] It is not clear, in particular, where institutional autonomy fits within the broader corpus of human rights given its collective character. Tensions between the individual, collective, and institutional characteristics of academic freedom—in such cases where individual academics may assert their academic freedom to research and teach in a way that is viewed as unacceptable by their faculty, institution or the wider academic community—may further fuel a sense of confusion about the nature of academic freedom and whether it can be justifiably identified as a human right at all.

Third, there are relatively few decisions or "Views" of the treaty bodies and judgments of regional human rights courts directly addressing the individual protection of academic freedom, especially in its institutional dimensions, as compared with the vast bodies of Views and jurisprudence on other areas concerning relevant rights, particularly freedom of expression, such as the protection of journalists.[11] There are some notable exceptions, however. In *Faurisson v France*, for instance, the Human Rights Committee held that there was no violation of an author's "freedom of academic research" under Article 19 of the ICCPR on freedom of expression as a result of legislation criminalizing the denial of the existence of Nazi concentration camps.[12] The author of the complaint, a Sorbonne professor of literature, had contended that the "Gayssot Act" infringed his freedom of expression and academic freedom and hence constituted "unacceptable censorship, obstructing and penalizing historical research."[13] In *Aduayom et al v Togo*, the Human Rights Committee found a violation of the provision in the case of university teachers who were prosecuted for having criticized the Togolese government.[14]

Fourth, there appears to have been a lack of interest in threats to academic freedom as a matter of political concern among the most senior figures of the UN system. When referring to the academic community in their official remarks and speeches, High Commissioners for Human Rights have tended to focus on academics' role as stakeholders, civil society partners

10 See Kristen Roberts Lyer and Aron Suba, *Closing Academic Space: Repressive State Practices in Legislative, Regulatory and Other Restrictions on Higher Education Institutions* (Washington, DC: International Centre for Not-for-Profit Law, 2019), 30–31.

11 Kaye, "Report of the Special Rapporteur," para. 21.

12 *Faurisson v France*, Communication No. 550/1993, UN Doc CCPR/C/58/D/550/1993 (1996).

13 *Faurisson v France*, para. 3.1.

14 *Adimayo M. Aduayom et al v Togo*, Communications Nos. 422–24/1990, UN Doc CCPR/C/51/D/422/1990 (1996).

in supporting human rights initiatives, or simply as hosts and/or the audience of the speaking event.[15] Successive UN secretaries-general have also not directly addressed attacks on academic freedom in their official remarks and speeches. For instance, the current UN secretary-general Antonio Guterres has chosen not to spotlight academic freedom through his interventions or comments. In contrast, while in office as secretary-general, Kofi Annan observed that "threats to academic freedom are often the beginning of broader assaults on human rights and liberty" at the 2005 Plenary Session of the Global Colloquium of University Presidents.[16] Years after leaving office, Annan also invoked the language of rights in his personal letter of support for Central European University's campaign to remain in Hungary in 2017.[17]

Fifth, academic freedom has often appeared as a niche and narrow area for human rights advocacy, with very few NGOs enjoying an explicit mandate and focus on it, as compared with those working in other areas connected with freedom of expression, such as media freedom or digital rights. The comparatively small community of advocates dedicated to academic freedom advocacy has undoubtedly influenced their potential for impacting the UN system, especially in relation to cases that have lacked a high profile. As a barometer of influence, consider that only ten civil society organizations made submissions to the expert consultation on the academic freedom of the Special Rapporteur on freedom of opinion and expression in 2020, and of those only two organizations headquartered in the United States—Scholars at Risk with its global purview, and Foundation for Individual Rights in Education (now Foundation for Individual Rights and Expression), which focuses on the United States—have explicit mandates on academic freedom.[18] In comparison, seventy-five NGOs made submissions to the Special Rapporteur's expert consultation on disinformation in 2021, and forty-two

15 See, e.g., Navi Pillay, "The International Human Rights Treaty System: Impact at the Domestic and International Levels," lecture at the Washington College of Law, October 1, 2013; Louise Arbour, "The Activities of the Office of the United Nations High Commissioner for Human Rights: Achievements and Challenges," statement presented to the United Nations University, November 9, 2004.

16 United Nations, "Secretary-General Stresses Importance of International Migration, Academic Freedom in Remarks to Colloquium of University Presidents," UN Doc SG/SM/9685 (2005).

17 Annan wrote: "At the heart of a rights based order, of free speech and of intellectual freedom are centres of higher learning that promote these values to its future leaders"; see "Letter to Professor Michael Ignatieff, President and Rector of Central European University," April 6, 2017.

18 OHCHR, "Calls for Input: Academic Freedom and Freedom of Opinion and Expression," www.ohchr.org/en/calls-for-input/report-academic-freedom-and-freedom-opinion-and-expression.

NGOs made submissions to the Special Rapporteur's expert consultation on sustainable development in 2023.

Into the Line of Sight?

These obstacles to the consideration of academic freedom clearly within the framework of international human rights law and a certain historical hesitancy of UN actors toward academic freedom have given way to greater recognition of and engagement with issues of academic freedom and institutional autonomy by the UN system in recent years. Since 2015, certain high-profile cases of attacks on academic freedom—such as Turkey, Hungary, and Hong Kong—have driven various UN actors to engage with challenges to academic freedom more directly and systematically, which has, in turn, shored up existing and emerging monitoring by civil society organizations and empirical research in the area.[19] This increased engagement in issues of academic freedom by UN human rights actors has been manifested through six key developments.

First, concerns about cases of threats to academic freedom and institutional autonomy have been more vocally expressed by the UN's senior leadership, specifically the High Commissioner for Human Rights, in recent years. Since 2015, High Commissioners Zeid and Bachelet have both called out threats to academic freedom, particularly in their updates to the Human Rights Council. In his September 2017 Opening Statement to the thirty-sixth session of the Human Rights Council, High Commissioner Zeid Ra'ad Al Hussein highlighted that "very large numbers" of Turkish academics, as well as journalists, judges, civil servants, and human rights defenders, had been "arrested and detained, and others dismissed or subjected to intrusive surveillance, censorship, threats, and violence." He also pointed to the undermining of academic freedom as a "vital aspect of freedom of expression" in Hungary. In her update on the situation in Nicaragua to the Human Rights Council in June 2022, the then outgoing High Commissioner Michelle Bachelet denounced the arbitrary cancellation of at least twelve universities in the country, following the reform of the Law of Autonomy of Higher

19 Scholars at Risk, *Free to Think 2022: Report of the Scholars at Risk Academic Freedom Monitoring Project* (New York: Scholars at Risk, 2023); Katrin Kinzelbach et al., *Free Universities: Putting the Academic Freedom Index into Action* (Berlin: Global Public Policy Initiative, 2021).

Education Institutions requiring academic programs of all universities to be approved by a central body, as "a new threat to academic freedom and university autonomy, an integral component of the right to education and freedom for scientific research and creative activity."[20] Such references to threats to academic freedom have given the issue a greater political profile and visibility at a high level within the UN system, allowing it to be seen as a distinct matter of legitimate concern for the human rights movement and UN bodies and mechanisms.

Second, the ICESCR's adoption of General Comment No. 25 on science and economic, social, and cultural rights in 2020 stands as a significant advancement in the normative understanding of academic freedom, although it does not refer to that term as such.[21] It certainly complements earlier authoritative interpretations of treaty bodies, the CESCR's 1999 General Comment No. 13 on the right to education and the Human Rights Committee's 2011 General Comment No. 34 on freedom of opinion and expression, in particular.[22] General Comment No. 25 recognizes that the "protection and promotion of academic and scientific freedom" encompasses a range of rights, "including freedom of expression and freedom to seek, receive and impart scientific information."[23] It also emphasizes the "robust protection of freedom for research" as a prerequisite for scientific develop-

20 See Ra'ad Al Hussein, "Sri Lanka Investigation Report," statement delivered via videolink to the Human Rights Council, September 30, 2015; OHCHR, "Hungarian Parliament Urged by UN Expert to Reconsider New Law Targeting Central European University," April 11, 2017; Ra'ad Al Hussein, "Statement to the 36th Session of the Human Rights Council in Geneva," September 11, 2017; Michelle Bachelet, "Statement to the 40th Session of the Human Rights Council in Geneva," March 6, 2019; Michelle Bachelet, "Finland, Sweden and Norway in Multilateral Cooperation: How Can We Secure the Legitimacy of Multilateral Cooperation? What Are the Tendencies in Europe and Globally? The Rule of Law," keynote speech, February 6, 2020; Michelle Bachelet, oral update on the situation of human rights in Nicaragua delivered to the 50th session of the Human Rights Council in Geneva, June 16, 2022.

21 See Committee on Economic, Social, and Cultural Rights, "General Comment No. 25," UN Doc E/C.12/GC/25 (2020), para. 13: "This freedom includes, at least, the following dimensions: protection of researchers from undue influence on their independent judgment; their possibility to set up autonomous research institutions and to define the aims and objectives of the research and the methods to be adopted; the freedom of researchers to freely and openly question the ethical value of certain projects and the right to withdraw from those projects their conscience so dictates; the freedom of researchers to cooperate with other researchers, both nationally and internationally; the sharing of scientific data and analysis with policymakers, and with the public, wherever possible."

22 Committee on Economic, Social, and Cultural Rights, "General Comment No 13." See also Human Rights Committee, "General Comment No. 34 on Freedom of Opinion and Freedom of Expression," UN Doc CCPR/C/GC/34 (2011).

23 Committee on Economic, Social, and Cultural Rights, "General Comment No. 25."

ment, and elaborates on states' positive duties to "respect the freedom indispensable for scientific research" under Article 15(3) of the ICESCR by unpacking and providing examples of the protections for researchers that the provision requires. It states:

> 13 ... The freedom includes, at least, the following dimensions: protection of researchers from undue influence on their independent judgment; the possibility for researchers to set up autonomous research institutions and to define the aims and objectives of the research and the methods to be adopted; the freedom of researchers to freely and openly question the ethical value of certain projects and the right to withdraw from those projects if their conscience so dictates; the freedom of researchers to cooperate with other researchers, both nationally and internationally; and the sharing of scientific data and analysis with policymakers, and with the public wherever possible.

In fleshing out the freedom for scientific research and creative activity, General Comment No. 25 strengthens key individualistic dimensions of academic freedom. As a General Comment, it potentially provides a valuable reference point and persuasive (albeit nonbinding) source of normative guidance for state authorities in fulfilling their positive obligations to create the conditions conducive to the "freedom for research" of individual researchers.[24] Furthermore, while there is a lack of research on the impact of General Comments of the CESCR generally and General Comment No. 25 specifically—in terms of references to these texts within the jurisprudence of national courts, regional human rights courts, the policies and programs of state governments, the outputs of national human rights institutions, and academic literature—General Comment No. 25 is likely to exert an influence internally upon other UN human rights bodies and mechanisms, especially given their emerging heightened receptiveness to issues of academic freedom.[25]

Third, legislative restrictions and political assaults on academic freedom have been addressed more consistently through the concluding observations

24 Alston, "The Committee on Economic, Social and Cultural Rights."

25 Alston, "The Committee on Economic, Social and Cultural Rights."

of several treaty bodies since 2015 than in previous years. The Human Rights Committee has expressed its concern about the adoption of legislation in Hungary "which imposes disproportionate restrictions on the operation of foreign-accredited universities" in 2018,[26] the absence of legal reforms necessary for academic freedom in Namibia in 2016,[27] and the assault on academic freedom in Hong Kong in 2013.[28] The CESCR has criticized the ties between the governance of universities and "political and partisan interests" in China, which has led to the dismissal of teaching staff and the expulsion of students, restricting the right to education, freedom of thought and opinion, and freedom of scientific research and creative activity in 2023,[29] and, using similar language and, with reference to General Comment No. 25, has recommended that Nicaragua ensured that "the academic governance of universities is not driven by partisan political interests" in 2021.[30] For its

26 Human Rights Committee, "Concluding Observations on the Sixth Periodic Report of Hungary," UN Doc CCPR/C/HUN/CO/6 (2011), para. 51: "The Committee notes with concern the amendment introduced in 2017 to Act CCIV of 2011 on National Higher Education ... While the Committee notes the explanation given by the State party delegation that this legislation applies to all accredited universities in its territory, the Committee notes a lack of sufficient justification for the imposition of such constraints on freedom of thought, expression and association, as well as academic freedom. The Committee is concerned that the constraints particularly affect the Central European University because of its links with George Soros (arts. 18, 19, 21, 22 and 26)."

27 Human Rights Committee, "Concluding Observations on the Second Periodic Report of Namibia," UN Doc CCPR/C/NAM/CO/2 (2016), para. 42: "The State party should carry out all necessary legal amendments to ensure that research may be carried out without State authorization and fully respect, protect and promote academic freedoms."

28 Human Rights Committee, "Concluding Observations on the Third Periodic Report of Hong Kong," UN Doc CCPR/C/CHN-HKG/CO/3 (2013), para 13: "The Committee is concerned about reports that Hong Kong, China, has seen deterioration in media and academic freedom, including arrests, assaults and harassment of journalists and academics (arts. 19 and 25)."

29 Committee on Economic, Social, and Cultural Rights, "Concluding Observations on the Third Periodic Report of China, Including Hong Kong, China, and Macao," UN Doc E/C.12/CHN/CO/3 (2023), para. 127: "The Committee urges Hong Kong, China, in cooperation with the State party, to review its legislation to ensure the full academic freedom of students, teachers and other university staff. The Committee regrets that it has not received any information regarding guarantees of academic freedom and is concerned about reports that the academic governance of universities is increasingly tied to political and partisan interests, which has led to the dismissal of teaching staff and the expulsion of students, restricting the right to education, freedom of thought and opinion, and freedom of scientific research and creative activity (arts. 13, 14 and 15)."

30 Committee on Economic, Social, and Cultural Rights, "Concluding Observations on the Fifth Periodic Report of Nicaragua," UN Doc E/C.12/NIC/CO/5 (2021), para. 48: "The Committee regrets that it has not received any information regarding guarantees of academic freedom and is concerned about reports that the academic governance of universities is increasingly tied to political and partisan interests, which has led to the dismissal of teaching staff and the expulsion of students, restricting the right to education, freedom of thought and opinion, and freedom of scientific research and creative activity (arts. 13, 14 and

part, the Committee on the Elimination of Racial Discrimination has recommended that Costa Rica "[take] the necessary steps to ensure that textbooks that have content with racist overtones are removed from the mandatory curriculum in primary schools" in 2015.[31] Although treaty bodies' concluding observations only speak to the states concerned, their level of specificity and foundation in human rights treaties establishes their legitimacy and wider influence upon the development of other outputs of UN human rights bodies, such as general comments and the reports of special procedures mechanisms.

Fourth, in recent years, states have begun to raise issues concerning academic freedom and institutional autonomy directly in the Universal Periodic Review (UPR) process in connection with the cyclic reviews of a handful of UN member states. Specifically, Uruguay and Slovenia urged Venezuela to stop interfering in universities and ensure the independence and autonomy of all universities in 2022 and 2016 respectively[32]; Belgium, Liechtenstein, and Germany called on Hungary to ensure the protection of the scientific freedom and autonomy of universities, including "in determining curricula, teaching, research, and management," in 2021[33]; and Uruguay and

15). The Committee recommends that the State party take the necessary measures to ensure respect for academic freedom and freedom of thought and opinion in universities as well as respect for freedom of scientific research and creative activity. The Committee recommends that the State party ensure that the academic governance of universities is not driven by partisan political interests and refers the State party to its General Comment No. 25 (2020) on science and economic, social and cultural rights. E/C.12/NIC/CO/5 (CESCR 2021)."

31 Committee on the Elimination of Racial Discrimination, "Concluding Observations on the Combined Nineteenth to Twenty-Second Periodic Reports of Costa Rica," UN Doc CERD/C/CRI/CO/19-22 (2015), para. 16: "The Committee recommends that the State party step up its efforts to ensure that the national education system fosters an awareness and fuller knowledge of the distinctive cultural practices of the Afro-descendent and indigenous populations and their contributions to Costa Rican history and culture with the aim of providing objective and educational information about all societies and cultures in the State party. The Committee also recommends that the State party guarantee academic freedom of expression by, inter alia, taking the necessary steps to ensure that textbooks that have content with racist overtones are removed from the mandatory curriculum in primary schools."

32 Uruguay recommended to Venezuela to "[cease] the intervention in universities and other higher education institutes and transform without delay the parallel system of non-autonomous universities so that they achieve full independence and academic freedom"; see UN Doc A/HRC/50/8 (2022). Slovenia recommended to Venezuela to reform Education Act to achieve compliance with international human rights law on academic freedom; see UN Doc A/HRC/34/6 (2016).

33 Belgium recommended to Hungary to "[ensure] protection of the scientific freedom and autonomy of universities and research institutes, including autonomy in determining curricula, teaching, research and management in line with its international obligations regarding academic freedom." Liechtenstein recommended Hungary to "[take] effective steps to protect freedom of expression, including of civil society

Haiti pressed Turkey to "ensure academic freedom and student" and "related rights" in 2020.[34] States' review of such threats to academic freedom remains inconsistent and unsystematic, arguably an indicator of a certain reluctance to consider issues of academic freedom as a human rights matter and clearly within the purview of the Human Rights Council. It remains remarkable that no state has thus far raised the deep and longstanding challenges to academic freedom and institutional autonomy in countries such as China, Russia, or Iran—a situation that is explained by the political leverage of these states. But recent years have also exposed a sense of potential—admittedly one that is hitherto largely untapped—for the UPR to facilitate more constructive dialogue between UN member states about their records on academic freedom.[35]

Fifth, UN special procedures mandate-holders, the centerpiece of the UN human rights system, have paid far greater attention to contemporary threats to academic freedom since 2014. The most significant contribution to the field by a UN special procedures mechanism is the report dedicated to the subject by Special Rapporteur on freedom of opinion and expression, David Kaye, to the seventy-fifth session of the UN General Assembly, which examined attacks and threats to academic freedom as a global phenomenon and offered a series of recommendations for states, international organizations, academic institutions, and civil society.[36] Though it recognizes and reaffirms that academic freedom issues engage a range of rights protections, the report emphasizes its freedom of opinion and expression dimensions, the freedom of opinion and expression-related challenges to it, and the requirements of international human rights law on freedom of opinion and expression toward ensuring its protection. In this sense, it is the most significant

---

actors and scholars, protect academic freedom, and ensure the autonomy of universities." Germany recommended Hungary to "[take] measures to effectively protect university autonomy in line with international human rights standards relating to academic freedom"; see UN Doc A/HRC/49/8 (2021).

34 Uruguay recommended to Turkey to "[align] anti-terrorism legislation and article 301 of the Criminal Code with international human rights standards, ensuring the protection of academic freedom and student rights." Haiti recommended to Turkey to "take all the necessary measures under domestic and international law in order to protect academic freedom at university level and related rights"; see UN Doc A/HRC/44/14 (2020).

35 On the value of the UPR, see generally Hilary Charlesworth and Emma Larking, eds., *Human Rights and the Universal Periodic Review: Rituals and Ritualism* (Cambridge: Cambridge University Press, 2015).

36 Kaye, "Report of the Special Rapporteur," paras. 54–59.

tool for civil society organizations' advocacy of academic freedom, and bolsters such work undertaken by NGOs working in the realm of free expression in particular. The report builds on General Comment No. 13 to define academic freedom as "the freedom of individuals, as members of academic communities (e.g., faculty, students, staff, scholars, administrators, and community participants) or in their own pursuits, to conduct activities involving the discovery and transmission of information and ideas, and to do so with the full protection of human rights law."[37]

Beyond this report, four UN special procedures mandate-holders have addressed academic freedom through an array of country reports. In 2021, the Special Rapporteur on the negative impact of unilateral coercive measures on the enjoyment of human rights highlighted the impact of unilateral sanctions imposed on Venezuela by the United States, the EU, the UK, and other states upon the exercise of academic freedom in that country. The implications of the sanctions included the "reported reluctance of foreign partners to cooperate with Venezuelan institutions, including universities ... affect[s] the right to education, academic freedom and cultural rights, and impede the delivery of humanitarian aid."[38] The Special Rapporteur also found that the "ability [of academics] to travel abroad to attend international conferences has been hampered because of flight, visa and money transfer restrictions due to sanctions, thus limiting possibilities for academic research."[39] In 2021, the Special Rapporteur on the situation of human rights in Belarus called upon the Government of Belarus to "reinstate in the Education Code the concept of and articles on academic freedom, and ensure its broad definition and application, in line with the principles of the European Higher Education Area."[40] In 2020, the Special Rapporteur on cultural rights urged the Polish government to ensure legislative frameworks fully respect academic freedoms, including the freedom to seek and impart information,[41] and, in 2014, the government of Bosnia Herzegovina to "pro actively encourage (and refrain from discouraging) meetings between aca-

37 Kaye, "Report of the Special Rapporteur," para. 8.

38 Alena Douhan, "Report of the Special Rapporteur on the Negative Impact of Unilateral Coercive Measures on the Enjoyment of Human Rights," UN Doc A/HRC/48/59/Add.2 (2021), paras. 73, 101.

39 Douhan, "Report of the Special Rapporteur," para. 73.

40 Anaïs Marin, "Report of the Special Rapporteur on the Situation of Human Rights in Belarus," UN Doc A/HRC/47/49 (2021), para. 101(l).

41 See UN Doc A/HRC/43/50/ADD.1 (2020).

demics and researchers in all fields, including history."[42] In 2019, the Special Rapporteur on the right to education expressed concern about teachers' academic freedom in Qatar.[43]

In addition, special procedures mechanisms have called out individual and systematic attacks on academic freedom and institutional autonomy through their communications to a range of states, since 2014—specifically Israel (2022),[44] China (2021),[45] Eritrea (2021),[46] Hungary (2017),[47] Turkey (2016),[48] Egypt (2016),[49] Thailand (2014),[50] and Tajikistan (2014).[51] All of these communications have been issued jointly by several mandate-hold-

42 The mandate holder also urged the state, among others, to "pay particular attention to academic freedoms and the country's higher education system, which should be free from political interference"; see UN Doc A/HRC/25/49/Add.1 (2014), para. 108.

43 See UN Doc A/HRC/44/39/ADD.1 (2020), paras. 32, 96.

44 OHCHR, "Information Received Concerning the New 'Procedure for Entry and Residency of Foreigners in Judea and Samaria Region,' Which May Have a Negative Impact on the Enjoyment of Academic Freedom in the Occupied Palestinian Territory," UN Doc OL ISR 7/2022 (2022), https://spcommreports.ohchr.org/TMResultsBase/DownLoadPublicCommunicationFile?gId=27249.

45 OHCHR, "Concerning the Enactment of the Law of the People's Republic of China on Safeguarding National Security in the Hong Kong Special Administrative Region, Also Known as the National Security Law (NSL)."

46 Concerning national service requirements obliging all secondary school students in the country to complete their final year at the Warsai Yekalo Secondary School, located in the Sawa military camp, and to undertake mandatory military training for approximately five months of that year, as well as regarding related practices and conditions that impact the right to education, academic freedom, and the right to not be discriminated in the field of education.

47 OHCHR, "Concerning the Recently Passed Bill T/14686 Amending Act CCIV of 2011 on National Higher Education Which Appears to Specifically Target the Central European University and Represents Undue Interference with Academic Freedom and Independence," UN Doc OL HUN 1/2017 (2017), www.ohchr.org/sites/default/files/Documents/Issues/Opinion/Legislation/OLHungary-CEU.pdf.

48 OHCHR, "Concerning Alleged Arrests, Interrogations and Termination of Positions of Turkish Scholars and Members of the Academic Community in Violation of Their Right to Freedom of Expression," UN Doc UA TUR 3/2016 (2016), https://spcommreports.ohchr.org/TMResultsBase/DownLoadFile?gId=32868. According to the information received, Turkish federal prosecutors had placed over 1,100 professors and researchers at eighty-nine academic institutions under pressure for having cosigned a public statement led by Academics for Peace entitled "We Will Not Be a Party to This Crime."

49 OHCHR, "Concerning Arrest and Detention of Journalist and Academic Ismail Alexandrani," UA EGY 1/2016 (2016), https://spcommreports.ohchr.org/TMResultsBase/DownLoadPublicCommunicationFile?gId=18020.

50 OHCHR, "Concerning Arrest and Confiscation of the Passport of Pavin Chachavalpongpun, an Academic Working in Japan," Communication No. 52101/604, https://spcommreports.ohchr.org/TMResultsBase/DownLoadFile?gId=32809.

51 OHCHR, "Concerning the Alleged Arrest, Detention and Enforced Disappearance of a Doctoral Student and Journalist Alexander Sodiqov," UN Doc UA TJK 4/2014 (2014), https://spcommreports.ohchr.org/TMResultsBase/DownLoadPublicCommunicationFile?gId=17967.

ers, except the one in Hungary, which was issued by the Special Rapporteur on freedom of opinion and expression alone. It is also interesting that the Special Rapporteur on the right education has only joined in the communications since 2021, suggesting an unwillingness of earlier mandate-holders to engage with the issue. All of the communications except those to Israel, Eritrea, and Egypt received replies from the state concerned. The communication in relation to China concerned the erosion of academic freedom in Hong Kong following the Law of the People's Republic of China on Safeguarding National Security in the Hong Kong Special Administrative Region (HKSAR), also known as the National Security Law (NSL) on June 30, 2020. Several Special Rapporteurs—on the right to education, freedom of opinion and expression, and freedom of peaceful assembly and association—expressed concern about "the disciplining of educators for their social activism and for exploring political issues in class, particularly in the university context, textbook censorship, the removal of educational components aimed at fostering critical thinking from a core secondary school curriculum, and an announced plan to insert national security components into almost all subjects in primary and secondary curricula."[52] The Permanent Mission of the People's Republic of China to the UN in Geneva issued a vigorous forty-page response, stressing that Hong Kong's "education institutions continue to enjoy academic freedom, which is an important value treasured by Hong Kong and a cornerstone of [the] higher education sector."[53]

Sixth and finally, there has been growing attention at the regional level on academic freedom as a human rights issue. The interpretation of human rights protections under regional human rights systems can be an important point of reference for considerations of the implications of international human rights law by UN mechanisms, as shown through the reports of special procedures mandate-holders.[54] Over recent years, academic freedom has emerged ever more clearly as a regional human rights issue in the Americas and especially through jurisprudence in Europe, in particular.[55]

52 OHCHR, "Communication to China," UN Doc AL CHN 9/2021 (2021), https://spcommreports.ohchr.org/TMResultsBase/DownLoadPublicCommunicationFile?gId=26592.

53 OHCHR, "Letter from Permanent Mission of the People's Republic of China to the UN in Geneva," November 11, 2021.

54 Kaye, "Report of the Special Rapporteur," paras. 21–23.

55 See also for the African regional context: The Kampala Declaration on Intellectual Freedom and Social Responsibility, 1990; The Juba Declaration on Academic Freedom and University Autonomy, 2007.

In December 2021, the Inter-American Commission on Human Rights ("IACHR") together with its Special Rapporteurs on freedom of expression and on economic, social, cultural, and environmental rights issued the "Declaration of Inter-American Principles on Academic Freedom and University Autonomy," which is said to "[contribute] to promoting a clear approach of academic freedom as an autonomous human right that plays an enabling role in ensuring democracy and the development of societies."[56]

While the European Court of Human Rights ("ECtHR") has furthered the individual aspects of academic freedom, the Court of Justice of the EU ("CJEU") has served to defend the institutional dimensions of academic freedom on the basis of an explicit protection of academic freedom within EU law. In the 2014 judgment in *Mustafa Erdoğan and Others v Turkey*, the ECtHR built on its traditional stance toward freedom of expression by asserting that academic freedom "is not restricted to academic or scientific research, but also extends to the academics" freedom to express freely their views and opinions, even if controversial or unpopular, in the areas of their research, professional expertise, and competence." This "may include an examination of the functioning of public institutions in a given political system and a criticism thereof."[57] In a similar vein, the ECtHR has also emphasized that, alongside NGOs and the press, academic researchers exercise a public watchdog function and therefore should be accorded a high level of protection in relation to the right of access to information.[58] Within the EU context, Article 13 of the Charter of Fundamental Rights of the European Union ("EU Charter") explicitly provides that "academic freedom shall be respected" and emphasizes that "research shall be free of constraint." In October 2020, the CJEU reinforced the institutional dimensions of academic freedom through its 2020 judgment concerning the restrictions on academic freedom of foreign-accredited institutions in Hungary in 2017.

56 Inter-American Commission on Human Rights, "IACHR Issues Declaration of Inter-American Principles on Academic Freedom and University Autonomy," December 9, 2021, www.oas.org/en/iachr/jsForm/?File=/en/iachr/media_center/preleases/2021/331.asp. See also David Gómez Gamboa and Ricardo Villalobos Fontalvo, "Academic Freedom: A View from the Inter-American System of Human Rights," *Netherlands Quarterly of Human Rights* 41 (2023): 74.

57 *Mustafa Erdogan and others v Turkey*, Nos. 346/04 and 39779/04 (May 27, 2014), para. 40.

58 See also *Kula v Turkey*, No. 2022/06 (June 19, 2019), para. 38; *Magyar Helsinki Bizottság v Hungary*, No. 18030 (November 8, 2016), para. 168; *Gillberg v Sweden*, No. 41723/06 (April 3, 2012), para. 93; *Sorguç v Turkey*, No. 17089/03 (June 23, 2009); *Kenedi v Hungary*, No. 31475/05 (May 6, 2009), paras. 42–45; *Başkaya and Okçuoğlu v Turkey*, Nos. 23536/94 and 24408/94 (July 8, 1999), paras. 61–67.

The CJEU decided that the Hungarian law on national higher education had violated its obligations under WTO law, EU law on services in the internal market, and provisions of the EU Charter on academic freedom (Article 13), the "freedom to found educational establishments with due respect for democratic principles" (Article 14(3)), and freedom to conduct a business (Article 16).[59] The European Parliament's recommendation on the defense of academic freedom, which was adopted in November 2018, had previously identified institutional autonomy alongside academic freedom as a "core higher education" and "core democratic" value, which both EU states and candidate countries should commit to.[60]

Conclusion

This chapter has acknowledged a certain shift in the approach and attitude of UN human rights bodies toward academic freedom, identifying normative and structural constraints on the engagement of such bodies with the subject, including the paucity of a single international legal framework, and spotlighting various developments since 2015 suggesting a more receptive and positive engagement with cases concerning academic freedom by these bodies. These developments—the more regular statements of concern from the High Commissioner for Human Rights concerning restrictions on academic freedom and institutional autonomy; the specific identification of the meaning of the freedom for research by CESCR's General Comment No. 25; the accumulating range of concluding observations and views of treaty bodies, UPR recommendations, and the reports of special procedures mechanisms, particularly the focused 2020 report of the UN Special Rapporteur on freedom of expression; and the context of a growing body of regional jurisprudence and policy texts in the area—mean that there is a richer pool of rhetorical reference points and international soft law tools available to civil society advocates to advance their positions, both in their engagement with the UN system and also before policymakers at the domestic level.

59 *European Commission v Hungary*, No C-66/18 (October 6, 2020).

60 European Parliament, "Recommendation on Defence of Academic Freedom in the EU's External Action" (2018/2117).

These outputs also provide a source for further research into the field, including the scholar-led project of "reimagining of academic freedom."[61] At the same time, the identified challenges to a more coherent and effective approach to academic freedom under international human rights law persist and could be addressed by UN actors in various ways: the CESCR or the Human Rights Committee could initiate a dedicated general comment on academic freedom, although given this is unlikely and also given the multiple treaty basis for academic freedom; some joint guidance could be offered by the key two treaty bodies working together, as done during the admittedly distinct context of the COVID-19 pandemic[62]; states could be bolder in using future UPR cycles to call out more regularly impediments to academic freedom and institutional autonomy in other states, including powerful ones, such as China and Russia; and senior UN leaders figures, including the secretary-general, could use their positions to call out systematic attacks on academic freedom. In addition, a resolution of the General Assembly or the Human Rights Council could work to bring together and reaffirm the various treaty bases for academic freedom and soft law outputs that have accrued since 2015, and thereby serve to signal a more systematic approach to addressing challenges of academic freedom by the UN system. The joint declaration by seventy-four countries expressing concern at rising attacks on academic freedom delivered at the fifty-second session of the Human Rights Council on March 29, 2023, appears a potential starting point for gathering up the necessary diplomatic support for such an initiative.[63]

---

61 Liviu Matei, "Is There a Need to Reimagine Academic Freedom?" *King's College London Presidential Series*, December 5, 2022.

62 See "Recommendations of UN Human Rights Treaty Bodies on Human Rights Approach in Fighting COVID-19," March 24, 2020; "Comprehensive, Inclusive and Universal COVID-19 Human Rights Policies Urgently Needed: UN Treaty Bodies' Statement on Human Rights Day," December 10, 2021.

63 "Joint Declaration by 74 Countries on Academic Freedom (Intervention by France) at the 52nd Session of the Human Rights Council," March 29, 2023, https://onu-geneve.delegfrance.org/Joint-declaration-on-Academic-freedom. The Joint Declaration was supported by Albania, Andorra, Argentina, Armenia, Australia, Austria, Belgium, Brazil, Bulgaria, Cabo Verde, Cambodia, Cameroun, Canada, Chile, Cyprus, Colombia, Comoros, Costa Rica, Croatia, Czech Republic, Denmark, Dominican Republic, Estonia, Equatorial Guinea, Germany, Finland, France, Gambia, Georgia, Greece, Guinea, Hungary, India, Ireland, Iceland, Israel, Italy, Japan, Jordan, Korea, Latvia, Lebanon, Liechtenstein, Lithuania, Luxemburg, Malta, Moldova, Monaco, Montenegro, the Netherlands, North Macedonia, Namibia, Nepal, New Zealand, Nigeria, Norway, Palestine, Paraguay, Peru, Poland, Portugal, Romania, Saudi Arabia, Serbia, Slovakia, Slovenia, South Africa, Spain, Sweden, Ukraine, the United Kingdom, the United States, Uruguay, and Vanuatu.

Part II

Diversity and the Democratization of Academic Freedom

Chapter 7

Nationalist Backlash to Antiracist Education

A Transnational Blueprint for Academic Unfreedom

Vincent Wong

Introduction

In a global era marked by surging racial nationalism[1] and penal populism,[2] antiracist and decolonial research, education, and training have been under increasing threat in academia across the world. Popular use of the universalizing language of liberal internationalism as the dominant frame in discussing these developments leaves gaps in our understanding as to what areas of academic freedom are under the greatest threat, why they are under threat, what levers of sanction and discipline are used to suppress certain areas, and

1 According to Chenchen Zhang, "Racial nationalism refers ... to a kind of exclusionary ethnic nationalism that defines national belonging primarily in ethnic and cultural terms, and that views ethno-cultural others as 'fundamentally threatening to the homogeneous nation-state.' ... Taking the forms of xenophobia, racism and Islamophobia, racial nationalism undergirds the discussion on issues of immigration, race and Muslims in both Western and Chinese societies." Chenchen Zhang, "Right-Wing Populism with Chinese Characteristics?" *European Journal of International Relations* 26 (2020): 99.

2 Harsha Walia, *Border & Rule: Global Migration, Capitalism, and the Rise of Racist Nationalism* (Halifax: Fernwood, 2021), 178.

for what ends. Such a frame risks contributing to overly abstracted conceptualizations of academic freedom (and unfreedom) that are unmoored from the realities of how power operates in educational institutions and attendant maldistributions of who can in fact claim and be protected by academic freedom and who cannot.

In this chapter, I put into conversation three very different jurisdictional contexts where nationalist backlash to, and suppression of, antiracist and decolonial education and scholarship is occurring. Specifically, it examines American anti–Critical Race Theory (CRT) campaigns, Chinese suppression of scholarship critical of its ongoing colonial suppression of non-Han native peoples in the Xinjiang Uyghur Autonomous Region (XUAR), and Israeli suppression of scholarship critical of its ongoing occupation of Palestinian territories through the case study of the "Spiro scandal" at the University of Toronto (UofT) Faculty of Law.[3]

No good politics of academic freedom can emerge without centering an analysis of broader societal power and subordination. This is particularly true in the areas of national security and antiracism, which form distinct grounds for both legal and political intervention in academic freedom. A national security threat engages certain types of legal grounds, particularly domestically (e.g., carceral responses to perceived counterterrorism, separatism, and extremism threats), while antiracism justifies other types of intervention (e.g., civil rights complaints, removing of curriculum, firings, cutting funding) and can operate powerfully on a transnational level as well.

I highlight three common elements in a transnational blueprint that can be observed in the creation, justification, and operation of selective nationalist attacks on academic freedom in antiracist and decolonial education. My highlighting of these common elements is *not* meant to suggest any sort of equivalence between their operation, historical context, and/or relative severity, but

3 I acknowledge my personal situatedness with respect to Israeli nationalist campaigns against academic freedom as one of the whistleblowers in the hiring committee during the Spiro Scandal at the UofT Faculty of Law, where a sitting Canadian Tax Court judge and top university administrators helped facilitate a clandestine lobbying campaign instigated by a former Israeli foreign ministry advisor and an Israeli-Canadian lobby group to derail the hiring of a prominent international human rights scholar for the directorship of a human rights program. See Richard Moon and Anver M Emon, "Misadministering Justice? The UofT Law School Case Takes a Strange Turn," *Centre for Free Expression*, September 16, 2021, https://cfe.ryerson.ca/blog/2021/09/misadministering-justice-u-t-law-school-case-takes-strange-turn; Canadian Association of University Teachers, "University of Toronto under Censure," *CAUT Bulletin*, May 2021, www.caut.ca/bulletin/2021/05/university-toronto-under-censure.

rather to advance our collective understanding of the distributive nature of academic freedom politics and its relationship to power, race, and colonialism. Unpacking these campaigns transnationally complicates and unsettles the dichotomy between authoritarian and liberal populist censorship, giving us a more nuanced foundation by which to protect academic freedom and knowledge production in the service of racial justice and collective liberation.

The Blueprint of Antiracist Academic Unfreedom

I posit that three (unexhaustive) common elements emerge among nationalist attacks on academic freedom in antiracist and decolonial scholarship, which I unpack in this section:

a. Creating a moral panic by demonizing antiracist education;
b. Obscuring power imbalances and dissuading critical inquiry by framing issues using floating signifiers such as "divisive," "sensitive," and "controversial"; and
c. Reframing conversations around structural injustice and disparity as "racism" against dominant groups within ethnonationalist projects.

Creating a Moral Panic by Demonizing Antiracist Education

In the realm of antiracist and decolonial education, I argue that the justification of censorship is primarily done in the *affective* realm of emotional incitement, taking the form of moral panic to vilify and demonize this education and its proponents. Without a public campaign of moral panic, authorities who promulgate laws and policies or engage in practices that prohibit or erode antiracist education, risk encountering significant internal and external backlash, loss of institutional prestige (particularly for universities), legal challenges, and loss of political capital.

In the United States, as of March 2023, a total of 203 local, state, and federal government entities have introduced 619 anti-CRT bills, resolutions, executive orders, opinion letters, statements, and other measures.[4] This anti-

4 UCLA School of Law Critical Race Studies, "CRT Forward," https://crtforward.law.ucla.edu/.

CRT censorship campaign has followed a white nationalist strategy of "racial McCarthyism." This strategy attempts to deliberately invoke moral panic by fusing two distinct but intertwining political apprehensions: a domestic white *racial* unease awakened in response to the George Floyd protests opposing police brutality and racial injustice in the summer of 2020, combined with a geopolitical McCarthyist anxiety in response to a rising, nominally socialist China. Working at the register of *affect* allows anti-CRT censorship campaigners to reframe those teaching about contemporary racial injustice and the true history of slavery and colonial racism in the United States as both unpatriotic and actual national security threats.

Racial McCarthyist apprehensions were front and center at the very beginning of the campaign's inception. During then President Trump's 2020 US Independence Day speech at Mount Rushmore, Trump connected domestic racial justice demands to foreign influence concerns by analogizing the George Floyd protests to a Mao-era "left-wing cultural revolution ... designed to overthrow the American Revolution."[5] But Trump's nationalist search for a political boogeyman to counter grassroots demands for racial justice ended two months later when he stumbled upon a Tucker Carlson interview on Fox News of conservative activist Christopher Rufo, who said that CRT was "neo-Marxist rhetoric" that had "pervaded every institution in the Federal government" and had become "the default ideology of the federal bureaucracy ... now being weaponized against the American people."[6] The Trump administration got to work immediately: only three days later, the Office of Management and Budget (OMB) issued a memo informing federal agencies that any training related to CRT or white privilege would be enjoined and defunded.[7]

The moral panic campaign now had its ideological anchor: a specific branch of antiracist scholarship that would be blamed for a hodgepodge of American

5 Donald Trump, "Remarks by President Trump at South Dakota's 2020 Mount Rushmore Fireworks Celebration | Keystone, South Dakota," *The White House*, July 4, 2020, https://trumpwhitehouse.archives.gov/briefings-statements/remarks-president-trump-south-dakotas-2020-mount-rushmore-fireworks-celebration-keystone-south-dakota/.

6 Sam Dorman, "Chris Rufo Calls on Trump to End Critical Race Theory 'Cult Indoctrination' in Federal Government," *Fox News*, September 1, 2020, www.foxnews.com/politics/chris-rufo-race-theory-cult-federal-government.

7 Russell Vought, "Memorandum for the Heads of Executive Departments and Agencies," *The White House*, September 4, 2020, www.whitehouse.gov/wp-content/uploads/2020/09/M-20-34.pdf.

social and cultural ills. Two after the OMB memo, Trump announced the establishment of the President's Advisory 1776 Commission[8]: a national commission entrusted to "promote patriotic education" and ensure that "our sons and daughters ... know that they are the citizens of the most exceptional nation in the history of the world." The impetus for this heavy-handed patriotic curriculum was ostensibly the threat of CRT, which he described as a "Marxist doctrine" that holds America as a "wicked and racist nation." He decried CRT "being forced into our children's schools," "imposed into workplace trainings," and "deployed to rip apart friends, neighbors, and families" in order to "impose a new segregation."[9] Connecting the dots between CRT and the need for a patriotic rewrite of American history, Trump painted a picture of traitorous conspiracy against the American national project: "Critical Race Theory, the 1619 Project, and the crusade against American history is toxic propaganda. Ideological poison, that if not removed will dissolve the civic bonds that tie us together, will destroy our country."[10]

Finally, before the month was out, Trump promulgated Executive Order (EO) 13950: Combating Race and Sex Stereotyping,[11] which continues to form the highly successful legislative blueprint by which American racial justice education and history has been censored under the auspices of opposing "CRT." EO 13950 language has formed the template for state and local initiatives, such as South Dakota's House Bill (HB) 1012, which explicitly prohibits postsecondary teaching, curricular content, and training that critically examines racism and sexism.[12] At the K–12 level, teachers have been fired or otherwise removed from teaching duties for sharing poetry on white

8 "Establishing the President's Advisory 1776 Commission, Executive Order 13958," Federal Register, November 2, 2020, www.federalregister.gov/documents/2020/11/05/2020-24793/establishing-the-presidents-advisory-1776-commission.

9 "Executive Order 13958."

10 Donald Trump, "Remarks by President Trump at the White House Conference on American History," *The White House*, September 17, 2020, https://trumpwhitehouse.archives.gov/briefings-statements/remarks-president-trump-white-house-conference-american-history/.

11 "Executive Order on Combating Race and Sex Stereotyping, Executive Order 13950," *The White House*, September 22, 2020, https://trumpwhitehouse.archives.gov/presidential-actions/executive-order-combating-race-sex-stereotyping/.

12 SD HB 1012, "An Act to Protect Students and Employees at Institutions of Higher Education from Divisive Concepts," 97th Leg Sess, 2022, https://sdlegislature.gov/Session/Bill/23006/236257.

privilege,[13] displaying Black Lives Matter banners outside their classrooms,[14] and implementing reflections on racial privilege as part of curricula,[15] while many more educators are being forced out due to constant harassment and antagonism from anti-CRT censorship groups.[16] These laws have also led to spikes in book bans. PEN America's Index of School Book Bans found that over a nine-month period from 2021 to 2022, 1,145 unique book titles were banned in an "unprecedented shift." Of those bans, 41 percent resulted from compliance with directives from state officials and lawmakers, with 33 percent addressing LGBTQ+ themes, 22 percent addressing race and racism, and 16 percent constituting history books or biographies.[17]

In the context of Israel-Palestine and Xinjiang, the moral panic to demonize antiracist and decolonial education relies heavily on the *specter of terrorism* and its racialization of the Muslim Other in carving a state of exception for academic freedom (and other related human rights). As Khaled Beydoun writes, "Islamophobia is now more than ever a global phenomenon, and the War on Terror has evolved into an imperial project that advances it across longitudes and latitudes,"[18] which is justified by the fundamental misrepresentation "that terrorism is a uniquely Islamic enterprise."[19]

Proximity to anti-Muslim terrorist racialization in vilifying and discrediting scholarship through moral panic figured prominently in the Spiro scandal at UofT's International Human Rights Program (IHRP). The memo that instigated the affair was authored by Gerald Steinberg of NGO Monitor, who opposed the hiring of Dr. Valentina Azarova due to her work

13 Emma Green, "He Taught a Ta-Nehisi Coates Essay. Then He Was Fired," *The Atlantic*, August 17, 2021, www.theatlantic.com/politics/archive/2021/08/matt-hawn-tennessee-teacher-fired-white-privilege/619770/.

14 Southern Poverty Law Center, "BLM Reprisal: Florida School District Terminates Teacher Who Stood Up for Black Students," August 5, 2021, www.splcenter.org/news/2021/08/05/blm-reprisal-florida-school-district-terminates-teacher-who-stood-black-students.

15 Jon Skolnik, "Fired over CRT: Missouri High School Teacher Accused of Teaching 'Critical Race Theory' Loses Job," *Salon*, April 13, 2022, www.salon.com/2022/04/13/fired-over-crt-missouri-high-school-teacher-accused-of-teaching-critical-race-theory-loses-job/.

16 Tyler Kingkade, "Critical Race Theory Battles Are Driving Frustrated, Exhausted Educators Out of Their Jobs," *NBC News*, July 12, 2021, www.nbcnews.com/news/us-news/critical-race-theory-battles-are-driving-frustrated-exhausted-educators-out-n1273595.

17 PEN America, "Banned in the USA: Rising School Book Bans Threaten Free Expression and Students' First Amendment Rights," September 13, 2022, https://pen.org/banned-in-the-usa/.

18 Khaled A. Beydoun, *The New Crusades: Islamophobia and the Global War on Muslims* (Oakland: University of California Press, 2023), 5.

19 Beydoun, *The New Crusades*, 8.

with Palestinian human rights organizations such as Al-Haq. This memo was passed down to members of the Israeli-Canadian lobbying organization Centre for Israel and Jewish Affairs (CIJA), who then enlisted former director Justice David E. Spiro to contact the university to convey these concerns.[20] The concerns found their way to the dean of UofT Law, who summarily canceled the hiring of Dr. Azarova. In the memo, Steinberg makes the Israeli nationalist argument that Al-Haq and other related Palestinian human rights organizations facilitated "campaigns that promote the double standards used to demonize Israel."[21]

Despite the very common (and indeed frequently recommended) practice of human rights professionals adopting a country/region-specific focus, Dr. Azarova's expertise and record of publication on the Israel-Palestine context is recharacterized by Steinberg as a "discriminatory focus on Israel."[22] Steinberg did not seem to recognize that the IHRP itself had for decades worked with Al-Haq as an important regional partner, having organized summer student fellowships and hosted speakers from the prominent human rights organization.[23] These tropes were taken a step further in the December 2020 submissions of pro-Israel group B'nai Brith Canada to the Canadian Judicial Council reviewing Justice Spiro's conduct. Expanding on the Steinberg memo, B'nai Brith claimed that Al-Haq was an "extreme anti-Israel organization" with "direct ties to the Popular Front for the Liberation of Palestine (PFLP)—a listed terrorist entity in Canada."[24] Attacks on Canadian human rights groups for their connections with local human rights NGOs critical of the Israeli government are of course nothing new. Montreal-based NGO Rights and Democracy was shuttered in the early 2010s as a result of pushback after awarding small grants to B'Tselem, Israel's leading human rights group, and its partner agency in the West Bank, Al-Haq, as well as Al Mezan in Gaza.[25]

---

20 Moon and Emon, "Misadministering Justice?"

21 *National Council of Canadian Muslims, et al v AG Canada*, T-1005-21, Certified Tribunal Record (July 13, 2021): 145, https://censureuoft.files.wordpress.com/2021/09/t-1005-21-certified-tribunal-record-cjc-july-13-2021.pdf.

22 *National Council of Canadian Muslims*, 145.

23 International Human Rights Program, "Speaker Series," https://ihrp.law.utoronto.ca/page/speaker-series.

24 *National Council of Canadian Muslims*, 99.

25 Haroon Siddiqui, "Siddiqui: Stephen Harper's Homegrown Human Rights Problem," *Toronto Star*, January 24, 2010, www.thestar.com/news/canada/2010/01/24/siddiqui_stephen_harpers_homegrown_human_rights_problem.html.

Presciently, the strategy of moral panic in deliberately framing Palestinian civil rights organizations as terrorist-adjacent for the purposes of state repression would find legal expression in October 2021 when the Israeli minister of defense designated six Palestinian civil society groups, including Al-Haq, as terrorist organizations under Israel's 2016 Anti-Terrorism Law.[26] Immediately after this designation, Israeli occupying forces raided and shut down the offices of numerous Palestinian organizations, including Al-Haq, seizing and/or destroying numerous documents and items under Article 319 of Israel's 1945 Emergency Regulations.[27]

Similarly, the attack on academic freedom in Xinjiang has been intimately tied to a consistent ideological campaign of racially othering Uyghurs and other Turkic Muslims by tying these populations to the specter of radical Islamic terrorism to inspire fear. After the 2009 Urumqi Riots and 2014 Kunming knife attacks, Xi Jinping pledged to implement a "strike hard" strategy through a "People's War on Terror" in Xinjiang. Within this strategy, the policy goal of eliminating terrorism was explicitly tied to eliminating separatism and extremism under the framework of the "Three Evils."[28] Understanding China's combined policy interests in combating terrorism, separatism, and extremism allows us to better understand the form in which the state socially constructs the "Other": as a racialized Muslim that is a threat because of their radical religious piety, resistance to assimilation, and native claims to the land that pose a direct challenge to Chinese territorial claims and sovereignty.

This racialized demonization of Uyghurs and other Turkic Muslims has allowed for carceral repression of academic freedom. At least several hundred Uyghur intellectuals (including professors, students, and cultural elites) have

26 UNOHCHR, "UN Experts Condemn Israel's Designation of Palestinian Human Rights Defenders as Terrorist Organisations," October 25, 2021, www.ohchr.org/en/press-releases/2021/10/un-experts-condemn-israels-designation-palestinian-human-rights-defenders. The other five organizations were Addameer; Defence for Children International, Palestine; the Union of Agricultural Work Committees; the Bisan Center for Research and Development; and the Union of Palestinian Women Committees.

27 Human Rights Watch, "Joint Statement: Over 150 Organizations Demand International Community Stand against Raids and Closures of 7 Palestinian Organizations," August 22, 2022, www.hrw.org/news/2022/08/22/joint-statement-over-150-organizations-demand-international-community-stand-against.

28 Joanna Smith Finley, "Security, Insecurity and Conflict in Contemporary Xinjiang: Has PRC Counter-terrorism Evolved into State Terror?" *Central Asian Survey* 38 (2019): 2.

been detained, imprisoned, or disappeared since China expanded its counterinsurgency efforts in the XUAR in 2016.[29] Many of these targeted scholars, such as renowned economics professor Ilham Tohti and seven of his students, who wrote on the dangers that totalitarianism and ethnonationalist chauvinism posed for non-Han Indigenous groups in China, including the Uyghur people.[30]

Sean Roberts argues that this silencing of academic freedom in the area of Uyghur cultural, linguistic, historical, and political knowledge production is a crucial part of the Han settler colonial project that seeks to coercively integrate Uyghurs into Chinese modernity through policies of mass incarceration and forced assimilation.[31] This has been supported by state media running programs, such as the documentary *The War in the Shadows: Challenges of Fighting Terrorism in Xinjiang*, which incite moral panic by reinforcing the idea that the teaching of Uyghur political history and past separatist movements against imperial Chinese dynasties constitute radical Islamic terrorism.[32] Chinese nationalist efforts to shut down Uyghur rights activists have also made their way to Western campuses. For instance, in February 2019, Chinese nationalist students at McMaster University in Hamilton, Ontario filmed verbally harassed Uyghur activist Rukiye Turdish during her lecture on mass incarceration of Uyghurs in China. Some of the students then contacted the Chinese Consulate in Toronto about the event and were told to see whether university officials attended and whether Chinese nationals had organized the talk. They later wrote that they sent photos to Chinese officials.[33]

---

29 Abdullah Qazanchi, "Briefing: The Disappearance of Uyghur Intellectual and Cultural Elites: A New Form of Eliticide," *Uyghur Human Rights Project*, December 2021, 1, https://uhrp.org/wp-content/uploads/2021/12/The-Disappearance-of-Uyghur-Intellectual-and-Cultural-Elites_2021-12-07-1.pdf.

30 Ilham Tohti, *We Uyghurs Have No Say: An Imprisoned Writer Speaks* (London: Verso Books, 2022).

31 Sean R. Roberts, *The War on the Uyghurs: China's Internal Campaign against a Muslim Minority* (Princeton: Princeton University Press, 2020), 4–5.

32 "The War in the Shadows: Challenges of Fighting Terrorism in Xinjiang," *CGTN*, April 2, 2021, https://news.cgtn.com/news/2021-04-02/The-war-in-the-shadows-Challenges-of-fighting-terrorism-in-Xinjiang-Z7AhMWRPyo/index.html.

33 Gerry Shih and Emily Rauhala, "Angry over Campus Speech by Uighur Activist, Chinese Students in Canada Contact Their Consulate, Film Presentation," *Washington Post*, February 14, 2019, www.washingtonpost.com/world/angry-over-campus-speech-by-uighur-activist-students-in-canada-contact-chinese-consulate-film-presentation/2019/02/14/a442fbe4-306d-11e9-ac6c-14eea99d5e24_story.html.

Using Floating Signifiers Such as "Divisive," "Sensitive," and "Controversial" to Obscure Power Imbalances and Dissuade Critical Inquiry

There are certain keywords, or "floating signifiers,"[34] that do much of the work to signal that the machinations and injustices of racism and colonialism cannot be discussed, researched, or acted against. The pantheon of floating signifiers in this context includes the words "divisive," "sensitive," and "controversial." These terms are effective in both obscuring the power imbalances inherent in processes of racial subordination and dissuading critical inquiry by signaling academic "redlines" where the benefits and protections of relative academic freedom fall away and educators can expect to experience significant professional and personal consequences. Thus, they become useful tools for nationalists as it is power adjacency and not truth or evidence that frequently dictates what is considered "divisive," "sensitive," or "controversial" in any particular context.

"Divisive" is the key floating signifier that has been codified in the US anti-CRT censorship campaign. For instance, EO 13950 prohibits discussions and training across a list of nine vaguely defined and broadly crafted "divisive concepts." These ideas include: that the United States might be fundamentally racist or sexist,[35] collective responsibility for legacies of systemic racism and sexism,[36] and any sort of discussion around racism and sexism that may cause individuals to "feel discomfort, guilt, anguish, or any other form of psychological distress on account of his or her race or sex."[37] By framing CRT and related antiracist training and education as "divisive," the Order is then able to, in the words of Christopher Rufo, "recodify [CRT] to annex the entire range of cultural constructions that are unpopular with

34 Floating signifiers are words or symbols that "have no determinant meaning without the experience of the particular experiencer"; see Carrie Menkel-Meadow, "The Power of Narrative in Empathetic Learning: Post-Modernism and the Stories of Law," *UCLA Women's Law Journal* 2 (1992): 301; Patricia J. Williams, *The Alchemy of Race and Rights* (Cambridge: Harvard University Press, 1992), 7.

35 "Executive Order 13950," s 2(a)(2).

36 "Executive Order 13950," s 2(a)(7).

37 "Executive Order 13950," s 2(a)(8).

Americans" with the goal of having "the public read something crazy in the newspaper and immediately think 'critical race theory.'"[38]

The preamble of EO 13950 does exactly this by describing "divisive" ideas associated with CRT as "anti-American" (invoking nationalist concerns), "subtle coercive pressure to ensure conformity of viewpoint" (invoking concerns about freedom of expression), and "malign ideology" that "threatens to infect core institutions of our country" (invoking an analogy to a virus that must be contained and destroyed).[39] That these divisive concepts are incoherent insofar as they have little to do with the real CRT (and in some cases are directly in opposition with core CRT tenets[40]) *is the point.* As Moria Donegan states: "The very opacity of the words [critical race theory] made them the perfect vehicle for what the right-wing wanted: a new vessel for white racial anxiety and grievance."[41]

The role of "divisive" in the anti-CRT censorship campaign is taken up by the term "controversial" in the case of the Spiro scandal and the broader campaign to censor teaching and research that is critical of Israeli colonial occupation in higher education. After the Spiro scandal broke in the media and attracted significant condemnation from the public, UofT hired former Supreme Court justice and counsel at Borden Ladner Gervais LLP, Thomas Cromwell, to conduct an internal investigation and publish his findings. The investigation revealed a wealth of additional damning facts surrounding the chain of emails and communications revealing Gerald Steinberg's efforts to enlist the help of CIJA and Justice Spiro to relay concerns about the candidate's research that was critical of Israeli policies under international law to Dean Edward Iacobucci.[42] Despite this wealth of new evidence, however, Cromwell stated that he "would not draw the inference that external influ-

38 Christopher Rufo (@realchrisrufo), March 15, 2021, https://twitter.com/realchrisrufo/status/1371541044592996352?s=20.

39 "Executive Order 13950," preamble.

40 For instance, the preamble of EO 13950 claims that CRT "ideology" advocates the view "that some people, simply on account of their race or sex, are oppressors." Yet CRT articulates a systemic analysis of racial subordination through law and policy that directly critiques the idea of race essentialism or the idea that racism can be best understood through individual bias and personal prejudice.

41 Moira Donegan, "What the Moral Panic about 'Critical Race Theory' Is About," *The Guardian*, June 17, 2021, www.theguardian.com/commentisfree/2021/jun/17/critical-race-theory-republicans-moira-donegan.

42 Vivian Cheng, "Criticisms over the Cromwell Report Erupt with CAUT Censuring U of T," *Ultra Vires*, May 17, 2021, https://ultravires.ca/2021/05/criticisms-over-the-cromwell-report-erupt-with-caut-censuring-u-of-t/.

ence played any role in the decision to discontinue the recruitment of the Preferred Candidate."[43]

In making this conclusion, Cromwell offers a conflicting assessment of the relationship between human rights work and controversy. Indeed, Cromwell begins by acknowledging the director of a human rights program must be "in the business" of tackling controversial issues,[44] yet concludes that Justice Spiro "simply shared the view that the appointment would be controversial with the Jewish community and cause reputational harm to the University"[45] in downplaying the seriousness of his intervention on the hiring. Cromwell then doubles down on the common sense of "controversy" as a justification for Justice Spiro's actions by stating that the controversial nature of the appointment of a human rights expert whose work was critical of Israel "would hardly be news to anyone who had taken a moment or two to look on the internet."[46] The weaponization of "controversial" to justify the benevolence of Justice Spiro's intervention was also picked up by the Canadian Judicial Council that used the abovementioned portions of the Cromwell report to conclude that Justice Spiro was simply "expressing concern that the appointment might subject the faculty to adverse criticism and publicity," thus exonerating him from sanction.[47] In another high-profile dehiring, "controversy" related to "anti-Israel bias" would play a key factor in Harvard Kennedy School's 2023 retraction of a fellowship offer to former Human Rights Watch director Kenneth Roth.[48]

Similarly, in the Chinese context, "sensitive" is the key floating signifier that has been used to shut down critical inquiry while marking publications and educators as legitimate targets of censorship. In particular, "sensitivity" has been used to sanction researchers who deviate from the Party line

43 Thomas A. Cromwell, "Independent Review of the Search Process for the Directorship of the International Human Rights Program at the University of Toronto, Faculty of Law," March 15, 2021, 6, https://ultravires.ca/wp/wp-content/uploads/2021/05/Report-of-the-Hon-Thomas-A-Cromwell-CC-%E2%80%93-March-15-2021.pdf.

44 Cromwell, "Independent Review," 8.

45 Cromwell, "Independent Review," 48.

46 Cromwell, "Independent Review," 48.

47 Canadian Judicial Council, "Report of the Review Panel Constituted by the Canadian Judicial Council Regarding the Honourable D. E. Spiro," April 13, 2021, para. 44, https://cjc-ccm.ca/sites/default/files/documents/2021/Report%20of%20the%20Review%20Panel%20-%20Spiro.pdf.

48 Sabrina Conza, "FIRE Criticizes Harvard for Rescinding Human Rights Champion Ken Roth's Fellowship," *FIRE*, January 6, 2023, www.thefire.org/news/fire-criticizes-harvard-rescinding-human-rights-champion-ken-roths-fellowship.

in areas where the impacts of Chinese colonialism and imperialism are most stark: namely Tibet, Xinjiang, and Taiwan. In 2012, the Xi administration expanded its restrictions on areas of university research and teaching under the framework of the so-called Seven No's: "civil society, civil rights, universal values, legal independence, press freedom, the bourgeois class with money and power, and the historical wrongs of the Party."[49]

At the extreme end of the spectrum, researchers of Xinjiang who delve into areas deemed too "politically sensitive" have been detained or disappeared. For instance, Exmet Momin Tarimi, a PhD candidate in history at Nanjing University, has been subject to ongoing extrajudicial detention since December 2017. Tarimi was a director and senior editor at the historical cultures department of the Xinjiang People's Press, authoring books on Uyghur historiography, including a translation of the history of East Turkestan's rise and fall that was immediately banned by authorities. Just prior to his detention, he was completing a doctoral dissertation on Yaqup Beg, a prominent historical figure who established the independent state of Yesttishar (Kashgaria) between 1865 and 1877. His dissertation question had been opposed by his supervisor at Nanjing University for being too politically sensitive in examining questions of self-determination in the region.[50]

The overwhelming level of political surveillance, policing, and carceral coercion around Xinjiang research creates conditions in China where the histories and analyses of colonial subjugation in the region are *preemptively terminated* by the state. Even within global Chinese studies, ideas around political sensitivity are increasingly being deployed to censor areas that touch on these topics. In 2017–18, it was discovered that, at the request of Chinese authorities, Cambridge University Press had blocked 315 articles on "sensitive topics" from *China Quarterly*'s Chinese website, Springer had removed more than 1,000 articles, and Taylor and Francis had removed more than eighty journals.[51] In 2019, scholar Timothy Grose revealed that his review of Tom Cliff's book *Oil and Water*—an ethnography about Han settler experiences in the XUAR—was rejected by Brill's *China and Asia: A Journal*

49 Zhidong Hao, "Commercialization and Corporatization vs. Professorial Roles and Academic Freedom in the USA and Greater China," in *Academic Freedom Under Siege: Higher Education in East Asia, the U.S. and Australia*, ed. Zhidong Hao and Peter Zabielskis (Cham: Springer, 2020), 15.

50 Qazanchi, "A New Form of Eliticide," 11–12.

51 Nicholas Loubere, "The New Censorship, the New Academic Freedom: Commercial Publishers and the Chinese Market," *Journal of the European Association for Chinese Studies* 1 (2020): 240–241.

in Historical Studies in part because he refused to remove a contextualizing opening paragraph on "concentration reeducation centres" in the region.[52] The editor-in-chief responded that this was justified on the basis that such a framing was "a political message," again suggesting that censorship could be engaged anywhere there was political sensitivity, without requiring further inquiry.[53] Like in other contexts, nationalism's prerogative in delineating what is divisive, controversial, or sensitive (and just as importantly, what is not), is a rhetorical technology of power that is easily weaponized to curtail academic freedom.

Reframing Conversations around Structural Injustice and Disparity as "Racism" against Dominant Groups within Ethnonationalist Projects

Another key element of antiracist academic unfreedom is the move to "reverse" racism—that is, to rebrand opposition to the racial oppression of materially subordinated groups in society as racism against dominant groups. This discursive move goes one step further when it substitutes an ethnonationalist state (e.g., Israel, China) in lieu of the dominant group (e.g., Jewish people, Han Chinese). The functional effect of this is to insulate these states from critique, scrutiny, and organized resistance by falsely conflating it with racial subordination against one's own ethnoracial group. Philosopher Jason Stanley describes this as groups in power using the "mask of nationalism of the oppressed" to "obscure the contradiction between a struggle for equal respect and a struggle for dominance."[54] The understanding of race as socially, historically, and geographically contingent—what Keith Aoki and Robert S Chang theorize as "racial microclimes"[55]—is thus entirely absent from this power-evasive analysis of race.

---

52 Timothy Grose, "How an Academic Journal Censored My Review on Xinjiang," *Modern Chinese Literature and Culture*, May 13, 2019, https://u.osu.edu/mclc/2019/05/16/how-a-journal-censored-by-review-on-xinjiang/.

53 Hao Xiaorong, "My Response to Timothy Grose's 'How an Academic Journal Censored My Review on Xinjiang,'" *Modern Chinese Literature and Culture*, May 16, 2019, https://u.osu.edu/mclc/2019/05/16/how-a-journal-censored-my-review-on-xinjiang-1/.

54 Jason Stanley, *How Fascism Works: The Politics of Us and Them* (New York: Random House, 2018), 106.

55 Robert S. Chang, "Keith Aoki's Theory of Racial Microclimes," *UC Davis Law Review* 45 (2012): 1913.

The best-known example of this reframing is likely the weaponization of anti-Semitism to silence and delegitimize critiques of Israeli policies. Under this line of argumentation, "Israel is the state of all Jews and to vilify the state or disparage its founding ideology, Zionism, is to vilify or disparage all Jews."[56] This deliberate and crucial conflation between anti-Semitism and anti-Zionism undergirds much of the attacks on academic freedom for scholars who teach critically on the Israel-Palestine conflict, particularly from human rights, antiracist, and decolonial lenses. Such attacks have escalated since 2016, when the International Holocaust Remembrance Alliance (IHRA) adopted its working definition of anti-Semitism that appended eleven illustrative examples, seven of which focus on the state of Israel, rather than on Jews as a group.[57] In perhaps the highest-profile case since, Kenneth Roth, long-term executive director of Human Rights Watch, had a fellowship revoked by the dean of the Kennedy School of Government for alleged "anti-Israel bias."[58] As part of substantiating this argument, Canary Mission (a website that hosts a blacklist of individuals in order to intimidate students, faculty members, and community activists engaged in Palestine solidarity work) refers heavily to Roth's opposition to the IHRA definition of anti-Semitism on the grounds that it "tries to equate antisemitism with much criticism of Israel and its abusive treatment of Palestinians."[59]

As detailed by Independent Jewish Voices Canada, the adoption of the IHRA definition by universities threatens academic freedom through censorship of "courses and curricular materials which frame the Israel/Palestine conflict in terms of settler colonialism or other types of anticolonial and anti-racist theory."[60] Faculty who have engaged in teaching and research in these areas reported:

---

56 Sheryl Nestel and Rowan Gaudet, "Unveiling the Chilly Climate: The Suppression of Speech on Palestine in Canada," *Independent Jewish Voices Canada*, October, 2022, 8, www.ijvcanada.org/wp-content/uploads/2022/10/Unveiling-the-Chilly-Climate_Final-compressed.pdf.

57 Independent Jewish Voice Canada, "How Not to Fight Antisemitism: A Critique of the International Holocaust Remembrance Alliance Working Definition of Antisemitism (IHRA-WDA)," October 2020, 14, https://static1.squarespace.com/static/5f52a48dcce98340e25350e2/t/5fff2d4e058b964b22eb8f33/1610558799440/IHRA+Report+v1.1+-+20201025.pdf.

58 Joseph Leone, "The Harvard Kennedy School's Anti-Palestinian Bias," *Jewish Currents*, January 26, 2023, https://jewishcurrents.org/the-harvard-kennedy-schools-anti-palestinian-bias.

59 "Kenneth Roth," *Canary Mission*, June 15, 2023, https://canarymission.org/individual/Kenneth_Roth.

60 Nestel and Gaudet, "Unveiling the Chilly Climate," 16.

> Restrictions on academic freedom, self-censoring of expression on Palestinian human rights, discriminatory treatment by academic publishing platforms, harassment by pro-Israel advocacy groups and media outlets, attacks from colleagues, political interference by university administration, classroom surveillance by pro-Israel student groups, and anti-Palestinian and anti-Arab racism.[61]

Indeed, the US anti-CRT campaign and the campaign to censor those in higher education critical of the Israeli settler colonial project have engaged in similar strategies when it comes to "reversing racism." In December 2019, some ten months before the anti-CRT EO 13950, then President Trump issued EO 13899, the Executive Order on Combating Anti-Semitism, which directly adopted the IHRA definition and its list of "Contemporary Examples of Anti-Semitism" as legal grounds for Title VI civil rights complaints.[62] Unlike EO 13950 however, EO 13899 was *not* repealed once the Biden administration came to power, despite its creation of significant new legal risks and chilling effects for antiracist scholars and Palestinian rights activists.[63]

Some US anti-CRT campaigners have also made use of reverse racism arguments when claiming that critical race theory and its interrogations of the history and contemporary manifestations of racial injustice are "antiwhite"—a view advanced by Christopher Rufo[64] as well as former House speaker Newt Gingrich.[65] However, this messaging has not had the same mass resonance that reframing support for Palestinian rights as anti-Semitism has had. Rather, anti-CRT censorship campaigners have legally codified reverse racism by centering the potential hurt feelings of white students to shut down antiracist teaching and research, a mainly affective stratagem. For instance, EO 13950 and other copycat measures prohibit concepts where individuals may feel "discomfort, guilt, anguish or any other form of

61 Nestel and Gaudet, "Unveiling the Chilly Climate," 2.

62 "Executive Order on Combating Anti-Semitism, Executive Order 13899," *The White House*, December 11, 2019, s 2(a)(ii), https://trumpwhitehouse.archives.gov/presidential-actions/executive-order-combating-anti-semitism/.

63 Gabriella Fried, "On the Outer Reaches of the Marketplace of Ideas: The Weaponization of Title VI against Palestinian College Activists," *Journal of Law and Policy* 30 (2021): 157.

64 Christopher Rufo (@realchrisrufo), May 26, 2021, https://twitter.com/realchrisrufo/status/1397620203387703299?s=20&t=qcjqlfrsLcSj7ktJ-k_exw.

65 Darragh Roche, "Newt Gingrich Says Liberals Push 'Cult of Anti-White Racism,'" *Newsweek*, July 12, 2022, www.newsweek.com/newt-gingrich-says-liberals-push-cult-anti-white-racism-1723682.

psychological distress on account of his or her race or sex" or feel that they "bear responsibility for actions committed in the past by other members of the same race or sex."[66] Yet as Christie Nold and Ursula Wolfe-Rocca write, the real concern of anti-CRT campaigners "is not that children will feel bad when learning about the fight for racial justice, but that children will feel good. Young white people with the capacity to act in solidarity with movements for justice are dangerous to white supremacy and its guardians."[67]

Like the deliberate conflation of anti-Semitism with criticism of Israel to silence work on Palestinian rights, Chinese ethnonationalists have been hard at work reframing support for Uyghur and other Turkic Muslims' rights in the context of accelerating colonial repression as either Sinophobic or manifestations of anti-Chinese racism. China's reverse racism narrative has found renewed resonance in the project to avenge the "century of humiliation" that undergirds Xi Jinping's "China Dream"[68] as well as rising anti-Asian racism globally in the wake of the COVID-19 pandemic that began in the city of Wuhan.

Perhaps uniquely in the case of China, the bait-and-switch move of replacing sympathy for racially subordinated communities with sympathy for ethnonationalist projects that themselves perpetrate systemic racial oppression has been significantly bolstered by Western "anti-imperialist"[69] media outlets that follow campist lines. In a high-profile example, in May 2021, state media outlet Xinhua published an interview with former UN mandate holder Alfred-Maurice de Zayas where the latter claims that legal arguments of genocide in the XUAR constitute "fake news," "vulgar Sinophobia," and a "geopolitical weapon" against China.[70] Xinhua's interview of de Zayas prominently features references to reporting by *The Grayzone*, an influen-

66 "Executive Order 13950," ss 2(a)(7)–(8).

67 Ursula Wolfe-Rocca and Christie Nold, "Why the Narrative That Critical Race Theory 'Makes White Kids Feel Guilty' Is a Lie," *Hechinger Report*, August 2, 2022, https://hechingerreport.org/opinion-why-the-narrative-that-critical-race-theory-makes-white-kids-feel-guilty-is-a-lie/.

68 Mark Metcalf, "The National Humiliation Narrative: Dealing with the Present by Fixating on the Past," *Education about Asia* 25 (2020): 43.

69 I put anti-imperialist in quotation marks due to the frequent failures of many of these outlets in expressing consistent positions against imperialism, instead myopically framing the West as the primary imperialist power in all situations. See Rohini Hensman, *Indefensible: Democracy, Counter-Revolution, and the Rhetoric of Anti-Imperialism* (Chicago: Haymarket Books, 2018), 11–15.

70 Chen Junxia and Xu Chi, "Genocide Accusations against China Sinophobic Propaganda, Says Former UN Expert," *Xinhua*, May 13, 2021, www.xinhuanet.com/english/2021-05/13/c_139943866.htm.

tial news website well known for misleading reporting, sympathetic coverage of authoritarian regimes, and conspiracy theories regarding Venezuela, Syria, Ukraine, and Xinjiang.[71] Specifically, *The Grayzone* published articles that characterize US policies to address unfree labor within camp-to-factory pipelines[72] in the XUAR as fundamentally "anti-China" and that actually hurt communities targeted by Chinese counterinsurgency since they "cost Uyghur workers their jobs."[73]

Conclusions

As can be gleaned from all three of these transnational examples, dominant groups and national governments have no problem weaponizing race (including curtailing and even directly attacking academic freedom) when it is done in service of protecting structures of racial hierarchy in their specific racial microclimes. The blueprint for nationalist attacks on antiracist scholarship relies on three elements: stirring up moral panic by presenting antiracist education as ideological extremism or the gateway to terrorism, using floating signifiers to preempt truthful discussion and analysis, and co-opting the moral weight of antiracism by framing education about structural racial injustice as "racism" against dominant groups.

This strategy has been so successful that it has since been imitated to varying degrees of success by the far-right government of Narendra Modi in India, as well as the Putin administration after Russia's full-scale military invasion of Ukraine in the forms of "Hinduphobia"[74] and "Russophobia,"[75] respectively. These developments unsettle the dichotomy that liberal scholar-

71 Caitlin Thompson, "Enter the Grayzone: Fringe Leftists Deny the Scale of China's Uyghur Oppression," *Coda*, July 30, 2020, www.codastory.com/disinformation/grayzone-xinjiang-denialism/.

72 Alison Killing and Megha Rajagopalan, "We Found the Factories Inside China's Mass Internment Camps," *Buzzfeed News*, December 28, 2020, www.buzzfeednews.com/article/alison_killing/xinjiang-camps-china-factories-forced-labor.

73 Max Blumenthal, "Xinjiang Shakedown: US Anti-China Lobby Cashed in on 'Forced Labor' Campaign That Cost Uyghur Workers Their Jobs," *The Grayzone*, April 30, 2021, https://thegrayzone.com/2021/04/30/xinjiang-forced-labor-china-uyghur/.

74 Max Daly, Shahar Habib Ghazi, and Phallavi Pundir, "How Far-Right Hindu Supremacy Went Global," *Vice*, October 26, 2022, www.vice.com/en/article/n7z947/how-far-right-hindu-supremacy-went-global.

75 "'Nothing but Racism': Putin Hits Out at Russophobia Spreading around the World," *TASS*, September 30, 2022, https://tass.com/politics/1516167.

ship in academic freedom frequently draws between liberal democratic and authoritarian settings.

As such, defenders of academic freedom are left with a self-fulfilling prophecy: censorship of antiracist education only works in the context of an *impoverished understanding* of racism. This is why ethnonationalists deliberately seek to target critical race theory and decolonial and postcolonial studies for delegitimization and censorship. Liberal internationalist solidarities around academic freedom and freedom of expression fail to fully capture and understand this, particularly in its attraction to power-neutral analyses that allow for false conflation between ideologies of racial subordination on one hand, and race-conscious equality on the other. Any meaningful politics of academic freedom thus requires an analysis that is attendant to questions of power, particularly when it comes to race and colonialism.

Chapter 8

Coloniality and Diversity of Academic Freedom

The African Context

Kwadwo Appiagyei-Atua

Introduction

The academic community is entitled to enjoy and exercise fundamental features of academic freedom, including institutional autonomy, self-governance, individual freedom of academics and students, and tenure for academics. The principal UN instrument on academic freedom—the ILO/UNESCO Recommendation Concerning the Status of Higher Education Teaching Personnel, 1997 (UNESCO Recommendation)—directly recognizes two types of academic freedom. First, the individual freedom of academics, which are broken down into five sets of freedoms:

i. freedom of teaching and discussion,
ii. freedom in carrying out research and disseminating and publishing the results thereof,
iii. freedom to express freely their opinion about the institution or system in which they work,

iv. freedom from institutional censorship, and
v. freedom to participate in professional or representative academic bodies.[1]

The UNESCO Recommendation recognizes "the institutional form of academic freedom," defined as

> that degree of self-governance necessary for effective decision-making by institutions of higher education regarding their academic work, standards, management and related activities consistent with systems of public accountability, especially in respect of funding provided by the state, and respect for academic freedom and human rights.[2]

The other pillars of academic freedom are also recognized in the document. Tenure, for example, is considered "one of the major procedural safeguards of academic freedom and against arbitrary decisions." Students' academic freedom is also recognized in the UNESCO Recommendation, though indirectly.[3] How these pillars are respected, protected, and fulfilled, however, is determined by the historical, sociocultural, and developmental factors of a particular country/region. These factors influence the environment for research, teaching, learning, dissemination, and application of research output and the ability to use knowledge to speak truth to power and to challenge orthodoxy.

In the African context, the present chapter contends that academic freedom has acquired a peculiar character of its own, as a result of these relative factors, which need to be taken into account in any assessment or review of the academic freedom architecture on the continent. It should also feature Africa's unique contribution to shaping a more diverse global architecture of academic freedom, which is not the preserve of a particular region, religion, race, or culture.

To unravel these factors, the first section of the chapter focuses on the origins of the university in premodern Africa, its purpose, and its relationship with the right to science and academic freedom. The next section covers the

---

1 UNESCO Recommendation, Arts. 25–30.

2 UNESCO Recommendation, Art. 17.

3 Kwadwo Appiagyei-Atua, "Students' Academic Freedom in African Universities and Democratic Enhancement," *African Human Rights Law Journal* 19 (2019): 151.

suppression and destruction of Africa's premodern university education by Europe and the subsequent establishment of the colonial university. The next section focuses on the role of the Bretton Woods institutions in influencing academic freedom in African universities through the implementation of structural adjustment programs (SAPs) and the reaction of African academics to the SAP. The place of internationalization is also captured here. The chapter then examines events flowing from the fall of the Berlin Wall, which triggered the introduction of academic freedom in a number of African constitutions. The final section covers the conclusion and recommendations for a reconceptualization of academic freedom to capture these African features.

Origins, Purpose of the University, and the Place of Academic Freedom

The view has been held that academic freedom is linked to the origins of university education in Europe, starting from Bologna. Perkin, for example, argues that it is "only in Europe from the 12th century onwards, did an autonomous, permanent, corporate institution of higher learning emerge and survive, in varying forms, down to the present day."[4] It is also stated that academic freedom is "embedded in the liberal script, as a norm intrinsic to the pursuit of enlightenment, individual self-determination, and scientific and social progress."[5]

These claims, however, have been questioned. Lulat, for example, argues that the origins of the modern university system (including think tanks and research libraries) can be traced to the Per-ankh (the House of Light) (circa 2000 BCE) and the Bibliotheca Alexandrina, circa 332 BCE[6] in Egypt. In addition, reference is made to Islamic higher education institutions—the madrasahs—which evolved into universities in North and West Africa, including the oldest existing and continually operating educational institution in the world, the al-Qarawiyyin University in Fez, Morocco (founded in 859 BCE). Another is

4 Harold Perkin, "History of Universities," in *International Handbook of Higher Education*, ed. James J. F. Forest and Philip G. Altbach (Cham: Springer, 2018), 159.

5 Tanja A. Börzel et al., "Science Friction: Patterns, Causes and Effects of Academic Freedom Contestations," www.scripts-berlin.eu/research/research-projects/General-Research-Projects/Science-Friction_-Patterns_-Causes-and-Effects-of-Academic-Freedom-Contestations/index.html.

6 Kwadwo Appiagyei-Atua, Klaus Beiter, and Terence Karran, "The Composite Theory: An African Contribution to the Academic Freedom Discourse," *South African Journal on Human Rights* 31 (2015): 320.

the University of Sankorey, Timbuktu, in the Mali Empire that contained the largest collection of books in Africa since the Bibliotheca Alexandrina.[7]

These institutions were established for the pursuit of truth, that is to advance human knowledge[8] through critical thinking and systematic inquiry to respond to societal needs.[9] This explains the development of bodies of knowledge in disciplines such as mathematics, philosophy, metallurgy, medicine, agriculture, astrology, and astronomy, that helped to sustain and enable precolonial African societies to thrive and develop their rich civilizations.[10] The existence of academic freedom in these institutions, therefore, could not be denied due to its inextricable link to the pursuit of truth.[11] Felix DuBois, for example, describes how inventions made by the University of Timbuktu were utilized by the kings of the time to address societal problems. He also identified academic mobility and intellectual exchanges among scholars in the universities then existed in Timbuktu, Fez, Tunis, and Cairo.[12]

Many of Africa's traditional centers of higher learning, its ancient academic traditions, and knowledge base, however, were subjected to epistemic violence, coinciding with the emergence of the Renaissance that sought to establish the superiority of Greece and Roman civilization over others.[13] This period also witnessed the "discovery" of the "New World" by Christopher Columbus, which in turn led to the establishment of the transatlantic slave trade, mercantilism, and colonialism.[14] As a result, thriving

---

7 Zulkifli Khair, "The World-Class University of Sankore, Timbuktu," *Muslim Heritage*, June 5, 2003, www.muslimheritage.com/topics/default.cfm?ArticleID=371.

8 Olufemi Taiwo, "On 'Post-Colonial Discourse': An Introduction," *Callaloo* 16 (1993): 743; Olufemi Taiwo, "Colonialism and Its Aftermath: The Crisis of Knowledge Production," *Callaloo* 16 (1993): 891.

9 Emmanuel Efem Etta and Francis Ibe Mogu, "The Relevance of Proverbs in African Epistemology," *LWATI: A Journal of Contemporary Research* 9 (2012): 186.

10 "Technological Developments in Pre-colonial Africa," *Confucian Weekly*, February 17, 2020, https://confucianweeklybulletin.wordpress.com/2020/02/17/technological-developments-in-pre-colonial-africa/; Kabiru Kinyanjui, "Culture, Technology and Sustainable Development in Africa," *Asian Perspective* 17 (1993): 269.

11 Y. G. M. Lulat, *A History of African Higher Education from Antiquity to the Present: A Critical Synthesis* (London: Bloomsbury Academic, 2005), 42; Félix Dubois, *Timbuctoo the Mysterious* (New York: Longmans, Green, 1896).

12 Dubois, *Timbuctoo the Mysterious.*

13 Dan-el Padilla Peralta, "Why 'Why Classics'?" *Stanford Department of Classics*, https://classics.stanford.edu/dan-el-padilla-peralta-why-why-classics; Deborah Yaffe, "The Color of Classics," *Princeton Alumni Weekly*, October 2021, https://paw.princeton.edu/article/color-classics.

14 Bernard S. Cohen, *Colonialism and Its Forms of Knowledge: The British in India* (Princeton: Princeton University Press, 1996); Lewis Pyenson, *Civilizing Mission: Exact Sciences and French Overseas Expansion 1830–1940* (Baltimore: The Johns Hopkins University Press, 1993); David Olusoga, "The Roots of

civilizations that had hitherto established diplomatic relations and shared knowledge with Europe suddenly became societies without history, legal identity, and civilization.[15] In place of the African university, mainly missionary schools were set up in pursuit of the Christianizing and civilizing mission, which, wittingly or unwittingly, came to form an important part of the colonial enterprise and contributed to mind colonialism.[16]

The Colonial University

Thus, at the time of independence, only eighteen universities were to be found in Africa. These could be grouped into four categories. One was linked to missionary activities, exemplified in the Fourah Bay College founded in 1827 in Sierra Leone. Second, there were those set up in settler colonies to educate citizens of the colonial powers that formed part of the colonial establishment.[17] Third, those universities were established in Liberia, after the declaration of its independence from the American Colonization Society in 1847.[18] The fourth type of university was set up when decolonization became imminent, such as the University College of the Gold Coast (now the University of Ghana) and the University College of Ibadan, Nigeria. The motive for their establishment

European Racism Lie in the Slave Trade, Colonialism—and Edward Long," *The Guardian*, September 8, 2015, www.theguardian.com/commentisfree/2015/sep/08/european-racism-africa-slavery.

15 Walter Rodney, *How Europe Underdeveloped Africa* (London: Bogle-L'Ouverture Publications, 1972); Damtew Teferra and Philip G. Altbach, "African Higher Education: Challenges for the 21st Century," *Higher Education* 47 (2004): 21; Sintayehu Kassaye Alemu, "Meaning, Idea and History of University/Higher Education: Brief Literature Review," *Forum for International Research in Education* 4 (2018): 218.

16 Examples include the Fourah Bay College in Sierra Leone founded in 1827 and recognized as one of the oldest colleges of higher education in Africa, and Liberia College, founded in 1863. However, it is important to note that these countries were created by freed slaves who had returned from America and were not former colonies.

17 The universities established in South Africa (which later evolved into the apartheid system): the University of Cape Town (1829), Stellenbosch University, South Africa (1903), the University of Pretoria (1909). The exception is the University of Fort Hare, which was established for Blacks in South Africa and other parts of the continent. Mandela, Tutu, Tambo, and other African nationalist leaders were trained there. Similarly, in Algeria, the University of Algiers, Algeria (set up in 1909), largely opened its doors to the French and other Europeans who, by the early twentieth century, formed a majority of Algiers' population.

18 The University of Liberia was born in 1862, and the Cuttington University in 1889 as Cuttington College by the Episcopal Church of the United States (ECUSA), which were formed to also cater to the needs of the mainly Americo-Liberian freed slaves.

was principally to train a corps of Europeanized elite to maintain, after colonialism, the politico-economic framework put in place by the colonialists.[19]

These colonial universities reproduced the patterns characteristic of the metropolitan universities, beginning as "university colleges" affiliated with the universities in London, Paris, and Louvain, among others. The suzerain nature of the relationship between the colonial and metropolitan universities denied the former any form of institutional autonomy. These modern "Westernized" universities played a central role in the invention and universalization of the "colonizer's model of the world" in Africa.[20]

Under these arrangements, university education in the colonies was linked to specific colonial political projects and resulted in constraining the free-thinking environment needed for the pursuit of truth.[21] According to Assalat, this led to the creation of the "captive mind"—"one that is imitative and uncreative and whose thinking is based on Western categories and modes of thought."[22] Paulin Hountondji also talks about the "external overdetermination of African intellectual life" that rendered regional intellectual and theoretical development redundant"[23] because truth was alleged to have been discovered already through the emergence of Europe's superior knowledge. Consequently, after denigrating African scientific knowledge, no significant effort was made to give a place of prominence to science in the university curriculum of the colonial university.[24]

Academic Freedom in the Independent African University

Africa's independence constitutions negotiated with the departing colonial authorities were structured on the principles of limited government, individ-

19 Kwadwo Appiagyei-Atua, Klaus Beiter, and Terence Karran, "The Capture of Institutional Autonomy by the Political Elite and Its Impact on Academic Freedom in African Universities," *Higher Education Review* 47 (2015): 48.

20 Sabelo J. Ndlovu-Gatsheni, *Epistemic Freedom in Africa: Deprovincialization and Decolonization* (London: Routledge, 2018).

21 Asquith Commission on Higher Education in the Colonies, 1945–8.

22 Syed Hussein Alatas, "Intellectual Imperialism: Definition, Traits, and Problems," *Southeast Asian Journal of Social Science* 28 (2000): 24.

23 Amina Mama, "Towards Academic Freedom for Africa in the 21st Century," *Journal of Higher Education in Africa/Revue de l'enseignement supérieur en Afrique* 4 (2006): 8.

24 Rohan Deb Roy, "Science Still Bears the Fingerprints of Colonialism," *Smithsonian Magazine*, April 9, 2018, www.smithsonianmag.com/science-nature/science-bears-fingerprints-colonialism-180968709/.

ual rights, and multiparty elections.[25] Academic freedom was not specifically enshrined in any, except in the case of Somalia's constitution.[26] Despite this absence, Africa's political leadership embraced and accepted academic freedom within the university space[27] while not being oblivious to the fact that the university remained colonized in terms of staff and curricula.[28]

A few years into independence in many African States, however, systemic efforts were made to undermine and reject the liberal democratic independence constitutions on the basis that they were impediments to the realization of "rapid development."[29] In this equation, human rights (and by extension, academic freedom) were identified as stumbling blocks to development that needed to be side-lined.[30] As a result, the African universities were reset or designed as "developmental universities."[31] This supposed new identity for the university was meant to help the new nations to use the universities as one of the tools to build the State's capacity to develop and manage their resources, alleviate the poverty of the majority of their people, and close the gap between them and the developed world.[32] This goal, like the colonial motive for the university, also represented a deviation from the pursuit of truth toward the subservience of higher education to State policy or market objectives.[33]

The pursuit of this objective involved the suppression of academics' self-determination in deciding what to research, what to teach, how to teach, and

25 Issa Shivji, "Three Generations of Constitutions in Africa: An Overview and Assessment in Social and Economic Context," paper presented at the Warsaw Conference on Constitutionalism, May 17, 2021.

26 It was not until the mid-1970s before independence came to the former Portuguese colonists, including Cape Verde (1975), Sao Tome and Principe (1975), Mozambique (1975), and Angola. Their independence constitutions embraced the freedom of science.

27 Appiagyei-Atua, Beiter, and Karran, "The Capture of Institutional Autonomy."

28 Appiagyei-Atua, Beiter, and Karran, "The Capture of Institutional Autonomy," 58.

29 John Mukum Mbaku, "Preparing Africa for the Twenty-First Century: Lessons from Constitutional Economics," *Constitutional Political Economy* 11 (1995): 139.

30 Rhoda Howard, "The Full-Belly Thesis: Should Economic Rights Take Priority over Civil and Political Rights? Evidence from Sub-Saharan Africa," *Human Rights Quarterly* 5 (1983): 467.

31 Eric Fredua-Kwarteng, "Africa: The Case for Developmental Universities," in *Understanding Global Higher Education: Insights from Key Global Publications*, ed. Georgiana Mihut, Philip G. Altbach, and Hans de Wit (Rotterdam: SensePublishers, 2017), 193.

32 Fredua-Kwarteng, "Africa: The Case for Developmental Universities."

33 Kirsten Roberts Lyer, Ilyas Saliba, and Janika Spannagel, "University Autonomy and Academic Freedom," in *University Autonomy Decline: Causes, Responses, and Implications for Academic Freedom*, ed. Kirsten Roberts Lyer, Ilyas Saliba, and Janika Spannagel (London: Taylor and Francis, 2023), 14–15.

who to be admitted to the university,[34] as well as the undermining of their involvement in self-governance and their ability to criticize the functioning of the university, these being critical ingredients of academic's right to academic freedom.[35] This posture led to the incorporation of the university into the organic structure of the one-party or military regime and the institutionalization of party or governmental control over the day-to-day affairs of the university.[36] It also represents an aspect of coloniality that is embedded in the exercise of vestiges of colonial power, the reproduction and application of this colonial power, and the endorsement of epistemic violence by the African State on the African university.

The Bretton Woods Institutions and Academic Freedom in Africa

The attack on the institutional autonomy of the African university was not only waged by the State but by other international actors, including the Bretton Woods institutions—the World Bank (WB) and the International Monetary Fund (IMF).[37] In line with the developmental university concept, these institutions introduced another approach to university education that has contributed to shaping the character of the African university, and by extension, its academic freedom architecture. That is the neoliberal policies embodied in marketization, commodification of knowledge, managerialism, and quality control,[38] under the SAP introduced in response to the

34 T. B. Davie, "Davie Academic Freedom Lecture," *University of Cape Town*, May 22, 1991, https://digitalcommons.nyls.edu/cgi/viewcontent.cgi?article=1575&context=fac_other_pubs.

35 UNESCO Recommendation, Arts. 25–30.

36 Appiagyei-Atua, Beiter, and Karran, "The Capture of Institutional Autonomy." See also C. R. M. Dlamini, "University Autonomy and Academic Freedom in Africa: Ex Africa semper aliquid novi?" *Comparative and International Law Journal of Southern Africa* 35 (2022): 79.

37 Paul Tiyambe Zeleza, "Academic Freedom in the Neo-Liberal Order: Governments, Globalization, Governance, and Gender," *Journal of Higher Education in Africa* 1 (2003): 149; Damtew Teferra, "The World Bank's Perspective on African Higher Education," *World Bank's New Africa Report* 54 (2009): 15.

38 Emmanuel Mogaji, Felix Maringe, and Robert Ebo Hinson, "Understanding the Market in Higher Education in Africa," in *Understanding the Market in Higher Education in Africa*, ed. Emmanuel Mogaji, Felix Maringe, and Robert Ebo Hinson (London: Routledge, 2021), 2; David Brancaleone and Stephen O'Brien, "Educational Commodification and the (Economic) Sign Value of Learning Outcomes," *British Journal of Sociology of Education* 32 (2011): 501.

economic downturn that African States faced in the 1970s.[39] These developments turned the IMF/WB into the new dictators of education policies for Africa with African governments using these funding relationships to further limit the institutional autonomy of universities and the academic freedom of academics and students.[40]

The reaction of academics in African universities to the severe impact of the SAP implementation on the university triggered a new dimension in the academic freedom discourse in Africa, reflected in the Dar es Salaam Declaration on Academic Freedom and Social Responsibility of Academics (1990) and the Kampala Declaration on Intellectual Freedom and Social Responsibility (1990). These emphasized the social responsibility of the academic community to promote rights and democracy in the larger society and thereby improve gown–town relationships. For example, the Kampala Declaration provides that "the struggle for intellectual freedom is an integral part of the struggle of our people for human rights."[41] This way, academic freedom would not be limited to producing knowledge to meet societal needs but also be used extramurally to enable the broader society to enjoy similar rights, commensurate with its own needs.[42] Zeleza also makes the case that African academics rarely perceive themselves solely as intellectuals for intellectualism's sake but as "public intellectuals" whose social responsibility attached to academic freedom is not just negative but implying a duty to take the gown to town.[43]

However, it is not only the international financial institutions that have contributed to shaping the academic freedom architecture in Africa. Equally worthy of mention is the role of universities from the Global North through internationalization—some reflecting legacies of colonial expansion that creates a center–periphery dichotomy in many internationalization programs. At the center are the "producers" and "suppliers" of knowledge and funding and at the periphery, the consumers—of knowledge and funding, which

39 Howard Stein and Machiko Nissanke, "Structural Adjustment and the African Crisis: A Theoretical Appraisal," *Eastern Economic Journal* 25 (1999): 399.

40 Teferra, "The World Bank's Perspective on African Higher Education."

41 The Kampala Declaration on Intellectual Freedom and Social Responsibility, 1990, preamble.

42 Appiagyei-Atua, Beiter, and Karran, "The Composite Theory," 315–329.

43 Zeleza, "Academic Freedom in the Neo-liberal Order," 151.

is subject to the dictates of the foreign university.[44] Where the research is jointly conducted, the theme is often chosen by the center and credit for the findings of the research is appropriated by the center. In some situations as well, we see the practice of "helicopter" research where the periphery is only involved in data collection and provision of logistics but denied participation in the analysis, and all credit for the findings is given to the center.[45] These practices have created relationships that, in the words of Kassaye are "asymmetrical, unethical, and unequal."[46]

The Fall of the Berlin Wall and Repercussions on Academic Freedom in Africa

The fall of the Berlin Wall in 1989 resulted in the return to multiparty democracy, the rule of law, and human rights in Africa, which was reflected in the reemergence of liberal constitutions. Unlike the independence constitutions, however, many of these new constitutions now include references to academic freedom. According to the breakdown, thirteen (23.6 percent) of the fifty-five African countries give explicit recognition to "academic freedom" in their constitutions. Next, in sixteen of such constitutions (21 percent) there is no explicit mention of "academic freedom" but some other form of freedom of science.[47] During this epoch, there was also an increased de jure recognition of academic freedom in legislation, flowing from the acknowledgment of the same in the national constitutions, and practice, there was a direct retreat from the university by government officials.

This development also saw attempts by African universities to enhance student participation in university governance and or to incorporate civic and citizenship education for students in universities. There is a reference to high levels of understanding of democracy by students and students' enlight-

44 Andrew Goss, *The Floracrats: State-Sponsored Science and the Failure of the Enlightenment in Indonesia* (Madison: University of Wisconsin Press, 2011).

45 Budiman Minasny and Dian Fiantis, "'Helicopter Research': Who Benefits from International Studies in Indonesia?" *The Conversation*, August 29, 2018, https://theconversation.com/helicopter-research-who-benefits-from-international-studies-in-indonesia-102165.

46 Sintayehu Kassaye Alemu, "An Appraisal of the Internationalisation of Higher Education in Sub-Saharan Africa," *Center for Educational Policy Studies Journal* 4 (2014): 71.

47 Kwadwo Appiagyei-Atua, Klaus Beiter, and Terence Karran, "A Review of Academic Freedom in Africa through the Prism of the UNESCO's 1997 Recommendation," *Journal of Higher Education in Africa* 14 (2016): 85.

ened view of university governance.[48] However, reforms to give a democratic space for students are largely cosmetic. For example, there is student dissatisfaction with and distrust in student leadership, infiltration and co-optation of student leadership, among others by governments; as well as attempts by university management to suppress student efforts to challenge authority on campus and sometimes off it.[49]

What is poignantly missing in this analysis, moreover, is the asymmetrical relationship between academics and students that "embeds learners' oppression" and creates a disabling environment for students from acquiring "democratic habits" in the classroom.[50] This gap is reflected in the Kampala Declaration that gives attention to students' academic freedom in just one of its articles dealing with participation in the development of academic programs.[51] Therefore, one finds a contradiction in the prodemocracy agenda of the African intellectual engendered by the reaction to the SAPs and the fact that African scholars omitted to first deal with the democratic deficit in the classroom.

This gap in the student–lecturer relationship, therefore, has had a huge impact on attempts by African universities to decolonize the curriculum, which should involve students, as exemplified in the "Rhodes Must Fall" movement in South African universities.[52] The decolonization of the curriculum is a critical part of academic freedom advocacy in Africa.[53] Decolonization here is simply about exposing the ills of colonialism in an attempt to undo their longstanding effects.[54]

48 Thierry M. Luescher-Mamashela et al., eds., *The University in Africa and Democratic Citizenship: Hothouse or Training Ground?* (Wynberg: Centre for Higher Education Transformation, 2011).

49 Luescher-Mamashela et al., eds., *The University in Africa and Democratic Citizenship.*

50 Chikumbutso Herbert Manthalu, Anthony Mavuto Gunde, and Victor Chikaipa, "Towards Communication for Equality in Education: Reconfiguring Pedagogical Relations in Teacher Education," in *Education, Communication and Democracy in Africa*, ed. Chikumbutso Herbert Manthalu, Victor Chikaipa, and Anthony Mavuto Gunde (London: Routledge, 2022), 33; Markos Tezera Taye and Ahmed Alduais, "Exploring the Practice of Academic Freedom and Active Learning in Ethiopia's Higher Education: A Case Study," *Athens Journal of Education* 9 (2022): 655. See also Appiagyei-Atua, "Students' Academic Freedom in African Universities and Democratic Enhancement."

51 The Kampala Declaration on Intellectual Freedom and Social Responsibility, 1990, Art. 7.

52 Amanda Castro and Angela Tate, "Rhodes Fallen: Student Activism in Post-Apartheid South Africa," *History in the Making* 10 (2017): 195.

53 P. du Plessis, "Decolonisation of Education in South Africa: Challenges to Decolonise the University Curriculum," *South African Journal of Higher Education* 35 (2021): 54.

54 Erik J. Olsson, "Academic Freedom and the Decolonisation of Knowledge: Curriculum Transformation in South Africa from a UNESCO Perspective," *Studies in Higher Education* 48 (2023): 1.

The Return of Illiberal Democracy

The return to democracy after the fall of the Berlin Wall has suffered some major setbacks and resulted in the stagnation of democracy or the fallback into illiberal democracy in Africa.[55] This development has had its impact on the respect for academic freedom. Among others, de facto, though the State has retreated from the university space, it has been using university management, tertiary education commissions, and other bodies as proxies to do their bidding.[56]

Many African governments continue to deprecate the knowledge and expertise of local academics, especially those who are critical of them in preference for the work of captive intellectuals whose research work supports the policy objectives of such governments. This trend has led to self-censorship on many African university campuses.[57] Also, there have been instances of reported attacks in Africa, rising from 14 percent of the world total in 2017 to 26 percent in 2021, for example.

Conclusion and Recommendations

This chapter has sought to highlight how the perpetration and perpetuation of mind colonialism and the imposition of the "superior knowledge" of Europe on Africa through the Christianizing and civilizing missions and the colonial curriculum propagated through the church, liberal ideology and the colonial university has resulted in the coloniality of higher education in Africa.[58] Thus, in spite of the formal end of colonialism, colonial-

55 Rachel Sigman and Staffan I. Lindberg, "Neopatrimonialism and Democracy: An Empirical Investigation of Africa's Political Regimes," *V-Dem Working Paper Series* 56 (2017).

56 Hajer Kratou and Lissa Laakso, "The Impact of Academic Freedom on Democracy in Africa," *Journal of Development Studies* 58 (2022): 809.

57 Wachira Kigotho, "Academic Freedom Remains under Threat in Africa—Report," *University World News*, November 9, 2022, www.universityworldnews.com/post.php?story=20221109073147468; John Higgins, "Relevance, Academic Freedom and the Academic Profession," *University World News*, September 9, 2021, www.universityworldnews.com/post.php?story=20210908130047567. See also Kronstad Felde et al., *Democracy and the Discourse on Relevance within the Academic Profession at Makerere University* (Cape Town: African Minds, 2021).

58 André Keet, Sahar D. Sattarzadeh, and Anne Munene, "An Awkward, Uneasy (De)coloniality Higher Education and Knowledge Otherwise," *Education as Change* 21 (2017): 1; Hanne Kirstine Adriansen and Lene Møller Madsen, "Capacity-Building Projects in African Higher Education: Issues of Coloniality in International Academic Collaboration," *Learning and Teaching* 12 (2019): 1.

ity reflecting the persistence of colonialism beyond the dismantlement of its direct administrative structures remains in many lives of Africans, including in higher education. Part of this coloniality is embedded in the exercise of vestiges of colonial power, the reproduction and application of this colonial power, and the endorsement of epistemic violence by the African State on the African university.

Thus, coloniality of higher education largely accounts for the nature of and the State in which academic freedom finds itself in Africa. This has contributed to compromising the use of the concept to promote knowledge production in order to advance social progress and enable the academic community to challenge orthodoxy, speak truth to power, and be involved in the decolonization of the curriculum, among others. It is trite knowledge that research helps to build a knowledge economy and to put knowledge capital at the center of development should be a priority. Yet, Africa produces less than 1 percent of global research output, placing the continent at the lowest ebb of research capacity and output in the world.

In light of the above, the chapter argues that these historical, cultural, political, and other factors have colored and influenced the environment for research, teaching, learning, dissemination, and application of research output and the ability to use knowledge to speak truth to power and challenge orthodoxy. Consequently, these developments have also influenced the type character, and features of academic freedom in African universities and the kind of advocacy that can be applied to promote and protect academic freedom as well as expand the frontiers for the application of academic freedom advocacy in Africa.[59] Therefore, I conclude that a conceptual and practical framework for a global shared reference for academic freedom does not yet exist. Such a framework will only exist when there is a shift from the idea of academic freedom being a European idea or a liberal script.

59 du Plessis, "Decolonisation of Education in South Africa."

Chapter 9

Freedom for All

Academic Freedom in a Pluralistic Society

Tamara Thermitus[1]

As *Mad Men*'s Don Draper once said, "If you don't like what's being said, change the conversation." This is what Afrodescendant people have wanted since the abolition of slavery. But how does one "change the conversation" when the racial contract continues to perpetuate the dominance of some groups over others,[2] notably by invoking academic freedom to shield remnants of the past?

Social Context: Universities as White Spaces

The white space, or *White Space*,[3] is composed of all the elements of a society in its material and symbolic dimensions. It is a space in which racism is reproduced by the professional class—those who systematically privilege, in discursive and sometimes coercive ways, Eurodescendants over nonwhites.[4]

---

1 The author thanks Professor Frédéric Mégret (McGill University) and Me Mireille Fournier (Sciences Po) for their insightful comments, and Nicolas Kamran for the translation.

2 Charles W. Mills, *The Racial Contract* (Ithaca: Cornell University Press, 1997), 3.

3 Elijah Anderson, *Black in White Space* (Chicago: Chicago University Press, 2022), 14–15, 251–252.

4 Amanda Carlin, "The Courtroom as White Space: Racial Performance as Non-credibility," *UCLA Law Review* 63 (2016): 462.

Universities have been active participants in the theoretical development of racial hierarchy.[5] Some say that they are the institutions where "prejudices were legitimized through deliberately biased studies."[6] Power there was concentrated in the hands of men of European descent,[7] who developed the principles and norms applicable to their institutions. It would therefore be hard to claim that the values governing universities are neutral or objective. As white spaces, they tend instead to ignore the very effects of their whiteness, which then allows them to position their norms as exercises in neutrality and reason—all while reinforcing the establishment of a white space. Jurist Barbara Flagg has named this process "the transparency phenomenon."[8] The culture of whiteness and the privileges that flow from it remain, paradoxically, omnipresent but invisible.

Although universities now have programs for diversity, equity, inclusion, and even antiracism, substantive change is still long overdue and carries its share of institutional risk. One need look no further than the mistreatment of Harvard's former president for proof of this. Claudine Gay was the first Black woman to head this institution, and her appointment was hailed as a major step forward in terms of "diversity."[9] Yet her downfall was brutal and abrupt, something akin to a social death.[10] Gay was forced into resignation following mounting criticisms of her defense of academic freedom on campus, a result of pressure from government, faculty, and alumni.[11] In

5 Efram Sera-Shriar, "Race," in *Historicism and the Human Sciences in Victorian Britain*, ed. Mark Bevir (Cambridge: Cambridge University Press, 2017), 70.

6 Ijeoma Oluom, *Mediocre* (New York: Seal Press, 2020), 97.

7 Isabelle Hachey, "Ça va trop loin (ou pas)," *La Presse*, April 1, 2022, www.lapresse.ca/actualites/chroniques/2022-04-01/ca-va-trop-loin-ou-pas.php.

8 Flagg notes that "transparency often is the mechanism through which white decisionmakers who disavow white supremacy impose white norms on blacks [namely the requirement to assimilate Black people in the pursuit of pluralism]." Barbara J. Flagg, "'Was Blind, but Now I See': White Race Consciousness and the Requirement of Discriminatory Intent," *Michigan Law Review* 91 (1993): 450, cited in Carlin, "The Courtroom as White Space," 450, 453, 459.

9 Stephanie Saul and Vimal Patel, "Harvard Names a New President, an Insider and Historic First," *New York Times*, December 15, 2022, www.nytimes.com/2022/12/15/us/harvard-president-claudine-gay.html.

10 Zaire Z. Dinzey-Flores, "This Is How Black Women Leaders Do Not Survive," *The Griot*, January 4, 2024, https://thegrio.com/2024/01/04/this-is-how-black-women-leaders-do-not-survive/: "Even when you have all the accolades, all the knowledge, all the skills and attributes, it is hard to know the way forward. How is success achievable when the scrutiny is so vast and extensive? This is how we die, even if it may have felt for a moment that we triumphed."

11 Claudine Gay, "Claudine Gay: What Just Happened at Harvard Is Bigger Than Me," *New York Times*, January 3, 2024, www.nytimes.com/2024/01/03/opinion/claudine-gay-harvard-president.html.

many ways, she was collateral damage for the broad backlash against diversity, equity, and inclusion (DEI) in the United States.[12] Once more, we must remain cognizant of the fact that "[when] a Black woman enters a leadership position, she is under immediate suspicion that she is going to focus on particular issues (e.g., DEI) regardless of the position she is in. [They] are more often questioned about the projects or activities (they) want to pursue, and don't always get the institutional support that others take for granted."[13]

Claudine Gay's "story reflects a pattern of adversity suffered not merely by her, but also countless other Black women in leadership positions."[14] Black women who have dared to occupy positions of power in white spaces have seen their presence characterized as deserving of suspicion. In those spaces, their credibility is quickly called into question, while intersectional sexism and racism, such as misogynoir,[15] only accentuate the racist treatment they face. Gay had been moving in circles of power in white spaces for years, constantly required to adduce evidence of her belonging within them. More evidence was required of her this time. This is part of the context in which the analyses of academic freedom must take place.

The Racial Contract at the Heart of Social Interaction

Held to the outer limits of knowledge and "civilization," Black people have been historically excluded from universities. Defined by the otherness,[16] they have been greeted with suspicion. Statistics show that the presence of Black

12 Charles Blow, "The Persecution of Harvard's Claudine Gay," *New York Times*, January 2, 2024, www.nytimes.com/2024/01/03/opinion/harvard-claudine-gay-politics.html.

13 Nadia E. Brown, "The Challenges Facing Black Leaders," *Good Authority*, January 12, 2014, https://goodauthority.org/news/challenges-facing-black-leaders-claudinegay-harvard/.

14 Kimberly Bryant, "Claudine Gay and the Black Girlboss Paradox," *Boston Globe*, January 9, 2024, www.bostonglobe.com/2024/01/09/opinion/claudine-gay-black-girlboss-paradox/.

15 Janice Gassam Asare, "Academia Is Failing Black Women: Examining Misogynoir within the Academy," *Forbes*, January 16, 2024, www.forbes.com/sites/janicegassam/2024/01/16/academia-is-failing-black-women-a-brief-examination-of-misogynoir-within-the-academy/?sh=3cfbd9213adc; Janelle Benjamin, "Harvard's Dr. Claudine Gay: Misogynoir on Full Display," *All Things Equitable*, January 5, 2024, www.allthingsequitable.ca/blog/harvard-president-claudine-gay-misogynoir-full-display.

16 Toni Morrison, *The Origin of Others* (Cambridge: Harvard University Press, 2017); Martha R. Mahoney, "Whiteness and Women—In the Practice and Theory: A Reply to Catherine Mackinnon," *Yale Journal of Law and Feminism* 5 (1993): 220.

intellectuals in Canadian universities remains sparse,[17] with Ibram X. Kendi noting how their credentials[18] are often contested through campaigns aimed at destroying their credibility.[19]

The notion of white space is not dissimilar to what Fanon called the space of the colonizer as opposed to that of the colonized.[20] The space of colonizer allows them to be seen and heard, but also to claim agency—a privilege denied to the colonized:

> Power is first and foremost the power to see or to not see—and in the latter case, to expunge reality, to strike it out, to blot it out, to bracket it, to de-realize. ... Seeing is therefore a foundational issue for the constitution of a common life and the recognition of likeness or, on the contrary, the entrenchment of difference. We might also say that seeing is at the root of all human interaction. But there is also a relationship between being driven into invisibility and remaining silent.[21]

As described by Charles W. Mills, this absence of recognition and representation is explained by the racial contract to which universities are party as social actors. This contract presupposes a degree of *white ignorance*, which disguises an unjust social order that maintains certain nonwhite subjects as socially "incapable" due to their subordination, a context in which the social construction of race plays an important role. White people are thus ignorant of Black people and race relations. For Raúl Pérez, this epistemological ignorance "[marginalizes] the history and memory of white racial domination and its impact on the present by putting white racism out of sight and out of mind."[22]

---

17 Frances Henry et al., *The Equity Myth: Racialization and Indigeneity at Canadian Universities* (Vancouver: University of British Columbia Press, 2017), 5.

18 Adria R. Walker, "'Racist, Vicious': Academics Decry Right-Wing Attacks on Claudine Gay," *The Guardian*, January 3, 2024, www.theguardian.com/education/2024/jan/03/racist-rightwing-attacks-claudine-gay-former-harvard-president.

19 Ibram X. Kendi, "The Crisis of the Intellectuals," *The Atlantic*, March 22, 2023, www.theatlantic.com/ideas/archive/2023/03/intellectualism-crisis-american-racism/673480/.

20 Frantz Fanon, *Les damnés de la terre* (Paris: La découverte, 2002), 42–45.

21 Achille Mbembe, "De la scène coloniale chez Frantz Fanon," *Rue Descartes* 58 (2007): 37–55.

22 Raúl Pérez, *The Souls of White Jokes How Racist Humor Fuels White Supremacy* (Stanford: Stanford University Press, 2022), 37.

The racial contract is defined as "that set of formal or informal agreements or meta-agreements ... between the members of one subset of humans, henceforth designated by ... 'racial' ... criteria ... as 'white.'"[23] The subset of human beings categorized as "nonwhite" is assigned a different and inferior moral status. They are construed as "subhuman," subordinates within the white political system. As such, only white people have the capacity to define social rules. Since they are considered to be deficient citizens, amoral or immoral people, bereft of reason, Black people are excluded from the social contract and do not stand to benefit from the political and moral contracts.

The moral and legal rules governing the conduct of white people in their mutual social interactions do not apply to their relationships with nonwhites, or only slightly. This racial contract grants privilege to white people.[24] In those societies that are infused with the legacy of slavery, of which all forms of racism are a manifestation, those benefiting from the racial contract consider themselves as the only moral and rational citizens. As such, this contract enables white people to seize and retain power by controlling the bodies, resources, and land of racialized and colonized peoples.

In short, the social contract consolidates white privilege. Politically speaking, the social contract envisions "abstract men without race" who are white, while the racial contract reveals how the social construct of race is deployed by white people to preserve their power and maintain their privilege.

Universities in Light of the Racial Contract

By ignoring or denying the effects of the racial contract, universities perpetuate historical oppression. Notions of neutrality, objectivity, and reasonableness (*common sense*) cloak privilege, rendering discriminatory and racist acts invisible to the naked eye.[25] In particular, universities embrace "democratic racism," which may be defined as an ideology in which democratic values such as justice, equality, and fairness can coexist with racism.[26]

---

23 Mills, *The Racial Contract*, 11.

24 Peggy McIntosh, "White Privilege: Unpacking the Invisible Knapsack," *The National SEED Project*, 1989, https://nationalseedproject.org/key-seed-texts/white-privilege-unpacking-the-invisible-knapsack.

25 Frances Henry and Carol Tator, *The Colour of Democracy: Racism in Canadian Society*, 3rd ed. (Toronto: Nelson Thomson, 2006), 18.

26 Henry and Tator, *The Colour of Democracy*, 22.

Scheurich and Young have identified certain expressions of racism in the academic world, noting how "racism in the academy goes beyond the individual, institutional and societal manifestations to also incorporate the epistemological and ontological constructs of racism." The authors note further "that epistemological racism is drawn from [broad] civilizational structures, the level that encompasses the deepest assumptions about the nature of reality (ontology) the ways of knowing that reality (epistemology), and (axiology) presumption about the real, the true and the good."[27] One way in which racism is stratified is through the Western Canon of "Great Works," uncritically taught in universities as if they represented an objective form of knowledge about the human condition. Discussions surrounding academic freedom cannot take place in the abstract, that is, by erasing the power dynamics at play. This freedom has a political dimension. Arguments in the matter carry the risk of obscuring how academic freedom unwittingly protects privilege.

Academic Freedom

The Supreme Court of Canada's holding in *McKinney* presents the university as a largely autonomous community in law, for academic freedom[28] is

27 Scheurich and Young quoted by Frances Henry and Carol Tator, "Theorical Perspectives and Manifestations of Racism in the Academy," in *Racism in the Canadian University: Demanding Social Justice, Inclusion, and Equity*, ed. Frances Henry and Carol Tator (Toronto: University of Toronto Press, 2009), 35.

28 The debate rages on in the United States. In March 2023, Dean Jenny Martinez of Stanford Law School took a stand in an open letter, stating that a "commitment to diversity, equity, and inclusion can and should be implemented in ways that are consistent with its commitment to academic freedom and free speech," a position grounded in the Chicago Statement. See Jenny S. Martinez, "SLS Memorandum on Academic Freedom," *Stanford Law School*, March 22, 2023, https://law.stanford.edu/wp-content/uploads/2023/03/Next-Steps-on-Protests-and-Free-Speech.pdf. Cornell University president Martha E. Pollack (pictured in her office with a photo of Nelson Mandela in prison) took the same position a few days later, rejecting a student resolution calling for trigger warnings to be issued in class when necessary. President Pollack believed such warnings risked encroaching on professors' freedom to select and present course material as they saw fit; see Katherine Rosman, "Should College Come with Trigger Warnings? At Cornell, It's a 'Hard No,'" *New York Times*, April 12, 2023, www.nytimes.com/2023/04/12/nyregion/cornell-student-assembly-trigger-warnings.html. This position has a blind spot: the marketplace of ideas. See Francis Dupuis-Déri, *Panique à l'université: Rectitude politique, wokes et autres menaces imaginaires* (Montreal: Lux Editeur, 2022), 157–160. As noted by Herbert Marcuse, the market is hardly ever a level-playing field; see Herbert Marcuse, *Tolérance répressive, suivie de Quelques conséquences sociales de la technologie moderne* (Paris: Homnisphères, 2008), 80–81. Academic freedom could thus be considered through this angle. Without this insight, reinstituting those traditions developed before the

"essential to our continuance as a lively democracy."[29] With that said, there is no universally accepted definition of academic freedom.[30] Historically speaking, two sources have helped define the notion, namely the declarations from the American Association of University Professors (AAUP) and the University of Chicago. The AAUP defined academic freedom within its 1915 and 1940 Statements of Principle on Academic Freedom and Tenure, setting forth how professors should be free to conduct their research and teaching as experts seeking to advance human knowledge.[31] The 1902 Chicago Declaration established the principle of complete free speech on all subjects as fundamental, a "principle [that] can neither now nor at any future time be called in question."[32]

With this being said, universities in this same period were persistently denying admission to prospective students on the grounds of race, ethnicity, sexual orientate, gender, and religion. One has no choice but to acknowledge how universities protected the interests of the dominant group (white men), thus ensuring that certain ideas could not be placed into proper context or fully challenged—and thus maintaining the racial contract. This state of affairs doubtlessly influenced dominant interpretations of academic freedom, interpretations that remain influential in contemporary academia.

---

emergence of ideas like Critical Race Theory and the racial contract will only maintain a devastating status quo.

29 *McKinney v University of Guelph*, 1990 CanLII 60 (SCC), [1990] 3 SCR 229 at 286–287.

30 Michel Bastarache, "Rapport du Comité sur la liberté académique de l'Université d'Ottawa," 2021, https://fr.scribd.com/document/537258893/Rapport-du-Comite-sur-la-liberte-academique-de-l-Universite-d-Ottawa#.

31 AAUP, "1915 Declaration of Principles on Academic Freedom and Academic Tenure," in *American Association of University Professors: Policy Documents and Reports*, ed. H.-H. Tiede (Washington, DC: American Association of University Professors, 2015); AAUP, "1940 Statement of Principles on Academic Freedom and Tenure with 1970 Interpretive Comments," in *American Association of University Professors: Policy Documents and Reports*, ed. H.-H. Tiede (Washington, DC: American Association of University Professors, 2015).

32 Office of the Provost, University of Chicago, "Report of the Committee on Freedom of Expression," 2014, https://provost.uchicago.edu/sites/default/files/documents/reports/FOECommitteeReport.pdf. In 2014, it was further emphasized that "the freedom to debate and discuss the merits of competing ideas does not, of course, mean that individuals may say whatever they wish, wherever they wish. The University may restrict expression that violates the law, that falsely defames a specific individual, that constitutes a genuine threat or harassment, that unjustifiably invades substantial privacy or confidentiality interests, or that is otherwise directly incompatible with the functioning of the University ... But these are narrow exceptions to the general principle of freedom of expression, and it is vitally important that these exceptions never be used in a manner that is inconsistent with the University's commitment to a completely free and open discussion of ideas."

This is why it is important to conceptualize academic freedom in light of the international instruments that offer new parameters for interpreting and circumscribing it.

The UNESCO Recommendation Concerning the Status of Higher Education Teaching Personnel (1997)

The Supreme Court of Canada has recognized the use of international instruments in interpreting legislation,[33] but they are also useful for better understanding the scope of the protections afforded by "rights" or "freedoms" such as academic freedom. At the outset, I will turn my attention to the 1997 UNESCO Recommendation concerning the Status of Higher Education Teaching Personnel (Recommendation), which recognizes that "the right to education, teaching, and research can only be fully enjoyed in an atmosphere of academic freedom and autonomy for institutions of higher education and that the open communication of findings, hypotheses, and opinions lies at the very heart of higher education and provides the strongest guarantee of the accuracy and objectivity of scholarship and research."[34]

The Recommendation refers to other UNESCO instruments, including the Convention against Discrimination in Education (1960),[35] "which recognizes that UNESCO has a duty not only to proscribe any form of discrimination in education but also to promote equality of opportunity and treatment for all in education at all levels."[36] It applies to "all those persons in institutions or programs of higher education who are engaged to teach and/or to undertake scholarship and/or to undertake research and/or to provide educational services to students or the community at large."[37]

33 *Baker v Canada (Minister of Citizenship and Immigration)*, [1999] 2 SCR 817 at para. 71: "The principles of the Convention and other international instruments place special importance on protections for children and childhood, and on particular consideration of their interests, needs, and rights. They help show the values that are central in determining whether this decision was a reasonable exercise of the H & C power."

34 UNESCO, "Recommendation Concerning the Status of Higher Education Teaching Personnel," 1997, preamble.

35 Convention against Discrimination in Education, December 14, 1960, 429 UNTS 93 (entered into force May 22, 1962). Note that Canada is not a party to the convention.

36 UNESCO, "Recommendation Concerning the Status of Higher Education Teaching Personnel," preamble.

37 UNESCO, "Recommendation Concerning the Status of Higher Education Teaching Personnel," Art. 1(f).

The Recommendation states that institutions should uphold academic freedom as well as fundamental rights. In particular, students must be "treated fairly and justly, and without discrimination."[38] Institutions must ensure that professors "are not impeded in their work in the classroom or their research capacity by violence, intimidation or harassment."[39] Policies and procedures must therefore be established to "ensure the equitable treatment of women and minorities and to eliminate sexual and racial harassment."[40]

Inter-American Commission on Human Rights: The Inter-American Principles on Academic Freedom and University Autonomy (2021)

December 2021 saw the publication of the Inter-American Commission on Human Rights' Inter-American Principles on Academic Freedom and University Autonomy, which aims to facilitate the development of normative and legal frameworks for academic freedom in the Americas.[41]

Inspired by the Universal Declaration of Human Rights,[42] these principles emphasize the importance of nondiscrimination in interpreting academic freedom. Indeed, this freedom should promote, protect, and guarantee "equally and without discrimination on any ground, including political or other opinions, ethnic-racial origin, nationality, age, gender, sexual orientation, gender identity and expression, language, religion, cultural identity, social origin, socioeconomic status, educational level, situation of human mobility, disability, genetic characteristics, mental or physical health condition, including those of infectious or contagious disease, mental impairment, and any other."[43]

Under these principles, academic freedom "encompasses the freedom of workers, employees, and students in academic institutions to express themselves with respect to said institutions and the educational system."[44] This

38 UNESCO, "Recommendation Concerning the Status of Higher Education Teaching Personnel," Art. 22(f).

39 UNESCO, "Recommendation Concerning the Status of Higher Education Teaching Personnel," Art. 22(h).

40 UNESCO, "Recommendation Concerning the Status of Higher Education Teaching Personnel," Art. 22(g).

41 Inter-American Commission on Human Rights, "Inter-American Principles on Academic Freedom and University Autonomy," 182nd Session, December 6–7, 2021.

42 Universal Declaration of Human Rights, GA Res 217A (III), UNGAOR, 3rd Sess., Supp. No 13, UN Doc A/810 (1948) 71.

43 Inter-American Principles on Academic Freedom and University Autonomy, principle III.

44 Inter-American Principles on Academic Freedom and University Autonomy, principle I.

recognition enables students to denounce those biases and behaviors that help consolidate the racial contract.

These principles take the *common good* as the core justification for academic freedom, which "enables the consolidation of democracy, pluralism of ideas, scientific progress, human and societal development."[45] Academic freedom is defined as a fundamental human right, related to the right to education, freedom of expression and association, and equality before the law. As such, "no discriminatory rule, act or practice based on such criteria suspected of discrimination, whether by state authorities or by private individuals, may in any way diminish or restrict the rights of a person in the exercise of his or her academic freedom."[46]

The convention sets forth a "proportionality" procedure when relevant rights conflict with one another, "[implying] that the adoption of any of these measures[47] must pursue aims that are not only legitimate under the American Convention on Human Rights, but also compelling."[48]

Academic Freedom and Freedom of Speech

In Canada, the scope of academic freedom encompasses the autonomy of universities and faculty from external pressures, including those levied by the State. Academic freedom is notably guaranteed by collective agreements and memoranda of understanding negotiated between faculty associations and university administrations. Although freedom of expression is not explicitly included within academic freedom, these freedoms are of course linked, and one cannot afford to ignore their similarities in scope and content.[49] With this said, academic freedom is complex: "It is a cluster of freedoms associated in various ways with various scholarly personnel and institutions. Freedom of expression is just one of those subsidiary freedoms."[50]

---

45 Inter-American Principles on Academic Freedom and University Autonomy, preamble.

46 Inter-American Principles on Academic Freedom and University Autonomy, principle III.

47 Measures restricting protected rights.

48 Inter-American Principles on Academic Freedom and University Autonomy, principle III.

49 Bastarache, "Rapport du Comité sur la liberté académique de l'Université d'Ottawa," 19–27.

50 Shannon Dea, "First Dispatch: Academic Freedom and the Mission of the University," *University Affairs*, September 5, 2018, www.universityaffairs.ca/opinion/dispatches-academic-freedom/first-dispatch-academic-freedom-and-the-mission-of-the-university/.

In *Zundel*, the Supreme Court underlined the core objectives pursued by freedom of expression, which are "promoting truth, political or social participation, and self-fulfillment."[51] Per the Alberta Court of Appeals, freedom of expression and academic freedom pursue similar aims:

> Academic freedom and freedom of expression are inextricably linked. There is an obvious element of free expression in the protection of academic freedom, whether limited to the traditional conception of academic freedom as protecting the individual academic professional or applied more broadly to promote discussion in the university community as a whole … In my view, there is no legitimate conceptual conflict between academic freedom and freedom of expression. Academic freedom and the guarantee of freedom of expression contained in the Charter are handmaidens to the same goals; the meaningful exchange of ideas, the promotion of learning, and the pursuit of knowledge.[52]

Academic freedom has some similarities with freedom of expression.[53] As such, academic freedom is also subject to those reasonable limits that can be justified in a free and democratic society.[54] Bearing in mind that academic freedom is not absolute, how should it be deployed in a social context that recognizes the importance of DEI?

DEI Policies

In the wake of the social movements sparked by the murder of George Floyd, the lack of representation of Black people in universities became the object of increased attention. Commitments were taken to remedy the situation and give concrete institutional expression to policies of DEI.[55]

DEI programs are not just human resources policies. Rather, they can be characterized as a means of implementing measures to redress the histori-

51 *R v Zundel*, [1992] 2 SCR 731 at 753.

52 *Pridgen v University of Calgary*, 2012 ABCA 139 at paras. 113–117.

53 Jean-François Gaudreault-DesBiens and Léa Boutrouille, "Les libertés universitaires dans une université inclusive," *Université de Montréal*, March 2020, www.umontreal.ca/public/www/images/diversite/documents/RAPPORTFINAL-LIBUNIV-JFGDLB-MARS_2020.pdf.

54 Linda Mckay-Panos, "Freedom of Expression at Canadian Universities: A Difficult Compromise?" *LawNow*, July 4, 2019, www.lawnow.org/freedom-of-expression-at-canadian-universities-a-difficult-compromise/.

55 See, e.g., McGill University, "Equity, Diversity & Inclusion (EDI) Strategic Plan 2020–2025," 2020, www.mcgill.ca/equity/files/equity/mcgill_strategic_edi_plan_2020-20251.pdf.

cal wrongs of discrimination.[56] Assumed to take on organizational change through the creation of more inclusive university campuses, DEI policies only take effect if they alter the structures in which they operate.

As potently questioned by Diana, "How does the University in which so many are committed to diversity manage to achieve so little on its behalf? ... The university has nothing whatsoever against diversity, as long as it doesn't interfere with the white masculinity status quo."[57] For DEI policies to be fully effective, the racial contract's effects must be countered through an exercise in decolonization so as to ensure the well-being of Black students—who inherit historical traumas with intergenerational consequences.

This is why universities must listen to the stories of those who have lived through anti-Black racism: their narratives can compensate for the epistemological deficit of universities.[58] Critical Race Theory teaches us this crucial insight.[59] To be truly transformative, DEI must take racial justice into account. From then on, it may become a policy of justice (social and racial), equity, diversity, and inclusion (JEDI), which would require deliberate action aimed at dismantling systemic racism to enable structural change. Only racial justice can allow racialized people to flourish within universities.

The Experiences of Black University Students and Faculty

Traces of History

The mobilization of Black students against racism at the university is nothing new. In 1969, six Black students attending Sir George Williams University filed complaints alleging that they faced discrimination from one of their

56 The Hon. Rosalie Silberman Abella, *Report of the Commission on Equality in Employment* (Ottawa: Human Resources and Skills Development Canada, 1984), 1–9.

57 Diana Relkel quoted by Henry and Tator, "Theorical Perspectives and Manifestations of Racism in the Academy," 15–16.

58 Aurélie Lanctôt and Jean-François Gaudreault-DesBiens, "'Si on m'avait écouté dès le début, si on avait écouté mon récit,' Le narrativisme comme legs de la Critical Race Theory dans la pensée juridique Canadienne," *Droit et société* 108 (2021): 337–350.

59 Richard Delgado and Jean Stefancic, *Critical Race Theory: An Introduction* (New York: New York University Press, 2001), 7; Carol A. Aylward, *Canadian Critical Race Theory: Racism and the Law* (Halifax: Fernwood, 1999); Kimberlé Crenshaw, "Twenty Years of Critical Theory: Looking Back to Move Forward," *Connecticut Law Review* 117 (2011): 1255.

professors.[60] The dismissal of their complaints led to the largest student protest in Canadian history at the time. Over two hundred students occupied the school's computer lab in an event that has since been erroneously characterized as a "riot," when in fact the mobilization sought to obtain justice.[61]

Fifty years on, it is now time for universities to seriously consider the concerns of their Black students and time to decolonize universities so as to better consider their multiracial and multicultural contexts. Black students are leading the way toward a vision of academic freedom more sensitive to their experiences and perspectives.[62]

The Experiences of Black University Students

Universities must create an environment that is conducive to the pursuit of knowledge, but also to the development of those analytical tools upon which critical thinking can be based.

While Canada's professoriate is homogeneous,[63] its students are remarkably diverse. Yet the privileged position of university faculty, often white, risks obscuring the violence concealed in certain institutional stances. Most white students come from a homogeneous social background and have rarely interacted with racialized people. And even when they do, their failure to understand racial (and therefore power) dynamics prevents them from fully grasping the experiences of Black students. This gap in understanding is at the root of social interactions marked by stereotyping and racism, leaving Black students to feel isolated and excluded.[64]

---

60 Sir George Williams University was the site of violent protests and a fourteen-day sit-in against racism. The events leading to the protest began in earnest in the spring of 1968, during which six Caribbean students accused their professor, Perry Anderson, of racist grading practices. See David Austin, *Nègres Noirs, Nègres Blancs* (Montréal: Edition Lux, 2015), 45–47, 168–198. See also Rinaldo Walcott, *On Property* (Windsor: Biblioasis, 2021), 79; Rinaldo Walcott and Idil Abdillahi, *BlackLife: Post-BLM and the Struggle for Freedom* (Winnipeg: Arbeiter Ring, 2019), 61–63.

61 In October 2022, Concordia University (formerly known as Sir George Williams) issued an official apology. Lucas Marsh, "Concordia Officially Apologizes for Mishandling 1969 Black Student Protests," *The Concordian*, November 7, 2022, https://theconcordian.com/2022/11/concordia-officially-apologizes-for-mishandling-1969-black-student-protests/.

62 Marlon Bailey et al., "Unsung, Underpaid, and Unafraid Black Graduate Students' Response to Academic and Social Anti-Blackness," in *Making Black Lives Matter: Confronting Anti-Black Racism*, ed. Kevin Cokley (San Diego: Cognella Academic Publishing, 2021).

63 "Canadian Universities Fall Short on Diversity," *Nature* 556 (2018): 399.

64 Marlon Bailey et al., "Unsung, Underpaid, and Unafraid Black Graduate Students," 241.

Anti-Black racism foments a sense of withdrawal among Black students, which can lead to dropping out of school. It should also be noted that Black women in universities face overlapping and intersectional forms of oppression.[65] Their limited presence in universities leaves them vulnerable to feelings of inadequacy, which then pushes Black students to constantly seek out the approval of others for the sake of proving their legitimacy.[66] This feeling of hypervigilance can affect one's academic performance, mental health, and interpersonal relationships. Their minority status on campus hinders their capacity to implement systemic changes and makes it more difficult for them to be heard.

In this environment, beyond experiencing a double consciousness[67] and carrying a racial burden,[68] Black students undergo race-related stress[69]—stress that can be vicarious in nature, such as the stress felt at the murder of George Floyd. The racial violence lived through racist incidents, or the mention of the N-word carries their share of race-related stress for those involved.

To survive, Black students involve themselves in the antiracist education of white students, resulting in an emotionally taxing experience that can have adverse effects on their academic performance.[70] Linked to their experience of otherness, this "tax" can also have negative effects on their physical and psychological health.

It should be further noted that the slim presence of Black faculty has repercussions on the dynamics of intragroup support, an element of social

65 These injustices must also be recognized; see Laurenda McKinney, Daphne Halkias, and Leah Hollis, "Vicarious Bullying and Career Progression of African American Women Academics: An Integrative Literature Review," *SSRN*, September 2, 2021, https://dx.doi.org/10.2139/ssrn.3916282; Wendi S. Williams and Catherine Lynne Packer-Williams, "Frenemies in the Academy: Relational Aggression among African American Women Academicians," *Qualitative Report* 24 (2019): 2009.

66 Marlon Bailey et al., "Unsung, Underpaid, and Unafraid Black Graduate Students," 243.

67 W. E. B. Du Bois, *Les âmes du peuple Noir* (Paris: La découverte, 2007), 11; Magali Besson and Matthieu Renault, *W. E. B. Du Bois, double conscience et condition raciale* (Paris: Éditions Amsterdam, 2021), 41, 49.

68 According to Laurentian University sociology professor Rachid Bagaoui, a person facing stigmatization can feel the racial burden. See Francesca Mérentié, "La charge raciale et la diversité ethnoculturelle," *Ici Radio-Canada*, September 1, 2019, https://ici.radio-canada.ca/nouvelle/1282296/charge-raciale-discrimination-racisme-diversite-ethnoculturelle-capsule-connais-ton-voisin.

69 Association for Behavioral and Cognitive Therapies, "Race-Based Traumatic Stress," www.abct.org/fact-sheets/race-based-traumatic-stress/.

70 Dnika J. Travis et al., "Emotional Tax: How Black Women and Men Pay More at Work and How Leaders Can Take Action," *Catalyst*, 2016, www.catalyst.org/wp-content/uploads/2019/01/emotional_tax_how_black_women_and_men_pay_more.pdf.

capital. These professors are overburdened with the work related to the support of Black students. This situation only increases the risk of burnout and professional alienation that stems from a racially toxic work environment.[71]

In their efforts to create a more hospitable environment, students, armed with their ability to think critically, challenge certain stances taken by their university and professors. They also challenge traditional understandings of academic freedom. It is within this context that we propose to analyze the use of the N-word in the setting of Quebec universities—and touch upon a debate that eventually led to the enactment of a provincial law on academic freedom.

Academic Freedom in the Quebec Context

In 2021, the Act Respecting Academic Freedom in the University Sector was enacted in the province of Quebec.[72] Some have claimed that this law runs counter to the fundamental principles underlying academic freedom. Indeed, the law has the effect of undermining university and faculty autonomy,[73] notably by transforming academic freedom into a political tool.[74]

While the Act's preamble refers to the aforementioned Recommendation and recognizes that the full exercise of academic freedom requires institu-

71 Zawadi Rucks-Ahidiana, "The Inequities of the Tenure-Track System," *Inside Higher Ed*, June 7, 2019, www.insidehighered.com/advice/2019/06/07/nonwhite-faculty-face-significant-disadvantages-tenure-track-opinion.

72 An Act Respecting Academic Freedom in the University Sector, RLRQ c L-1.2.

73 "Mieux protéger la liberté académique," report presented by the University of Montreal as part of the Committee on Citizen Relations' public consultation on Bill 32, May 9, 2022, 3. More recently, the Quebec government blocked the appointment of a professor to the board of the Institut national de la recherche scientifique, despite the professor having been nominated for the position by her colleagues at the institution. The government rationale for denying her the position hinged on the professor's alleged links to Adil Charkaoui, an Imam suspected and formerly detained by the Canadian government for terrorism. Her colleagues in the Quebec university sector have been steadfast in her defense, with the Teachers' Union accusing the government of "political interference," and the Quebec Federation of University Professors claiming that the government's decision was in violation of provincial law; see Marie-Michele Sioux, "Une prof de l'INRS disqualifiée en raison de 'liens' avec Adil Charkaoui, selon Québec," *Le Devoir*, January 26, 2024, www.ledevoir.com/politique/quebec/806073/prof-inrs-disqualifiee-liens-adil-charkaoui-selon-quebec. See also Frédérick Nadeau, "La belle ironie, ou quand la CAQ s'ingère dans les affaires universitaires," *Le Devoir*, January 26, 2024, www.ledevoir.com/opinion/libre-opinion/806008/libre-opinion-belle-ironie-ou-quand-caq-ingere-affaires-universitaires.

74 François Lemieux, "Mot en 'N': François Legault veut 'défendre la liberté d'expression," *Métro*, February 13, 2021, https://journalmetro.com/actualites/national/2615784/francois-legault-defense-liberte-dexpression/; Alex Mahoudeau, *La panique woke, anatomie d'une offensive réactionnaire* (Paris: Éditions textuel, 2022), 124.

tional autonomy, the Act fails to mention the Recommendation's measures on antidiscrimination. Though Canada is a signatory to the Inter-American Principles, no mention is made of them. Such omissions should give rise to some serious questions, especially considering how the very impetus for this piece of legislation was to respond to Black student discontent with a professor's use of the N-word.

This Act ignores the social context set out earlier, ignoring in particular how universities are becoming increasingly diverse.[75] Yet this demographic shift should be prompting us to ask more questions. As per the Act's preamble, why are some forms of discourse deemed "ideological" and others not?[76] We can note the effects of the racial contract and the transparency phenomenon. The traumatic experiences of Black students and the race-related stress they suffer are a blind spot for this law.

One of this Act's effects is to give academic freedom precedence over other fundamental rights, such as freedom from discrimination and the right to a healthy learning and work environment. In this context, one should note that the Act prohibits universities from requiring "trigger" or "content warnings"[77] from their professors.[78] As such, minorities' (a vulnerable group protected by the constitution) demands are ignored, running counter to the very foundations of academic freedom and the democracy it is supposed to protect.[79] This is despite how minority issues "play a central role in political life and permeate the functioning of all institutions and constitutional law."[80]

---

75 Report presented by McGill University as part of the Committee on Citizen Relations' public consultation on Bill 32, May 9, 2022, 3.

76 The Act's preamble "defines the right to university academic freedom as the right of every person to engage freely and *without doctrinal, ideological or moral constraint* in an activity through which the person contributes to carrying out the mission of such an educational institution."

77 On racial trauma, triggers, and their consequences on the brain, see Janeé M. Steele and Charmeka S. Newton, *Black Lives Are Beautiful, 50 Tools to Heal from Trauma and Promote Positive Racial Identity* (New York: Routledge, 2023), 25–27.

78 An Act Respecting Academic Freedom in the University Sector, RLRQ c L-1.2, Art. 4(5).

79 Many academic freedom policies drafted in compliance with the Act only reinforce this harmful situation for Black students. See, e.g., "McGill Draft Policy on Academic Freedom," February 2, 2023, www.mcgill.ca/provost/files/provost/mcgill_universitys_draft_policy_on_academic_freedom.pdf; "Statement on McGill University's Draft Policy on Academic Freedom," *McGill Black Faculty & Staff Caucus*, April 12, 2023, www.blackfacultycaucus.mcgill.ca/statements.

80 José Woehrling, "Les trois dimensions de la protection des minorités en droit constitutionnel comparé," *Revue de droit de l'Université Sherbrooke* 34 (2003): 93.

Black student demands for the prohibition of the N-word seek to build upon the evolution of human rights, particularly with regard to the social constructs of race and gender. Legal interpretations of academic freedom must take the racial contract into account if racial justice is to become a tangible reality. In fact, the common good justifies an interpretation of academic freedom that is supportive of social cohesion in a pluralist democracy. A relationship based on mutual listening must be at the heart of racial justice policy.

We must ask whether professors and the institutions in which they work can use academic freedom to counter the demands of students from historically excluded groups. The use of academic freedom as an excuse to ignore their demands for racial justice reveals how certain discourses, certain historically charged words, are valued to the detriment of equality rights, running counter to the Recommendations and Principles set out earlier.

The N-Word: A Case Study

"I believe that words are things ... I think they stick on the walls, they go into the upholstery, they go into your clothes, and finally, into your very body."[81]

The N-word is rooted in a system of racial hierarchy and privilege, a system that enables dehumanization. After the abolition of slavery, the N-word became a racial slur, remaining a part of an enduring power structure.[82] As noted by Raúl Pérez, the power of words is part of "how race and racism worked as a political and ideological tool for ruling-class whites in power by creating and maintaining social division and control within white-dominated societies."[83]As a vector for stereotypes transmitted from generation to generation, its mention is an act of violence that revives trauma and enforces the racial contract.[84] Alluding to the N-word in reference to a Black person

81 Lynn Okura Bey, "Maya Angelou on the Dangerous Power of Racist Words," *Huffpost*, August 11, 2016, www.huffpost.com/entry/maya-angelou-dangerous-words_n_57ab8af3e4b0ba7ed23ed49b.

82 Ijeoma Oluo, *So You Want to Talk about Race* (New York: Seal Press, 2018), 134–141.

83 Pérez, *The Souls of White Jokes*, 6.

84 Kevin Cokley, "The Psychological Impact of Racist Slurs: The Painful History and Consequences of the Weaponization of the N-Word," *Psychology Today*, May 13, 2021, www.psychologytoday.com/us/blog/black-psychology-matters/202105/the-psychological-impact-racist-slurs#:~:text=The%20lesson%20to%20be%20learned%20here%20is%20simple%3A,to%20the%20cumulative%20racial%20trauma%20of%20Black%20people.

has consequences not only for the person targeted by the racial epithet but also for those who hear the word.

Even today, Black people are forced to confront this word and the attitudes that derive from it. Being called the N-word or living in a space in which the word is used corresponds to an "N-word moment," that is, a moment in which the lack of respect owed to Black people can have detrimental effects on one's life.[85] Continuing to use the N-word allows an oppressive world to stand firm in its rights and privileges. As an institution, the university should neither participate in nor defend such violence.

Allowing the use of the N-word in an academic context is to entrench racially charged conversation in a space where systemic racism has yet to be erased.[86] Moreover, regardless of the context in which it is used, tolerating this word has serious repercussions on the university's institutional culture.

Yet this is exactly what happens when academic freedom is invoked to justify the use of the N-word. On the one hand, we allow students to suffer direct or indirect racial violence within the university. On the other hand, the university imposes a supplementary form of violence by preventing students from denouncing this racial violence—imposing upon them a silence "in support of academic freedom."

*Vallières' White N*****s of America*

Pierre Vallières' *White N*****s of America*[87] is at the heart of this controversy. If it is brought up so often, it is due to the important role of the book in shaping the "Quebec subconscious." It is time to puncture its myths once and for all.

Having since become a classic of Quebec literature, Vallières' *White N*****s of America* was published in 1968, advancing a thesis that continues to influence Quebec politics today. If this book is problematic, it is not only due to its hyperbolic title. It is also because the book sets forth an implausible interpretation of lived experience in Quebec, failing to consider the existence of a French Canadian elite and the experiences of Black people in

85 Anderson, *Black in White Space*, 18–19.
86 Elsa Dorlin, *Se défendre. Une philosophie de la violence* (Paris: Zones, 2017), 175.
87 Pierre Vallières, *Nègres blancs d'Amérique* (Montréal: Typo, 1994).

Quebec since the early seventeenth century.[88] By ignoring Quebec's colonial history, Vallières feeds into a pernicious myth: that there was no slavery in New France or the British colony of Quebec. He omits the enslaved people Olivier Lejeune[89] and Marie-Angélique Joseph,[90] *N***** Rock*,[91] and the basic fact that the articles of the Capitulation of Montreal determined the fate of enslaved people living in eighteenth-century Quebec.[92]

Vallières defines Quebec identity by drawing upon the struggles of American enslaved people, but equates the Quebec worker's status to that of a "N*****": "The liberation struggle by the Americans blacks nevertheless arouses growing interest among the French-Canadian population, for the Quebec workers are aware of their condition as N****, as exploited, as second-class citizens. Have they not been, even since the establishment of New France in the seventeenth century, the servants of the imperialists, the white N**** of America?"[93] Although the lived experiences of the Québecois reseme ble those of second-class citizens, designating them as "N*****s" ignores how the systemic racism experienced by Black people differs from the discrimination faced by Québecois, who, as whites, have always benefited from some degree of privilege, namely that of never having been chattel. In short, slavery is much more than poverty or being confined to low-paying work: it is the absence of freedom, being considered as an object to be owned by others and never as a subject of rights.

Vallières uses "race," or the word "N*****," to speak of social class—but it is impossible to deracialize the word "N*****," which has been constructed as central to racial and colonial power dynamics. In doing this, Vallières empties "N*****" of its historical meaning, erasing the history of anti-Black racism in Quebec. As such, his "amalgamative drive and the settler commonsen-

---

88 Fernande Roy, "Nègres blancs d'Amérique," *Mythes 1959–2009* 51 (September 2009): 34–52; Austin, *Nègres Noirs, Nègres Blancs*, 23–30; Marcel Trudel, *Deux siècles d'esclavage au Québec* (Montréal: Biblio Québécoise, 2009).

89 Olivier Lejeune, "Répertoire du patrimoine culturel du Québec," www.patrimoine-culturel.gouv.qc.ca/rpcq/detail.do?methode=consulter&id=27849&type=pge.

90 Afua Cooper, *La pendaison d'Angélique* (Montréal: Les éditions de l'homme, 2007); Denyse Beaugrand-Champagne, *Le procès de Marie Joseph Angélique* (Montréal: Libre expression, 2004).

91 Rolland Viau, *Ceux de N***** Rock* (Montréal: Libre Expression, 2003).

92 Capitulation of Montreal 1760, Art. 47, https://ville.montreal.qc.ca/memoiresdesmontrealais/files/article-47-de-la-capitulation-de-montreal-1760.

93 Pierre Vallières, *White N*****s of America: The Precocious Autobiography of a Quebec Terrorist*, trans. Joan Pinkham (Toronto: Monthly Review Press and McClelland & Stewart, 1971), 21.

sicality of his class-conscious humanism and antiracism simply add a series of shades to his de-racialized and '(br)otherly' catalog of nè***s; Vallières thus remains firmly rooted in the white supremacist, antiblack, and settler colonial logic of his original appropriative gesture."[94]

Even as he draws inspiration from the Black Panthers, influenced as much by Frantz Fanon as by Malcolm X, Vallières leeches off the Black experience and appropriates it for his own ends. It is one thing to draw inspiration from the Black freedom struggle, but quite another to reclaim their history for one's own myth-making purposes.[95] It is through his silences and omissions that Vallières is complicit in the consolidation of racial hierarchies.[96] With his privileged status as a white man, he gets to decide who figures most prominently in history. He marginalizes Black people once again, relegating them to a mere footnote in history, censoring their narratives.

Vallières has paved the way for a sort of generalized amnesia in Quebec, a province whose motto is "Je me souviens" ("I remember"). This amnesia is a political choice: "the wilful and selective process of sifting and filtering to find the memories that fit the narrative you are committed to" and, for the rest, "excising, negating and delegitimizing" those who contradict the national narrative.[97] Even today, racialized Québecois suffer the conz sequences of this truncated history. The premier's refusal, on behalf of the Quebec government, to acknowledge systemic racism is only a manifestation of a history entangled in the Vallières myth.

This position taken by Quebec, which has consistently advocated for its recognition as a nation, is particularly embarrassing when considering the availability of clear definitions for system racism against Africans and people of African descent, most notably the one proposed by the UN High Commissioner for Human Rights. This definition of systemic racism, "including as it relates to structural and institutional racism, is understood

94 Bruno Corneiller, "The Struggle of Others: Pierre Vallières, Quebecois Settler Nationalism, and the N-Word Today," *Discourse: Journal for Theoretical Studies in Media and Culture* 39 (2017): 50.

95 Wendell Nii Laryea Adjetey, *Cross-Border Cosmopolitans: The Making of a Pan-African North America* (Chapel Hill: The University of North Carolina Press, 2023), 167.

96 Michel-Rolph Trouillot, *Silencing the Past: Power and the Production of History* (Boston: Beacon Press, 2015).

97 Gary Younge, "Lest We Remember: How Britain Buried Its History of Slavery," *The Guardian*, March 29, 2023, www.theguardian.com/news/ng-interactive/2023/mar/29/lest-we-remember-how-britain-buried-its-history-of-slavery.

to be the operation of a complex, interrelated system of laws, policies, practices, and attitudes in State institutions, the private sector, and societal structures that, combined, result in direct or indirect, intentional or unintentional, de jure or de facto discrimination, distinction, exclusion, restriction or preference on the basis of race, color, descent or national or ethnic origin. Systemic racism often manifests itself in pervasive racial stereotypes, prejudice, and bias and is frequently rooted in histories and legacies of enslavement, the transatlantic trade in enslaved Africans, and colonialism."[98] It is clear that the N-word is clearly a manifestation of "pervasive racial stereotypes, prejudice, and bias and is frequently rooted in histories and legacies of enslavement."

The Case of Verushka Lieutenant-Duval: A Moral Panic

During one of her lectures, the University of Ottawa lecturer Verushka Lieutenant-Duval uttered the N-word in reference to Vallières and his book. As a contract-based employee of the university, she was soon suspended from her position. A moral panic-fueled media storm swept through Quebec, as Black students were said to have "attacked" a vulnerable teacher.[99] This event also highlighted the notion of a "hierarchy of credibility" as defined by sociologist Howard Becker, a hierarchy that results in "our propensity to believe those with the power or higher status."[100]

Everything had to be done to protect this woman, preserve the established order of things, and maintain the status quo—and all this within a media context that is not or only performatively representative of Quebec diversity. When racialized minorities are included in media, they rarely hold anything more than a marginal influence on news content.

The case of Lieutenant-Duval has come to symbolize the "attack" on academic freedom. Public discourse, fueled by the government, forged a social crisis out of thin air. The incident was depicted as a transgression of domi-

98 United Nations High Commissioner for Human Rights, "Promotion and Protection of the Human Rights and Fundamental Freedoms of Africans and of People of African Descent against Excessive Use of Force and Other Human Rights Violations by Law Enforcement Officers," UN Doc A/HRC/47/53 (2021), para. 9.

99 Judith Lussier, *Annulé(e): réflexions sur la cancel culture* (Montréal: Cardinal, 2021), 43–63.

100 Victor Ray, *On Critical Race Theory* (New York: Penguin Random House, 2022), 85.

nant values. This is a moral panic based primarily on a fear of "racial" and cultural differences.

Moral panics have been theorized by Stanley Cohen and Stuart Hall.[101] According to Cohen, they tend to emerge out of those power struggles in which facts are manipulated to bolster the dominant position. Per Hall, this kind of panic illustrates how elites "consciously and deliberately fabricate moral panics, both to reinforce and justify social control mechanisms and to divert attention away from important issues and problems."[102]

Putting this panic into motion ostracized those Black students who had merely asked that their professor not use the N-word, even as their calls for racial justice only sought recognition of their dignity and of their right to a safe and healthy learning environment.[103] For some, all calls for social or racial justice are either expressions of "cancel culture,"[104] or an assault against "academic freedom" by historically marginalized groups.

This case illustrates how the individual realities and interests of elites influence media coverage and government responses to social issues. This state of affairs corresponds to how Henry and Tator's description of the links between the media outlets and the political, economic, and cultural elites that dictate media coverage and legislative responses.[105] Building upon van Dijk's work, these authors have found that editorials are aimed at elites, particularly politicians. A nonrepresentative media therefore influences the legislative agenda.

The Discourse of Victimhood

Lieutenant-Duval has been portrayed as the victim of an attack perpetrated by a horde of Black students: the collective unconscious longs to protect this woman from Black bodies—an impulse not unlike the one underlying the practice of lynching, punishments once reserved for the Black men who dared to even speak to a white woman.[106] Ironically, by advancing the discourse of victimhood as a counter to demands for justice and emancipa-

101 See Dupuis-Déri, *Panique à l'université*, 51.
102 Dupuis-Déri, *Panique à l'université*, 52.
103 Mahoudeau, *La panique woke*, 21.
104 Lussier, *Annulé(e)*, 27–37.
105 Frances Henry and Carol Tator, *Discourses of Domination: Racial Bias in the Canadian English-Language Press* (Toronto: University of Toronto Press, 2002), 26, 235.
106 Timothy B. Tyson, *The Blood of Emmet Till* (New York: Simon & Schuster, 2017).

tion, the media and the State have marginalized those who make demands for racial justice as radicals, enemies of universalism, or activists hijacking the antiracist movement. Paradoxically, the use of this counterdiscourse by members of the majority (Eurodescendants) presents themselves as victims.

On Censorship

For some, asking for the N-word to not be uttered is not only an attack on Vallières' work but an act of censorship. These people forget that censorship requires power. As Éric Fassin has noted, "The term censorship is misleade ing: to prohibit, one must have the power to prohibit. Thus, 'the ultimate recourse of minorities, beyond simple interpellation, is rather a boycott' and not an act of censorship. It's about using their weight to accredit or discredit, value or devalue, legitimize or delegitimize. In short, it's about playing the democratic game of values. Let's not reduce this politicization to a challenge to freedom of expression. On the contrary, it widens the circle of those who are entitled to this fundamental right."[107]

Brandishing "censorship" aims to silence those who already have little or no voice. Discourses of censorship, victimhood,[108] moral panic,[109] "us" and "them,"[110] and national identity only aim to preserve a status quo in which the majority remains free to oppress.[111] All these discourses run counter to the values upheld by academic freedom and its central place in democracy. Furthermore, deploying the moral panic of "wokeness" when describing the students' demands leaves much damage in its wake. In addition to demonizing a liberation movement (the Black American Woke movement), concrete policies have been marshaled in service to this moral panic. Indeed, the media's treatment panic of "wokeness" is akin to "[ridiculing] important issues."[112] As noted by Alex Mahoudeau, referring to the moral panic of "wokeness" as but a means to counter "any change that challenges or denat-

107 Dupuis-Déri, *Panique à l'université*, 163; Éric Fassin, "Qui annule qui? Contextualiser la polémique contre le cancel cultulre," *Médipart*, August 28, 2020.

108 Frances Henry and Carol Tator, *The Colour of Democracy: Racism in Canadian Society*, 4th ed. (Toronto: Nelson Education, 2009), 13.

109 Henry and Tator, *The Colour of Democracy*, 14.

110 Henry and Tator, *The Colour of Democracy*, 14.

111 Henry and Tator, *The Colour of Democracy*, 17.

112 Mahoudeau, *La panique woke*, 138.

uralizes social hierarchies"[113] warns us against overlooking the ever-growing "phenomenon of institutionalizing moral panics."[114]

The N-Word: A Word That Wounds

The discourse of racism denial is brandished to silence the voices of Black people, thus perpetuating an imbalance of power.[115] By discrediting their trauma (racial gaslighting),[116] the suffering of Black students gets erased. Yet words create worlds. Though archaic, the N-word still carries the charge of hatred.[117] The word is not a word. It is at best a concept, and at worst an assault on peoples' psychological integrity.

As the standard bearer of white supremacy and the racial contract, this word only reinforces Black peoples' sense of exclusion or self-exclusion.[118] The word ultimately acts as an obstacle to the presence of Black people in universities and society.

I was told that during the University of Ottawa incident, the only Black professor in a Montreal university's faculty was verbally abused by his colleagues. He broke down in tears. Against the academic freedom invoked by his white colleagues, this Black professor's dignity held little weight. Although the N-word was not used against him, some of his colleagues saw fit to mount a defense of existing power structures. The use of the N-word became a source of collateral damage. These professors ignored the institutional privileges that had allowed them to consider their experiences as "universal," thereby discrediting the experiences of "others" and extending their privilege.[119] By refusing to grasp the racist significance of the N-word, pro-

113 Mahoudeau, *La panique woke*, 139.

114 Mahoudeau, *La panique woke*, 133–135.

115 Henry and Carol Tator, *The Colour of Democracy*, 11.

116 Sheila Wise Rowe, *Healing Racial Trauma, the Road to Resilience* (Downers Grove: Intervarsity Press, 2020), 15; V. E. Johnson et al., "'It's Not in Your Head': Gaslighting, 'Splaining, Victim Blaming, and Other Harmful Reactions to Microaggressions," *Perspectives on Psychological Science* 16 (2021).

117 Tamara Thermitus, "L'excellence ne met pas à l'abri du racisme," *Pivot*, July 18, 2022, https://pivot.quebec/2022/07/18/lexcellence-ne-met-pas-a-labri-du-racisme/.

118 Christian Prince, "How Saying the N-Word Keeps White Supremacy Alive," *Medium*, February 28, 2023, https://medium.com/@cprincejr/how-saying-the-n-word-keeps-white-supremacy-alive-b72891b867a8.

119 Harris analyzes Whiteness as the consolidating social force of White power. Cheryl I. Harris, "Whiteness as Property," *Harvard Law Review* 106 (1993): 1707.

fessors at that university engaged in Whitesplaining.[120] Ignoring the experiences of blacks is a hermeneutical injustice: "when a gap in collective interpretative resources puts someone at an unfair disadvantage when it comes to making sense of their social experience."[121] This type of injustice is "caused by structural prejudice in the economy of collective hermeneutical resources."[122]

For some professors, the use of the N-word as an insult should be prohibited and sanctioned. However, if reference is made to a work or historical document containing the word, its use should be permitted, since its use is tied to the subject matter being taught. Such an approach overlooks how, at the time these works were created, racism was socially acceptable; to use the word today is to replicate this state of affairs. Moreover, this approach refuses to see how using this word can have vicarious or ripple effects on others.

David Raban, the student who filed a complaint against University of Chicago law professor (and noted free speech advocate) Geoffrey Stone when the latter used the N-word, noted how his professor, "as a white man, repeated a word used by white people to perpetuate the subjugation of Black Americans for hundreds of years. He trivialized the world's history and the lived experience of Black students. He employed the word to highlight a white student's reprehensible treatment of a Black student. He lent credence to the false stereotype that Black men are prone to violence."[123]

For Raban, Stone's use of the N-word showcased what some call the *stereotype threat*,[124] that is, the detrimental impact on performance that occurs when an individual's poor performance is at risk of confirming a task-relevant stereotype.[125] Black students targeted by this threat, who are led to believe that they only represent their racial group, conclude on some level that they have no agency—which is ultimately dehumanizing.

The case of Geoffrey Stone is quite interesting. He no longer uses this word when teaching. He finally recognized that using the N-word was caus-

120 Catriona Elder, "'Whitesplaining': What It Is and How It Works," *The Conversation*, September 30, 2015, https://theconversation.com/whitesplaining-what-it-is-and-how-it-works-48175.

121 Miranda Fricker, *Epistemic Injustice: Power and the Ethics of Knowing* (New York: Oxford University Press, 2007), 1.

122 Fricker, *Epistemic Injustice*, 1.

123 David Raban, "Racism Thrives at the Law School", *Chicago Maroon*, March 5, 2019, https://chicagomaroon.com/26727/viewpoints/op-ed/racism-thrives-law-school/.

124 Kristal Hines Shelvin et al., "Stereotype Threat in African American Children: The Role of Black Identity and Stereotype Awareness," *Revue internationale de psychologie sociale* 27 (2014): 175–204.

125 Rokhaya Diallo, *Ne reste pas à ta place* (Vanves: Marabout, 2019), 75.

ing real harm to his students, whether white or Black. Now a grandfather of Black children, Stone is able to grasp the unsettling effects of the N-word. Through his experience, he seems to have become aware of his blind spots and privileges. With that being said, this example is ultimately one of how members of a group sharing the same social capital or "race" struggle to grasp the full scope of racism.[126]

The Repercussions of Using the N-Word

The notion of "words that wound" has been analyzed by Judith Butler and subsequently by Claire Oger, who notes how "the power of a name to wound [is grounded in] the sedimentation of the uses of the name that freezes its repetition."[127] For her part, Mari J. Matsuda highlights the suffering experienced by the victim of a racist remark like the N-word.[128] She notes that to avoid their exposure to racist interactions, Black people sometimes quit their jobs, leave their homes, and avoid certain public spaces. She underscores how the N-word creates "inner turmoil."

One should not lose sight of how the mere rejection of a racist mark does not prevent it from being stored in one's psyche: this is what gives rise to internalized racism. From the victim's perspective, the wounds inflicted by the N-word are neither random nor isolated. The word supplements and overlaps with the multiple forms that racism can take, reinforcing the existing conditions of racial domination. Just like blackface, the N-word is "more than the denigration and dehumanization of Blackness. It [is] also a powerful form of racism that player a key role in the formation of a sense of 'whiteness.'"[129]

Racism is an experience of psychic destruction that robs Black people of their dignity and humanity. It inflicts personal, psychological, and spiritual wounds. The use of the N-word contributes to this "spirit murder."[130]

---

126 Julie W. de Sherbinin, "White Professors Can Help Uproot Racism," *Chronicle of Higher Education*, May 7, 2004, www.chronicle.com/article/white-professors-can-help-uproot-racism/.

127 Claire Oger, "Judith Butler, Le pouvoir des mots. Politique du performatif," *Mots. Les langages du politique* 81 (2006): 125–129.

128 Mari J. Matsuda, "Public Response to Racist Speech: Considering the Victim's Story," *Michigan Law Review* 87 (1989): 2320.

129 Pérez, *The Souls of White Jokes*, 17.

130 Patricia Williams, "Spirit-Murdering the Messenger: The Discourse of Fingerpointing as the Law's Response to Racism," *University of Miami Law Review* 42 (1987): 127.

Can Academic Freedom Justify the Use of the N-Word?

Considering the devastating effects of this word, could a Black person's right to fully participate in the academic experience be sacrificed in the name of allowing dominant groups to use the N-word? No. Such an interpretation of things, which ignores the rights and freedoms of Black people, must be rethought in light of the need to implement JEDI within universities.

The Black student and faculty demand to prohibit the use of the N-word goes to the very heart of education. They have the right to a healthy learning and work environment, and the right to demand that their search for knowledge do not contribute to their further alienation.

Conclusion

For universities to fully grasp the advances in knowledge regarding the social construction of race, the ramifications of the racial contract within the various structures of these institutions must be understood. This exercise is necessary if our democratic ideals are to become a reality for the Black students and faculty, who are the most burdened by the N-word's harmful effects. There is no intellectual duty to use dehumanizing words. On the contrary, universities must take student trauma into account and move with tact and sensitivity to foster a healthy work environment for racialized people.

The racial contract reveals the social contract's blind spots. Emancipation viewed from the faulty perspective of a decontextualized academic freedom will only benefit white people. This is what the racial contract reveals. Armed with this critical insight, we must then approach academic freedom within its proper context and deconstruct it in order to dismantle the racial contract. In this sense, Black professors and students cannot be present in merely symbolic or performative functions. With the lived experience of racism, they can instead elucidate the full consequences of the racial contract and explain to their fellow professors and students how white supremacy and systemic racism emerge within their institutional contexts.

These narrative experiences make up a wealth of knowledge that can be used to inform pedagogical approaches, which is why institutions must therefore make every effort to avoid assimilating their students and censoring their stories. Academic freedom cannot be used to silence or further marginalize the voices of Black and other minority students and faculty, but must instead be interpreted in its proper context so as to guarantee all members of the community full participation in academic life.

Since universities have actively participated in the social and political construction of racial hierarchy, is it not time to truly remedy the historical exclusion of Black people from universities? Is it not time to foster the kind of environment that allows Black people to live out their academic experiences without being exposed to trauma? Advancing history means actively working against racism. As Sven Lindqvist writes in *Exterminate All the Brutes*. "You already know enough. So do I. It is not knowledge we lack. What is missing is the courage to understand what we know and to draw conclusions from it."[131]

131 Sven Lindqvist, *Exterminate All the Brutes* (New York: New Press, 1996), 1.

Chapter 10

Academic Freedom and Social Justice in Quebec

Sophie Bisping

Introduction

The debate around academic freedom in Quebec has taken on a growing importance in recent years, culminating in the passing of Bill 32—An Act Respecting Academic Freedom in the University Sector—in June 2022. This bill was drafted in response to what many in the governmental and public spheres saw as the dangers of student-led pressures on academic spaces. While discussions about academic freedom were already happening, the public discussion took a new turn in October 2020, after a professor at the University of Ottawa, Ms. Lieutenant-Duval, used a racial slur when quoting a text in the context of a course on gender representation in the visual arts.[1] Complaints from students led to her suspension,[2] which sparked a debate in the academic community and beyond on the place to be given to students' demands in the name of social justice. The event was divisive and

1 Étienne Lajoie and Boris Proulx, "La professeure Lieutenant-Duval soutient qu'elle ignorait le caractère délicat du mot en n," *Le Devoir*, August 31, 2022, www.ledevoir.com/societe/751533/la-professeure-lieutenant-duval-plaide-qu-elle-ignorait-la-sensibilite-du-mot-en-n.

2 Léa Carrier, "L'affaire Lieutenant-Duval en arbitrage: L'Université d'Ottawa persiste et signe," *La Presse*, August 29, 2022, www.lapresse.ca/actualites/2022-08-29/l-affaire-lieutenant-duval-en-arbitrage/l-universite-d-ottawa-persiste-et-signe.php.

led to a group of 579 professors across Canada writing a letter of support.[3] English-speaking media initially focused on the racism present in the event, while French-speaking media had a heavier focus on the threats to academic freedom that it represented. This event and other similar ones, including at McGill University, led to the establishment of the *Commission sur la liberté académique* in March 2021, presided by Justice Michel Bastarache, and ultimately to the Quebec government's decision to approve Bill 32.[4]

The public discussion around academic freedom so far has polarized around two main views. One side puts forth that the suspension of Ms. Lieutenant-Duval was emblematic of a climate of insecurity in universities. A group of essays published by Ottawa University professors, *Liberté Malmenée*,[5] and a longer essay by McGill University professors, *Liberté universitaire et justice sociale*,[6] both contend that the teaching staff self-censors and decides not to teach material that could contain problematic words or ideas in fear of going through a similar fate as Mrs. Lieutenant-Duval. For these authors, we are currently in a deep crisis of academic freedom, characterized by a pursuit of social justice to the detriment of academic rights.[7] Parallel to this argument runs the concern that university administrations do not provide enough support for their employees against student pressures and are bending to unreasonable student demands to satisfy the needs of a student body that is increasingly treated as a clientele.[8] These two books distinguish themselves from more extreme political views, often associated with right-wing politics, claiming that students' complaints are a violation of

3 "Université d'Ottawa: La professeure suspendue reçoit l'appui de 579 collègues," *La Presse*, October 20, 2020, www.lapresse.ca/actualites/education/2020-10-20/universite-d-ottawa/la-professeure-suspendue-recoit-l-appui-de-579-collegues.php.

4 Isabelle Arseneau and Arnaud Bernadet, *Liberté universitaire et justice sociale* (Montréal: Editions Liber, 2022). The commission's final report was published in December 2021; see Alexandre Cloutier et al., *Reconnaître, protéger et promouvoir la liberté universitaire: Rapport de la Commission scientifique et technique indépendante sur la reconnaissance de la liberté académique dans le milieu universitaire* (Québec: Gouvernement du Québec, Ministère de l'Enseignement supérieur, 2021).

5 Anne Gilbert, Maxime Prévost, and Geneviève Tellier, eds., *Libertés Malmenées: Chronique d'une Année Trouble à l'Université d'Ottawa* (Montréal: Leméac Éditeur, 2022).

6 Arseneau and Bernadet, *Liberté universitaire et justice sociale.*

7 Léa Carrier, "Affaire Lieutenant-Duval: La crise à l'Université d'Ottawa vue de l'intérieur," *La Presse*, February 23, 2022, www.lapresse.ca/actualites/education/2022-02-23/affaire-lieutenant-duval/la-crise-a-l-universite-d-ottawa-vue-de-l-interieur.php.

8 Arseneau and Bernadet, *Liberté universitaire et justice sociale*, 29.

free speech and are a symptom of a radical left, and instead reclaim a critique of student protests from a more liberal perspective.[9]

Another side of the debate argues that the danger of censorship is exaggerated, and the few instances when it might happen are either justifiable on moral grounds or do not quite meet the threshold to be considered censorship. Francis Dupuis-Déri's essay *Panique morale* à *l'université*, published in August 2022, describes a moral panic that has taken hold of professors, creating a sensationalist but false image of a crisis in universities.[10] Proponents of this view have also maintained that responding to students' complaints can be important to prevent further harm.[11] They suggest that the focus on censorship obscures valid demands made by activists and that discussions about academic freedom in higher education "risk overshadowing racism and anti-racist activism."[12]

In the last two years, this debate has increasingly been presented as entailing an adversarial relationship between students on one side, and professors and universities' administrations on the other. This has led to a public understanding of academic freedom as a value needing to be defended *against* student movements, and as competing with social justice aims. Student voices have often been sidelined in this debate compared to professors' and public commentators'. The reality is more complex. Far from being a monolith, individual students have aligned themselves with both sides of the debate.[13] Simultaneously, student associations have published consultation reports that offer alternative answers to a potential crisis of academic freedom in

9 Commentator Mathieu Bock Coté has espoused this opinion, arguing that the "woke left" is ideologically dominant in universities and contributing to a society-wide "racialized regression"; see Mathieu Bock-Côté, "François Legault Contre La Gauche Woke," *Le Journal de Montréal*, February 13, 2021, www.journaldemontreal.com/2021/02/13/francois-legault-contre-la-gauche-woke. Unfortunately this view is quite widespread in the broader public debate in Quebec.

10 Francis Dupuis-Déri, *Panique à l'université: rectitude politique, wokes et autres menaces imaginaires* (Montréal: Lux éditeur, 2022).

11 Léa Carrier, "L'université, les wokes et les menaces imaginaires," *La Presse*, September 4, 2022, www.lapresse.ca/actualites/education/2022-09-04/l-universite-les-wokes-et-les-menaces-imaginaires.php; Willa Holt, "Quebec's 'Cancel Culture' Debate Misses the Point," *Ricochet*, April 22, 2021, https://ricochet.media/en/3619.

12 Holt, "Quebec's 'Cancel Culture' Debate Misses the Point."

13 "Les étudiants et la liberté universitaire," *La Presse*, February 15, 2021, www.lapresse.ca/debats/courrier-des-lecteurs/2021-02-15/les-etudiants-et-la-liberte-universitaire.php.

Canadian universities.[14] The multiauthored report *Avis jeunesse: regards sur la liberté académique* published in 2022 and the University of Montreal Student Associations' public statement on academic freedom both call for a depolarization of the question.[15] They emphasize the importance of contextualizing academic freedom as exercised within institutional pressures, and through the positionality of singular professors and students.

Inspired by these reports, this contribution first contextualizes the student demands that have manifested themselves in Quebec universities, before seeking to rework the conceptual relationship between academic freedom and social justice to address the underpinning concerns of both sides of the debate. Transnational histories are interwoven in the background of the Quebec debate, from student protests aiming to decolonize academia in South Africa, to debates on barring certain speakers from public platforms in the UK. Disentangling these histories will be the focus of the first section of this chapter. Contextualizing the current adversarial relationship between students and university administrations will help envisage other perspectives on the values promoted by each side. The second section attempts to rethink the tension between social justice and academic freedom by foregrounding the obligations that are inherent to the definition of academic freedom. This leads to a definition of academic freedom that includes working toward one aspect of social justice, namely epistemic justice. The concluding section evaluates the pitfalls of broadening the definition of academic freedom to include moral aims such as epistemic justice.

I ultimately argue that whether understood as parallel concerns or as concentric ones, the aims of academic freedom and social justice are not contradictory: they interact in complex ways but are not in conflict. Loosening up the conceptual bounds of academic freedom provides alternatives to the apparent deadlock between the need for an antiracist and inclusive education and the freedom to teach any material. By situating student movements in current discussions on academic freedom in Quebec, I show that clearly

14 "Les étudiants et la liberté universitaire"; Meriem Khatem, "Liberté Académique En Contexte Universitaire," *Fédération des Associations Étudiantes du Campus de L'Université de Montréal*, https://cdn-contenu.quebec.ca/cdn-contenu/adm/min/education/publications-adm/enseignement-superieur/organismes-lies/14_FAE__CUM_20210709.pdf?1629733516; Nabil Jaafari et al., *Avis Jeunesse: regards sur la liberté académique* (Montreal: Institut du Nouveau Monde, 2022).

15 Khatem, "Liberté Académique En Contexte Universitaire"; Jaafari et al., *Avis Jeunesse: regards sur la liberté académique.*

defining the relation between the concepts of academic freedom and epistemic justice will be beneficial for the pursuit of both social justice within academia, and a shared definition of academic freedom among students, professors, and university administrations.

Contextualizing the Tension between Academic Freedom and Social Justice

Two movements in the 2010s have had transnational echoes in the Quebec debate about academic freedom. One is the wave of student protests first in South Africa, then globally, to decolonize their institutions. The other is the renewed discussion around the practice of "no-platforming" in the UK, which has influenced the methods used by students to make their voices heard. No-platforming, or deplatforming, consists of denying individuals the possibility to present their views in public forums (particularly academic institutions) on the basis of the "perceived abhorrent or misguided nature of the individual's views."[16]

Global Protests to Decolonize Academia

Student demands to shape course content and teaching methods are rooted in a global history of decolonial protests. The latest wave of student protests aiming for an active decolonization of the university was initiated with the Rhodes Must Fall campaign at the University of Cape Town in South Africa. The protesters not only asked for changes to the curriculum but also for the decommissioning of colonial and apartheid symbols and the right to free education.[17] The campaign resulted in the 2015 removal of a statue of Cecil Rhodes, a zealous supporter of British imperialism who served as prime minister of the Cape Colony in the late nineteenth century. These protests, in turn,

16 Uwe Peters and Nikolaj Nottelmann, "Weighing the Costs: The Epistemic Dilemma of No-Platforming," *Synthese* 199 (2021): 7231.

17 Sabelo J. Ndlovu-Gatsheni, "El Movimiento Estudiantil 'Rhodes Debe Caer' (Rodhes Must Fall): Las Universidades Sudafricanas Como Campo de Lucha," *Tabula Rasa* 25 (December 2016): 195.

inspired others in the UK,[18] India,[19] and the United States,[20] with slogans such as "Decolonize Your Curriculum" or "Why Is My Curriculum White."

Generally, these protests ask for a decolonization of academia through various avenues, including redrafting course syllabi and changing research methodologies to reconsider the colonial lines along which academic knowledge has developed. The desire to decolonize the production of knowledge has always accompanied larger political movements of decolonization, as education and research were themselves an integral part of colonial projects. Indeed, European colonizers in the nineteenth and twentieth centuries strengthened their power by creating higher education institutions and research hierarchies that "used under-education, biased and exploitive research practices, and racist theories of knowledge as tools of colonial subjugation."[21] In more recent years, the sociologist Walter Mignolo has argued that Western epistemology still shapes the production of knowledge in ways that propagate colonial structures of power.[22] Scholars Shose Kessi, Zoe Marks, and Elelwani Ramugondo have further proposed that the history of student activism reflects the pace of decolonization, as they embody the tension between demands for change from a younger generation and the institutional resistance to this change.[23] Recognizing this, the Federation of Student Associations of the University of Montreal calls for a definition of academic freedom that prioritizes decolonizing knowledge.[24]

Today, actions such as removing symbols glorifying a colonial past or including racialized authors in syllabi inscribe themselves both in a decolonizing project and in a critique of the continued structural inequality and

---

18 Aamna Mohdin, "Protesters Rally in Oxford for Removal of Cecil Rhodes Statue," *The Guardian*, June 9, 2020, www.theguardian.com/world/2020/jun/09/protesters-rally-in-oxford-for-removal-of-cecil-rhodes-statue.

19 Vamsee Juluri, "Decolonising the Curriculum," *The Hindu*, July 20, 2017, www.thehindu.com/opinion/op-ed/decolonising-the-curriculum/article19319381.ece.

20 "Decolonize Your Syllabus | University of Portland," https://college.up.edu/gwsm/decolonize-your-syllabus.html.

21 Shose Kessi, Zoe Marks, and Elelwani Ramugondo, "Decolonizing Knowledge within and beyond the Classroom," *Critical African Studies* 13 (2021): 2.

22 Walter D. Mignolo, "Introduction: Coloniality of Power and De-colonial Thinking," *Cultural Studies* 21 (2007): 156; Walter D. Mignolo, "Coloniality Is Far from Over, and So Must Be Decoloniality," *Afterall: A Journal of Art, Context and Enquiry* 43 (March 2017): 38.

23 Kessi, Marks, and Ramugondo, "Decolonizing Knowledge within and beyond the Classroom."

24 Khatem, "Liberté Académique En Contexte Universitaire," 3.

racism of academia.[25] Despite protests, universities have not been proactive in their attempts to decolonize curricula. For some activists, the slow and grudging response of higher education administrators to student demands reflects a reluctance to address colonialism's impact on present-day racism.[26] It was only after the Black Lives Matter movement sparked discussion about the intersecting forces of colonialism and racism that the Rhodes statue at Oxford University was taken down, despite student campaigns having started five years earlier.[27]

The decolonial critique of higher education is not only voiced by students. In Canada, the Truth and Reconciliation Commission's calls to action on education also brought forth these concerns, including a call for law schools to require students to train in antiracism.[28] In Montreal, calls to take down statues that glorified the history of colonialism were also made by civil society groups.[29] One of the statues targeted was that of James McGill, who gave his name to McGill University and owned Black and Indigenous slaves.[30] The Quebec debate on academic freedom needs to be resituated as happening in reaction to these movements as well. Indeed, university administrations' reactions to decolonizing demands have been perceived by some professors as imposing restrictions on their academic freedom.

For example, one response by universities has been to set in place equity, diversity, and inclusion (EDI) policies, to work against the way in which "processes of academic selection and recruitment reflect, reproduce and amplify social inequalities."[31] Indeed, reports informing these policies have revealed that the university experience was "not one of equitable access for many of

25 Mariam Aiyad, "On Decolonizing Academia," *The Footnote*, October 4, 2021, https://the-footnote.org/2021/10/04/on-decolonizing-academia/.

26 David Batty, "Only a Fifth of UK Universities Say They Are 'Decolonising' Curriculum," *The Guardian*, June 11, 2020, www.theguardian.com/us-news/2020/jun/11/only-fifth-of-uk-universities-have-said-they-will-decolonise-curriculum.

27 Kessi, Marks, and Ramugondo, "Decolonizing Knowledge within and beyond the Classroom," 5.

28 Truth and Reconciliation Commission of Canada, *Calls to Action* (Winnipeg: Truth and Reconciliation Commission of Canada, 2015).

29 Cecilia Keating, "Montreal's Monuments to Colonialism," *Ricochet*, September 8, 2017, https://ricochet.media/en/1949.

30 Claire Loewen, "Taking Down Statue of James McGill Is Only One Step in Fighting Systemic Racism, Students Say," *CBC News*, June 14, 2020, www.cbc.ca/news/canada/montreal/james-mcgill-petition-1.5611769.

31 Jana Bacevic, "Epistemic Injustice and Epistemic Positioning: Towards an Intersectional Political Economy," *Current Sociology* (2021): 2.

the Black students, faculty and staff."[32] In reaction, universities committed to goals such as increasing the representativeness of the student body and the workforce.[33] Yet these policies have been criticized by both professors and student groups.

Some professors have criticized EDI policies for bringing perfunctory changes to attract more student clientele, and for creating pressures to conform with standards that are not adapted to their research fields.[34] For example, Yves Gingras and Arnaud Bernadet decry the use of EDI criteria in the allocation of research grants, arguing that they represent social norms that should not dictate research inquiries and that their application is arbitrary.[35] Simultaneously, some students argue that EDI policies come from higher levels of university administrations and fall short of a more transformative understanding of decolonizing education, and of working toward present-day goals of social justice such as the distribution of wealth, opportunities, and privileges within society. The 2022 Divest McGill campaign foregrounded these overarching goals with the slogan "Democratize, Divest, Decolonize," which aimed to show the interconnection between democratizing university administrations, divesting from fossil fuel energies, and decolonizing teaching content and methods.[36] These critiques point to the role and power of university administrations in determining both the students' and the professors' experiences of academic freedom in universities. While administrative decisions impact students and professors immensely, the most visible clashes have taken place between students and their professors. Students have thus increasingly made direct claims to professors to change what is being taught and how the university is being administered, aiming toward an overarching aim of social justice.

---

32 Angélique Willkie, "Chair of the President's Task Force on Anti-Black Racism," 2022, www.concordia.ca/provost/initiatives/task-force-anti-black-racism.html.

33 "McGill University Equity, Diversity & Inclusion (EDI) Strategic Plan 2020–2025," www.mcgill.ca/equity/files/equity/mcgill_strategic_edi_plan_2020-20251.pdf.

34 Arnaud Bernadet and Martin Drapeau, "EDI, la 'business' de la vertu universitaire," *Le Devoir*, January 28, 2023, www.ledevoir.com/opinion/idees/779593/inclusion-edi-la-business-de-la-vertu-universitaire.

35 Yves Gingras and Arnaud Bernadet, "La mise au pas de la recherche," *La Presse*, November 18, 2022, www.lapresse.ca/debats/opinions/2022-11-18/la-mise-au-pas-de-la-recherche.php.

36 Divest McGill, "Occupy McGill," www.divestmcgill.ca/occupymcgill.

Academic Freedom, No-Platforming, and Cancel Culture

It has not been the substance of these demands as much as the methods that have been perceived as a restriction of academic freedom, though some academics might feel that any effort to orient their teaching material and research is displaced. Especially controversial is the practice of no-platforming, when students block an individual from speaking at a university based on their moral or political views. This practice emerged in the UK in the 1970s, as a reaction to the rise of a far-right and fascist political party (the National Front) attempting to recruit students on university grounds.[37] Student groups argued that they should be denied a platform on campus, which led some universities, upon the suggestion of student unions, to adopt a "no-platform policy" for far-right groups.

While the practice was already criticized back then, these debates erupted once more in the UK in the 2010s when speakers were prevented from using a platform because of their Islamophobic discourse.[38] The use of this method by students gave rise to similar criticisms in Quebec and the UK, and the UK Parliament also passed a bill on academic freedom entitled the Higher Education (Freedom of Speech) Act of 2021, with Article 1 specifically demanding that universities protect the free speech of invited speakers on campus grounds.

Opponents of the method contend that it is fundamentally contrary to the principle of open public discourse that lies at the heart of a democracy.[39] However, no-platforming is not seen by all as an affront to academic freedom. Some supporters argue that it can be justified as a harm prevention measure,[40] and others contend that the intellectual rigor demanded by universities already excludes speakers who are not vetted by the academic

37 Evan Smith, *No Platform: A History of Anti-fascism, Universities and the Limits of Free Speech* (Abingdon: Routledge, 2020).

38 Smith, *No Platform.*

39 Judith Suissa and Alice Sullivan, "How Can Universities Promote Academic Freedom? Insights from the Front Line of the Gender Wars," *Impact* 27 (2022): 2.

40 Arianne Shahvisi, "Privileges and Responsibilities Regarding Speech on Campus," in *The Value and Limits of Academic Speech: Philosophical, Political, and Legal Perspectives*, ed. Donald Alexander Downs and Chris W. Surprenant (London: Routledge, 2018), 266.

community,[41] an argument that will be further explored in the following section of this chapter.

While they can overlap, no-platforming is distinct from the more American phenomenon of "call-out culture," sometimes also called "cancel culture," though the use of this term implicitly expresses a negative perception of the phenomenon.[42] "Canceling," as opposed to no-platforming, is a more widespread action or reaction. It refers to the act of withdrawing support for public figures, and denotes "a form of online shaming on social media platforms."[43] It is the fear of being "canceled" that often leads to the self-censorship referred to at the onset of this chapter. It is worth asking if the deplatforming of a speaker ever occurs without a parallel movement of "canceling" the speaker on social media, but it is important to conceptually separate these two processes. Conflating the practice of no-platforming with "cancel culture" obscures some valid demands made by student activists. Journalist Willa Holt has argued that the focus on cancel culture foregrounds the danger of researchers being censored by a reactionary student body, without acknowledging the issues that led to the deplatforming taking place.[44] No-platforming and the social justice demands of students become equated with censorship, further antagonizing relations between students and their professors and administrations.

With social media facilitating transnational networks of activism, contemporary student demands in Quebec are informed by these global trends. Disentangling these influences shows how the apparent tension between academic freedom and social justice may be conflating the methods of no-platforming and the phenomenon of "canceling" with the substantive demand of decolonizing higher education. Keeping these histories in mind, the next section attempts to ease this tension by positing that academic freedom per definition can include social justice demands.

---

41 Robert Mark Simpson and Amia Srinivasan, "No Platforming," in *Academic Freedom*, ed. Jennifer Lackey (Oxford: Oxford University Press, 2018), 186.

42 Ligaya Mishan, "The Long and Tortured History of Cancel Culture," *New York Times*, December 3, 2020, www.nytimes.com/2020/12/03/t-magazine/cancel-culture-history.html.

43 Sara Atske, "Americans and 'Cancel Culture': Where Some See Calls for Accountability, Others See Censorship, Punishment," *Pew Research Center: Internet, Science & Tech*, May 19, 2021, www.pewresearch.org/internet/2021/05/19/americans-and-cancel-culture-where-some-see-calls-for-accountability-others-see-censorship-punishment/.

44 Holt, "Quebec's 'Cancel Culture' Debate Misses the Point."

Redefining Academic Freedom and Its Obligations

Academic freedom is usually defined in the 1997 UNESCO Recommendation Concerning the Status of Higher Education Teaching Personnel as "the right, without constriction by prescribed doctrine, to freedom of teaching and discussion, freedom in carrying out research and disseminating the results thereof, freedom to express freely their opinion about the institution or system in which they [higher education teaching personnel] work, freedom from institutional censorship and freedom to participate in professional or representative academic bodies."[45] Quebec's Bill 32 (An Act Respecting Academic Freedom in the University Sector 2022) relies on this definition.[46]

It is clear from this definition that the protection of academic freedom overlaps with other concepts, such as the freedom of expression, institutional autonomy, or the right to disseminate knowledge. Around the world, these rights have been used to defend academics against undue pressures, especially where there are no provisions targeting the protection of teaching and research. As other contributions in this volume show, the debate around student movements situates itself in a much larger constellation of issues around academic freedom and the pressures it endures from governmental and corporate forces. But academic freedom is more than the sum of its parts. It is a right vested in a group and in individuals belonging to this group. This right also entails obligations. Indeed, the UNESCO definition's preamble states that "higher-education teaching personnel, like all other citizens, is expected to endeavor to enhance the observance in society of the cultural, economic, social, civil and political rights of all peoples" and furthermore that higher education institutions need to "meet social and economic changes."[47] These elements inform the UNESCO member states' duty to "promote equality of opportunity and treatment for all in education at all levels, including the conditions under which it is given."[48]

---

45 UNESCO, "Recommendation Concerning the Status of Higher Education Teaching Personnel," 1997.

46 An Act Respecting Academic Freedom in the University Sector, 2022, vol. 21, www2.publicationsduquebec.gouv.qc.ca/dynamicSearch/telecharge.php?type=5&file=2022C21A.PDF.

47 UNESCO, "Recommendation Concerning the Status of Higher Education Teaching Personnel."

48 UNESCO, "Recommendation Concerning the Status of Higher Education Teaching Personnel."

A more recent definition of the concept from the 2020 European Higher Education Area's Statement on Academic Freedom reiterates these obligations. Beyond the freedom to learn, to teach, and to research without fear of reprisal, it adds that academic freedom "must be framed by rigorous scientific and professional standards, respect for the rights of others, ethical conduct and the awareness of the impact of research on humans and their environment," additionally linking it to the necessity of equitable access and accountability for public funds.[49] These seemingly disparate values are to be taken comprehensively, as none individually guarantees academic freedom. For example, institutional autonomy may only reflect the transfer of responsibilities from public authorities to higher education institutions, without securing the protection of academic freedom.[50] This autonomy must therefore be paired with public accountability, such as financial transparency in the disbursement of public funds for research.[51]

The obligations framing academic freedom are particularly helpful to understand the social justice claims of some student movements in Quebec, specifically the value of equitable access—both the equitable access to education, and to the academic profession. For many, meaningful academic freedom requires equitable access to the academic community. This is premised on the idea that if only some individuals can become university researchers, the freedom they exercise in their capacity as academics is somewhat vitiated because of the lack of freedom of other individuals to become part of this community. Indeed, while academic freedom is a collective right, access to this group is still defined by power structures that often reflect racial inequalities in society.[52] If the obligation of equitable access is to be taken seriously, it should therefore include working against barriers of access that are created by societal inequalities, working toward what philosopher Miranda

49 Rome Ministerial Communiqué, *Statement on Academic Freedom* (Rome: European Higher Education Area, 2020), http://ehea.info/Upload/Rome_Ministerial_Communique_Annex_I.pdf.

50 Pavel Zgaga, "Reconsidering University Autonomy and Governance: From Academic Freedom to Institutional Autonomy," in *University Governance and Reform: Policy, Fads, and Experience in International Perspective*, ed. Hans G. Schuetze, William Bruneau, and Garnet Grosjean (New York: Palgrave Macmillan), 19.

51 Klaus D. Beiter, Terence Karran, and Kwadwo Appiagyei-Atua, "Academic Freedom and Its Protection in the Law of European States," *European Journal of Comparative Law and Governance* 3 (2016): 273.

52 Bacevic, "Epistemic Injustice and Epistemic Positioning."

Fricker has named epistemic injustice, defined broadly as unfairness related to knowledge.

Someone suffers from epistemic injustice when their credibility is undermined by the biases of their audience.[53] Fricker describes two types of epistemic injustice: testimonial and hermeneutical. One suffers from testimonial injustice when their audience unfairly assesses their credibility because of a prejudice. Conversely, one suffers a hermeneutical injustice when there is a gap in collective understanding that "puts someone at an unfair disadvantage when it comes to making sense of their social experiences."[54] For example, this could happen when one is a victim of sexual harassment in a context where this concept is not recognized as valid. In academia, the systematic misrepresentation of a community's contribution to knowledge production can entail testimonial injustice, as it denotes the exclusion of certain communities from being perceived as capable of valuable knowledge production.

Ensuring equal access to the academic community could mean ensuring that potential participants are not disadvantaged by systemic biases that impair their credibility. This broader conceptualization of academic freedom necessitates a decolonial lens to understand how systemic biases against some communities are rooted in colonial histories of research hierarchies. Students and academics arguing that curricula should be revised to include more diverse voices and pedagogy thereby participate in an attempt to repair the epistemic injustice that has been created by colonial relationships that have systematically devalued or appropriated work done by racialized authors. Movements to decolonize higher education work toward breaking down these invisible barriers of access to institutions and to the academic community.

In Canada, this injustice is often expressed in the lack of consideration given to Indigenous ways of knowing. Indigenous academics at the Wilfrid Laurier University in Waterloo therefore suggest implementing an "Indigegogical" rather than a pedagogical approach to teaching materials. This method is centered on land-based education, Indigenous methodologies, and traditional teachings. It aims to be a "decolonizing practice that builds on the resurgence of Indigenous ways of knowing, teaching and

53 Miranda Fricker, "Introduction," in *Epistemic Injustice: Power and the Ethics of Knowing*, ed. Miranda Fricker (Oxford: Oxford University Press, 2007), 1.

54 Fricker, "Introduction," 2.

learning."[55] The value of equitable access to academic freedom could be construed as including redressing the epistemic wrongs suffered by Indigenous communities. Furthermore, if these communities' perspectives are omitted in defining what it means to be socially responsible as a researcher, these obligations might not be fully understood and fulfilled.

In abstraction, the argument presented here does not conflict with more conventional understandings of academic freedom, and many universities endorse the notion of increasing representation through their EDI policies. Beyond epistemic justice, the underlying obligations of academic freedom could also allow for the more divisive method of no-platforming. In line with this, Simpson and Srinivasan argue in favor of no-platforming as an exercise of the duty incumbent on academics in the promotion of academic freedom.

As a right vested in a professional community, many consider that academic freedom requires academic work of a certain standard of quality, which is defined by peers.[56] For Simpson and Srinivasan, the purpose of academic freedom is not just to "protect the speech of academics, but also to protect academics' rights to determine which views and speakers have sufficient disciplinary credentials to receive a hearing in academic contexts."[57] Collective quality control is part of academic freedom. Therefore, if a speaker is denied a platform based on the "negative appraisal of her credibility and the content of her views," it is not an affront to the intellectual freedom of the institution. Universities already routinely exclude the speech of nonexperts from academic platforms to ensure the pursuit of disciplinary expertise.[58] This process does not take place without intense debate, as disagreements within the academic community about disciplinary expertise are part of the development of this expertise. This can be permissible because effective research and teaching "requires that communicative privileges be given

55 Wilfrid Laurier University, "Centre for Indigegogy," www.wlu.ca/academics/faculties/faculty-of-social-work/centre-for-indigegogy/index.html.

56 Robert Post, *Democracy, Expertise, and Academic Freedom a First Amendment Jurisprudence for the Modern State* (New Haven: Yale University Press, 2012); Milica Popovic, Liviu Matei, and Daniele Joly, *Changing Understandings of Academic Freedom in the World at a Time of Pandemic* (Vienna: Global Observatory on Academic Freedom, 2022), 57.

57 Simpson and Srinivasan, "No Platforming," 186.

58 Simpson and Srinivasan, "No Platforming," 198.

to some and not others, based on people's disciplinary competence."[59] This crucially distinguishes academic freedom from freedom of expression. Free speech extends to all forms of expression, while academic freedom does not.[60] Conflating free speech and academic freedom entails that all opinions are equally legitimate, which can undermine the scientific authority of academics.

This view supports no-platforming in instances where, after student demands, disciplinary experts confirm that the speaker does not fulfill the required standards, even if the latter remains debated.[61] However, it is harder to defend this practice in cases where the disciplinary standards remain deeply contested. In these cases, the controversy revolves around "who gets to claim and wield disciplinary authority,"[62] and ultimately on who has the most compelling argument. While these instances often result from student demands (and sometimes from professors' as well), this should not discredit them. Students, especially at the graduate level, are part of the academic community, albeit with different rights and obligations than fully fledged researchers. Though their voices may be less well placed to understand ways in which a discipline may grow, they also have a legitimate role to play in the formation of disciplinary standards. They may be less driven by the "disciplinary inertia and methodological conservatism"[63] that can affect their teachers and institutions, as shown by the slow reaction of universities to answer demands to remove colonial symbols from their campuses. Student protests are as old as the academic institution itself, with students historically raising issues that previous generations have overlooked.[64] Though they are not experts, they can help the growth of their disciplines by suggesting heretofore ignored views in the teaching materials, and by

59 Simpson and Srinivasan, "No Platforming," 196.

60 Robert Quinn, "What Is Academic Freedom?" *Alexander von Humboldt Foundation*, 2021, www.humboldt-foundation.de/en/explore/newsroom/dossier-philipp-schwartz-initiative/what-is-academic-freedom.

61 Simpson and Srinivasan, "No Platforming," 199.

62 Simpson and Srinivasan, "No Platforming," 203.

63 Simpson and Srinivasan, "No Platforming," 204.

64 Comité école et société, *Réflexion Sur La Liberté Académique Incluant Les Enjeux Du Racisme et de La Discrimination Systémiques* (Montreal: FNEEQ-CSN, 2021), https://fneeq.qc.ca/wp-content/uploads/2021-11-17_Dossier-Liberte%CC%81-acade%CC%81mique_CF2.pdf.

"demanding less attention be given to views that should in fact no longer be taken seriously."[65]

Student activism also knows excesses and its methods are not always conducive to a productive redefinition of disciplinary standards. However, the quickness of public opinion in defending academic freedom against students' actions too often displays an indifference to the systemic discrimination at hand and the reasonableness of students' demands. If we adopt a definition of academic freedom that foregrounds the obligations of equitable access and of safeguarding disciplinary expertise, it is possible to understand student movements to decolonize academia and to prevent the platforming of some speakers as part of fulfilling these obligations. Proponents of a narrower definition of academic freedom that does not foreground any type of obligation may see this tendency as unduly constraining academics' freedom to teach. The next section argues that even a narrower definition of academic freedom does not conflict with the aims of epistemic justice.

Responding to Objections to a Broad Definition of Academic Freedom

Advocates of a narrow definition of academic freedom might argue that overexpanding its conceptualization would be detrimental to its protection, including through legislative action. Furthermore, they might hold that epistemic justice and academic freedom have fundamentally different aims and should thus be pursued in parallel but separately.

Academic freedom historically protects institutions and their actors from undue influence by the state.[66] Some might argue that it is not the universities' role to work toward justice and equitable access—those goals are better tackled by legislatures and the judiciary, or at least by university administrations rather than faculty members. Epistemic justice can be understood as falling within the broader duty of the state to ensure political freedom rather than specifically universities. For Fricker, epistemic justice is a condition for political freedom because an individual suffering from an unjust lack of credibility is unable to contest violations of their freedoms. They will

65 Simpson and Srinivasan, "No Platforming," 204.
66 Quinn, "What Is Academic Freedom?"

lack the fair treatment needed to prove that their rights have been violated. Epistemic justice is thus "a compound constitutive condition not only of contestation, but of non-domination."[67] In this sense, it might be argued that working toward conditions for political freedom is an important goal for public institutions including higher education, but not necessarily congruent with or even related to academic freedom.

Tasking universities with the goal of epistemic justice might itself seem an undue influence on their role in supporting the development of knowledge, a support that tends to be portrayed as amoral and unbiased. This perception is misguided—though universities are independent, funding bodies such as companies or governments influence the directions in which knowledge develops by granting funding to specific topics. Behind these funding decisions are moral convictions as well. A recent (and problematic) example is the *Programme d'appui* à *la laïcité*,[68] which provides grants to researchers studying secularism under the condition that their research promotes the Quebec model as defined by the statute An Act Respecting the Secular Nature of the State, and that it generates "positive outcomes for the government of Quebec."[69]

Positing that universities should not take on the role of pursuing justice therefore obscures the fact that academic pursuits are taking place within a society's evolving norms, where different freedoms are balanced against one another. The definition of academic freedom expands and constricts depending on the context, but it is flexible and intersects with many other rights. Foregrounding its obligations highlights that it not only includes negative liberties (to be free from restrictions from the state, for example), but also positive ones: to be free to determine disciplinary standards, or free to ensure equitable access to the academic community.[70] In that sense, the pursuit of epistemic justice can be one of the positive obligations inherent to one's belonging to the academic community—or could at least be considered

67 Fricker, "Epistemic Justice as a Condition of Political Freedom," 1324.

68 Secularism Support Program—my translation.

69 Gouvernement du Québec, "Programme d'appui à la laïcité," November 16, 2022, www.quebec.ca/gouvernement/politiques-orientations/laicite-etat/programme-dappui-a-la-laicite.

70 See the report *Réflexion sur la liberté académique incluant les enjeux du racisme et de la discrimination systémiques* by the Fédération nationale des enseignantes et des enseignants du Québec (FNEEQ) for a useful and detailed examination of the positive and negative liberties inherent to academic freedom in the context of systemic discrimination.

as a liberty that some institutions or individuals can willingly take. While it is not a primary aim of academic freedom, it is also not in opposition to it and can be pursued as a parallel goal. It is important not to create a hierarchy between those freedoms—and be wary of polarizing discourses that cast them as conflicting values.

The Quebec public debate portrays students demanding social and epistemic justice as directly impairing the academic freedom of their professors. This picture obscures the complex dynamics that exist between university administrations and their teaching staff. Indeed, the university is already a place where institutional frameworks have been developed to work against epistemic biases and toward epistemic justice in the form of EDI policies of institutions. These policies have been criticized because they require researchers to include in their inquiries criteria that can seem extraneous to their fields.[71] But this minimizes the extent to which failure to have an eye to the obligations of EDI creates the risk that the current norm in academia will be maintained.[72] This status quo is one where, if nothing else, there are still wide inequalities in the representation of minorities in academic positions of power,[73] and where systemic racism continues to create barriers to higher education in Quebec.[74] Of course, it is also important to remember that increasing representation of marginalized communities is only one of the many ways to improve this status quo and that an overemphasis on this method risks an essentialization of identities that could arguably be detrimental to a truly decolonized university space. Still, the tension between inclusion and epistemic justice is a productive one.

Conclusion

Contextualizing student movements in their transnational influences, expanding a definition of academic freedom to include epistemic justice,

71 Gingras and Bernadet, "La mise au pas de la recherche."

72 Rémi Quirion, "Réplique: Réflexion sur le lien entre science et société," *La Presse*, December 8, 2022, www.lapresse.ca/debats/opinions/2022-12-08/replique/reflexion-sur-le-lien-entre-science-et-societe.php.

73 Bacevic, "Epistemic Injustice and Epistemic Positioning: Towards an Intersectional Political Economy."

74 "Des actions pour promouvoir l'accès des communautés noires aux professions de la santé," *UdeM Nouvelles*, May 12, 2022, https://nouvelles.umontreal.ca/article/2022/09/20/des-actions-pour-promouvoir-l-acces-des-communautes-noires-aux-professions-de-la-sante/.

and recognizing students as agents in defining disciplinary standards might help reconcile the two sides of the debate presented at the onset of this chapter. Both sides can benefit from a broader understanding of academic freedom. Academics protesting perceived censorship might be able to redirect more specific criticism at when and where disciplinary standards should be changed. Alternatively, those arguing that there is a false sense of crisis might gain from reflecting on the legitimate demands to decommission certain symbols, words, and even authors. This might help defuse the adversarial relationship that has been created between students, teaching staff, and university administrations, and refocus the discussion on how to move forward. Thankfully, a number of voices, both students' and professors', suggest ways in which all actors can work together to prevent further polarization of the debate and collectively define the values that higher education institutions should promote.[75]

75 Jaafari et al., *Avis Jeunesse*; Alexandre Beaupré-Lavallée, "Academic Freedoms: We Need to Fix This Ourselves," *University Affairs*, April 23, 2021, www.universityaffairs.ca/opinion/its-never-just-academic/academic-freedoms-we-need-to-fix-this-ourselves/.

Chapter 11

The Simultaneous, Crucial Pursuit of Academic Freedom and Equity, Diversity, and Inclusion through a Relational Approach

Angela Campbell[1]

Academic freedom is anchored in origin and purpose to the protection of unorthodox ideas and minority perspectives—and, by extension, to the holders of those perspectives—within institutions of higher learning. This protection is understood as essential to the pursuit of knowledge and inquiry, the goal that lies at the heart of knowledge discovery, production, and dissemination. Contemporary conversations about academic freedom have, however, pitched it as competing with institutional obligations to uphold and promote the rights of underrepresented groups on university campuses, notably via equity, diversity, and inclusion (EDI) initiatives. Hence, a core question that challenges contemporary universities is whether, and under what circumstances, academic freedom might be bridled to prevent or halt harm. This question can be further finessed by exploring who bears vulnerability in campus contexts and interrogating whether universi-

1 I am deeply indebted to McGill DCL candidate Vishakha Wijenayake for sterling research and feedback that helped develop this chapter. I also thank the editors of this collection, Frédéric Mégret and Nandini Ramanujam, for inviting me to be a contributing author and for their insightful comments on earlier drafts. I further acknowledge research funding provided by McGill University.

ties ought to intervene in curbing the exercise of academic freedom when the harm in question affects socially oppressed groups and whether such harm should be interpreted with enough breadth to tolerate instances of injury to feelings or the compromise of emotional and psychological safety.

Faced with such a question, typically arising in the context of fraught campus controversies, universities face a seemingly intractable debate between two opposing camps. A first posits that ideas and their expression can inflict real harm and violence, which in turn warrants institutional intervention, especially but not exclusively when members of socially oppressed groups experience harm.[2] EDI, centered on the goal of promoting access to and belonging within institutions of higher education for members of these groups,[3] can thus be invoked as a shield against expression understood to be harmful. An opposing view holds that a university must reflect openness to and curiosity about all concepts and arguments, even those that

2 See, e.g., Jennifer Saul, "Beyond Just Silencing: A Call for Complexity in Discussions of Academic Free Speech," in *Academic Freedom*, ed. Jennifer Lackey (Oxford: Oxford University Press, 2018), 119; Mary Kate McGowan, "On Political Correctness, Microaggressions, and Silencing in the Academy," in *Academic Freedom*, ed. Jennifer Lackey (Oxford: Oxford University Press, 2018), 136; Bernard Shapiro, "The Role of Universities in a Changing Culture," in *Academic Freedom and the Inclusive University*, ed. Sharon E. Kahn and Dennis Pavlich (Vancouver: University of British Columbia, 2001), 30; Saba Fatima, "I Know What Happened to Me: The Epistemic Harms of Microaggressions," in *Microaggressions and Philosophy*, ed. Lauren Freeman and Jeanine Weekes Schroer (London: Routledge, 2020), 163; Azeezat Johnson and Remi Joseph-Salisbury, "'Are You Supposed to Be in Here?' Racial Microaggressions and Knowledge Production in Higher Education," in *Dismantling Race in Higher Education: Racism, Whiteness and Decolonising the Academy*, ed. Jason Arday and Heidi Safia Mirza (Cham: Springer, 2018), 143. It is worthwhile noting that calls to limit academic freedom do not only stem from those who support the rights of minorities and excluded communities. See, e.g., "Map: Where Critical Race Theory Is under Attack," *Education Week*, September 2, 2021, www.edweek.org/policy-politics/map-where-critical-race-theory-is-under-attack/2021/06.

3 This objective is questioned not only by scholars concerned with EDI as contributing to mission drift within universities but also by critical scholars who speak to the challenges of implementing meaningful EDI programs, some of whom suggest that a university's EDI efforts seek to mask or dilute the discriminations faced by members of disadvantaged communities while failing to take the transformative actions needed to root out structural biases. See Sara Ahmed, *On Being Included: Racism and Diversity in Institutional Life* (Durham: Duke University Press, 2012); Richard Hall et al., "Struggling for the Anti-racist University: Learning from an Institution-wide Response to Curriculum Decolonisation," *Teaching in Higher Education* 26 (2021): 902; Ebony Omotola McGee, "Interrogating Structural Racism in STEM Higher Education," *Educational Researcher* 49 (2020): 633; M. Neelika Jayawardane and Rinaldo Walcott, "Diversity Efforts in Universities Are Nothing but Façade Painting," *Al Jazeera*, May 7, 2021, www.aljazeera.com/opinions/2021/5/7/diversity-efforts-in-universities-are-nothing-but-facade-painting; Paul Gorski, "Avoiding Racial Equity Detours," *Educational Leadership* 76 (2019): 56.

might be subjectively or objectively offensive.[4] For this group, academic life must accept the free exchange of ideas that encourages or at least permits these ideas to be argued, tested, and debated, regardless of their propensity to engender controversy.

Advocates on each side of this debate commonly present their positions with an absolutism and conviction that can be jarring. Particularly striking is the sense one gets, listening to or reading these advocates, that theirs is the position marked by moral superiority and absolute truth. Proponents do not seem shy to show disdain for those with more nuanced or contesting positions. In consequence, the debate is oversimplified, with each side risking self-caricature, compromising the important arguments they each make.

Often university constituents turn to those at their helm, seeking decisive intervention. Yet while university leaders—presidents and principals, provosts, and deans—are charged with listening to and carefully considering varying sides of a debate, in all but the simplest of cases they cannot altogether set aside one line of argument in preference to another. That is, they do not have the prerogative of dismissing arguments promulgated about academic freedom, the latter being a core value animating the mission of higher education. Neither can universities ignore or refrain from acting to address historic institutional practices that have perpetuated structural inequities by limiting opportunities for higher education and social advancement for historically dominated groups. Both of these realities—the need to preserve academic freedom and the imperative to embed equity—matter to universities, even when they seem to be at odds. How, then, can academic institutions pay attention and give credence to divergent positions on this issue while avoiding the trap of prioritizing one over the other?[5]

---

4 See, e.g., Joanna Williams, *Academic Freedom in an Age of Conformity: Confronting the Fear of Knowledge* (London: Palgrave Macmillan, 2016), 4. The author argues that speech codes, antiharassment policies, and equality and diversity initiatives, while well intentioned, have the effect of privileging intellectual safety and comfort over academic freedom. See also William M. Bowen, Michael Schwartz, and Lisa Camp, *End of Academic Freedom: The Coming Obliteration of the Core Purpose of the University* (Charlotte: Information Age, 2014), 146: "Political correctness can give rise to scholarship that does not seek the truth (however conceived or defined) or even argues the issues, but rather increases the power and influence of particular moral, political, or individual positions or groups." John Fekete, "Academic Freedom versus the Intrusive University," in *Academic Freedom and the Inclusive University*, ed. Sharon E. Kahn and Dennis Pavlich (Vancouver: University of British Columbia, 2001), 78.

5 In Canada, academic freedom and EDI are issues recently positioned as competing with one another. See, e.g., Jessica Murphy, "Toronto Professor Jordan Peterson Takes on Gender-Neutral Pronouns," *BBC News*, November 4, 2016, www.bbc.com/news/world-us-canada-37875695; Konrad Yakabushi, "The

In this chapter, I argue for an approach that moves away from rights-based arguments, which have been centered in recent campus debates about academic freedom and EDI in North America. Within these debates, academic freedom and EDI have each been positioned as individual liberty and free speech rights tied to the autonomy and self-fulfillment of their respective holders set against the collective rights of a certain group or community and identity politics.[6] This framing of the debate as a competition of rights incites institutions to wade into the conflict by determining which of these prevails or trumps the other. The invariable result is an identification of winners and losers, which ultimately proves unhelpful to developing more nuanced, less polarized engagement on one of the toughest contemporary social challenges for today's Western universities.

What if, instead, our discussions about academic freedom and EDI distanced themselves from rights and instead zeroed in on *relationships*? Such an approach, which draws on feminist relational theory, would seek to identify connections deserving of protection and preservation in university settings.[7] It would at the same time foreground the obligations of different actors, accounting for the formal and informal power that they hold about each other. A relational understanding of rights and autonomy might thus permit greater nuance in situations where academic freedom and EDI appear to be in tension.

University of Ottawa Throws Academic Freedom under the Bus," *Globe and Mail*, October 21, 2020, www.theglobeandmail.com/opinion/article-the-university-of-ottawa-throws-academic-freedom-under-the-bus/; "Concordia Students Launch Petition Condemning Film Professor's Use of N-Word in Class", *CBC News*, August 6, 2020, www.cbc.ca/news/canada/montreal/concordia-film-professor-use-of-n-word-in-class-1.5676992. Of course, academic freedom also protects the development and expression of critical social perspectives that center antioppression theory and praxis. The point has emerged in American contexts where private or public interests are alleged to interfere with so-called social justice or "activist" scholarship. See, e.g., Margaret Sullivan, "Why It's So Important That UNC Trustees Give Nikole Hannah-Jones the Tenure She Deserves," *Washington Post*, June 29, 2021, www.washingtonpost.com/lifestyle/media/unc-nikole-hannah-jones-tenure/2021/06/28/cb51a03e-d82a-11eb-bb9e-70fda8c37057_story.html. Thus, while this chapter focuses on situations in which arguments arise over whether academic freedom and EDI appear unaligned, it acknowledges the reality that, in some circumstances, these values will be mutually nourishing.

6 Nadine Strossen, *Resisting Cancel Culture: Promoting Dialogue, Debate and Free Speech in the College Classroom* (Washington, DC: American Council of Trustees and Alumni, 2020); Fekete, "Academic Freedom versus the Intrusive University." For a nuanced reading of this rights-based analysis, see Judith Butler, "Exercising Rights: Academic Freedom and Boycott Politics," in *Who's Afraid of Academic Freedom?* ed. Akeel Bilgrami and Jonathan R. Cole (New York: Columbia University Press, 2019), 293.

7 See, e.g., Jennifer Nedelsky, *Law's Relations: A Relational Theory of Self, Autonomy, and Law* (Oxford: Oxford University Press, 2012).

Critical feminist scholars over several decades have developed theories of rights in relationships, which interrogate traditional liberal approaches to rights as tethered to individualism. Orthodox liberalism casts rights as invocable as political "trumps" that protect each of us from state or private encroachment, or as requiring a "balancing" when they compete with one another. By contrast, a relational interpretation of rights moves away from this atomistic understanding and sees the human capacity for autonomy and agency as necessarily dependent on, and existing within, social contexts and relationships. Developed from work that first emerged more than three decades ago, relational theory was originally understood as tied to feminist and care-based ethics.[8] Over time, concerns about essentializing experiences and identities along gender lines prompted a more refined discourse based on relationships and relationality.[9]

Understanding rights as existing within human relationships generates four principles that help examine the issues considered in this chapter. *First*, human agency can only be actualized in the context of healthy interpersonal relationships. As such, caring for those relationships so they are marked by trust, generosity, and empathy is essential to a fulsome expression and exercise of rights. In this way, relationships—rather than the individuals who are parties to them—are "at least the primary, if not the most fundamental, units of moral concern."[10] A *second* principle is related to the first. It posits that social relations will exert an impact on a person's ability to exercise agency.[11] Accordingly, while liberal theories position individuals as consistently already ready and able to exercise rights, relational perspectives cast each of us as dependent, vulnerable, and reliant vis-à-vis one another, such that our capacity for autonomy is tied to the broader notion of social inter-

8 Carol Gilligan, *In a Different Voice: Psychological Theory and Women's Development* (Cambridge, MA: Harvard University Press, 1982).

9 Nel Noddings, *Caring: A Relational Approach to Moral Education* (Berkeley: University of California Press, 2013), cited in Thaddeus Metz and Sarah Clark Miller, "Relational Ethics," in *The International Encyclopedia of Ethics*, ed. Hugh LaFollette (Hoboken: Wiley-Blackwell, 2016), 6.

10 Metz and Miller, "Relational Ethics," 7.

11 There is some debate here within the discipline about the extent to which social connections affect individual agency, with some philosophers taking the view that the former influences the latter and others arguing that the former is constituted of the other. See Marina Oshana, "Is Social-Relational Autonomy a Plausible Ideal?" in *Personal Autonomy and Social Oppression*, ed. Marina Oshana (London: Routledge, 2014), 3; John Christman, "Relational Autonomy, Liberal Individualism, and the Social Constitution of Selves," *Philosophical Studies: An International Journal for Philosophy in the Analytic Tradition* 117 (2004): 143.

dependence. *Third*, understanding rights as "socially embedded" or as existing "within relationship" calls for the explicit recognition of obligations as the necessary corollary of rights. As one author has stated, rights call for "answerability." In other words, one who holds rights also holds responsibilities.[12] Thus, both rights and responsibilities ought to be shaped with reference to the relationships in which they exist. *Fourth*, relational autonomy resists the precept that the sage exercise of judgment calls for logical and impartial moral reasoning, to the exclusion of emotion. Instead, proponents of relational theory intentionally make room for personal and emotional elements within analyses and decisions. As such, within a relational framework, the subjective (emotions, identities, experiences) will matter, especially as it shapes interpersonal connections.[13]

This chapter does not undertake to contest or further refine relational theories of rights. Instead, it draws on this conceptualization to propose an approach to contemporary academic freedom and EDI debates, which concerns itself first and foremost with the relationships that lie at the heart of the academic missions of Western universities: that is, producing, advancing, and disseminating knowledge through teaching and research.

Because I believe it is both more interesting and instructive to ground discussions about concepts and theoretical frameworks with reference to examples, I begin the essay (first section) with a case study. I use this case study throughout the text as a reference point to examine how a relational framework can guide—from both analytic and governance perspectives—approaches to academic freedom in higher education institutional settings. Thus, following the presentation of the case study, I discuss a principal relationship at the heart of many situations where academic freedom ostensibly clashes with EDI in a university setting: that between professor and students (second section). Here, I consider how an approach that aims to cultivate that relationship could inform our approach to academic freedom. Finally, I explore (third section) the feminist argument that rights are not only relational but also nestled within larger social frameworks. In higher education,

12 Andrea C. Westlund, "Rethinking Relational Autonomy," *Hypatia* 24 (2009): 28. According to the author, a key component of autonomy is the "the disposition to hold oneself answerable to external critical perspectives on one's action-guiding commitments."

13 Lucy-Ann Buckley, "Relational Theory and Choice Rhetoric in the Supreme Court of Canada," *Canadian Journal of Family Law* 29 (2015): 265.

the university provides that framework. I thus consider how universities might work to nourish positive professor–student relationships that foster learning and discovery even in circumstances of tension and controversy.

While I focus here on the professor–student relationship, I do not intend to suggest that this is the only or even the most important connection that deserves attention in debates emerging within and about higher education. Besides students and professors, myriad other groups—such as labor and student associations, alumni, parents, and external communities—have varied and intersecting connections with one another. These are connections that university leaders must appreciate and account for in developing and implementing university policies. For the purposes of this essay, however, I consider the parties that will have the most direct and immediate interest in questions arising from the case study presented on academic freedom and EDI. Moreover, as I have suggested earlier, the health of this relationship both depends on and stands to be affected by the university context in which it is situated.

Having set out this background, I turn to a discussion of the case study that will ground the analysis developed throughout the balance of this chapter.

Case Study

This case study is fictional. It draws on themes arising in several different incidents emergent in universities across North America, especially over the last decade or so. I have decided to build this case study on the issue of sexual violence as this topic relates to my disciplinary expertise and is one that can generate intense reactions and perspectives in higher learning settings. Having worked on sexual violence policies and their application in my home institution, I am aware of how challenging the issue can be in university settings. Moreover, while commonly framed as a gendered issue, sexual violence has transversal and intersectional implications; it is a topic that affects everyone, albeit in different ways.

With this rationale in mind, I invite the reader to consider the following scenario.

Professor X is a criminal law scholar and tenured professor. Part of her research focuses on so-called rape-shield laws, which exist in many Western jurisdictions.[14] These laws generally prohibit, in the context of criminal sexual assault trials, defense counsel from questioning a complainant about their sexual history. The laws seek to protect complainants who testify from being discredited through the introduction of evidence about their sexual past, which contemporary law deems irrelevant to determining the guilt or innocence of the accused.

Professor X's view on rape-shield laws goes against the grain. In her writing and teaching, she has expressed the view that these laws have the effect of denying procedural fairness to the accused. For Professor X, the defense's ability to adduce any evidence to show that the accused reasonably believed that the complaint consented to sexual activity should be admissible. This is true even if that evidence relates to the complainant's sexual history. Excluding that evidence, according to Professor X, is a denial of an accused's constitutional right to a fair trial.

Professor X's views have sometimes prompted lively debate in her class, "Criminal Justice 135." This year, things became intense. Initially, three of her students met with Professor X to present "a demand from students." They indicated that, because the professor's views on rape-shield laws are "triggering" to survivors of sexual assault, Professor X ought to skip this topic when it came time to teach it. The students presented an alternate "demand" should Professor X refuse the first. The alternate demand was framed as follows: teach the material factually and without reference to her own views on the matter.

Professor X thanked the students for raising their views, which she stated reflected those of some students she had taught years prior. She went on to state, "I will not be deviating from the manner in which I have taught this material in the past." The conversation ended there.

Shortly thereafter, the students wrote to Professor X's chair to request that a guest lecturer be brought in as a substitute for Professor X on the module in "Criminal Justice 135" related to sexual assault. The reply from the chair was cursory and indicated there would be no substitution of the instructor.

Students subsequently wrote an "Open Letter to the Students of Criminal Justice 135," which they circulated on social media. It read:

> Students of Criminal Justice 135: You are called to stand in solidarity with millions of sexual violence survivors worldwide, including those on

14 Criminal Code, RSC 1985, c C-46, s 276.

> our campus, whose sense of self-worth, safety, and truth is compromised by the likes of our instructor, Professor X. If Professor X had her way, the shreds of protection survivors have in the criminal justice system would be eviscerated. Professor X lacks empathy for those of us who are survivors. She invalidates us. She must not be allowed to teach us Criminal Justice 135, a mandatory course. By allowing Professor X to retain this teaching privilege, the university negates our basic right to safe and dignified learning spaces. We call on you to write the Chair to demand that Professor X be removed from teaching mandatory courses and that she be required to follow sensitivity training related to sexual violence and consent. Until that happens, we will wear black to Professor X's classes as a symbol of our grief. We call on you to join us.

Professor X learns of this social media campaign, which has received many "likes" and expressions of support. She connects with her department chair demanding that the university intervene to protect her reputation and support her mental health. She reveals that she herself is a survivor of a violent sexual assault during her undergraduate years. She claims to be unable to return to the classroom without demonstrated support from her university. She asks that the institution reprimand the students and require them to withdraw their open letter.

The Professor–Student Relationship

The most obvious relationship at stake in this case study is that between Professor X and her students. Here, a singular focus on rights—whether of the professor or her aggrieved learners—neglects the ramifications of the exercise of these rights. Notably, rights-based claims open minimal, if any, space for thinking concomitantly about the parties' duties vis-à-vis one another. Likewise, zeroing in on rights fails to consider the adverse ramifications of such claims, notably the potential instability that conflicting claims will invariably inject into the learning environment. A shift to a focus on the relationships among the protagonists is not only worthwhile but necessary for the learning environment in question to function as a site where healthy exchange and learning—even if marked by disagreement or discord—can occur.

What, then, would a shift away from concentrating on rights to a focus on relationships look like in this scenario? A relational approach to rights helps us identify two key elements that would support a way forward. A first calls for acknowledging and validating the experiences and emotions—in addition to the intellectual concepts—at play, through an approach and actions rooted in *empathy*. Second, relational perspectives require an analysis of rights through a lens that concomitantly examines the *responsibilities* of the parties to the relationship concerned. This two-pronged approach can be made more concrete by examining it with reference to the different players in the relationship at issue here.

Professor X

Professor X's manner of engagement with her students, as outlined in the case study, privileges her freedom to share, through her teaching, a controversial position that she formed through her research. Her right to take and communicate this position seems clearly within the remit of free expression and academic freedom. At the same time, her approach stands to undermine objectives core to the mission of higher education, namely, learning, discovery, testing new ideas, and advancing student knowledge and capacity. Arguably, by insisting on her right to impart her controversial views, especially if she is not at the same time acknowledging the impact of doing so on at least some of her students, she risks alienating those students and thus curtailing their learning.

By contrast, a relational approach would invite Professor X to consider her responsibilities in addition to her rights. Once aware that some of her students are not at ease with her argument on rape-shield legislation, a more promising approach would acknowledge students' differing views, emotions, experiences, and perspectives while providing a rationale for the professor's position on the subject matter.[15] This approach does not call for Professor X to abandon the topic or be silent about her views in its regard. But it does prompt a discussion with students about why the material is important. It should also nudge Professor X to think critically about pedagogy. That is,

15 For similar approaches, see Terri E. Givens, *Radical Empathy: Finding a Path to Bridging the Racial Divides* (London: Policy Press, 2021); Sigal Ben-Porath, "Campus Free Speech in Polarised Times," *Law, Culture and the Humanities* 19 (2020): 1.

knowing that at least some of her students are adversely affected by her take on the topic of rape-shield laws, a thoughtful approach would call for classroom techniques that encourage all students' fulsome engagement. Those techniques would proactively welcome students and facilitate their engagement within the learning space regardless of their views on the matter concern or whether these accord with their instructor's.

Further, a relational approach, which centers both rights and responsibilities, calls for reflection on how the exercise of one's rights will impact others.[16] For Professor X, this would mean considering how at least some survivors might interpret and be affected by her critique of rape-shield laws. Looking even further ahead, Professor X would be wise to consider her own resilience, given the predictable objections to her work. That is, while Professor X has the freedom to advance arguments some will find controversial or even distasteful, that freedom is not accompanied by a right to be shielded from pointed criticism. Of course, when such criticism moves into the terrain of bullying or harassment, protection may be in order. But leaning on academic freedom to justify the advancement of unorthodox arguments requires one also to be ready and willing to face foreseeable resistance and objection, even when the latter becomes loud, sharp, and public. And of course, it remains critical for those who bear the privilege and responsibility of university teaching to be aware of and sensitive to the evolving nature of the student body. Time and place will play a significant role in the scope of deference students will bring to their relationships with their courses and the people who deliver them. This means that instructors ought to be prepared for varying degrees of opening, questioning, and critique by students, which ought to be welcomed while also ensuring that students understand the importance of and deploy evidence-based argument and respectful engagement.

A focus on responsibilities also would facilitate recognition that an instructor who perseveres with an absolute focus on rights and freedoms might fall short of her own duties to her learners, the duty of faculty to

16 Although not from a relational approach, the following articles emphasize the importance of responsibility and duties of academics in the exercise of academic freedom: Heather Douglas, "Scientific Freedom and Social Responsibility," in *Science, Freedom and Democracy*, ed. Péter Hartl and Adam Tamas Tuboly (London: Routledge, 2021), 68; Stuart Chambers, "Academic Freedom Entails Both Individual and Social Responsibility," *Academic Matters*, January 14, 2021, https://academicmatters.ca/academic-freedom-entails-both-individual-and-social-responsibility/.

respect students' right to dignity and freedom of expression.[17] In our case study, Professor X's terse response to her students, and insistence on teaching her material in the manner to which she was accustomed, contributed to circumstances that stood to detract from the learning environment. The cascade of events that ensued from Professor X's initial encounter with her students would have the result of enmeshing all learners in the course in a potentially hostile classroom context, regardless of their individual views on rape-shield laws. It also risked creating a major distraction from a core principle of criminal justice, namely, the right of an accused person to robust protection from the state's bluntest instrument (penal law), which in most Western legal traditions is constitutionally enshrined. This is an irony given that Professor X's position was entirely rooted in concern for that principal.

A relational approach also might probe Professor X to consider her connections and duties to her discipline and to the professional field in which she trains her students. As a professor of criminal justice, Professor X has a responsibility to be mindful of the various circumstances and scenarios her students will encounter postgraduation. Although her teaching ought to be marked by diligence, care, and equity, Professor X would do her students no favors by leaving aside controversial topics or perspectives. Students of criminal justice must understand the rules of evidence and criminal procedure, even if some aspects of acquiring that understanding are difficult or troubling. It is thus crucial, in thinking about academic freedom, to situate analyses within collegial and disciplinary contexts, and the various networks and obligations that exist therein. A law professor has to teach, and a law student has to learn, core juridical doctrines and tenets. It is only by understanding and engaging with these doctrines and tenets that scholars and students alike can begin to think about them critically, assess whether they yield just outcomes, and work to transform them where they fail to do so.

Drawing on a relational approach, which at once creates space for recognizing divergent experiences and emotions while at the same time centering responsibilities alongside rights, Professor X stood to do better at centering her students' learning. This approach would have been possible regardless of Professor X's views on some of her student's critiques. Focusing on pre-

17 On academic freedom of students, see Bruce Macfarlane, *Freedom to Learn: The Threat to Student Academic Freedom and Why It Needs to Be Reclaimed* (London: Routledge, 2017).

serving her relationship with students, which is grounded in the vocation of teaching, Professor X could have demonstrated that her students' claims, rooted at least in part in emotion and experience, are worthy of being taken seriously in academic contexts. Further, while under no obligation to share her own identity and experience as a survivor, this factual element complicates the discourse that all too often, in the context of campus debates, sets up reductive "us vs. them" or "ally vs. foe" camps. As a result, the nuance and messiness inherent to human identity and human relationships risk being neglected, even though grappling with these complexities is a crucial part of the learning that can happen through rich and robust campus dialogue.

Professor X's Students

Having looked at how a relational approach might have shaped Professor X's engagement with her students, I turn now to the converse question: How would an emphasis on relationship have affected the students' ability to preserve their basic right to safe and dignified learning spaces?[18] Before delving into this question, I think it is helpful to draw a distinction between formal and informal power. *Formal* power refers to the power that accompanies institutional positions that afford knowledge, access, and influence related to institutional governance and formal decision-making within institutions.[19] *Informal* power refers to the influence exercised outside of institutional systems and can be equally or more impactful than formal power in affecting outcomes.[20] A good example of formal power within higher education settings is the power a graduate supervisor exercises when she assesses her student's dissertation or writes a reference letter for that student. A good example of informal power is the influence that can be exerted by students through petitioning institutional actors and by relying on mainstream or social media campaigns to shine a light on institutional challenges and shortcomings.

18 John Palfrey, *Safe Spaces, Brave Spaces* (Cambridge, MA: MIT Press, 2018); Karin K. Flensner and Marie Von der Lippe, "Being Safe from What and Safe for Whom? A Critical Discussion of the Conceptual Metaphor of 'Safe Space,'" *Intercultural Education* 30 (2019): 275; Eamonn Callan, "Education in Safe and Unsafe Spaces," *Philosophical Inquiry in Education* 24 (2016): 64.

19 José M. Peiró and José L. Meliá, "Formal and Informal Interpersonal Power in Organisations: Testing a Bifactorial Model of Power in Role-Sets," *Applied Psychology: An International Review* 52 (2003): 14.

20 Peiró and Meliá, "Formal and Informal Interpersonal Power in Organisations," 14.

When thinking about the professor–student relationships, some might reject the proposition that students hold any power and that they could be compelled to bear responsibility to sustain the health of this relationship. Those who hold this view might even use terms such as "institutional gaslighting" and "victim-blaming" if asked to identify the obligations of students in the Professor X case study. There is some political utility to terms like this; they draw attention to and underscore the strength of emotion and conviction at play in a debate. Less helpful are absolutist or incendiary labels that serve to depict power as existing solely in its formal, institutionalized form. That approach does little to cultivate critical campus relationships, especially in situations of controversy and conflict. It also can minimize the actual power of the student body at large and its ability to publicize episodes to which it objects.

Without question, students have far less formal power than their professors. At the same time, students do enjoy some formal power vis-à-vis faculty, for example, in the context of assessing their instructors in the context of course and teaching evaluations. They also might enjoy considerable informal power.[21] Students' political capital and energy have allowed them to lead social movements over time.[22] Thus, while students are the beneficiaries of the relationships of trust and a duty of care in higher educational settings, they also hold responsibilities within this context.

Student responsibility translates, in the context of the case study presented here, into a duty to engage with their instructor with empathy and openness to hearing her perspectives.[23] Just as students have every right to expect respect and civility in their interactions with professors, the reverse is true. Here, a focus on relationships could have spurred the students to

21 The issue of whether a faculty member is tenured or untenured will also have some influence over the degree of power—be it formal or informal—students might exercise in her regard. See Saul, "Beyond Just Silencing," 120.

22 James Paterson, "Student Activism on the Rise," *NEA Today*, March 9, 2021, www.nea.org/advocating-for-change/new-from-nea/student-activism-rise; Our Turn National Action Plan, "Students for Consent Culture," www.sfccanada.org/action-plan; Karen Bartko and Emily Mertz, "Edmonton Students Rallying for Action on Climate Change Converge on Alberta Legislature," *Global News*, September 27, 2019, https://globalnews.ca/news/5959833/edmonton-student-climate-change-protest/.

23 I acknowledge the persuasive critique that has been levied against this proposition, underscoring the inequity of asking students who are racialized or otherwise from minority groups to show empathy and civility in the face of injustice. See Heather Igloliorte et al., "Killjoys, Academic Citizenship and the Politics of Getting Along," *Topia* 38 (2017): 187; Chanda Prescod-Weinstein, "Tone Policing & the Sound of Equality in STEM," *Medium*, December 5, 2019.

begin by explaining their goals, that is, to learn the subject matter in question within a setting that did not leave them feeling psychologically vulnerable. Furthermore, students could have asked Professor X about the rationale for her controversial views on rape-shield laws, thereby demonstrating curiosity about Professor X and a presumption of good faith.

Put simply, like Professor X, the students missed the chance to frame the challenge before them as circulating around a common goal: to teach and learn in a way that at once preserved the professor's academic freedom and the students' psychological safety. As witnessed in many other campus debates, the entrenchment of each party's own position deepened the undermining of the other's ability to enjoy their respective freedoms. An alternate approach, focused on conciliation through caring for the necessary connection between the parties, could well have generated a richer outcome for all that would have furthered the academic goals in this setting.

The social media dimension of the case study is also important. The tactic of "calling out" or denunciation through public platforms is not new or unusual. While social media can contribute to participatory democracy and the advancement of social justice in some critical ways, it rarely allows for nuanced or contextualized interaction. And while calls to organize through social media can be effective at spurring quick and powerful mobilization, in the situation under study here, the costs of this rapidity merit reflection.

The drafters of the open letter were entitled to express themselves as they did. Likewise, any student who heeded the open letter's call to wear black to class was within their right to do so. While the extent to which students enjoy academic freedom remains relatively undertheorized—at least compared to faculty members—students have a right to freedom of expression, conscience, and association. This is the right Professor X's students exercised. But the way they did so stood to wield lasting and potentially irreparable damage on their relationships with a professor. It also carried a real risk of dividing students within the class, some of whom might disagree with the framing of the open letter. Those students might deeply resent being forced either to conform by wearing black to class or to appear to support Professor X by not doing so. Among those students, some might perceive the cost of making this choice as too great and simply abstain from attending class. Hence, the result is a compromise of at least some students' freedom to learn, and that is problematic.

An approach focused on relationships should not be seen as curtailing student power in this case. Instead, it would force a recognition that students' freedoms are best preserved by recognizing the social context in which they learn and engage with one another and their professors. That is, by leaning exclusively on the "basic right to safe and dignified learning spaces" to ground a call for Professor X's removal or silence, the students' open letter pitted their rights and their professor's academic freedom as zero-sum, impossibly coexisting. That oversimplified approach removed the potential for creative, conciliatory problem-solving that could have been achieved through a focus on the relationship between the parties. In turn, a relational approach would have made space for explicitly recognizing the deep emotions at play and the responsibilities of each party to achieve the objective of creating an effective and psychologically safe environment for teaching and learning.

What's more, a relational approach could acknowledge the reality that vulnerability is transversal and can exist even for the party that seemingly holds greater power in each context (here, Professor X). Vulnerability also exists for those affected by conflict despite not being the protagonists of the storyline (here, all students in "Criminal Justice 135"). A recognition of vulnerability and frailty as a universal complicates the analysis but is essential to meaningful and textured approaches to human relationships that seek to avoid or mitigate harm. In this context, such an approach makes room to recognize Professor X, the apparent antagonist, as herself a member of the same group—survivors—that the letter-writers claimed to represent. All of this is of course complicated and more difficult to reconcile conceptually than the predominant approach of the day, which calls upon us to look at a situation and determine which parties' rights should prevail. But the methodology proposed herein promises deeper authenticity, care, and reflection of true human experiences and conditions, and of the varied, and sometimes ephemeral, forms of power that can exist in institutions of higher education.[24]

24 Martha Albertson Fineman, "The Vulnerable Subject," *Yale Journal of Law and Feminism* 20 (2008): 1; Martha Albertson Fineman, "The Vulnerable Subject and the Responsive State," *Emory Law Journal* 60 (2010): 251; Martha Albertson Fineman, "The Limits of Equality: Vulnerability and Inevitable Inequality," in *Research Handbook on Feminist Jurisprudence*, ed. Robin West and Cynthia G. Bowman (Elgar Online, 2019); Nina A. Kohn, "Vulnerability Theory and the Role of Government," *Yale Journal of Law and Feminism* 26 (2014): 1. See also Judith Butler, Zeynep Gambetti, and Leticia Sabsay, eds., *Vulnera-*

Social Frameworks

Rights are not exercised solely within private settings and relationships. They also exist within—and their capacity to be enjoyed is affected by—social and institutional frameworks. This reality is always true, regardless of whether that framework is a family, the workplace, or a public institution. In the context explored here, it is the university.

Thus, for the purposes of the analyses traced throughout this essay, it is critical to look beyond Professor X and her students' direct interactions to also consider the institutional context that frames this relationship.[25] The university, while not a party to the professor–student relationship, plays a critical role in shaping it. Notably the university setting gives students and their professors access to one another. The university also determines the obligations and freedoms of these parties, both in the abstract and in relation to each other. Finally, the university has a duty to intervene, course-correct, and sometimes even impose sanctions where this is warranted to protect the interests of a party whose rights have been compromised, pursuant to appropriate processes. For these reasons, universities cannot be understood as bystanders to academic freedom discussions and controversies that unfold in teaching or research settings. Rather, universities have a key role to play in such situations and must take up this role in a proactive, principled, and procedurally oriented manner so as to uphold the relationships that are crucial to their academic mission.

Most likely would agree that universities have some role to play, and some responsibilities to shoulder, in relation to questions pertaining to academic freedom. When controversy arises, campus actors—regardless of the position they espouse—often will look to university leadership for answers and actions. There is thus some consensus about the existence of institutional roles in such situations. Consider the case study: Professor X and the students alike called for institutional action to support their interests and position.

---

bility in Resistance (Durham: Duke University Press, 2016); Benjamin Davis, "Precarity and Resistance: A Critique of Martha Fineman's Vulnerability Theory," *Hypatia* 36 (2021): 1.

25 Ahmed, *On Being Included*; Maki Kimura, "Non-performativity of University and Subjectification of Students: The Question of Equality and Diversity in UK Universities," *British Journal of Sociology of Education* 35 (2014): 523.

More fraught, however, is the issue of what shape the university's role and responsibility should take in these situations. It is this question—that is, the nature and scope of a university's obligations where the exercise of academic freedom appears at odds with matters of equity and inclusion—that is at the root of extensive tension and debate. To address this question, I suggest that the university's role includes three main responsibilities, which relate to resource allocation, communication, and courage. In the discussion that immediately ensues, I describe these responsibilities and link each to the relational understanding of rights explored earlier, and to the Professor X case study.

Decisions about how an institution engages in *resource allocation* signal institutional priorities. The designation of resources within universities is increasingly focused on EDI as a means to foster student wellness and academic success. This is appropriate for a range of reasons. If, however, universities are serious about allowing the pursuit of knowledge and ideas even where some proposed concepts or arguments might engender offense, it is worth considering the resources needed to permit debates to occur even while institutions simultaneously affirm their commitments to student wellness. Concretely, this means allocating resources to student wellness and to free debate and exchange, even when these two goals appear to be at odds with each other.

For instance, consider a case where members of the Queer campus community and their allies contest and feel harmed by an invited speaker who takes the view that gender-nonconforming or gender-questioning children should be medically treated to accept their biological sex. How can an institution address this situation in a way that allows the speaker space on campus, repugnant as some might find the views pronounced, while also showing support to 2SLGBTQ+ members of the campus community? While challenging, there are in fact no bounds on the ideas that can be formulated in this context. They could include: robust population-specific support for those who feel harmed by the ideas in question; extending institutional support for concurrent events specifically designed by, with, and for the 2SLGBTQ+ campus community; recognition of the hurt and anger the invited speaker will have caused even if there is no institutional obstruction to stop the event; mediated discussions between those who feel hurt and those who organized the talk, each of whom likely believes their rights are at risk; facilitated dialogue about the history, meaning, importance, and limits of free expression and academic freedom, and why its erosion presents such a threat, including to socially oppressed groups; and facilitated dialogue about gender identity and the harms and oppressions that continue to be experienced by trans or gender nonconforming or nonbinary people worldwide, including within our own communities.

Likewise, in the context of the Professor X case study, such approaches would have worked to show support for individuals and the relationships in question. For example, enhanced support for students through the campus sexual violence support staff/center, or a facilitated discussion between Professor X and her learners, would have demonstrated that the university took seriously students' concerns while not standing in the way of a faculty member's academic freedom. Such approaches would have called upon time, energy, people, creativity, and money—all resources in short supply even in the most established of higher education institutions. At the same time, the allocation seems worthwhile, bearing the potential to strengthen relationships at the heart of the university's mission while affirming its commitment to both academic freedom and EDI.

Universities further have a responsibility to *communicate* clearly and consistently about expectations that attend members of the campus community and the principles that guide institutional decisions. This is true at both the level of campus-wide communications and those that occur when administrative leaders interact with and make decisions that affect individual campus actors. Reinforcing key values—which usually circulate the concepts of respect, responsibility, equity, and excellence—helps provide a touchstone for campus actors about the requirements they are expected to uphold vis-à-vis conduct. It also provides a reference point for universities when called upon to provide reasons for decisions in controversial cases. On the issue of academic freedom, these values underpin the breadth of protection extended to the freedom to pursue and express ideas as well as any limits on that freedom. Where to draw a line that separates academic freedom from intolerable expression is a contested question. Yet, there ought to be a consensus that where academic freedom veers into the terrain of research misconduct, harassment, or discrimination, the university has a duty to step in and take measures to uphold its obligations vis-à-vis institutional integrity and equity.

In Professor X's case study, the university has minimal institutional presence. The two moments of contact include the chair's response to students' request to replace Professor X for the class on rape-shield legislation, and the communication from Professor X to her chair requesting institutional support and intervention. In this example, the university arguably missed opportunities to set expectations through effective communication with key stakeholders. Notably, we have no evidence of how the university in question might have endeavored to commit itself both to academic freedom and the creation of inclusive learning environments. Moreover, after being contacted by students, the chair's "cursory" response suggested minimal regard for their position. The chair also failed to provide reasons for the decision not to replace Professor X. This response hence did little to cultivate confidence and trust. It was not anchored to an approach that favored relationship building in this classroom setting. Finally, while we do not know how the university would have responded to Professor X's communiqué seeking intervention and protection, ideally it would have prioritized the instructor's well-being and that of her students, inviting exploration to identify a path forward that would at once uphold the responsibility to teach the content in question, while at the same time supporting and striving for inclusion of all class members, including Professor X.

A final call on universities relates to the theme of *courage*. It is not easy to tell a student who is genuinely hurt and aggrieved that the conduct causing their distress is permissible and that the institution will not proscribe it. Likewise, it is hard to tell a professor that the way they have chosen to exercise academic freedom undermines some students' learning experience, or that the university will not intervene to curb students' expression of discontent in the classroom setting, even though the instructor finds it rattling. Universities in North America are under consistent, intense pressure to take positions on controversial topics. Success in navigating such circumstances requires a principled approach that resists succumbing to public pressure and criticism while also showing openness to necessary change that serves the needs and interests of a campus community. All of this takes tremendous institutional courage.

In the case study, student groups and sexual violence survivor advocates seek the institutional curbing of the instructor's freedom to share her controversial scholarly views with her students. But Professor X will also have supporters, within and beyond the classroom, even if she does not go looking for them. These may well include some students who may be frustrated that their peers claim to speak in their name. Those supporters, likely frustrated with so-called cancel culture and a perceived trend toward "coddling" university students,[26] may press the university to do more than refrain from interfering with Professor X's teaching. Quite possibly, they would seek the university's express support of their colleague and denunciation of the students' tactics as tantamount to harassment or defamation of Professor X.

Neither of these positions—one challenging, the other supporting, Professor X—can effectively guide institutional leaders seeking to find a way through situations like the one the case study offers. More constructive for those leaders is the recall of the institution's core mission focused on inquiry, discovery, and knowledge. In the classroom context, this can only be pursued where the relationship between teacher and learner allows for the presentation and exchange of ideas and views. Universities thus have a vested interest in protecting and supporting that relationship.

Controversial cases, like that of Professor X, require institutions to sift through calls for posturing and positioning to determine the true interests that compel attention and action. This in turn calls for careful listening to campus stakeholders with a view to informing measures that seek to establish and preserve trust and understanding within the relationships—like that between professors and their students—which are core to a university's academic mission. That kind of careful listening can be difficult. It requires institutional leaders to hear stories of lived experiences of pain and exclusion, to make space for positions that we as individuals might find unpalatable, to recognize that an institution's past or current stance on a given question is misguided, to identify divides and the hard work needed to bridge them, to admit to having more questions than answers, and to slow down, even in situations of apparent urgency or crisis. Such an approach focused on relationship building is much more complex, nuanced, resource-intensive, and demanding than naming a winner and a loser in a perceived contest of

26 John McWhorter, "Academics Are Really, Really Worried about Their Freedom," *The Atlantic*, September 1, 2020, www.theatlantic.com/ideas/archive/2020/09/academics-are-really-really-worried-about-their-freedom/615724/; Pippa Norris, "Closed Minds? Is a 'Cancel Culture' Stifling Academic Freedom and Intellectual Debate in Political Science?" HKS Working Paper No. RWP20-025, *SSRN*, https://ssrn.com/abstract=3671026; Mark Carl Rom and Kristina Mitchell, "Teaching Politics in a Call-Out and Cancel Culture," *PS: Political Science & Politics* 54 (2021): 610.

rights. Just the same, this way forward, which calls for administrative gumption, offers greater promise for an institutional context that fosters healthy and nourishing relationships that facilitate the rights and interests of different stakeholders, even in situations where these rights and interests appear to compete.

Conclusion

This chapter proposed an analytical framework to contemplate and engage in discussions about the intersections between the values of academic freedom on one hand, and EDI on the other, in contemporary campus settings. Conventional approaches to this topic are anchored to perspectives that prioritize individual rights. These approaches have presented academic freedom and EDI as operating at cross-purposes. This essay contemplated an alternate analytical lens for exploring the sites where academic freedom and EDI meet by privileging relational theory.

Drawing on a case study that served as a consistent point of reference, this essay considered how academic freedom and EDI can be meaningfully and simultaneously pursued even in situations where these values appear to clash. The case study centered on Professor X and her students, divided over whether the former should be permitted to share her scholarly views in her classroom since, for at least some students, doing so would compromise the psychological safety and inclusiveness of their learning environment.[27] Conventional approaches to a situation like this would involve examining the rights of each party directly concerned (Professor X, her students) and the strength of their respective claims, leading to a conclusion about which ought to prevail. The analysis developed herein traced a different course. It centered the relationships that are of deepest concern to the situation at

27 While in this chapter some of Professor X's students interpret her position on rape-shield laws as "unorthodox," the reality is that it is the rape-shield laws to which Professor X objects that in fact run against the grain of foundational criminal justice principles. Such principles establish an accused's right to present a fulsome defense through all available evidence, to which the rape-shield laws present an important limitation. The point here is not to offer a suggestion on the moral value of liberalism's approach to criminal law or on the rape-shield exception. Rather, it is to highlight the risks of absolutist moralistic positioning on topics that can elicit a range of nuanced and justified positions, as well as the evolving nature of disciplinary standards that require due regard as we endeavor to uphold academic freedom while concurrently seeking to establish rich and inclusive learning environments.

hand, assessing how these can be meaningfully sustained. It further explored the social context in which the debate unfolds and examined the role of institutional players—here, the university—in framing key relationships.

This analysis illuminated how zeroing in on core relationships within the academy can ground a refined approach that allows one to uphold academic freedom without subverting one's commitment to EDI. The work involved in taking such an approach is nuanced and complex. It calls for empathy on the part of the actors concerned and a focus on responsibilities over rights. The analysis demonstrated that our ability to exercise meaningfully our individual rights is contingent on our ability and willingness to engage with others, even those whose interests appear to threaten or undercut our own objectives and freedoms.

Beyond private relationships, the analysis developed in this essay calls for an examination of the social framework in which they are situated. Thus, in debates about academic freedom and EDI, we are advised to zoom out and look at what institutions of higher education can and must do to preserve the relationships that are crucial to the concomitant preservation and pursuit of both academic freedom and EDI. The institutional work will be grounded in thoughtful decisions about resource allocation, developing and delivering clear communications about institutional values and commitments, and having the courage to live by those values and commitments, even when pressured to act otherwise.

This chapter does not purport to put to bed debates about academic freedom and EDI as campus values. It has merely emphasized that both of these values merit focus and energy in contemporary higher education settings. It proposes a framework that offers an alternative to our default approach that has, until now, typically juxtaposed these values in opposition to each other, forcing decisions that lead to prioritizing one while the other gives way. It has suggested a framework that seeks to enable the simultaneous foregrounding of these two values through a focus on core relationships in academe. The approach demands greater resources—notably time, creativity, compassion, and energy—than many university leaders and decision-makers feel they have at their disposal, especially when operating in the throes of a public campus controversy or crisis.

But as stressed herein, all institutions including universities allocate their resources according to the things they value most. In the context of contemporary higher education, it is difficult to imagine values more deserving of recognition and care than academic freedom and EDI, both of which are essential to establishing academic settings that foster ambition, rigor, and inclusion for scholars and students alike.

Part III

Between Authoritarianism and Populism: State Interference with Academic Freedom

Chapter 12

The Crisis of Academic Freedom at the Beginning of the Twenty-First Century

Europe in a Plural World

Liviu Matei

The Predicaments of University Governance and Academic Freedom at the Beginning of the Twenty-First Century: National, Regional, or Global?

The end of the Cold War marked the beginning of a period of exuberance in many parts of the world in politics and economy as well as in the theoretical discourse in the social sciences.[1] There was exuberance in higher education as well. This was in part a reflection of the perception of accelerating democratic advancements in higher education during this time, such as with regard to access (what appeared as significant and continuously increasing enrolments), further internationalization and liberalization of academic cooperation, and progress in university governance, such as with regard to

1 Christian Scheinpflug, *The Rise and "Fall" of the Vision of a Post-Cold War New World Order* (Munich: GRIN Verlag, 2013).

institutional autonomy.[2]

In this context of positive perceptions and high expectations about progress and democratic freedoms in higher education, academic freedom was largely taken for granted and neglected as a subject of scholarly inquiry and intellectual and policy re-elaboration or updating, at a time when new concepts and models were emerging in other domains of higher education and some of the older ones went through a process of rekindling. That was the case in Europe with the advent of new or significantly modified concepts or models such as degree structures, degree types (e.g., new, European models of bachelor's, master's, and PhD degrees emerged), quality assurance and accreditation (e.g., European standards and guidelines for quality assurance were adopted in 2005 and revised in 2015), student mobility and international cooperation, and so on.[3] This was a time when Europe, possibly more than other regions of the world, saw remarkable, unprecedented developments in higher education.[4] These developments were made possible to a significant extent by the emergence after 1998–9 of the continental-wide Bologna Process and the related project of the European Higher Education Area (EHEA).[5]

At the beginning of the twenty-first century and in particular after the Great Recession of 2007–9, the mood started to change, moving away from the exuberance of the 1990s. Powerful public policy narratives, such as "knowledge society," "democratization," and, in Europe, "European integration," which had previously helped mobilize significant political and general public support for higher education and contributed to bringing it toward the forefront of the public policy agendas, ran out of steam. The ascendance of populism in undemocratic and democratic political regimes alike added

2 Liviu Matei and Julia Iwinska, "Diverging Paths: University Autonomy and Academic Freedom in the European Higher Education Area," in *European Higher Education Area: The Impact of Past and Future Policies*, ed. Adrian Curaj, Ligia Deca, and Remus Pricopie (Cham: Springer, 2018), 345.

3 European Commission, *Standards and Guidelines for Quality Assurance in the European Higher Education Area (ESG)* (Brussels: European Commission, 2015).

4 Liviu Matei, "Charting Academic Freedom in Europe," in *European Higher Education Area: Challenges for a New Decade*, ed. Adrian Curaj, Ligia Deca, and Remus Pricopie (Cham: Springer, 2020), 455.

5 The Bologna Process, launched formally with the Bologna Declaration of 1999, is a voluntary intergovernmental process in higher education based on jointly agreed principles, objectives, and standards. As of fall 2022, there were forty-nine European states implementing the Bologna Process, including Belarus and Russia, which were suspended in April 2022 following Russia's invasion of Ukraine. The EHEA, as a common European space for dialogue and practice in higher education, is considered a result of the Bologna Process.

to this noxious mix. As a consequence, trends in higher education started to change, even reverse. Enrolment and participation rates were capped, public funding was cut in many countries (although not in all), and, already before the COVID-19 pandemic and the war in Ukraine, new limitations to international cooperation started to be put in place. Higher education governance—how higher education institutions are structured, organized, and managed as autonomous organizations—started being affected negatively through an array of attempts at restrictions or actual restrictions, even direct repression. The less supportive atmosphere and hampering turn of events culminated in bringing entire national higher education systems to a halt through severely repressive means, such as in Myanmar and Afghanistan in 2021.

Academic freedom as a particular aspect or area of higher education governance was also affected negatively in many parts of the world. Multiple challenges to academic freedom remain, globally, until today.[6] However, while the democratic recession affecting the university is global, there are also important national and regional specificities that need to be considered. A differentiated analysis helps identify important nonglobal facts and trends, including some positive developments and reasons for hope. In particular, it can be argued that a regional dimension can be very important in understanding the dynamics of academic freedom. For our purposes here, Europe represents a relevant and important unit of analysis.

In Europe, the new atmosphere and trends that replaced the immediate post–Cold War economic, political, and public ethos exuberance went somewhat unnoticed in higher education until a few events occurred that served as wake-up calls. They include the chilling, mass repression against universities, students, academics, and administrators in Turkey in the aftermath of the attempted coup of 2016.[7] There were many reactions in the EHEA. However, although Turkey was a member of the EHEA, no European-level gesture or initiative meant to safeguard academic freedom helped significantly in that situation. In part, that was the case because there was no common ground in Europe, in the EHEA, regarding academic freedom. Turkey remained a full member of the EHEA, its membership largely undisturbed

6 Michael Ignatieff and Stefan Roch, eds., *Academic Freedom: The Global Challenge* (Budapest: CEU Press, 2017).

7 Muzaffer Kaya, "Turkey's Purge of Critical Academia," *Middle East Report* 288 (2018): 25.

despite the brutal, undemocratic actions of its government against higher education and academic freedom. At the same time, however, the beginning of a realization emerged that this space of dialogue and practice that was the EHEA lacked a shared, up-to-date, and effective conceptual reference for academic freedom.[8] For lack of such a reference, even a discussion about infringements of academic freedom in Turkey was difficult, if not impossible in the framework of EHEA, let alone action to address them.

Another case, that of Central European University (CEU), a US and European-accredited university forced out of Hungary following a series of attacks launched in 2017 by the populist-authoritarian government of an EU country, became not only a *cause célèbre* in the global fight for academic freedom but also the most visible syndrome of the new trends in Europe's higher education. As will be discussed in the next section, developments in Hungary, a EU country reported democratic, had a further chilling effect on academic freedom and in higher education more generally beyond just the case of CEU, and sent wake-up ripples of an even higher magnitude.

After a relatively long period of unprecedented positive developments in higher education on the continent, including in certain segments of university governance (such as university autonomy), Europe woke up to the reality of what we propose to call a continental-wide "crisis of academic freedom." This, it can be argued, is not a global crisis, nor can it be explained by national-level developments in Europe.

The Crisis of Academic Freedom in Europe: How the EHEA Matters

The crisis of academic freedom that unfolded in Europe after the Great Recession, more markedly after 2015, has multiple dimensions. They can be grouped into two intertwined categories: empirical (political, legal, and regulatory) and intellectual.

Political attacks of varying intensity were inventoried during this time, originating usually with the ruling political forces in the respective country. Such are the cases of Turkey and Hungary, mentioned earlier. In Hungary,

8 Liviu Matei, "Academic Freedom, University Autonomy and Democracy's Future in Europe," in *Academic Freedom, Institutional Autonomy and the Future of Democracy*, ed. Sjur Bergan, Tony Gallagher, and Ira Harkavy (Strasbourg: Council of Europe, 2020), 35.

CEU was not the only institution targeted in the dominant political discourse and by concrete, "dedicated," legislative, and regulatory initiatives. The entire higher education sector was targeted by discursive attacks, at first, followed by restrictive legislative and regulatory steps. Amid the Recession, Viktor Orbán, the long-term serving prime minister of Hungary, stated that his country could not compete internationally as an EU member state and based on knowledge and advanced education, as the European consensus in higher education and around the concept of knowledge economy or society asserted at that time.[9] Rather, he demanded that Hungary built a competitive edge based on "manual labor" while denouncing the EU as a "colonizing power." Anchored on this new ideological stand that takes a distance from the previously dominant policy narratives in Europe (knowledge society, democratization, Europeanization), he further affirmed that Hungary didn't need more higher education, but less; it didn't need more students, but fewer (and it didn't need more Europe, but less). More higher education was declared a waste, economically, and a national danger, politically. Higher education institutions and individuals who in the name of university autonomy and academic freedom opposed the new political direction were denounced as enemies of the nation, including in well-orchestrated media campaigns reminiscent of Nazi or communist propaganda. In the end, all higher education institutions were placed under one-party government control through an extensive package of legal and administrative measures.[10] They included the appointment of a government commissar (officially called "chancellor") in every public university, with veto rights over the rector (the chief executive officer) and the Senate (the highest internal governance body).[11] The constitution was amended easily and repeatedly after 2011, taking advantage of the ruling party's supermajority in parliament. The principles of academic freedom and university autonomy were all but abolished and replaced with

9 Károly Füzessi, "Can Europe Make It? Higher Education under Threat in Hungary," *Open Democracy: Free Thinking for the World*, February 11, 2013, www.opendemocracy.net/en/can-europe-make-it/higher-education-under-threat-in-hungary/.

10 Attila Chikán, "Key Developments in Hungarian Higher Education," in *Academic Freedom: The Global Challenge*, ed. Michael Ignatieff and Stefan Roch (Budapest: CEU Press, 2017), 113.

11 Gergelyi Kováts, "Recent Developments in the Autonomy and Governance of Higher Education Institutions in Hungary: The Introduction of the 'Chancellor System,'" in *Central European Higher Education Cooperation Conference Proceedings*, ed. József Berács et al. (Budapest: Corvinus University of Budapest Digital Press, 2015), 26.

government control in higher education and science, and the supremacy of Christian identity and national pride over scientific truth.[12]

Hungary and Turkey were the most extreme, but not the only cases. Hungary, in particular, was not an odd and atypical instance but rather a pacesetter, a country adopting quicker and more ruthlessly positions and measures that were later contemplated, tried, or put into practice by other countries or political forces on the continent.[13] In Western Europe, attacks against academics, research, and higher education institutions coming from populist or extreme right political forces have been noted, like in Germany, or from moderate, centrist government parties, like in France and the UK.[14] In a striking case of a populist, politically partisan outbreak, the then minister responsible for higher education launched a scathing attack against the entire French higher education sector in 2020–1, accusing all universities of *Islamo-gauchisme* (Islamo-leftism), of undermining national security in France by undertaking research and education in disciplinary areas and fields that should be off-limits in the eyes of the government and some of its supporters in the academe, and which should therefore be banned, such as postcolonial studies or critical race theory.[15]

In all these cases, new political and policy narratives translated into new types of political position-taking, which in turn tended to transform into new regulations and laws restricting academic freedom. In some case, like Hungary or Turkey, this has indeed happened; in the case of France not really, primarily because the higher education sector itself and parts of the civil society resisted and repelled successfully the attempts at new legislation or regulations. Attacks there thus remained contained largely within discourse, although not without a certain chilling effect. In the UK, to mention another symptomatic case, a bill on "higher education (freedom of speech)"

---

12 István Kenesei, "University Autonomy in Hungary in Perspective," in *Academic Freedom: The Global Challenge*, ed. Michael Ignatieff and Stefan Roch (Budapest: CEU Press, 2017), 123.

13 More recently, in 2022–3, the governor and the state legislature of Florida in the United States copy-pasted from Viktor Orbán's playbook, using the tactics of the "rule by law," "law with destination," and electoral super-majorities to restrict university autonomy and the freedoms of education and research. That makes Hungary a pacesetter beyond just Europe.

14 Andreas Fulda and David Missal, "Mitigating Threats to Academic Freedom in Germany: The Role of the State, Universities, Learned Societies and China," *International Journal of Human Rights* 26 (2022): 1803.

15 Michel Wieviorka, *Racisme, antisémitisme, antiracisme: apologie pour la recherche* (Paris: La Boîte à Pandore, 2021).

was under consideration in the parliament since 2021, was passed in 2022, and received "royal assent" in 2023, in a political context influenced by disputes around the so-called culture wars. This piece of legislation conceptualizes and codifies academic freedom as freedom of speech alone, implicitly restricting in this way the scope of academic freedom.[16] The bill excludes largely students from the scope of academic freedom and overshadows, if not simply ignores, important tenets of academic freedom such as the right to choose research questions and methods without fear of reprisal, or the relevance of standards of academic rigor and integrity—all in the name of a highly politicized and legalistic understanding of freedom of speech, otherwise important democratic freedom already protected in the national legislation, and for all citizens. The law is expected to be accompanied by a new set of regulations to be enforced by courts, by the Office for Students, and by a "champion of free speech," a newly created position housed in this regulatory agency.

Different European countries have been affected in different ways by the new winds in politics, public policy, and higher education. In some of them, like Austria or Germany, the commitment to academic freedom remains strong irrespective of the political color of the governments, and strong in the face of challenges from the extremes. National-level legal and regulatory protection of academic freedom remains effective in many other countries. And yet, the European crisis of academic freedom affected them all—because they are members of the EHEA, a common space for dialogue and practice in higher education with significant substance, in spite of its many imperfections and some skewed characteristics. The EHEA ties together the work of higher education institutions from all European countries like never before, functioning as a supranational area with imperfect but strong and consequential common values, standards, even rules, and institutions.

To give an example: Norway has one of the best national legal systems for the protection of academic freedom in the world. However, when a Norwegian master's student wants to go to Hungary to undertake gender studies within the Erasmus mobility program of which both countries are members and which operates based on multilaterally agreed-upon princi-

16 Liviu Matei and Shitij Kapur, "Academic Freedom Is Not Freedom of Speech for Academics," *Times Higher Education*, November 24, 2022, www.timeshighereducation.com/opinion/academic-freedom-not-freedom-speech-academics.

ples that should make it possible to study anywhere in Europe, that would not be possible because a decree of the Hungarian government from 2018 restricts, if not outright bans, accreditation of gender studies in Hungary. In this case, the right of Norwegian students to choose their areas of study, theoretically an important tenet of academic freedom, is infringed in the EHEA through the decision of public authorities from another country. This is not only the case with gender studies or social sciences. For political reasons, the Hungarian government stopped a PhD program in mathematics and its applications cotaught by academic staff from the Alfréd Rényi Institute of Mathematics of the Hungarian Academy of Sciences, one of the most prestigious mathematics centers in the world.[17] If a student from another European country wanted to come to Budapest to study mathematics with these outstanding researchers in a unique program, that would not be possible either.

The crisis of academic freedom in Europe is also an intellectual crisis, not only a political, legal, or regulatory one. In the years following immediately after the fall of the Berlin Wall, academic freedom was taken for granted. There was no systematic reflection on the concept itself or work to update it to reflect the new realities emerging in politics, economy society, and higher education. Europe reached the point where not only it lacked a conceptual reference for academic freedom that was shared, but it also lacked one that was up-to-date and effective. That, in turn, led to difficulties in codification, monitoring, and practice in the entire EHEA. The existing conceptualizations and codifications of academic freedom in Europe could not be applied in the case of Turkey or Hungary, to name just these two examples, in part because they were outdated and ineffective in the face of the new realities on the continent.

---

17 Liviu Matei, "The Virtues of Cooperation, Complementarity and Competition in Higher education in Time of Crisis," in *The Three Cs of Higher Education: Competition, Collaboration and Complementarity*, ed. Rosalind M. O. Pritchard et al. (Budapest: CEU Press. 2019), 253. The program was run since the early 2000s with funding and accreditation provided by CEU but teaching and supervision provided mainly by the Rényi Institute, which was otherwise not authorized to teach and grant degrees. At about the same time with the attacks against CEU, the Hungarian government also began attacking the research institutes of the Hungarian Academy of Sciences, which were eventually reorganized into a "network" under the direct control of the government. In this context, and even before CEU moved to Vienna, the Rényi Institute was forced by the government to stop the cooperation within this PhD program, which had to be closed down.

The EHEA is not only a supranational space for cooperation in the form of exchanges of students and staff. It is also a space for intellectual and professional innovation, which made possible the emergence of new and highly consequential concepts, models, and tools in European higher education. It is true that these are implemented with varying degrees of commitment and efficiency across all or some of the forty-nine member countries. Yet, they influence deeply the work of higher education institutions, students, and academics, of all other relevant stakeholders, such as professional associations, international organizations, and public authorities active in higher education throughout the continent. Such common elements include the EHEA standards and guidelines for quality assurance applied across Europe, mentioned in the previous section; the European Quality Assurance Register for Higher Education (a common institution of the EHEA); the European Credit Transfer and Accumulation System (ECTS); the Bologna degree structure and the new European models of master and doctoral education; the European model of university autonomy, and so on.[18] In 2020, a list of common European "fundamental values of higher education" was adopted by ministerial delegations representing the forty-nine EHEA countries,[19] adding an important element to the conceptual architecture of the EHEA. These values are currently being defined in separate statements being issued as common commitments of all EHEA member countries.

A particularly striking case study illustrates how powerful models and common conceptual references developed in the EHEA while academic freedom was neglected. The European University Association (EUA) has promoted since 2007–8 a new model of institutional autonomy. This model became very influential within and also outside the EHEA.[20] This "autonomy project," focusing on the freedoms of the university as an institution rather than of the individuals (students, staff) working in the university, led to the creation of an Autonomy Scorecard, in use until today as a measurement instrument across the EHEA. The project was explicitly meant only to produce a tool for monitoring autonomy, not as a conceptual model.[21] We

18 Matei, "Charting Academic Freedom in Europe."

19 European Higher Education Area, "Rome Ministerial Communiqué," www.ehea.info/Upload/Rome_Ministerial_Communique.pdf.

20 Matei and Iwinska, "Diverging Paths."

21 Thomas Estermann and Terhi Nokkala, *University Autonomy in Europe I: Exploratory Study* (Brussels: European University Association, 2009); Thomas Estermann, Terhi Nokkala, and Monika Steinel, *Uni-*

argue, however, that it has achieved exactly that: articulating and promoting a European model of university autonomy.[22] The team developing the tool and the organization supporting it (EUA) nonetheless decided from the beginning, programmatically, not to deal with academic freedom. This clear missed opportunity is symptomatic of the neglect of academic freedom in the EHEA.[23]

Many unconnected, older references to academic freedom continued to exist during this time, including in national and international legislation. However, these do not work or do not work well for the EHEA. They could not address the need for an up-to-date, shared, and effective *European reference* for academic freedom and thus cannot help much in addressing the crisis of academic freedom in the EHEA specifically. There are different explanations for why older references don't work. For example, when Wilhelm von Humboldt set forth the modern understanding of academic freedom at the beginning of the nineteenth century, the focus was on the relationship between the emerging nation-state and the university. Today, more than two hundred years later, the state is not the only key variable in the equation of academic freedom. In part, Europe began struggling with understanding and protecting academic freedom for lack of a clear and effective conceptualization that accounts for the international and supranational dimensions of higher education in this new, sui generis construction that is the EHEA. European higher education institutions operate in an environment in which national legislation, regulations, and practices are increasingly supplemented by supranational models, references, and rules. These need to be considered when academic freedom is conceptualized, codified, regulated, and practiced today.

Among the existing international references, one of the most comprehensive is the 1997 UNESCO Recommendation concerning the Status of Higher Education Teaching Personnel. The Recommendation has been ratified by many countries around the world. However, very few people—academics, students, university administrators, or public authorities—have even

versity Autonomy in Europe II: The Scorecard (Brussels: European University Association, 2011); Enora Bennetot Pruvot and Thomas Estermann, *University Autonomy in Europe III: The Scorecard* (Brussels: European University Association, 2017).

22 Matei and Iwinska, "Diverging Paths."

23 The author served as a member of the advisory board of the project.

heard about it. This UNESCO Recommendation is not effective because it is not implemented anywhere. Maybe it is not even implementable.

One final exemplary case illustrating the need for a shared, up-to-date, and effective reference for academic freedom in Europe is linked with the above: in 2017, the EU Commission referred Hungary to the European Court of Justice (ECJ) for infringement of academic freedom in the case of CEU. In its deliberations and ruling, the Court made recourse to commercial legislation, for lack of sufficient, effective, and shared European legal references about academic freedom itself. The ECJ ruled that Hungary has infringed upon the right of CEU to establish and deliver commercial services, rather than conduct education and research.[24] One should be concerned when cases involving core academic freedoms are entirely or primarily mediated through commercial freedoms.

Additional evidence can be provided to support the assertion that an up-to-date, shared, and effective concept for academic freedom was missing in the EHEA. It can also be proven that a common reference for academic freedom is both needed and possible, in particular, given that other common, up-to-date, and effective higher education models, concepts, and references exist and work effectively, including the closely related concept of university autonomy. Moreover, efforts are already underway aimed at putting forward and implementing a common, adapted, and effective EHEA reference for academic freedom.

European Efforts to Address the Crisis of Academic Freedom: The "Fundamental Values Project"

Although not officially presented as such, several European-wide efforts are underway to address the crisis of academic freedom in the EHEA. They attempt to address the crisis in all its dimensions (political, legal-regulatory, and intellectual) and novel ways, given the sui generis, unprecedented nature of the EHEA itself, and the constitutional and political specificities of the EU. The most effective to date and the most "European" such effort is taking place within the framework of the Bologna Process. This is an intermin-

24 The EU Charter of Fundamental Rights was also mentioned in the verdict. The charter states that "academic freedom shall be respected" without any indication as to what academic freedom is or how to protect it. The charter is an EU document, not applicable in the other European countries.

isterial coordinated endeavor that has resulted already in the adoption of a European-wide reference for academic freedom.

Following a few years of preparation, in October 2020 ministerial delegations representing all forty-nine EHEA countries (all European countries, except Monaco and San Marino, but including Russia and Belarus) adopted a Statement on Academic Freedom,[25] which can be considered the first EHEA common reference for academic freedom. In this statement, a longer conceptual reference for academic freedom was outlined, framed as a "fundamental value of higher education," along with five other values. Consecutively, the Bologna Follow-Up Group (BFUG), the main coordination body of the Bologna Process, set up a Working Group on Monitoring Fundamental Values of Higher Education tasked with proposing an EHEA-wide monitoring mechanism for these fundamental values of higher education, including academic freedom, to be considered for formal adoption in 2024 when ministerial delegations will meet again.[26] In other words, this endeavor does not limit itself to proposing a conceptual reference for academic freedom (expected to be shared, up-to-date, and effective within the EHEA), but aims to create a framework for implementing it in practice and monitoring its implementation, using the soft law approach that characterizes the Bologna Process. Within this endeavor, we can discern its intellectual (new conceptual elaboration), political, and legal-regulatory dimensions, which mirror the dimensions of the crisis, as analyzed earlier.

In the statement, academic freedom is framed as a value, which is rather intriguing given that most often academic freedom is conceptualized and regulated as either a human right, a fundamental right, or a governance principle. The EHEA's choice to frame academic freedom as a value has both epistemological relevance and tactical justification. The promoters of this initiative we propose to call "the fundamentals values of higher education project" wanted very much to be able to put forward a set of new and effective guiding principles for academic practice and cooperation in Europe. It can be inferred (although this was never stated by the group) that having realized the challenge represented by the lack of a common, up-to-date, and

25 European Higher Education Area, "Rome Ministerial Communiqué."

26 European Higher Education Area, "Work Plan of the Bologna Follow-Up Group 2021–2024," www.ehea.info/page-work-plan-2018-2020. The author is a member of this group in an independent expert capacity.

effective reference for academic freedom, they decided to propose such a reference in the form of a value, rather than a legal right principle. It is a lot easier to bring together around the same table all countries of Europe (including Hungary and Turkey, France, and the UK) to discuss and agree on values than on arcane, maybe impossible continental-wide legislation. Defining academic freedom as a value was a tactical choice to find a workable niche to address the crisis of academic freedom in the EHEA by reaching a common understanding or conceptual reference for it, adapted to the current times and EHEA realities.

Of course, framing academic freedom as a shared ("fundamental") value across such a large and diverse cultural, political, and legal geography comes with new challenges. Is it possible to regulate, implement, and monitor values? Is it the case that values imply acknowledging and respecting cultural diversity and traditions? Can this lead to relativism (everybody may claim to have their values or understanding of values)? Moreover, if ministers of the forty-nine countries defined a short set of six *European* fundamental values that include academic freedom, does this mean that other regions of the world don't share or don't have the same values? If "their" values are different than "our" values, in which way? Does a European solution to the crisis that frames academic freedom as a regional value help address the predicaments of academic freedom globally as well? What do "fundamental" values mean and how come only six such values (depending on how one is counting) were retained? These do not include truth or solidarity in academia as separate values, for example.

It is difficult and too early to know whether this EHEA "fundamental values of higher education project" will succeed or not. What can be said already is that it is clearly, although not officially, designed to address the predicaments, the crisis we would say, of academic freedom in Europe.

In another, somewhat parallel effort to address challenges to academic freedom, the EU Commission launched in 2022 its project aimed at developing indicators for monitoring academic freedom, although only in the EU countries and only in the area of research (not including education).[27] This project was triggered by the concern for protecting academic freedom in

27 European Commission, "Deepening the ERA through Protecting Academic Freedom in Europe—Action 6," https://era.gv.at/public/documents/4589/06_-_Academic_freedom_in_europe_explanatory_document_revised.pdf.

Europe under the auspices of another document that endeavored to put forward a common reference for academic freedom, the Bonn Declaration on Freedom of Scientific Research,[28] adopted in 2020 by the ministers responsible for research of EU countries (not the broader EHEA).

In yet another effort to address the crisis, the Panel for the Future of Science and Technology of the European Parliament is striving to include provisions with legal (constitutional) value about academic freedom, also focusing on research, into the very treaty of the EU, the closest there is to a EU Constitution,[29] or adopt separate EU legislation for the protection of academic freedom.

Addressing the Crisis of Academic Freedom: Europe in a Plural World

While identifying and scrutinizing these recent attempts in Europe to address the crisis of academic freedom, we can also ask how Europe compares with the rest of the world. What are the implications of the fact that European dynamics emerged, as opposed to national or global dynamics, including both specific challenges to academic freedom and efforts to address them? Partial answers to these questions have been suggested in this chapter.

An important observation is that at least some of the actors involved in the process of generating a common European reference for academic freedom along with a monitoring mechanism for it are mindful of the obvious fact that Europe is not alone in the world. An analysis of "who is involved" is not available to date and it will not be attempted in this chapter either. However, they include influential organizations such as the Magna Charta Observatory[30] (an organization initially founded in Europe, now global), the Council of Europe, the EUA, the European Student Union, the BFUG, rep-

28 "Bonn Declaration on Freedom of Scientific Research," www.bmbf.de/bmbf/shareddocs/downloads/files/_drp-efr-bonner_erklaerung_en_with-signatures_maerz_2021.pdf?__blob=publicationFile&v=1.

29 European Parliament, "Panel for the Future of Science and Technology," www.europarl.europa.eu/stoa/en/home/highlights.

30 The Living Values Project of the Magna Charta Observatory launched in 2015 influenced significantly the EHEA fundamental values project; see Observatory Magna Charta Universitatum, "Living Values in Higher Education Institutions," www.magna-charta.org/activities-and-projects/living-values.

resentatives of national governments, as well as a few "independent experts," mostly from Europe. For the most part, their work to date has focused on Europe and with some sense of urgency. Questions regarding cooperation with the rest of the world when addressing challenges to academic freedom have been raised occasionally but have not been answered systematically in this framework.

Other questions regarding the impact in the EHEA of developments and realities outside Europe have also been asked only occasionally. Some participants have argued that there was no need for new conceptual references or codifications of academic freedom, even less so with a European character. They warned about what they see as the danger of questioning existing international (global) human rights legislation and regulations with regard to academic freedom, arguing that what we need is to implement what we have, not question it. The real challenge, they imply, is in the implementation of existing international human rights standards within which academic freedom is grounded,[31] and education (more people should know about existing international regulations and references), not the creation of new references, codifications, and tools, possibly leading to relativism.

At times, the place of Europe in the world, in a plural world when it comes to academic freedom, is framed using security language. The EU has issued guidelines regarding how to address foreign interference in higher education.[32] The UK draft Bill on Higher Education (Freedom of Speech) mentioned earlier includes provisions meant to address foreign interference in higher education as well. Both have China in mind, rather than the world as a whole. They are indicative of the effort to reconceptualize and regulate academic freedom in a new era of regional integration (post-Brexit EU) and as part of new geopolitical realities.

A largely missing dimension of this discussion relates to the notion of decolonizing academic freedom. The perception that academic freedom is a concept of European or Western origin and an exclusively positive contribution to the rest of the world is rarely questioned. The idea that Europeans

31 Scholars at Risk, "Academic Freedom and Its Protection under International Law," *Scholars at Risk*, December 8, 2021, www.scholarsatrisk.org/resources/academic-freedom-and-its-protection-under-international-law.

32 See, e.g., European Commission, *Tackling R&I Foreign Interference: Staff Working Document* (Luxemburg: Publications Office of the European Union, 2020).

have a lot to learn from the rest of the world regarding academic freedom (not only from the United States) is rarely mentioned. This is, however, an idea promoted by a few institutions in Europe, such as the Global Observatory Academic Freedom[33] (represented in the EHEA Working Group of Fundamental Values).

If the analysis regarding the European crisis of academic freedom put forward in this chapter is reasonably accurate, it suggests that the belief in the possibility of a specific European approach to addressing this crisis has to do with a conviction regarding the reality of an intellectual, policy and regulatory substance of the EHEA. It is EHEA that creates elements of European specificity, and also the need and possibility to generate and implement a shared and effective new conceptual reference for academic freedom. However, even without institutionalized common regional education spaces, other regions may be pushed to develop region-specific forms of promotion of academic freedom.

33 Central European University, "Global Observatory on Academic Freedom," https://elkana.ceu.edu/global-observatory-academic-freedom.

Chapter 13

A Tale of Two Stories

Visible and Less Visible Assaults on Academic Freedom in France

Stéphanie Hennette Vauchez

Introduction

This chapter provides a personal perspective on the general issue of academic freedom based on reflections triggered by recent attempts to discipline academic freedom in France—some highly conspicuous and some less visible than others. It starts by recounting a rather blatant and conspicuous governmental assault on academic freedom that occurred in 2020 and 2021 when executive leaders suggested that a current of "Islamo-leftism" had come to "gangrene" French universities and warranted inquiry. It then recounts in the first person the ways in which the author's findings in the framework of a collaborative research project on the standards of judicial review over administrative orders taken during the 2015–17 antiterrorist state of emergency led to tensions with the *Conseil d'Etat*—the highest administrative court. These tensions eventually led to a redrafting of the legal agreement that the *Conseil d'Etat* requires researchers who claim access to its internal databases to sign, with the agreement now containing a number of provisions that are questionable with respect to academic freedom. It reads stories through the lens of both an institutional and political culture of unease with external intellectual critique.

The Visible: Academic Freedom and Republican Integralism

In June 2020, as he was starting to communicate on what was then called the bill against "separatisms,"[1] President Emmanuel Macron called academia "culpable" of encouraging "separatism" from republican values.[2] In an intervention in reaction to the global protests triggered by the killing of George Floyd by the Minneapolis police, Macron deplored that academia was encouraging "the ethnicization of social issues" and claimed that this was leading to new forms of "separatism" causing ominous threats to divide the Republic. A few months later, the minister of education used harsher language to express similar ideas. Jean-Michel Blanquer spoke of "intellectual forms of complicity with terrorism" that he claimed were prevalent in academia. As one of the major promoters of the catch-all label of "Islamo-leftism,"[3] he used it to describe an array of academic works and inquiries that he read as attacks on what he claimed to be the "French model" of "republicanism" and "universalism." Blanquer announced his determination to show extreme firmness toward all those who "while believing to be progressives, are making the bed of terrorism."[4] Finally, the minister of higher education, Frédérique Vidal, delivered the *coup de grâce* when she announced her decision to endow the French CNRS (Centre national pour la recherche scientifique) with the task of investigating and reporting on academic research in France, with a view to distinguish between "academic research"

---

1 The proposed bill eventually led to the adoption of the 2021 Act "comforting the principles of the Republic."

2 Camille Stromboni, "Comment Emmanuel Macron s'est aliéné le monde des sciences sociales," *Le Monde*, June 30, 2020, www.lemonde.fr/societe/article/2020/06/30/comment-emmanuel-macron-s-est-aliene-le-monde-des-sciences-sociales_6044632_3224.html.

3 Several authors have claimed that this anti-Islam rhetoric takes root in the Cold War; see, e.g., Russell Johnson, "Islamo-Leftism?" *University of Chicago Divinity School*, March 1, 2021, https://divinity.uchicago.edu/sightings/articles/islamo-leftism.

4 Mathilde Durand, "'Ce qu'on appelle l'islamo-gauchisme fait des ravages,' dénonce Jean-Michel Blanquer," *Europe 1*, October 22, 2020, www.europe1.fr/politique/ce-quon-appelle-lislamo-gauchisme-fait-des-ravages-denonce-jean-michel-blanquer-4000366.

and "activism" and better assess "Islamo-leftism" that she also claimed was "gangrening" universities.[5]

These interventions form a series of unprecedented attacks on academic freedom emanating from the highest ranks of the executive branch. In doing so, government officials were reacting to singular events. On October 16, 2020, high school teacher Samuel Paty fell victim to the murderous madness of an eighteen-year-old Chechen refugee who claimed to be acting in the name of Allah. This horrific act profoundly shocked the country and certainly led the government to affirm its determination to reinforce public authorities' arsenal of measures to not only combat terrorism but also prevent radical political ideologies and movements from taking root. This is the immediate context against which the important Act Comforting the Principle of the Republic that came into force in August 2021 needs to be read. These declarations of Macron, Blanquer, and Vidal also illustrate, however, a broader political shift. As *laïcité*, as well as "republican values" more generally, have become a key component of the rhetoric of fighting terrorism and security, they are increasingly turned into a tool wielded against a variety of forms of speech (including academic scholarship) that appear to be critical of said republican values.

Numerous legal developments that have taken place since the beginning of the twenty-first century have tainted *laïcité* with security (in French, "sécuritaire") overtones.[6] Broadly reconstrued as requiring religious neutrality or discretion (if not as the antonym of religion), *laïcité* is increasingly referred to as a crucial component of the public policy toolkit in the prevention of religious radicalization. The 2004 Act prohibiting public school students from wearing religious signs was certainly a breakthrough in this respect. The subsequent 2010 Act prohibiting the concealment of the face in public spaces (colloquially referred to as the "burqa ban") was also presented as part and parcel of a broader effort to contain religious radicalization in society at large. The repeated terrorist attacks that have taken place since 2015

5 Soazig Le Nevé, "Frédérique Vidal lance une enquête sur 'l'islamo-gauchisme' à l'université," *Le Monde,* February 16, 2021, www.lemonde.fr/societe/article/2021/02/16/frederique-vidal-lance-une-enquete-sur-l-islamo-gauchisme-a-l-universite_6070195_3224.html; Ishaan Tharoor, "France and the Spectral Menace of 'Islamo-Leftism,'" *Washington Post,* February 21, 2022, www.washingtonpost.com/world/2021/02/22/france-macron-islamo-leftism/.

6 Philippe Portier, "The Illiberal Turn of French Laïcité," *Reset Dialogues on Civilizations*, December 22, 2020, www.resetdoc.org/story/the-illiberal-turn-of-french-laicite/.

further favored associations and amalgamations between Islam and terrorism. Already in the wake of the January 2015 killings at Charlie Hebdo, Montrouge, and a Jewish supermarket, government officials, political leaders, and much of the media had framed the attacks as caused by the forgetfulness and ignorance of the principle and culture of *laïcité* (secularism) or claimed that heightened/better education to and enforcement of *laïcité* was the remedy to homegrown terrorism. This narrative of *laïcité* as a key element of the response to terrorism only grew stronger as more attacks continued to unfold—in November 2015 at the Stade de France and Bataclan, in 2016 in Nice or St Etienne du Rouvray, as well as in other instances. A robust public policy aiming to combat religious radicalization, once focused on specific social spaces such as schools and prisons, was swiftly mainstreamed throughout all public policy domains.[7]

In 2021, the parliament adopted the Act Comforting the Principles of the Republic. Prime Minister Jean Castex had very symbolically chosen to present the bill as simultaneously placing *laïcité* at center stage and directing against one enemy, "radical Islam."[8] The bill was formally introduced on the 9th of December 2020, the date of the 115th anniversary of the Law of 1905 proclaiming the separation of churches and the State and commonly read as the bedrock of the French regime of *laïcité*. The Act also further pushed the securitization of *laïcité* through a variegated set of measures. Throughout the country, representatives of the State (*préfets*) can now judicially challenge acts of local authorities through expedited procedures if they believe they threaten the religious neutrality of public services. Hence the decision of the *préfet* of the department of Vienne to challenge a municipal ruling adopted by the city of Grenoble with a view to allow the wearing of "burkinis" in municipal swimming pools.[9]

---

7 Laurent Bonelli and Francesco Ragazzi, "La lutte contre la 'radicalisation': Genèse et expansion d'un nouveau lieu commun administratif en France et dans l'Union Européenne," *Archives de politique criminelle* 41 (2019): 119.

8 Olivier Faye, Nicolas Chapuis, and Alexandre Lemarié, "Jean Castex: L'ennemi de la République, c'est une idéologie politique qui s'appelle l'islamisme radical," *Le Monde*, December 9, 2020, www.lemonde.fr/politique/article/2020/12/09/jean-castex-l-ennemi-de-la-republique-c-est-une-ideologie-politique-qui-s-appelle-l-islamisme-radical_6062698_823448.html.

9 His challenge was upheld by the *Conseil d'Etat*, for the decision to allow modest swimwear was indeed deemed to violate the requirement of neutrality of public services, since it had been motivated by and tailored to the specific needs of a particular group of the population: CE, réf. June 21, 2022, n° 464648.

The 2021 Act also determines that any association that applies for public funding must sign a contract of republican commitment (*contrat d'engement républicain*) by which it commits to respect a list of republican principles lest the funding be discontinued, and the association be requested to reimburse illegally perceived funds. The list of principles includes *laïcité* as well as "freedom," "equality," "human dignity," and even "ordre public"[10]—all of which are fuzzy and indeterminate enough for many academics and human rights organizations to have expressed the fear that arbitrary decisions would ensue.[11] Take, for instance, the recent Poitiers affair, whereby the *préfet* of Vienne ordered the mayor of the city to withdraw the public funds it had awarded a local association (named *Alternatiba*), on the grounds that their advertising of "civil disobedience workshops" constituted a failure to respect "ordre public."[12]

The 2021 Act also upended the legal regime of homeschooling, largely because of its purported risks in terms of religious radicalization. Once a choice families were free to make, homeschooling has now become illegal in principle, and can only be made available exceptionally upon administrative authorization.[13] The law further specifies that municipal authorities can only grant such authorization in a limited number of circumstances (e.g., when homeschooling is required for health reasons, or because the children have an intense and semi-professional practice of sports or arts that is incompatible with regular school attendance, or due to the family's traveling lifestyle, or for "any situation specific to a given child").[14]

---

10 See Décret n° 2021-1947 du 31 décembre 2021 pris pour l'application de l'article 10-1 de la loi n° 2000-321 du 12 avril 2000 et approuvant le contrat d'engagement républicain des associations et fondations bénéficiant de subventions publiques ou d'un agrément de l'Etat.

11 See, e.g., Observatoire des libertés associatives, "Promotion et défense des libertés associatives," www.lacoalition.fr/Observatoire-des-libertes-associatives.

12 On the pending legal challenge opposing the municipality to the préfet: Aurore Coulaud, "Désobéissance civile; Subventions d'Alternatiba: le bras de fer se poursuit entre la maire de Poitiers et le préfet de la Vienne," *Libération*, February 13, 2023, www.liberation.fr/environnement/subventions-dalternatiba-le-bras-de-fer-se-poursuit-entre-la-maire-de-poitiers-et-le-prefet-de-la-vienne-20230213_LC-45Z2A7RBCHDI3EEQMQW7ZD5E/.

13 Religious schools also became subjected to heightened controls and their freedom of establishment has been subjected to intensified checks: Loi n°2018-266 du 13 avril 2018 visant à simplifier et mieux encadrer le régime d'ouverture et de contrôle des établissements privés hors contrat. In the same vein, the 2021 Act comforting the principles of the republic later limited families' freedom to choose homeschooling to educate their children; that choice is now conditional upon administrative approval.

14 In its initial version, the proposed bill explicitly mandated that religious, political, or philosophical beliefs were invalid grounds for a choice to homeschool—and that administrative authorization ought to

Political theorist Jean-Fabien Spitz has recently offered a powerful critique of the renewed centrality of *laïcité* as well as "republican values" more generally in French political discourse. As he describes this new rhetoric as a form of "integralism," Spitz claims that the insistence on republican values is but a cover for the unprecedented levels of social and economic violence that result from the neoliberal agenda that is increasingly being pursued by the State: because it fails to justify the ever-increasing levels of inequality it produces, neoliberalism invokes—albeit hypocritically—universal moral values in an attempt to gain an axiological dimension.[15] In his reading, *laïcité* has become a sort of collateral victim of neoliberalism, now wielded as a magic card in the face of an array of challenges it was never conceptually or historically supposed to speak to.

Understanding these broader dynamics allows us to identify the parallel ways in which this increasingly central concept of *laïcité* disciplines citizens and society at large and academia in particular. As the policy goal of preventing terrorism increasingly led to the notion that it was necessary to prevent the dissemination of "radical ideas" that "threaten the Republic," a number of topics of academic inquiry and research have been framed as problematic. In particular, scholarship critical of republican narratives has become suspect in the eyes of segments of the political sphere—with, as recalled earlier, members of the government going as far as to suggest that it may indeed become the breeding ground of terrorism. The Minister of Education Jean-Michel Blanquer thus designated a very broad range of suspicious fields of academic inquiry in that respect, a list in which he included postcolonial studies, gender studies, antidiscrimination, intersectionality, race studies, and the like. He spoke of a necessary "combat" to be waged against these ideas that are also presented as generated by a North American intellectual matrix.[16]

---

be denied if such reasons motivated a family's request. The final version of the act no longer contains this language, but this genealogy illuminates the subtext of these provisions, which clearly echoes the prime minister's choice to fight a battle against "radical Islam."

15 Jean-Fabien Spitz, *La République? Quelles valeurs?* (Paris: Gallimard, 2022).

16 "Interview de Jean-Michel Blanquer," *Journal du Dimanche*, October 25, 2020: "Il y a un combat à mener contre une matrice intellectuelle venue des universités américaines et des thèses intersectionnelles, qui veulent essentialiser les communautés et les identités, aux antipodes de notre modèle républicain qui, lui, postule l'égalité entre les êtres humains, indépendamment de leurs caractéristiques d'origine, de sexe, de religion. C'est le terreau d'une fragmentation de notre société et d'une vision du monde qui converge avec

Blanquer's discourse did, of course, manage to secure some forms of support in academia. Shortly after one of his interventions describing institutions of higher education (especially in the social sciences) as infiltrated by such perverse ideologies, over a hundred intellectuals coauthored an op-ed in the national press expressing their support of his views.[17] For them "indigenist, racialist and 'decolonial' ideologies" (all of them imported from North American campuses where "wokism" is purportedly raging) are not only "well present" in universities. They are also, they claim, "feeding a hatred of 'whites' and France." In February 2021, another move by seventy-six academics occurred when an "Observatory of Decolonialism" was founded with a view "to put an end to the hijacking of research and the transmission of knowledge." The observatory held its inaugural conference in January 2022, with a keynote delivered by Jean-Michel Blanquer and the concluding remarks by a high-ranking official of the Ministry of Higher Education.[18] Many of the scheduled talks addressed the necessary critique of critical social sciences.

In May 2022, Macron was reelected for a second mandate. He did not reappoint Blanquer and Vidal in his cabinet. In the meantime, a legal challenge had been initiated by six academics against Vidal's plan to launch an investigation into the alleged takeover of "Islamo-leftism" in academia. The claimants argued that the minister had overstepped her powers; and within the court proceedings, the Ministry of Higher Education was requested to communicate all the documents related to the investigation that had been announced. The ministry was, however, to communicate anything for, they claimed, no action or indeed investigation had ever followed the minister's announcement.[19] The case was thus declared moot. The minister's words

les intérêts des islamistes. Cette réalité a gangréné notamment une partie non négligeable des sciences sociales françaises."

17 "Une centaine d'universitaires alertent: 'Sur l'islamisme, ce qui nous menace, c'est la persistance du déni,'" *Le Monde*, October 31, 2020, www.lemonde.fr/idees/article/2020/10/31/une-centaine-d-universitaires-alertent-sur-l-islamisme-ce-qui-nous-menace-c-est-la-persistance-du-deni_6057989_3232.html.

18 For a critique, see Monique Selim, "De la légitimation politique d'une trappe identitariste," *L'Homme et la société* 1–2 (2021): 7.

19 Soazig Le Nevé, "Enquête sur 'l'islamo-gauchisme' à l'université: histoire d'une vraie fausse annonce," *Le Monde*, March 29, 2023, www.lemonde.fr/societe/article/2023/03/29/enquete-sur-l-islamo-gauchisme-a-l-universite-histoire-d-une-vraie-fausse-annonce_6167488_3224.html; Fabien Jobard, "L'islamo-gauchisme est un excès de pouvoir," in *La savante et le politique: Défense et illustration des libertés académiques*, ed. Eric Fassin and Caroline Ibos (Paris: Flammarion, 2024).

did, however, have a very real chilling effect. As Eric Fassin and others have noted: "The result of this campaign is that there are a number of research projects that have been abandoned, vocations discouraged, dissertations that will not come to fruition, articles and books that will not be published, funds that have not been allocated, job offers that have not been made."[20]

The Invisible: Researchers' Access to Sources

I now turn to another illustration of the challenges that academic freedom is facing in contemporary France beyond this broader "republican" chilling effect, by sharing a first-hand account of some difficulties researchers may experience in their freedom to access relevant sources. Access to sources is, of course, a very broad question. To the extent that their political or economic interests may come into conflict with the dissemination of scientific studies, private and public authorities alike may exercise pressure on academics.[21] And while such threats and pressure may reach incommensurable proportions in authoritarian regimes, democracies are not immune.[22] And because, for a researcher, access to relevant sources of inquiry is crucial, it is important to think of hindrances and threats to academic freedom that may occur upstream from more conspicuous pressures on the publication of scientific results and analyses or the use of legal procedures (libel, defamation, or privacy) to silence academics (or whistleblowers, for that matter).[23] Yet, from bureaucratic hurdles to outright obstacles, access to relevant resources

---

20 Anne-Laure Amilhat Szary et al., "L'enquête sur 'l'islamo-gauchisme' à l'université n'aura pas lieu et n'avait pas lieu d'être," *Le Monde*, March 29, 2023, www.lemonde.fr/idees/article/2023/03/29/l-enquete-sur-l-islamo-gauchisme-a-l-universite-n-aura-pas-lieu-et-n-avait-pas-lieu-d-etre_6167487_3232.html. More dramatically, as Fassin again has noted, these governmental assaults on critical social sciences as a threat to the republic have also resulted in unleashing threats and violence against academics; see Eric Fassin, "Qui est complice de qui? Les libertés académiques en peril," *Blog Mediapart*, November 1, 2020, https://blogs.mediapart.fr/eric-fassin/blog/011120/qui-est-complice-de-qui-les-libertes-academiques-en-peril.

21 Joan W. Scott, *Knowledge, Power and Academic Freedom* (New York: Columbia University Press, 2018); Michael Ignatieff and Stefan Roch, eds., *Academic Freedom: The Global Challenge* (Budapest: CEU Press, 2017).

22 For a specific reflection on the challenges met by researchers in the field of social sciences who investigate sensitive political topics in democratic regimes, see Marwan Mohammed, "La fragilité juridique des chercheurs en sciences humaines et sociales face aux Etats démocratiques," in *Liberté de la recherche: Conflits, pratiques, horizons*, ed. Mélanie Duclos and Anders Fjeld (Paris: Kimé, 2019), 135.

23 Olivier Leclerc, "Overarmed or Underdressed? Whistleblowers between Anti-discrimination Law and Freedom of Expression," *International Journal of Discrimination and the Law* 23 (2023): 265.

can be barred in multiple ways. This section focuses on the access of French scholars to a specific category of legal sources that are often assumed to pose no particular challenge in terms of access but that can nonetheless run into the resistance of public authorities to academic inquiry: court decisions.

Before all else, a little bit of context is warranted. In France, court decisions have only recently been classified as open data. A 2016 Act prescribed they systematically be made accessible to the general public once they have been anonymized.[24] Respecting this basic privacy requirement for both the stock and flux of all court decisions, as well as designing the proper logistical tools for enabling access have, however, proved to be challenging goals—and close to ten years after this initial legislative commitment, the process is still underway. It is expected to be completed by 2025.[25] Until well into the 2010s, however, the only openly accessible database for court rulings was exhaustive for rulings by the supreme courts only (*Conseil d'Etat* and *Cour de cassation*),[26] while appellate and first-degree judgments were only available in a piecemeal fashion. As a consequence, any legal research project that needed to access, analyze, and classify the entirety of court decisions on any given topic in order to exhaustively document the judicial treatment of a particular issue, concept or question necessitated for the research team to request access to the internal databases of administrative, judicial (or other) courts.

In 2016, a few months into the antiterrorist state of emergency (SOE) that had been declared by President Hollande after the November attacks in Paris and the Stade de France, the Human Rights Law Center (CREDOF)[27] of University Paris Nanterre initiated a collaborative research project on the use of this emergency regime. The research project was supported and funded by the *Défenseur des droits*—the constitutional authority for the protection of fundamental rights. One of the project's goals was to scrutinize the standards of judicial review that apply to administrative measures such as house arrest or house search orders. The project's design supposed access and anal-

24 Loi n°2016-1321 du 7 octobre 2016 pour une République numérique.

25 See also Décret n° 2020-797 du 29 juin 2020 relatif à la mise à la disposition du public des décisions des juridictions judiciaires et administratives. In principle, court decisions are to be made publicly available within two (administrative courts) to six (judicial courts) months of the ruling.

26 As a high court separate from both the judicial and administrative courts system, the *Conseil constitutionnel* has long made all its decisions available on its own website.

27 Centre de recherches et d'études sur les droits fondamentaux.

ysis of all the (administrative) court decisions that challenges to the state of emergency measures had led to. The research team that I headed thus applied for authorization to access the administrative courts' internal database. Such requests are to be addressed to the *Conseil d'Etat*, the highest administrative court. Ours was granted and we were soon able to schedule appointments with the relevant department and start working and collecting data. At each of our visits, we were only met with openness and cordiality. As a principal investigator for the project, I had to sign an agreement stipulating the terms of our right to access.

In the meantime, the topic we were researching was growing in political salience. As we initiated the project, in January 2016, the first attempt by several human rights organizations to have a court enjoin the president of the Republic to lift the state of emergency had failed. The organizations claim that the conditions of clear and imminent danger that might have justified the declaration of an SOE in November were no longer met and that it was thus necessary to put an end to what was to remain a temporary legal framework allowing the executive to deal with exceptional circumstances (in the particular case, terrorist attacks) had not convinced the court. The *Conseil d'Etat* declared itself incompetent to deliver such an injunction to the chief of State.[28] Subsequently, the state of emergency was repeatedly renewed and prolonged for little short of two years. It only formally came to an end on the 1st of November 2017. During that time, concerns relative to the risks of normalization of emergency measures, increased human rights restrictions, and competence creep of the executive only grew bigger.

In this context, our research project and the findings it would lead to was drawing the attention and interest of numerous actors: human rights organizations and institutions, both national and international, were eager to understand exactly what this SOE regime was about, how it operated, and whether it was (or not) being tamed and controlled by courts. The study we were doing was going to provide a unique perspective on these and other questions. We were thus having sustained conversations with leading civil society organizations (Human Rights Watch, Amnesty International, *Ligue des droits de l'Homme*, among others) as well as with the office of the newly appointed UN Special Rapporteur for the protection and promotion

28 CE, ref. January 27, 2016, n° 396220.

of human rights in the fight against terrorism—who had, remarkably and because of her interest in this prolonged SOE, chosen France as the country of her first official visit at the outset of her mandate.[29] We were also in contact with journalists and several media outlets who were eager to learn about our findings and conclusions.

In terms of our project's calendar, our final report to the *Défenseur des droits* was due in May 2018. However, as is often the case with publicly funded research, we were to write an intermediary report—which we did in October 2017. On that basis, we agreed to meet with journalists who were running reports on the topic and to share some of our intermediary conclusions. We met with representatives of two important daily newspapers (*Libération* and *Le Monde*) and communicated some statistical elements based on the analysis of the over seven hundred court decisions we had drawn from the administrative courts' internal database: percentage of cases involving specific types of SOE measures (house arrest vs. house searches, for instance), the percentage of cases in which administrative authorities were defeated, and so on. We also discussed some instances of cases where we felt the standard of judicial review had been wanting. The newspapers published articles echoing our findings.[30]

As the principal investigator of the project, I immediately received an email from the *Conseil d'Etat*, complaining that I had breached the agreement granting us (me and the entire research team) access to the administrative courts' internal database. The agreement did stipulate that we were under the obligation to communicate the final research report to the *Conseil d'Etat*. While we were well aware of this obligation—one that is very common indeed in the contemporary economy of academic research—we had felt that our intermediary report and results were only due to our funder (the *Défenseur des droits*) and not to other institutions we had been interacting with. I explained this to the *Conseil d'Etat* but hardly convinced them. I sub-

29 See Fionnuala D. Ní Aoláin, "Report of the Special Rapporteur on the Promotion and Protection of Human Rights and Fundamental Freedoms while Countering Terrorism on Her Visit to France," OHCHROR, 40th Sess., UN Doc A/HRC/40/52/Add.4 (2019).

30 Sonya Faure and Pierre Alonso, "Etat d'urgence: des travers dans l'Etat de droit," *Libération*, June 21, 2017, www.liberation.fr/france/2017/06/21/etat-d-urgence-des-travers-dans-l-etat-de-droit_1578625/; Anne Chemin, "Conseil d'état: quand les recours n'aboutissent pas ou peu," *Le Monde*, October 11, 2017, www.lemonde.fr/idees/article/2017/10/11/conseil-d-etat-quand-les-recours-n-aboutissent-pas-ou-peu_5199605_3232.html.

sequently received a formal letter of disapproval signed by the secretary-general herself, accusing me of playing with words and of breaching the elementary code of conduct between researchers and public institutions.

After this episode of tension, we continued to work on our project. As it did come to an end in 2018, we of course complied with the requirement of sending the final report to all parties including the *Conseil d'Etat*; and never really heard back from them.[31] They never invited us to present our work, even when they later thematized their annual series of open seminars on states of emergency—other academics were invited, but none who had done the (unique) kind of work we had, and none that could seriously claim to have analyzed the level of judicial scrutiny exercised by administrative courts during states of emergency.[32] They also hardly referenced our work in the subsequent annual report they authored on the same topic.[33]

More twists and turns were to follow. By the end of 2017, I was also taking part in another—unrelated—collaborative research project. This project's topic was religion, secularism, and courts. Because once again the design was to provide in-depth studies of some specific areas of case law, this project's principal investigator also requested for the research team she had gathered to be granted access to the same administrative courts' internal database. This time, the request was denied. More accurately, the *Conseil d'Etat* asked her to renew her request after a few months, as (we were told) the agreement stipulating the terms and conditions for academics' access was being redrafted. Finally, in June 2018, the principal investigator's request was granted, under the revised convention.

Although none of the work packages I was personally involved in required access to the internal database, I was able to read the new agreement as a member of the research project—and indeed, to compare it to the one I had signed in 2016 in the framework of my SOE project. The new agreement was much stricter. In fact, some of its provisions raise a number of questions with respect to academic freedom. For instance, Article 1 of the agreement indicates that researchers' access to internal databases may be granted "given the

31 Stéphanie Hennette Vauchez, ed., *Ce qui reste(ra) toujours de l'urgence* (Paris: Éditions Varenne, 2018).

32 "'Les états d'urgence': nouveau cycle annuel de conférences du Conseil d'Etat," *Conseil d'Etat*, September 18, 2020, www.conseil-etat.fr/actualites/les-etats-d-urgence-nouveau-cycle-annuel-de-conferences-du-conseil-d-etat.

33 "Les états d'urgence: la démocratie sous contrainte," *Conseil d'Etat*, September 29, 2021, www.conseil-etat.fr/publications-colloques/etudes/les-etats-d-urgence-la-democratie-sous-contraintes.

interest of the research project for the administrative courts' system." Article 4 stipulates that the researchers pledge to only use accessed data for the purposes of the research project. Other provisions further echo the agreement's relatively restrictive nature:

> Art. 6: The co-contractor undertakes to provide the managers of the … Conseil d'Etat, at least fifteen days before any distribution or publication, whatever its form and medium, with a copy of the file of the academic work for which the provision of the service has been agreed, even if this distribution or publication occurs at an intermediate stage.
> Art. 9: The State Council may terminate the present agreement without prior notice in the event of a breach by the co-contractor of any of its stipulations. In this case, the co-contractor will not be able to use the data [from the Ariane and Ariane archives databases] that it has collected.

As it explicitly rebuts the argument I had previously made according to which the results we had communicated to the press on our SOE research were only included in an intermediary (rather than final) research report, this redrafted version of the agreement suggests that it might be a direct answer to my initial disagreement with the *Conseil d'Etat.*

Academic Freedom and the Acceptability of Critique

This story is arguably very specific and idiosyncratic. There are however many reasons why it is emblematic of more structural hindrances to academic freedom that are surely to be found in various national settings. The mere existence of an agreement that legal academics need to sign in order to gain access to meaningful databases of legal rulings is, in and of itself, problematic. Firstly, it constrains researchers to position themselves as applicants, and therefore in a position unequal to the courts—here, the Supreme Administrative Court—as it is ultimately the *Conseil* that holds the power to grant them access or not. The power imbalance exists regardless of whether these requests are generally agreed to or not (they are). It is only reinforced by the new version of the agreement, as the earlier quotes of specific provisions show: even though the *Conseil* is by no means an academic institution, it has empowered itself to deny access to projects (or researchers?) that *it* deems lack interest. The new provisions pertaining to the researchers' obligation to communicate any results or findings to the *Conseil d'Etat* also testify to a desire to control the use of data—which, it is important to recall, only consists of court rulings that are, in principle, delivered in the name of the people and supposed to be public.

Secondly, this narrow and specific issue of the conditions under which researchers may access databases internal to court systems illustrates the weakness of a culture of critique within the French institutional system. Surely, the *Conseil d'Etat* is a very peculiar institution, one that is closely related to the State—historically, institutionally, and sociologically.[34] It is also, however, the Supreme Administrative Court and, to that extent, a major locus and field of inquiry for many legal (and other) scholars, especially those who are interested in judicial oversight of the executive branch.

In March 2021, the *Conseil d'Etat* found itself under an unusually high level of scrutiny as it was projected at the forefront of the new (sanitary) state of emergency created and declared by the government in March 2020 in the face of the COVID-19 pandemic. Because of the structure of powers in the French regime, most of the pandemic-related measures were governmental executive orders that the *Conseil d'Etat* was competent to review if and when they were challenged. The *Conseil* thus had to review numerous high-profile orders such as, emblematically, the March 2020 decree by which the government issued a general lockdown and stay-at-home order[35]—and many more. A year later, as the first statistics compiled by legal scholars and investigative journalists started to become available, the *Conseil* was criticized for its leniency and lack of bite vis-à-vis the executive.[36] The figures were, indeed, troubling—to the extent that the issue left the somewhat padded walls of scientific journals and publication and became a story for the general press: the *Conseil d'Etat* and its relationship to the executive, especially under the state of emergency, was the main topic of a ten-page story in the weekly magazine published by the main national newspaper *Le Monde*. Emblematically, as he

34 Antoine Vauchez and Pierre France, *The Neoliberal Republic* (Ithaca: Cornell University Press, 2021); Danièle Lochak, *Le role politique du juge administratif français* (Paris: Librairie générale de droit et de jurisprudence, 1972).

35 These orders were upheld; see CE, ref. March 22, 2020, n°439674; CE, December 22, 2020, n° 439800.

36 Further details in Stéphanie Hennette Vauchez, "Taming the Exception? Lessons from the Routinization of States of Emergency in France," *International Journal of Constitutional Law* 20 (2022): 1793.

was interviewed by journalists, the head of the *Conseil* essentially discarded all questions and critique, disqualifying them as "partisan" and "political."[37]

Conclusion

In this chapter, I have argued that scholars interested in threats to academic freedom, particularly as they manifest themselves in democracies, must pay attention not only to obvious, top-down threats instilled by a particular political climate of hysteria but also to some of the more subtle ways in which the executive, as well as the courts, can make research on sensitive issues more complicated than it needs to be. France provides a vivid illustration of a State that, in the wake of a terrorist campaign, has been tempted by a blanket reassertion of one of its foundational myths ("Laïcité") to deal with both actual and imagined radicalization. In the process, it has put obstacles in the way of critical but significant and useful research on the all-sensitive resort to a state of emergency. Researchers on academic freedom should be attuned to the polymorphous reality of such insidious threats.

37 Laurent Telo and Grégoire Biseau, "On sait d'où viennent ces critiques, balaye-t-il. Ce sont des considérations partisanes et politiques," *Le Monde*, March 12, 2021, www.lemonde.fr/m-le-mag/article/2021/03/12/crise-sanitaire-affaire-duhamel-entre-soi-le-quart-d-heure-warholien-du-conseil-d-etat_6072824_4500055.html?random=683684709.

Chapter 14

Academic Freedoms in Modern Russia

"Dawn" and "Dusk" of the Higher School of Economics[1]

Andrey Shcherbovich

Academic Rights in Russia in Connection with Other Constitutional Rights

Intellectual rights derive from the freedom of creativity, established by Article 44 of the Constitution of the Russian Federation. In its second chapter, this article proclaims that everyone (regardless of citizenship) is guaranteed freedom of literary, artistic, scientific, technical, and other types of creativity and teaching. The same article provides the constitutional foundations for protecting intellectual property in the Russian Federation.[2] The following aspects of intellectual rights and freedoms are subject to consider-

1 **Disclaimer.** Having been at the Higher School of Economics for seventeen years, starting from my student days, I hardly accepted my dismissal as a fact of my biography. The Department of Constitutional Law, where I was first a graduate student, then a teacher and assistant professor, ceased to exist due to the adoption of amendments to the constitution of the Russian Federation and the events that followed. Because of this, I had to leave Russia with the support of the Scholar Rescue Fund of the Institute of International Education. I am currently a visiting fellow at the Center for Human Rights and Legal Pluralism at McGill University (Montreal, Canada). However, this chapter presents the facts as I know them.

2 The Constitution of the Russian Federation (adopted by popular vote on December 12, 1993 with amendments approved during the all-Russian vote on July 1, 2020).

ation within the framework of this article.

Freedom of teaching means the teacher's right to choose and determine the teaching methods of the subject, correct them, select additional material, and express their attitude to the information that constitutes the teaching subject. It is the freedom to determine the nature, plan, and style of reading a topic. Freedom of expression also ensures freedom of teaching since this opinion is expressed primarily within the framework of the taught subject. No one, including the administration of the educational institution, parents and legal representatives of students, authorities, and local governments, has the right to try to influence the expression of thoughts, positions, and points of view of the teacher on specific issues of the subject and related topics. The only exception is the violation by the teacher of legislation and the norms of pedagogical ethics.

We can understand freedom from interference in professional activities somewhat more broadly—we mean freedom from interference not only when it comes to merely teaching work. It is also relevant in those areas where scholars are active in addition to teaching (participation in the work of methodological associations, conferences, educational work, verification of creation, development of programs, participation in the development of local acts, duty in the organization, work at the examination point, etc.)[3]

The need to present several alternative points of view both in the media and in the university context can be understood as a right to protection from total propaganda on problems of public and political life. It involves a guarantee of freedom of thought, freedom of expression, information, and communication. Total propaganda is prevalent during political crises and military conflicts and can pose a severe threat to civil society and the rule of law. Freedom of thought is traditionally viewed primarily in connection with freedom of conscience and other religious human rights. This connection can be traced, in particular, in such cases of the European Court of Human Rights as *Lautsi v Italy* or *Nikishina v Russian Federation*.[4] However,

3 S. V. Barabanova et al., "Commentary to the Federal Law of December 29, 2012, N 273-FZ, on Education in the Russian Federation."

4 *Lautsi and Others v Italy*, No. 30814/06 (March 18, 2011); *Nikishina v Russia*, No. 45665/99 (September 12, 2000).

Arrowsmith v The United Kingdom deals with secular convictions, namely pacifism and refusal to military service.[5]

The rights to freedom of thought, conscience, and religion, in general, are not easily separated from each other. According to the *Explanatory Dictionary of Constitutional Terms and Concepts*, freedom of thought, although close, is somewhat different from freedom of speech. It is no coincidence that in the European Convention for the Protection of Human Rights and Fundamental Freedoms, these two freedoms are classified under different articles: freedom of thought is combined with the other freedoms: conscience (Article 9) and speech of expression (Article 10). Only when someone professes their faith or beliefs can the state know about their existence or character. At the same time, when a person professes his religion or beliefs, such a confession, in many cases, is subject to protection under Article 9 or 10 of the convention.[6]

As noted by M. K. Basharatyan, a review of scientific commentaries on the Constitution of the Russian Federation allows us to single out two main approaches to the interpretation of the relationship between freedom of thought and freedom of speech. According to the first approach, freedom of thought and freedom of speech are not separated and, thus, freedom of thinking does not exist as an independent right. A second approach suggests that these rights are determined independently, and different content is attributed to the freedom of thought and expression. Freedom of thinking can be defined as the state-guaranteed protection of a person from "unlawful influence on his brain or consciousness with medications or technical means, illegal experiments." Also, it is guaranteed freedom for everyone to form their own opinions and beliefs without state intervention, excluding ideological violence or control over the individual.[7]

Thus, the content of freedom of thought is much broader and concerns religion and the political convictions of a person, irrespective of whether they are manifested publicly. Here we can trace its connection with the constitutional freedom of speech and the right of access to information. "Propaganda" seeks to interfere with individuals' worldviews and therefore

5 *Arrowsmith v The United Kingdom*, No. 7050/75 (November 12, 1978).

6 M. A. Krasnov and V. A. Kryazhkov, *Explanatory Dictionary of Constitutional Terms and Concepts* (Moscow: Gorodets, 2006).

7 M. K. Basharatyan, "Freedom of Thought: Legal Analysis," *Law and Politics* 1 (2007): 10.

potentially interferes with freedom of thought. Total propaganda threatens freedom of both speech and thought. According to the *Newest Political Science Dictionary*, political propaganda (in Latin, propaganda is subject to dissemination) is the act of disseminating specially prepared information and, as a rule, populist ideas. Its goal is to foster a confident attitude toward political institutions, leaders, and the political system as a whole and to develop specific models of political behavior.[8] It should be noted that despite the existence of a constitutional ban on socially dangerous propaganda and the abundance of normative definitions of various types of propaganda, there is no legal definition of political propaganda.

According to the renowned expert on academic freedom Dmitry Dubrovsky, in the modern world the fundamental academic rights and freedoms are the right to teach and learn. This protects knowledge from the influence of ideology and the preservation of science's logic and function as a critical understanding of society and the state. The idea that science should be free is not an abstract requirement and all states try to use science for their own political goals. Often behind this is a desire not only to control science but also to explain what scientists need to do. The main task of academic freedom is to protect scientists from such state control.[9]

This is the idea laid down in the Magna Charta of Universities, adopted in Bologna on September 18, 1988. According to the document, the university is an autonomous institution underlying societies, differently organized by the peculiarities of geography and historical traditions; it creates, studies, evaluates, and transmits culture through scientific research and teaching from generation to generation. Research and education must be morally and intellectually independent from political authorities and economic pressures.[10] We should note that the Higher School of Economics (HSE), which is the subject of the present case study framework, is not among the signatories of this charter.

Nonetheless, the HSE has approved its Declaration of Values, according to which the university proclaims academic freedom and political neu-

8 D. E. Pogorely, V. Yu. Fesenko, and K. V. Filippov, eds., *The Latest Political Science Dictionary* (Rostov on Don: Phoenix, 2010), 197.

9 Dmitry Dubrovsky, "Academic Rights and Freedoms," *Postnauka*, February 20, 2019, https://postnauka.ru/video/95734.

10 Magna Charta of Universities, 1988.

trality. It states that the university welcomes the free exchange of views and ideas based on the principles of strict scientific approach, mutual respect, and partnership, respects the opinion of each member of the faculty, and considers the right to express one's point of view inalienable. In academic research, it is unacceptable for a university to impose a particular scientific school's educational approaches and standards. In expert support and empirical analysis of socioeconomic processes, the university should be free from political and ideological dogmas. The university should not restrict staff and students from forming and expressing their political views. At the same time, any discussion of politics within the university's walls should be based on research, impartial, and rely on meaningful arguments.[11]

Civil society institutions have other interests in implementing modern education, which involves direct and constant cooperation with foreign partners. Foreign agent legislation makes it very difficult for such organizations to carry out externally funded advocacy work. Under the law on public associations, a nonprofit organization performing the functions of a foreign agent means a Russian nonprofit organization that receives money and other property from foreign states, their bodies, international and foreign organizations, foreign citizens, stateless persons, or persons authorized by them. Also, the law refers to Russian legal entities receiving funds and other property from these sources (except for open joint stock companies with state participation and their subsidiaries), and which participate, including in the interests of foreign sources, in political activities carried out on the territory of the Russian Federation.[12] The academic community may have difficulties implementing the law restricting educational activities. Schools and universities have the right to participate in international cooperation only if there is an agreement from the Ministry of Education or the Ministry

11 The HSE Declaration of Values was approved; see "HSE Declaration of Values," www.hse.ru/news/life/105019933.html.

12 Federal Law of 20.07.2012 N 121-FZ, "On Amendments to Certain Legislative Acts of the Russian Federation Regarding the Regulation of the Activities of Non-commercial Organizations Performing the Functions of a Foreign Agent."

of Education and Science of Russia, respectively.[13] An exception was made only for schools and universities operating on the federal level.[14]

Academic History of the HSE

The HSE was created by the prime minister of the Russian Federation, Yegor Gaidar, in 1992, initially as a university dedicated to teaching economics. The institution aimed to develop a cadre of professionals to support the development of the market economy in new Russia. Subsequently, the HSE received a national research university status and has formed more than twenty faculties, schools, and directions, from economic to technical and humanitarian. The HSE had earned a reputation of being a liberal university and fostered a space for perspectives from across the political spectrum. The university projected this sense of liberalism because these views coexisted without political manipulation and interference. The HSE had successfully developed an international network of peer institutions, adopting a range of best practices in research and teaching.

Political repression at the HSE began in 2019 after the elections to the Moscow City Duma, where the HSE vice rector Valeria Kasamara ran. In September of that year, the student magazine *Doxa* published an article about the rector of the Russian State Social University (RSSU) Natalya Pochinok, who was also a candidate in the elections to the Moscow City Duma. The article revealed violations in Pochinok's dissertation, as well as details about her political career. In response, the rector of the RSSU filed a complaint to protect the business reputation of the university. The magazine was awarded the status of a student organization, which left it without several privileges. The position allowed the *Doxa* editorial staff to interview teachers and students and conduct events at the university, including briefings, interviews, and training sessions.[15]

13 Federal Law of 05.04.2021 N 85-FZ, "On Amendments to the Federal Law on Education in the Russian Federation."

14 M. A. Fedotov, "The Eye Blurred, the Ear Sweetened," *Novaya Gazeta*, March 29, 2021, https://novayagazeta.ru/articles/2021/03/27/glaz-zamylilsia-ukho-zasakharilos.

15 Y. Onodera, "'Blatant Act of Censorship': HSE Excluded *Doxa* Magazine from Its Student Organizations for Reputational Damage," *The Village*, December 3, 2019, www.the-village.ru/city/news/368859-vshe-bez-doxa.

The situation has continued to worsen since. The founder and permanent rector of the HSE, Yaroslav Kuzminov, suddenly announced his resignation on July 1, 2021. He explained this by saying that twenty-eight years as a rector was too much, and that he never liked the administrative activity. However, the resignation must be seen in a context where HSE has been systematically losing its well-deserved image as the "most liberal university," curtailing student and professorial freedoms. There is a suspicion that the resignation was imposed and that Kuzminov was tired of compromises, people who know him say.[16]

In November 2021, two more HSE professors were dismissed. They were Sergei Pashin, a well-known lawyer in Russia, a retired federal judge, and Gennady Esakov, head of the Department of Criminal Law. They were fired for criticizing the Russian justice system in their lectures. The contract with Pashin, a retired federal judge, was terminated on December 24, 2021. He confirmed that he was not resigning on his initiative. Pashin is a member of the Moscow Helsinki Group.[17] At the end of December 2021, it became known that the former head of the Federal Security Service (FSB) for the Belgorod Region, Sergei Rozhkov, was appointed vice rector of the HSE. He will oversee the HSE Security Directorate.[18] In other words, a gradual process of replacement of the institution's cadre has led to a subtle but unmistakable erosion of its independence.

Overview of the 2020 Constitutional Amendments

In addition, the Department of Constitutional and Municipal Law of the national research university HSE soon found itself in the heart of the storm and ceased to exist. To understand why, one must understand the context

---

16 Anastasia Yakoreva et al., "I'm Not Sure if I'll Finish My Studies with Another Rector: How HSE Fired Yaroslav Kuzminov, Who Built One of the Best and Freest Universities in the Country—And Then Sacrificed His Freedom," *Meduza*, July 2, 2021, https://meduza.io/feature/2021/07/02/ne-uverena-chto-douchus-pri-drugom-rektore.

17 "'Blessed Are Those Banished for the Truth': Two Law Professors Were Fired from the HSE after Criticizing Russian Courts," *Novaya Gazeta*, https://novayagazeta.ru/articles/2021/11/27/blazhenny-izgnannye-za-pravdu-dvoikh-professorov-prava-uvolili-iz-vshe-posle-kritiki-rossiiskikh-sudov-news.

18 The former head of the FSB of the Belgorod region became the vice rector of the HSE; see www.znak.com/2021-12-19/byvshiy_glava_ufsb_belgorodskoy_oblasti_stal_prorektorom_vshe.

and notably the adoption of amendments to the Constitution of the Russian Federation in July 2020.

The president of the Russian Federation, Vladimir Putin, announced the need to amend the constitution on January 15, 2020, in his address to the Federal Assembly of the Russian Federation. This annual address is provided for by Article 84 of the Constitution. According to Vladimir Putin, the situation prevailing more than a quarter of a century ago amid a severe internal political crisis has since changed dramatically. The president of the Russian Federation insisted that the constitutional amendments were quite reasonable and essential for the further development of Russia as a rule-of-law state emphasizing the freedoms and rights of citizens, human dignity, and well-being.

The main goal of the amendments is nonetheless undeniably to strengthen the sovereignty of the Russian Federation by actually rejecting the priority of international law. Recall that according to part 4 of Article 15 of the Constitution of the Russian Federation, the generally recognized principles and norms of international law and international treaties of the Russian Federation are an integral part of its legal system. If an international treaty of the Russian Federation establishes rules other than those provided for by law, then the rules of the international treaty are supposed to be applied. President Putin insisted, however, that the sovereignty of the Russian people must be unconditional and in particular that the country's unity should be reestablished and seized back from the oligarch clans who had usurped state functions. Russia would return to international politics as a country whose opinion cannot be ignored.[19]

We should note that Russia uses a hybrid system for adopting amendments to the Constitution of the Russian Federation. It is impossible to amend chapter 1, which regulates the foundations of the constitutional system of the Russian Federation, or the second, which governs human and civil rights and freedoms. The ninth chapter describes the procedure for adopting amendments and changes to the Constitution of the Russian Federation. According to the constitution itself, to change the provisions of these chapters, it is only possible to adopt a new constitution via the convening of a

19 "President's Address to the Federal Assembly on January 15, 2020," www.kremlin.ru/events/president/news/by-date/15.01.2020.

Constitutional Assembly. A corresponding federal constitutional law has not been adopted about this body. The Constitutional Assembly is not authorized by itself to amend the Constitution of the Russian Federation. The assembly must confirm the invariability of the Constitution of the Russian Federation or submit the draft of the new constitution to a referendum.

We should pay special attention to the term "referendum." Even the original Constitution of the Russian Federation in 1993 was not adopted by referendum. At the time of its adoption, there was no federal constitutional law on a referendum in the Russian Federation. The procedure for adopting amendments to the constitution does not allow any voting. A referendum is envisaged if the Constitutional Assembly deems it necessary to adopt the draft of the new constitution (i.e., to make any amendment to chapters 1, 2, or 9). The chairperson of the Central Election Commission of the Russian Federation, E. A. Panfilova, stated that the voting should not have taken place at all. In her opinion, this law has already been adopted, and this process is already legitimate in itself.[20] However, a vote was carried out.

When preparing the amendments, the committee met under the chairmanship of a member of the Federation Council of the Russian Federation, Andrei Klishas, known as the coauthor of several laws regulating the internet in Russia. At the end of 2018, Andrei Klishas became the author of three bills to control the Internet.[21] On the network, they were called the "package of laws" by Klishas: laws have already entered into force punishing "fake news" and "insulting representatives of the authorities on the Internet," as well as the primary law "on the sovereign Internet."[22] The committee on amendments to the constitution included lawyers and public figures from many other areas, musicians, actors, and athletes. However, representatives of the political opposition, negatively disposed toward the constitutional amendments, were not among them.

These amendments had the effect of allowing Putin to be elected for the post of president of the Russian Federation at least two more times. The procedure for adopting the amendments was of a package nature. The Central

---

20 "Putin's Will to Hear the Opinion of the People Is Worthy of Great Respect," *Mediazona*, March 20, 2020, https://zona.media/news/2020/03/20/uvazhenie.

21 Resolution No. 244/1804-7 on the Procedure for All-Russian Voting on the Approval of Amendments to the Constitution of the Russian Federation, March 20, 2020.

22 Pyotr Kozlov and Andrey Soshnikov, "Does Senator Klishas Consider Himself a 'Gravedigger of the Runet?'" *BBC Russian Service*, April 12, 2019, www.bbc.com/russian/features-47894622.

Electoral Commission initiated the vote only to legitimize the amendment to nullify the limit on presidential terms.[23] At the same time, the authorities never advertised this particular amendment during the public campaign of support. The advertisement of the revisions to the constitution focused on social aspects of the amendments such as the indexation of pensions and even the protection of animals from cruelty or the idea that marriage is between a man and a woman, issues that are not ordinarily included in the subject of constitutional and legal regulation in Russia. All in all, the idea was to force acceptance of the package of amendments in a "single block" in violation of the provisions of the federal law on the procedure of adoption and entry into force of amendments to the Constitution of the Russian Federation that anticipates that there should be a single law for each constitutional change.[24] In this case, the amendments were not in any way connected. The adoption of the amendments by the package, then, was essentially an act of populism to ensure the adoption of the entire package of revisions.

The Fate of the Department of Constitutional Law

The lecturers of the Department of Constitutional Law of the national research university HSE, many of whom stood at the origins of Russia's democratic, constitutional development, disagreed with these amendments and the way they were adopted. The amendments were also criticized by the Venice Commission of the Council of Europe for Democracy through Law. In terms of the procedure for adopting the amendments, the Venice Commission concluded that the speed of preparing such large-scale amendments was inconsistent with their depth, taking into account their impact on society. This meant that there was not enough time for proper consultation with civil society before the amendments were adopted by parliament. The Venice Commission concluded that they disproportionately expanded the president of the Russian Federation's powers while eliminating some of the mechanisms of checks and balances initially provided for in the constitution. The extensive scope of immunity, coupled with the rules of proce-

23 "New Term for the President: What Is Important to Know," *RBK*, www.rbc.ru/politics/10/03/2020/5e675bfb9a79475945of67eb.

24 Federal Law of 03/04/1998 N 33-FZ, "On the Procedure for the Adoption and Entry into Force of Amendments to the Constitution of the Russian Federation."

dure for removal from office, which makes it very difficult to remove the president from power, raises serious questions about the accountability of the president.[25]

Professor Elena Lukyanova, who was also later dismissed from the HSE, agreed with the conclusions of the Venice Commission. In an interview with the radio station "Echo of Moscow," she said this is an engaging, correct, and professional fashion. It has been a long time since she read documents that would leave her with deep professional satisfaction.[26] At the end of 2018, the author of this article stated that Russia does not need a reform of the constitution.[27]

It is worth noting that it was not the first time that the Department of Constitutional and Municipal Law ended up in the crosshairs of the Russian government. An earlier case that occurred back in 2017 involved a memorial plaque in honor of the Soviet dictator Joseph Stalin. The Department of Constitutional and Municipal Law made a statement about its categorical disagreement with the installation of this plate. "The other day, we were struck by the news that in the building of the Moscow State Law Academy named after Oleg Kutafin, The Academy hung a memorial plaque dedicated to Stalin's speech. We, the collective of the Department of Constitutional and Administrative Law of the national research university HSE, will not condone this. We want to state that while this board hangs in the building of the Moscow State Law Academy, not a single member of the department will participate in scientific and other events held by the Academy."[28]

Following this, four lecturers of constitutional law have been dismissed from the Faculty of Law of the HSE. Elena Lukyanova, Irina Alebastrova,

---

25 Council of Europe, "Venice Commission Adopts New Opinion on 2020 Constitutional Amendments and the Procedure for Their Adoption in the Russian Federation," www.coe.int/ru/web/moscow/-/venice-commission-adopts-new-opinion-on-2020-constitutional-amendments-and-the-procedure-for-their-adoption-in-the-russian-federation.

26 Council of Europe, "Opinion on Draft Amendments to the Constitution (as Signed by the President of the Russian Federation on 14 March 2020) Related to the Execution in the Russian Federation of Decisions by the European Court of Human Rights, Adopted by the Venice Commission on 18 June 2020 by a Written Procedure Replacing the 123rd Plenary Session," June 18, 2020, www.venice.coe.int/webforms/documents/?pdf=CDL-AD(2020)009-e.

27 Federal Law of 03/04/1998 N 33-FZ, "On the Procedure for the Adoption and Entry into Force of Amendments to the Constitution of the Russian Federation."

28 A. Gatinsky, "HSE Professors Refused to Work with Moscow State Law Academy Because of the Plaque in Honor of Stalin," *RBK*, June 28, 2017, www.rbc.ru/society/28/06/2017/59537a5b9a79470a1d73d040.

Elena Glushko, and Andrey Shcherbovich (the article's author) were fired, with immediate effect. They were then informed about the dissolution of the Department of Constitutional Law by email on July 1, the day of voting on amendments to the Constitution of the Russian Federation. The Faculty of Law liquidated the Department of Constitutional and Municipal Law. Its long-term leader, Mikhail Krasnov, was transferred to a research professor position. The goal was to eliminate, together with the department, a small but close-knit community of people who supported the democratic tradition in constitutional law, and who were ready to defend the importance of democratic institutions. The department's teachers trained good specialists and caring and responsible citizens of their country. The gradual establishment of ideological control over higher education in the humanities contradicts the still valid constitutional provision on freedom of teaching, weakens Russian higher education, and extinguishes free thought.

The faculty fired from the HSE and then created the Free University, a free community of educators who offer quality university courses to students who want to listen to them. The Manifesto of the Free University states: "Our task is to rebuild the University, freeing teachers from all administrative dictatorship. If the University can no longer be free, a new free university is needed. Here the paths of the University and the state diverge. We are not state and not competing with state educational institutions. We do not have a campus. We will teach from home. We will teach from libraries. We will train in summer schools. We will not stop defending the freedom of knowledge and leave our students. We cannot be expelled from the University because the University is us."[29]

29 Free University Manifesto, https://freemoscow.university/.

Chapter 15

Challenges of Academic Freedom in India

Considering the Human Rights Education Framework for Amplifying Marginalized Student Voices

Nidhi Sadana Sabharwal and Brigid Freeman

Introduction

Internationally applicable "civil, political, social and cultural rights" are understood to involve "freedom of thought, conscience, religion, expression, assembly and association."[1] Freedom from censorship, discrimination, repression, and interference is intrinsic to democracy and the everyday practice of secular values such as equality and social justice. In the sphere of higher education, conceptions of academic freedom, informed by Humboldtian ideals, have evolved over time, vary between jurisdictions, and remain contested.[2] Tierney and Sabharwal have emphasized the importance of the free-

1 UNESCO, "Recommendation Concerning the Status of Higher Education Teaching Personnel," 1997, Art. 26.

2 Rold Von Lüde, "From Humboldt to Market: Competition and Excellence as New Governance Principles in the German University System," in *State and Market in Higher Education Reforms*, ed. Hans G.

dom to teach, undertake, and disseminate research, study, learn, and discuss without fear or concern of retribution.[3]

Academic freedom involving sensitive issues concerning caste-based inequalities and gender-based injustices becomes even more critical on socially diverse higher education campuses. Social diversity among the higher education student body signifies a plurality of ideologies and values. Plurality influences the ways in which issues of inequality and injustice are discussed by diverse peer groups, and interactions take place in classrooms and more generally on campuses. For students from socially excluded groups, the use of academic freedom to build understanding and critical analysis of social oppression and its consequences becomes important. It is only when everyone understands and agrees on principles of equality, social justice, and nonviolence that students from marginalized groups feel welcomed and higher education classrooms and campuses start to become inclusive.

However, tension points exist around the ways in which academic freedom is exercised to meet its goal of creating inclusive campuses. These tensions arise when the use of academic freedom is caught between a diverse student body, a homogeneous management and faculty composed primarily of a privileged social group, and the prevalence of systemic social inequalities and injustices, as is the case in India. Given this context, this chapter asks: What challenges exist with regard to achieving the goal of academic freedom while concurrently making India's higher education campuses more inclusive?

Discussions on academic freedom necessitate an understanding of the dimensions of challenges facing students from marginalized social groups on higher education campuses and the responsibility of faculty members to internalize the varied purposes of their academic freedom. These purposes include the creation of a civic learning environment by management and faculty for realizing inclusive classrooms and campuses, free of fear or concern about retribution including censorship, direct and indirect discrimination, repression, or interference.

Based on empirical evidence, this chapter argues that academic freedom must be accompanied by academic responsibility, which allows for the mar-

---

Schuetze (Leiden: Brill, 2012), 149; Akeel Bilgrami and Jonathan R. Cole, eds., *Who's Afraid of Academic Freedom?* (New York: Columbia University Press, 2015).

3 William G. Tierney and Nidhi S. Sabharwal, "Academic Freedom in the World's Largest Democracy," *International Higher Education* 86 (2016): 15–16.

ginalized voices of students from socially excluded groups to be amplified and their participation rights respected. It puts forward the important role of human rights education to advance the goals of academic freedom in creating a civic learning environment. Such an environment can act as a mechanism for protecting responsible academic freedom and creating democratic spaces on socially diverse higher education campuses.

Higher Education in India

In order to situate the chapter, it is useful to offer some background context on higher education in India. Higher education participation in India has increased manifold over recent decades and campuses have undergone significant demographic change. India's higher education system, traditionally a domain of the elite, entered a stage of massification as the gross enrollment ratio (GER) increased from 6 percent in the 1990s to 27 percent in 2020, in large part due to growth in private higher education provision.[4] With this shift toward massification, the proportion of higher education graduates in India's large population increased. India has grown to be the second largest higher education system after China (50.2 million in 2020); well ahead of the United States (18.8 million in 2020).[5]

In 2020–1, 41.3 million students enrolled in Indian higher education, through 1,100 universities, 43,800 colleges, and 11,300 standalone institutions. With massification, access has broadened. By 2020–1, over half of the Indian higher education student population comprised traditionally marginalized groups including 14 percent Scheduled Castes (SC; former untouchables), 6 percent Scheduled Tribes (ST; indigenous groups), and 36 percent from Other Backward Classes (OBC; lower castes in the caste hierarchy). Women's participation had grown, constituting 49 percent by 2020–1; however, Muslim students remain underrepresented, constituting 5 percent (1.9 million) compared to their representation more broadly (14 percent

4 N. V. Varghese and Nidhi S. Sabharwal, "The Future of Higher Education in India from Massification to Universalization," *CPRHE Research Papers* 16 (2022); N. V. Varghese and Garima Malik, "Institutional Autonomy in Higher Education in India," *University News* 53 (2015): 115.

5 UNESCO Institute of Statistics, "Enrolment by Level of Education (Dataset 2023)," http://data.uis.unesco.org/Index.aspx?DataSetCodeEDULIT_DS&popupcustomisetrue&langen.

in 2011).[6] India has a long history of campus-based activism, with student unions frequently affiliated with major political parties.[7]

Change through Policy and Commissions

Equitable Access to Education

Targeted legislation and numerous public policies have been introduced to promote equitable access at all levels of education. Importantly, this includes the Right to Education Act 2009 framing school education as a fundamental human right along with Education for All (EFA) programs.[8] Following these developments, the number of secondary school graduates eligible to transition to higher education has grown. At the higher education level, public policies have favored affirmative action initiatives emphasizing access. Most notably this includes the implementation of a centrally mandated quota system for admissions (i.e., reservation of seats for students from marginalized groups) and relaxation of entry-level eligibility criteria (i.e., low cutoff marks). Higher education institutions also provide student support, mostly in the form of scholarships, fee concessions, and student hostel accommodation. Many of these initiatives target SCs, STs, and OBCs, while others are available preferentially for girls and women, and religious minorities (i.e., Muslims, Christians, Sikhs, Buddhists, and Zoroastrians).

Despite such interventions, achievements of inequitable access remain overshadowed by persistent challenges students from socially excluded groups face after they have been admitted. If one of the main obligations of higher education institutions is to provide an inclusive learning environment that teaches students about tolerance and civil discourse through open discussion and debate, then gaining an understanding of these chal-

6 Government of India, Ministry of Education, "All India Survey of Higher Education 2020–2021," https://aishe.gov.in/aishe/BlankDCF/AISHE%20Final%20Report%202020-21.pdf.

7 Niraja Gopal Jayal, "Academic Freedom in India," in *University Autonomy Decline: Causes, Responses, and Implications for Academic Freedom*, ed. Kirsten Roberts Lyer, Ilyas Saliba, and Janika Spannagel (London: Routledge, 2023), 64.

8 Monisha Bajaj, *Schooling for Social Change: The Rise and Impact of Human Rights Education in India* (London: Continuum, 2012); Monisha Bajaj, ed., *Human Rights Education: Theory, Research, Praxis* (Philadelphia: University of Pennsylvania Press, 2017).

lenges is imperative.[9] Tensions faced by such students manifest themselves in two dominant forms. First, caste-based prejudices influence socioacademic interactions between marginalized students and their peers, teachers, and management; second, feelings of marginalization in classroom discussions regarding social justice issues. These tensions will be discussed in more detail throughout this chapter.

Institutional Autonomy and Academic Freedom

Following India's independence, important education commissions and policies highlighted institutional autonomy, academic freedoms, and rights afforded to faculty members. The Radhakrishnan University Education Commission of 1948 referred to freedom of conscience and differentiated between the role of the State in funding and controlling academic policies and practices. This early commission affirmed the importance of self-governing higher education institutions and emphasized the right of teachers to speak freely regarding controversial issues.[10] Two decades later, the Kothari Commission of 1964–6 affirmed the importance of institutional autonomy and again positioned faculty members' right to critical thinking and dissent as integral to the role of the university. This report argued that "universities are pre-eminently the forum for a critical assessment of society—sympathetic, objective, unafraid—whose partiality and motives cannot be suspected."[11] In 2009, the important Yashpal Committee report lamented the erosion of academic freedoms in preceding years, for example, observing that "organized youth [and] ... the official machinery of the university has been deliberately used to obstruct or subvert the possibility of peaceful debate and inquiry."[12] The Radhakrishnan, Kothari, and Yashpal Commissions each highlighted the importance of freedom of thought for teachers, emphasizing their pur-

9 Geoffrey R. Stone, "A Brief History of Academic Freedom," in *Who's Afraid of Academic Freedom?* ed. Akeel Bilgrami and Jonathan R. Cole (New York: Columbia University Press, 2015), 1.

10 Sarvepalli Radhakrishnan, *The Report of the University Education Commission (1948–1949)* (New Delhi: Ministry of Education, 1962).

11 Kothari Commission, *Report of the Educational Commission (1964–66): Education and National Development* (New Delhi: Ministry of Education, 1966), 275–276.

12 Yashpal Committee, *The Report of the Committee to Advise on Renovation and Rejuvenation of Higher Education in India* (New Delhi: Government of India, 2009), 16.

suit and practice of truth as the basis through which democratic ideals of equality, liberty, and fraternity could be achieved.

The National Education Policy (NEP2020), representing a transformational change agenda for India's school and higher education systems and institutions, anticipated that "faculty will be given the freedom to design their own curricular and pedagogical approaches ... including textbook and reading material selections, assignments, and assessments."[13] Further, while not explicitly referring to academic freedom, NEP2020 stated that "empowering the faculty to conduct innovative teaching, research, and service" is a "key motivator and enabler for them to do truly outstanding, creative work."[14] Chattopadhyay has argued that NEP2020 hinges on institutional and teacher autonomy, coupled with the institutionalization of accountability.[15]

Challenges to Academic Freedom in Indian Higher Education

As India's higher education system has grown, academic freedom has suffered.[16] In recent years India's position on the Academic Freedom Index has declined overall, with particular concerns relating to campus integrity, institutional autonomy, and academic and cultural expression. Scholars have suggested that this "decline ... started from a comparatively high level during India's democratic period and is now associated with rapidly accelerating autocratization."[17] Scholars have suggested there has been an increase in assaults on academic freedom in Indian higher education since 2014, including increased deployment of India's antiterrorist Unlawful Activities

13 Brigid Freeman, *Internationalisation at Home and Abroad: Leveraging the National Education Policy 2020* (Pariprekshya: National Institute of Educational Planning and Administration, 2022), 40. See also Brigid Freeman, *India's National Education Policy 2020 and Australia's Education Engagement: Key Findings from Roundtables* (Melbourne: Australia India Institute, 2021).

14 Freeman, *Internationalisation at Home and Abroad*, 40; Freeman, *India's National Education Policy 2020.*

15 Saumen Chattopadhyay, "Academic Freedom, Institutional Autonomy and Institutionalising Accountability: A Reflection on the National Education Policy 2020," *JMC Review* 4 (2020): 1.

16 Nandini Sundar, "Academic Freedom and Indian Universities," *Economic & Political Weekly* 53 (2018): 48; Chattopadhyay, "Academic Freedom, Institutional Autonomy and Institutionalising Accountability"; David Kaye, "Report of the Special Rapporteur on the Promotion and Protection of the Right to Freedom of Opinion and Expression," UNGAOR, 75th Sess., UN Doc A/75/261 (2020).

17 Friedrich-Alexander-Universität Institute of Political Science, "Academic Freedom Index Update 2023," www.pol.phil.fau.eu/2023/03/02/academic-freedom-index-update-2023/.

(Prevention) Act (UAPA) against faculty and students.[18] The *Free to Think Report of the Scholars at Risk Academic Freedom Monitoring Project* argued that in India "state and higher education actors have used arrests, prosecutions, dismissals, and other coercive means to punish and silence scholars and students whose academic work, views, or associations the government finds displeasing."[19] Sundar has also highlighted the role of student groups acting as provocateurs.[20]

Challenges to Faculty Member's Rights

Reported instances of challenges to faculty member's rights at Indian higher education institutions are numerous and growing. They range from censorship of books and interference with university syllabi; denial of permission to present; disruption of seminars, meetings, and events on campus; arrest and criminal charges; physical attacks; termination, suspension, and/or resignation; and denial of research visas and restrictions on academic exchanges.[21] In multiple examples, the curriculum has been disrupted by objections from university management, or teacher and student organizations.[22] For example, Delhi University's Standing Committee of Academic Council recommended the removal of Kancha Ilaiah's *Why I Am Not a Hindu, God as Political Philosopher, and Post-Hindu India* as the content of the book was seen as controversial.[23] Manonmaniam Sundaranar University, Tirunelveli,

18 Kusha Anand and Laraib Niaz, "The Precarious State of Academic Freedom in Higher Education: The Case of India and Pakistan," in *Research in the Social Scientific Study of Religion: Lesser Heard Voices in Studies of Religion*, ed. Ralph W. Hood and Sariya Cheruvallil-Contractor (Leiden: Brill, 2022), 281; Dimitar D. Gueorguiev, "Introduction: Progress under Threat—Academic Freedom in Asia," in *New Threats to Academic Freedom in Asia*, ed. Dimitar D. Gueorguiev (New York: Columbia University Press, 2023), 1; Jayal, "Academic Freedom in India."

19 Scholars at Risk, *Free to Think: Report of the Scholars at Risk Academic Freedom Monitoring Project* (New York: Scholars at Risk, 2021), 68.

20 Sundar, "Academic Freedom and Indian Universities."

21 Nandini Sundar and Gowhar Fazili, "Academic Freedom in India: A Status Report," *The India Forum*, www.theindiaforum.in/article/academic-freedom-india; "Six Tables That Tell the Story of Academic Unfreedom in India," *The Wire*, October 4, 2022, https://thewire.in/rights/six-tables-that-tell-the-story-of-academic-unfreedom-in-india.

22 "Students Call Off Ambedkar Jayanti Event after TISS 'Denies Entry' to Sujat Ambedkar," *The Wire*, April 14, 2022, https://thewire.in/caste/tiss-ambedkar-jayanti-sujat-ambedkar.

23 Saikat Ghosh, "Decision to Remove Kancha Ilaiah's Books from Delhi University's Political Science PG Syllabus Is RSS-Motivated," *The Leaflet*, October 29, 2018, https://theleaflet.in/decision-to-remove-kancha-ilaiahs-books-from-delhi-universitys-political-science-pg-syllabus-is-rss-motivated/.

removed Arundhati Roy's *Walking with the Comrades* following objections on the ground that it justified the actions of groups that engaged in antistate activities.[24] A faculty member who used popular media to question their university's implementation of affirmative action policy may face disciplinary action. This instance occurred when a faculty member from a government-supported public university wrote a newspaper article in support of students from disadvantaged social groups. The article raised doubts and questioned his university's compliance with affirmative action policies. However as a result he was accused of damaging the institution's reputation and was threatened with disciplinary measures.[25] In some instances, complaints have been taken to the High Court, including an objection by the right-wing student organization (ABVP) to a reading included in a University of Delhi history syllabus.[26]

Challenges to Student's Rights

Academic freedom of students in Indian higher education institutions has been framed in terms of choices, where students have the freedom to choose to apply to study in different institutions, courses, and delivery modes.[27] However, there are numerous reported instances of challenges to students' rights manifest as disruption of seminars, meetings, and events on campus; arrest of students; physical attacks on students; suspension and/or expulsion of students; and bans on student groups.[28] For example, the Ambedkarite Students' Association (ASA), representing marginalized students (i.e., SC, ST, OBC, and religious minorities), canceled their planned celebrations where management refused entry to Tata Institute of Social Sciences, Mumbai, to journalist Sujat Ambedkar, grandson of Dr. B. R. Ambedkar.

---

24 "Arundhati Roy Book Removed from Syllabus of TN University over Alleged Support for Maoists," *New Indian Express*, November 12, 2020, www.newindianexpress.com/states/tamil-nadu/2020/nov/12/arundhati-roy-book-removed-from-syllabus-of-tn-university-over-alleged-support-for-maoists-2222838.html.

25 Jayal, "Academic Freedom in India."

26 Jayal, "Academic Freedom in India."

27 Saumen Chattopadhyay, "Academic Freedom and Employability: A Neoliberal Agenda to Guide Education Reform," *Social Scientist* 41 (2013): 69; Chattopadhyay, "Academic Freedom, Institutional Autonomy and Institutionalising Accountability."

28 Sundar and Fazili, "Academic Freedom in India: A Status Report"; "Six Tables That Tell the Story of Academic Unfreedom in India."

The ASA claimed management's refusal was "deeply ... discriminatory and casteist ... against the entire Dalit community."[29]

In another instance, an event exploring "The Idea of the University" at Delhi University hosted by the left-wing All India Students Association (AISA) was allegedly disrupted by the right-wing student organization (ABVP). Faculty argued that "the obvious casualty in the process is the right to speak freely."[30] In another example, management at Sai Homeopathic Medical College and Nityanand Hospital disallowed an enrolled Muslim student entry to campus for wearing a hijab.[31] In extreme cases, students from marginalized groups have resorted to suicide in response to hostile treatment, suspension, and harassment by university administration, faculty, and other students. Cases such as this have led to a nationwide outcry.[32]

There are other examples where students' academic freedoms have been challenged. For example, in 2016 the ruling government in Gujarat reportedly dictated topics around government schemes as suitable for PhD theses.[33] In other instances, criminal charges have been brought against students for allegedly defamatory statements concerning issues sensitive to the government (e.g., Kashmir, Hindu gods, the Citizenship [Amendment] Act).[34] A Jawaharlal Nehru University (JNU) PhD student was charged with, among other matters, reading inappropriate literature for his MPhil, including Paul Brass's *Forms of Collective Violence: Riots, Pogroms and Genocide in Modern India*.[35] Talks at higher education institutions focusing on issues concerning caste and gender discrimination, democracy, and the constitution have reportedly been subject to protests and bans invoking the "heckler's

29 "Students Call off Ambedkar Jayanti Event after TISS 'Denies Entry' to Sujat Ambedkar."

30 Ajoy Ashirwad Mahaprashastra, "ABVP Allegedly Attacks Delhi University Students, Journalist at Public Meeting," *The Wire*, October 28, 2016, https://thewire.in/uncategorised/abvp-allegedly-attacks-delhi-university-students-journalist-public-meeting.

31 Sukanya Shantha, "Don't Wear a Hijab if You Want to Study Here," *The Wire*, March 25, 2018, https://thewire.in/education/dont-wear-a-hijab-if-you-want-to-study-here.

32 Bharat Rathod, "Caste Conflicts on Campuses: Examining Diversity Research to Transform Indian Universities into Inclusive Learning Spaces," *Journal of Social Inclusion Studies* 5 (2019): 129.

33 Jayal, "Academic Freedom in India"; Bharat Yagnik and Ashish Chauhan, "Gujarat Govt Gives Universities List of Topics for PhD Theses," *Times of India*, April 26, 2016, https://timesofindia.indiatimes.com/india/Gujarat-govt-gives-universities-list-of-topics-for-PhD-theses/articleshow/51986510.cms.

34 Sundar and Fazili, "Academic Freedom in India"; "Six Tables That Tell the Story of Academic Unfreedom in India."

35 Nandini Sundar, "When Universities Become Objectives of Counterinsurgency," *The Wire*, March 26, 2021, https://thewire.in/education/when-universities-become-objects-of-counterinsurgency.

veto."[36] Incidents involving faculty at elite Indian higher education institutions abusing students from Dalit and Adivasi backgrounds have also been reported, and there are multiple examples of student resistance against casteism on campus.[37]

Many of these examples involved management and faculty pushback against academic endeavors and activities of marginalized students. Examining such issues, Rathod concluded that "the evidence demonstrates ... a range of discriminatory practices and behaviors by higher caste individuals and the higher castes-controlled institutions" against Dalit students.[38]

Dimensions of Challenges Facing Students from Socially Excluded Groups on Higher Education Campuses

While achieving higher education equity has been a major goal of various Government of India education policies and commissions, and an important principle underpinning diversification of the student body, challenges persist for students from socially excluded groups who enter higher education. This section discusses empirical evidence from a large-scale national study on the nature and forms of challenges that threaten the social justice goals of academic freedom in Indian higher education.[39] The study was carried out in twelve higher education institutions located across six major states including Bihar, Delhi, Karnataka, Kerala, Maharashtra, and Uttar Pradesh. The empirical research followed a mixed methodology approach with primary data collected through a survey, focus groups, and in-depth interviews. The survey was administered to over 3,200 students, while focus group discussions were conducted with students from marginalized groups (i.e., SCs, STs, OBCs, women, and minorities). In-depth interviews were carried out with faculty members, faculty in charge of cells and committees, and institutional leaders. Secondary data was sourced from administrative records. The empirical study found that campus tensions faced by students from socially

36 Sundar, "Academic Freedom and Indian Universities."

37 See, e.g., Ananya Bhattacharya, "'Bloody Bastards': India's Elite IITs Have a History of Deep-Rooted Casteism," *Quartz India*, April 27, 2021, https://finance.yahoo.com/news/bloody-bastards-india-elite-iits-100341453.html; Sundar, "Academic Freedom and Indian Universities."

38 Rathod, "Caste Conflicts on Campuses," 131.

39 Nidhi S. Sabharwal and C. M. Malish, "Diversity and Inclusion in Higher Education: A Study of Institutions in Selected States of India," *CPRHE Research Report* (2016).

excluded groups on higher education campuses stem primarily from two channels: exclusion from curriculum content and pedagogy, and teachers' negative conceptions of diversity.

Exclusion from Curriculum Content and Pedagogy

In India's higher education system, what gets taught in the classroom (i.e., the curriculum) is centrally prescribed by the government or the curriculum development committees to a greater extent than in more decentralized systems.[40] Students from socially excluded groups reported that their experiences were not reflected in the curriculum. These students reported that, in group discussions, the curriculum overrepresented the life world and cultural practices of dominant socioreligious groups, while theirs remained largely invisible. This aspect is particularly felt by students from religious minorities.

Furthermore, it is striking that a much higher proportion of students from the SC group (39 percent) than from the ST/OBC group (28 percent) reported that teachers rarely encouraged students to respect diverse beliefs and perspectives in their classrooms. A significant majority of teachers in Indian higher education institutions are from privileged socioreligious groups.[41] Students from marginalized groups also reported that the dominant pedagogy, the lecture method, and the lack of classroom discussion involving diverse perspectives and alternative opinions exacerbated their sense of exclusion. Clearly, opportunities to encourage constructive interactions among various social groupings in higher education classrooms are being lost.

Teachers' Negative Conceptions of Diversity

Faculty members frequently had low expectations regarding the academic talents of students from underprivileged social groups, particularly the SCs and STs, and harbored bias against these pupils. Several faculty members

40 Tierney and Sabharwal, "Academic Freedom in the World's Largest Democracy."

41 Nidhi S. Sabharwal, Emily F. Henderson, and Roma Smart Joseph, "Hidden Social Exclusion in Indian Academia: Gender, Caste and Conference Participation," *Gender and Education* 32 (2020): 27; Anand and Niaz, "The Precarious State of Academic Freedom in Higher Education."

appeared to hold a meritocratic ideology, believing that increased student diversity resulting from quota admission systems and relaxed eligibility criteria—rather than merit—was harming the quality of higher education. Faculty members frequently failed to take into consideration the rights of students from underprivileged social groups enrolled through affirmative action initiatives such as reservations.

As a result, students from marginalized groups, most notably SCs and STs, feel excluded from higher education. Diverse perspectives are frequently not respected in classroom discussions, and prejudice and stereotypes influence teacher–student socioacademic interactions. Peer group interactions unnecessarily reflect students' social identities. These findings are consistent with research that has highlighted challenges facing students from socially excluded groups on higher education campuses in India, including poor treatment and discrimination.[42]

These challenges increase the responsibility of faculty members to question dominant ideologies, encourage discussions on foundational principles, and allow diverse perspectives to be debated. Only when everyone in the classroom understands the principles of equality, social justice, and nonviolence can the academic freedom of the marginalized be realized and learning proceed without fear or concern of retribution. The presence of democratic spaces to be able to freely discuss and critically analyze multiple forms of social inequalities and injustices can help develop a shared understanding.

Human Rights Education for Advancing Social Justice Goals

The multifaceted issues facing higher education students from socially excluded groups suggest there is scope to promote a greater understanding of human rights and academic freedom in order to advance social justice goals. This would involve expanding the notion of academic freedom afforded uni-

42 Samson Ovichegan, "Social Exclusion, Social Inclusion and Passing: The Experience of Dalit Students at One Elite Indian University," *International Journal of Inclusive Education* 18 (2013): 359; Anoop Kumar Singh, "Defying the Odds: The Triumphs and Tragedies of Dalit and Adivasi Students in Higher Education," in *Beyond Inclusion: The Practice of Equal Access in Higher Education*, ed. Satish Deshpande and Usha Zacharias (London: Routledge, 2013), 186; Nidhi S. Sabharwal et al., "Diversity, Academic Performance, and Discrimination: A Case Study of a Higher Educational Institution," *IIDS Working Paper Series* 8 (2014); Rathod, "Caste Conflicts on Campuses."

versities teachers, and students in terms of institution and course choice, to student engagement with curriculum, pedagogy, and teacher–student socio-academic interaction. Where human rights education is introduced, a civic learning environment that safeguards the social justice goals of academic freedom emerges. What follows presents elements of the human rights education framework that could more broadly be deployed to address current tensions around academic freedom, particularly for students from marginalized groups as they navigate higher education classrooms and campuses.

We argue that even where education policy interventions have stipulated that academic freedom be valued and protected, this has not been sufficient. In the context of a social mismatch between student and faculty composition, where what gets taught in the classroom is more or less centrally prescribed by regulatory authorities developing and approving curriculum, we affirm the important role of education that promotes human rights in creating a civic learning environment for teachers and students on higher education campuses.

Human Rights Education Framework

International conventions and declarations obligate states to guarantee the rights of persons facing inequality and injustice including women, religious and sexual minorities, people with disability, refugees, displaced and trafficked persons. Framing of human rights by the UN Human Rights Commission in the years following the Second World War broadly encompassed economic, social, and political inequality and, more particularly, racial antidiscrimination. Bajaj explained that through this lens, "human rights led to justice by challenging unequal hierarchies of power, amplifying the voices of the weak, and working to eliminate the root causes of conflict: poverty, discrimination, and exploitation."[43]

The right to human rights education was first codified in the 1948 Universal Declaration of Human Rights and reinforced by international treaties on civil, political, economic, social, and cultural rights that India is party to.[44] According to the Universal Declaration of Human Rights, edu-

43 Bajaj, *Human Rights Education*, 229–230.

44 The Universal Declaration of Human Rights, when read with the 1966 International Covenant on Civil and Political Rights (ICCPR) (in force from 1976) and 1966 International Covenant on Economic So-

cation aims to promote "understanding, tolerance, and friendship among different nations, racial or religious groups."[45] Gibson and Grant argued that such human rights instruments "provided a new common language for contesting injustice."[46] Subsequent supranational agreements have reiterated the importance of human rights education and intercultural understanding. First, the 1989 UN convention obligated states to promote education for "the development of respect for human rights and fundamental freedoms … in the spirit of understanding, peace, tolerance, equality of sexes, and friendship among all peoples, ethnic, national and religious groups and persons of indigenous origin."[47] This convention also asserted the right to an education that promotes respect for cultural identity, language, and values. Second, the 2011 UN declaration envisaged education promoting observance of human rights, peace, and fundamental freedoms "by providing persons with knowledge, skills, and understanding and developing their attitudes and behaviors, to empower them to contribute to the building and promotion of a universal culture of human rights."[48]

At the global level, several initiatives have embraced these principles. For example, the UN World Programme, launched in 2004, aimed to advance human rights education to build inclusive, peaceful societies.[49] These governance instruments and initiatives anticipated human rights education acknowledging the rights of teachers and students, including students' participation rights and empowerment and, more recently, progress toward achievement of the Sustainable Development Goals (SDGs).[50]

---

cial and Cultural Rights (ICESCR) (in force from 1976), together form the International Bill of Human Rights.

45 Universal Declaration of Human Rights, GA Res 217A (III), UNGAOR, 3rd Sess., Supp. No 13, UN Doc A/810 (1948) 71, Art. 26(2).

46 Melissa L. Gibson and Carl A. Grant, "Historicizing Critical Educational Praxis: A Human Rights Framework for Justice-Oriented Teaching," in *Human Rights Education: Theory, Research, Praxis*, ed. Monisha Bajaj (Philadelphia: University of Pennsylvania Press, 2017), 234.

47 Universal Declaration of Human Rights, 1948, Art. 29.

48 Universal Declaration of Human Rights, 1948, Art. 2(2).

49 United Nations, "Fourth Phase (2020–2024) of the World Programme for Human Rights Education," www.ohchr.org/en/resources/educators/human-rights-education-training/world-programme-human-rights-education/phase4.

50 Audrey Osler and Juanjuan Zhu, "Narratives in Teaching and Research for Justice and Human Rights," *Education, Citizenship and Social Justice* 6 (2011): 223.

Influence of Human Rights Framework on Indian Constitution, Policy, and Programs

The Constitution of India, in force from 1950, enshrined fundamental rights including the right to equality, the right to freedom, the right against exploitation, the right to freedom of religion, cultural and educational rights, and the right to constitutional remedies. While not explicitly protecting academic freedom, the constitution stipulated that "no citizen shall be denied admission into any educational institution maintained by the State or receiving aid out of State funds on grounds only of religion, race, caste, language or any of them."[51]

The constitution and supranational legal instruments, including the Universal Declaration of Human Rights, have informed the establishment of Government of India ministries (e.g., Ministry of Minority Affairs), enforcement mechanisms (e.g., National Human Rights Commission), and institutions (e.g., Indian Institute of Human Rights). They have also energized India's national education regulatory authorities such as the University Grants Commission and National Council of Educational Research and Training.[52] Government-commissioned reports have also promoted human rights education. For example, the 1985 Sikri Committee report, *Blueprint for Promotion of Human Rights in India at All Levels*, gave some impetus, while the National Human Rights Commission and University Grants Commission produced model human rights education curriculum and foundation course materials.[53]

Policies have also reinforced the role of higher education in engendering human rights. The Kasturirangan Committee's Draft National Education Policy 2019 affirms that higher education institutions "will develop an understanding of our Constitutional values, and the disposition and capacities for their practice, amongst all their students. The curricula of (all) programs, in tandem with the overall culture and the environment of the [higher education institution], will enable this. The duties and rights in action, of all citi-

51 Constitution of India, 1950, Art. 29(2).

52 Monisha Bajaj and Rachel Wahl, "Human Rights Education in Postcolonial India," in *Human Rights Education: Theory, Research, Praxis*, ed. Monisha Bajaj (Philadelphia: University of Pennsylvania Press, 2017), 147.

53 Kumar Kumar, "The Relevance of Human Rights Education in Indian Society," *Yojana*, http://yojana.gov.in/public-account3jan.asp.

zens of India, informed by these values will also be highlighted, [including] commitment to equality, justice, and fairness; embracing diversity, plurality, and inclusion."[54] More recently, NEP2020 mooted increased institutional autonomy and emphasized human and constitutional values as guiding principles for programs, including the democratic spirit, pluralism, equality, justice, liberty, equality, and fraternity.

India's human rights education programs are now provided variously at undergraduate and postgraduate levels, through regular, distance learning, and, more recently, online modes. Such programs are provided through different disciplinary lenses including political science, law, sociology, economics, and history emphasizing human rights and duties and human rights law. Programs differ in scope and intensity throughout India.[55] For example, the Savitribai Phule Pune University Human Rights Education Programme explores human rights and duties, the human rights of women, socially and economically disadvantaged people, and vulnerable groups (i.e., stateless persons, sex workers, migrant workers, and HIV/AIDS victims).[56] The National Human Rights Commission runs training programs in conjunction with some Indian education institutions and makes available online human rights education resources from the Indira Gandhi National Open University. Such programs frequently highlight three dimensions: knowledge about human rights; values, beliefs, and attitudes underpinning a human rights lens; and actions to defend human rights and avoid abuses.[57]

Somewhat similarly, peace education programs have been introduced by some institutions, with India's National Council for Educational Research and Training envisioning such programs emphasizing responsible citizenship and social justice while promoting a secular, democratic culture. India's

54 Kasturirangan Committee, *Draft National Education Policy 2019* (New Delhi: Ministry of Human Resource Development, 2019), 231.

55 Sheeraz Ayoub Kuchy and T. Thilagavathy, "Human Rights Education in India: Importance, Present Status and Future Actions," *Asia Pacific Journal of Research* 1 (2016): 120; Bajaj, *Human Rights Education.*

56 Other examples include the Jamia Millia Islamia Master of Arts (Human Rights and Duties Education), Jawaharlal Nehru University (Human Rights Studies Programme), Banarus Hindu University (Master of Laws, Human Rights, and Duties Education), and National Law School of India University (human rights law units in Bachelor of Arts/Bachelor of Laws [Hons.], Postgraduate Diploma in Human Rights Law).

57 Indian Institute of Human Rights, "Education: A Tool for the Elimination of Human Rights Violations," www.rightsedu.net/about_us.htm#.

peace education programs frequently critique structures of violence, respond to intergroup and societal violence and conflict, and/or concentrate on pluralism, character building, and values education. For example, peace education programs include Communalism Combat in Mumbai primary schools and Centre for Dialogue and Reconciliation teacher training in the northern India region of Kashmir.[58]

India's experiences of violence relating to Dalits and religious minorities and cultural and structural violence (e.g., income inequality and discrimination on the basis of caste, religion, gender, language, and sexual identity) have encouraged the introduction of human rights and peace education programs.[59] These programs have some synergies with citizenship education more broadly defined, which has been established at school and higher education levels. Thorat and Sabharwal posit that citizenship education "prepare[s] students to become effective citizens by enhancing [their] knowledge regarding issues pertaining to inequalities, poverty, discrimination, injustices, and inculcating democratic values of equality, liberty, fraternity and skills needed to participate in effective democratic engagement."[60] Expanding the provision of such programs using a human rights education framework to develop democratic classrooms and campuses would go some way to addressing the limitations of existing academic freedoms of universities, teachers, and students in higher education institutions.

Conclusion

This chapter has examined the challenges of academic freedom in India and proposed the adoption of a human rights education framework to amplify marginalized student voices and assure their academic freedom, to realize human rights. Furthermore, human rights education can provide protection to faculty members whose academic freedom has been violated while advocating for students from marginalized social groups. In Indian higher education, tensions around academic freedom are situated between a large diverse

58 Monisha Bajaj and Maria Hantzopoulos, *Educating for Peace and Human Rights: An Introduction* (London: Bloomsbury, 2016).

59 Bajaj, *Schooling for Social Change*; Bajaj and Hantzopoulos, *Educating for Peace and Human Rights.*

60 Sukhadeo Thorat and Nidhi S. Sabharwal, "Education for Civic Learning: Bring It at Core of Learning," *University News* 53 (2015): 61.

student population, homogeneous faculty and management composed primarily of privileged socioreligious groups, and the prevalence of systemic social inequalities and injustices. Some of these tensions manifest themselves in students from marginalized groups feeling excluded from curriculum and by pedagogy. They may also feel excluded by teachers' negative conceptions of diversity. Empirical analysis revealed dominant factors including teacher's apparent meritocratic ideology, perceptions regarding India's quota admission system, and relaxed eligibility criteria for marginalized groups.

In the context of Indian higher education when there is a social mismatch between student and faculty composition, and what gets taught in the classrooms is typically prescribed centrally, we have argued that academic freedom must be accompanied by academic responsibility. Higher education should promote human rights and fundamental freedoms, including students' full participation and empowerment, regardless of caste, gender, religion, language, sexual identity, disability, or citizenship. Democratic spaces must be created by institutions, management, teachers, and all students where marginalized student voices can be spoken and amplified. In such an environment, persistent tensions around exclusion from the curriculum, pedagogy, and teacher–student (and student–student) interactions can start to be addressed.

Despite prominent Government of India education policies and important education commissions having recognized the centrality of institutional autonomy and academic freedoms for universities, faculty, and students, challenges remain for students from socially excluded groups. This chapter makes two recommendations: first, extending the conception of academic freedom more fully to higher education students; second, expanding human rights education opportunities through civic learning environments free of censorship, discrimination, repression, or interference, affording discussion regarding caste-based inequalities, gender-based injustices, and violence. These two recommendations we argue would go some way to allowing marginalized voices to be heard.

CHAPTER 16

China's Rising Threats to Global Academic Freedom

Spectrum, Impacts, and Response

TENG BIAO AND CATHERINE MALANGA

THE DETERIORATING SITUATION IN CHINA AND ABROAD

Academic freedom is under attack worldwide—from Turkey to Afghanistan, from Russia to Kenya.[1] According to the most recent Academic Freedom Index (AFI), academic freedom is in retreat for over 50 percent of the world's population and is stagnating in 152 out of 179 countries, often at far too low a level.[2]

In mainland China, all media, schools, universities, publishing, and think tanks are controlled by the Chinese Communist Party (CCP). The Chinese authorities have employed "a range of tactics to intimidate, silence, and punish academics and students. They include limits on internet access, libraries, archives, publishings, and publication imports that impair research and learning; orders to ban discussion and research on topics the party-state deems controversial; surveillance and monitoring of academic activity that

1 Scholars at Risk, *Free to Think: Report of the Scholars at Risk Academic Freedom Monitoring Project* (New York: Scholars at Risk, 2023).

2 Katrin Kinzelbach, Staffan I. Lindberg, Lars Pelke, and Janika Spannagel, *Academic Freedom Index 2023* (Gothenburg: V-Dem Institute, 2023).

result in loss of position and self-censorship; travel restrictions that disrupt the flow of ideas across borders; and the use of detentions, prosecutions, and other coercive tactics to retaliate against and constrain critical inquiry and expression."[3] In 2013, the Briefing on the Current Situation in the Ideological Realm, famously known as Document No. 9, prohibits intellectuals, particularly teachers, from promoting "Western Constitutional Democracy," "universal values," "civil society," "civil rights," "free press," "the Party's historical mistakes," and so on.[4] China's relentless campaign against Uyghur intellectuals and Muslim cultural elites has resulted in nearly 312 Uyghurs held in arbitrary detention.[5] In schools, Chinese students are encouraged by the authorities to report critical speech by the teachers.[6] School teacher Li Tiantian was threatened with being held in a psychiatric hospital after making remarks that supported Song Gengyi's statements regarding the 1937 Nanjing Massacre.[7]

Academic freedom inside China has consistently been undermined. Given China's one-party system and general human rights record, the situation is getting worse. Yet, this chapter will focus on how the Chinese authorities threaten academic freedom and free speech beyond its borders, with a focus on, but not limited to, the United States.

Case Studies: China's Threats to Global Academic Freedom

Infringements on academic freedom can take numerous forms. For decades, the CCP's infringement on academic freedom and free speech has transcended borders, from disinformation, harassment, and spying, to physical attacks and overseas abductions.

3 Scholars at Risk, *Obstacles to Excellence: Academic Freedom & China's Quest for World-Class Universities* (New York: Scholars at Risk, 2019).

4 "中央秘密文件视宪政与人权为威胁," *New York Times*, August 20, 2013, https://cn.nytimes.com/china/20130820/c20document/dual/.

5 "The Disappearance of Uyghur Intellectual and Cultural Elites: A New Form of Eliticide," *Uyghur Human Rights Project*, December 8, 2021, https://uhrp.org/report/the-disappearance-of-uyghur-intellectual-and-cultural-elites-a-new-form-of-eliticide/.

6 David Bandurski, "Informants in the Chinese Classroom," *China Media Project*, September 27, 2018, https://chinamediaproject.org/2018/09/27/informants-in-the-chinese-classroom/.

7 Qiao Long, "Teacher Sent to Psychiatric Hospital in China's Hunan after Backing Massacre Comments," *Radio Free Asia*, December 20, 2021, www.rfa.org/english/news/china/teacher-history-12202021123228.html. Note: Song Gengyi taught at a university in Shanghai and was later fired.

Visa Denial

Various visa denial cases illustrate China government's global measures to silence academic discourse. Fears of visas to China being rejected for Chinese colleagues or family still in China also drive academics and students to self-censor. Accomplished professors Perry Link and Andrew Nathan were banned from entering China in 1996 and 2001 because of their long-time support of Chinese prodemocracy activists.[8] In 2001, Link was detained and questioned upon arriving in Hong Kong because of his involvement in the book *The Tiananmen Papers*. In Xinjiang—China's vast western region home to a majority Muslim population and the eye of the Uyghur genocidal campaigns—international scholars have been barred from travel. Thirteen US scholars and authors of *Xinjiang: China's Muslim Borderland*—an academic book published in 2004 of a collection of essays about the experience of Muslims living in Xinjiang—were banned from entering China.[9] Professor Edward Friedman had a similar experience.[10] Through China's increasing use of visa denial and denial of entry as a punishment against scholars, journalists, and other individuals who speak or write in ways the Chinese officials deem politically offensive, there is a growing concern that intellectuals might censor themselves to maintain access to China.

Disinformation and Propaganda

China has all but eliminated the independent Chinese-language media outlets that once served communities in the United States through a mix of co-option and aggressive expansion of its own competitors.[11] As China also seeks to grow its global reach in media, it has severely limited the ability of the United States and other news media outlets to operate in China. The situation of Chinese-language media in other countries is similar or worse.

---

8 Andy Newman, "Professor Barred from China," *New York Times*, August 14, 1996, www.nytimes.com/1996/08/14/nyregion/professor-barred-from-china.html.

9 Daniel de Vise, "U.S. Scholars Say Their Book on China Led to Travel Ban," *Washington Post*, August 20, 2011, www.washingtonpost.com/local/education/us-scholars-say-their-book-on-china-led-to-travel-ban/2011/08/17/gIQAN3C9SJ_story.html.

10 Anastasya Lloyd-Damnjanovic, "A Preliminary Study of PRC Political Influence and Interference Activities in American Higher Education," *Woodrow Wilson International Center for Scholars*, digital file.

11 Hoover Institution, *Chinese Influence and American Interests* (Stanford: Hoover Institution, 2018), 109.

China has bought out or infiltrated non-Chinese media all over the world. Joshua Kurlantzick found that China has "become a global media and disinformation superpower through an arsenal of tactics, including state media, disinformation campaigns and digital infrastructure."[12]

The CCP instrumentalizes its global media influence through censorship, propaganda, and control over content delivery systems, aiming to "tell a good Chinese story." China's toolbox for propaganda includes but is not limited to purchasing foreign media, conducting disinformation campaigns, expanding Chinese state media, and producing pro-Beijing content. Censorship is encouraged in China's efforts to incentivize self-censorship and deploy physical assaults and verbal abuse. Becoming a leading force in digital television and gaining worldwide mobile market share encourages foreign investment in China and strategic engagement abroad. Still, these measures also marginalize, demonize, or entirely suppress anti-CCP voices and incisive political commentary that present the Chinese government and its leaders in a negative light.

Expulsion

In addition to visa denial, foreigners who are critical of Beijing can be expelled before their visas expire. China expelled David Missal, a German student who studied in Beijing. The decision was linked to a documentary Missal was making about human rights lawyers for his master's program.[13] Elliot Sperling, a US professor on Tibetan history at Indiana University, was dragged by border officials after landing in Beijing from New York for interrogation.[14] After this, he was put back on the plane to leave Beijing, despite carrying a valid one-year tourist visa. Sperling has spent time supporting Ilham Tohti, an ethnic Uyghur economics professor charged with separatism by Chinese authorities. Sperling's forced removal and interrogation signifies China's attempts to silence international advocates of individuals or groups that the Chinese government denounces. Banning a scholar from

12 Liam Scott, "How China Became a Global Disinformation Superpower," *Coda*, December 6, 2022, www.codastory.com/disinformation/kurlantzick-book-china-global-media-offensive/.

13 "China Expels German Journalism Student," *Deutsche Welle*, August 12, 2018, www.dw.com/en/german-student-david-missal-expelled-from-china-after-making-human-rights-film/a-4505020.

14 Edward Wong, "China Denies Entry to an American Scholar Who Spoke Up for a Uighur Colleague," *New York Times*, July 7, 2014, www.nytimes.com/2014/07/08/world/asia/us-scholar-who-supported-uighur-colleague-is-denied-entry-to-china.html?r=0.

entering China after many years of studying Chinese and building a network in China causes extreme professional, social, and emotional suffering.

Disinvitation, Cancelation, and Censorship

The CCP operates Confucius Institutes worldwide[15]; however, as of March 2023, there remain only thirteen Confucius Institutes in the United States, with a total of 108 in the process of or are already closed.[16] While marketed as educational programs and centers that fund Chinese language, history, and culture courses, CIs in reality are vehicles of the Chinese government's propaganda schemes.

In August 2022, Confucius Institutes at various universities in the UK began screening staff to ensure those hired have no political views or sentiments that might go against the CCP.[17] Sonia Zhang, a former Confucius Institute teacher at McMaster University, said she had to sign a contract that indicated that Falun Gong practitioners, like herself, were barred from the teaching post.[18] The CCP's primary tool of influence abroad comes with control over curriculum and hiring in overseas institutions, leaving these schools vulnerable to censorship of important and wide-ranging discussion topics. These include not only Confucius Institutes but also, possibly, any institutions or projects that involve funding or cooperation from the PRC or the institutions or companies related to the PRC.

Informants and Spying

A study by the Wilson Center asserts that the PRC's influence and interference in activities in American higher education pose challenges to global academic freedom through overseas spying. Chinese intelligence officers and

15 The global Confucius Institute program was initially launched under China's Ministry of Education in 2004. It consists of campus-based language and culture partnerships.

16 "How Many Confucius Institutes Are in the United States?" *National Association of Scholars*, March 22, 2023, www.nas.org/blogs/article/how_many_confucius_institutes_are_in_the_united_states.

17 Louisa Clarence-Smith, "Chinese Institutes at UK Universities 'Screening out Undesirable Staff,'" *The Telegraph*, August 13, 2022, www.telegraph.co.uk/news/2022/08/13/chinese-institutes-uk-universities-screening-undesirable-staff.

18 Tom Blackwell, "Chinese Government's Confucius Institute Holds Sway on Canadian Campuses, Contracts Indicate," *National Post*, March 11, 2020.

diplomats are monitoring campuses across the United States with online surveillance and an array of informants motivated by money, ambition, fear, or authentic patriotism. A small amount of PRC students in American universities have monitored classmates and activities on campus, probed faculty for information, and engaged in intimidating and abusive conduct toward other members of the university community.[19] A comment in class about the Tiananmen massacre or a speech at a rally about Tibet can result in retaliation against students and their relatives back home.

In 2023 alone, VOA, a US international radio broadcaster, has interviewed at least five Chinese students studying in the United States and Australia whose parents, who are civil servants or employees of state-owned enterprises in China, have received official threats from the Chinese government over remarks or actions by their children studying abroad.[20]

Economic Coercion

The CCP's manipulative powers over global free speech have been tied to economic coercion—a threatened or actual imposition of economic costs by a state on a target aiming to extract policy concession.[21] Many Western universities and think tanks are afraid of criticizing China because they benefit from the Chinese government directly or indirectly. Every year Chinese students bring huge benefits to the United States. The economic impact of Chinese students in the United States was $15.9 billion in 2019. Chinese students in the UK account for €1.7 billion in tuition fees yearly. The University of Glasgow has a 31 percent share of total tuition fees from Chinese students. After awarding an honorary doctorate to the Dalai Lama, the University of Calgary's accreditation was revoked by the Chinese government.[22] Beijing stopped government funding programs at the University of California, San

19 Lloyd-Damnjanovic, "A Preliminary Study of PRC Political Influence."

20 Xiao Yu, "The State Security Not Only Monitors the Speeches of Chinese Students Studying Abroad, but Also Coerces Them to 'Take Crimes and Make Meritorious Service' as Undercover Agents," *VOA*, www.voachinese.com/a/china-s-secret-police-tries-to-recruit-chinese-students-in-america-20201030/5640534.html.

21 Matthew Reynolds and Matthew Goodman, *Deny, Deflect, Deter: Countering China's Economic Coercion* (Washington, DC: Center for Strategic and International Studies, 2023), digital file.

22 J. Michael Cole, "University off PRC's Approval List after Dalai Lama Honored," *Taipei Times*, February 7, 2010, www.taipeitimes.com/News/front/archives/2010/02/07/2003465412.

Diego (UCSD) after the university invited the Dalai Lama to give a commencement speech in 2017.[23]

Sanctions

In March 2021, China's Foreign Ministry blacklisted ten European Union individuals and four entities in response to Brussels' sanctions against Chinese officials over the human rights abuses committed in Xinjiang.[24] The ministry released a statement stating that among the ten individuals sanctioned by China and prohibited from entering the mainland, Hong Kong, and Macao of China were two scholars: Adrian Zenz of Germany, and Bjorn Jerden of Sweden. In 2022, Beijing decided to sanction Miles Yu Maochun, along with his close family members.[25] Yu is a dissident and a professor who served as a key China adviser under the former secretary of state Mike Pompeo. In addition, a US library and a think tank were added to an increasingly long list of sanctions and retaliation because they hosted meetings that angered Beijing.[26]

Lawfare

Lawfare is the use of legal systems and institutions to damage or delegitimize an opponent or to deter an individual's expression of opinions. Lawsuits were used to target academics or others whose work illuminates China's human rights abuses. For example, companies from Xinjiang have—no doubt at state direction—filed a lawsuit in a Xinjiang court against researcher Adrian Zenz, one of the most outspoken scholars critical of the Uyghur genocide.[27]

---

23 Elizabeth Redden, "Is China Punishing a U.S. University for Hosting the Dalai Lama?" *Inside Higher Ed*, September 20, 2017, www.insidehighered.com/news/2017/09/20/china-punishing-american-university-hosting-dalai-lama.

24 Tom Daly, "China Hits Back at EU with Sanctions on 10 People, Four Entities over Xinjiang," *Reuters*, March 22, 2021, www.reuters.com/business/aerospace-defense/china-hits-back-eu-with-sanctions-10-people-four-entities-over-xinjiang-2021-03-22/.

25 "China Sanctions 2 US Citizens over Raising Tibet Human Rights Issue," *Outlook*, December 24, 2022, www.outlookindia.com/international/china-sanctions-2-us-citizens-over-raising-tibet-human-rights-issue-news-247821.

26 Huizhong Wu, "China Sanctions Reagan Library," *AP News*, April 7, 2023, https://apnews.com/article/china-sanctions-taiwan-us-dc6e2a198f3777dceca272e1d3395f2b.

27 Eva Dou, "Academic Faces Chinese Lawsuit for Exposing Human Rights Abuses in Xinjiang," *Washington Post*, March 10, 2021, www.washingtonpost.com/world/asia_pacific/china-sanctions-uighurs-xinjiang/2021/03/10/dd57f8c8-814a-11eb-be22-32d331d87530_story.html.

Due to his work and findings, Zenz is encouraged to remain outside of China to evade being sued by companies in the Xinjiang region. This lawsuit and its threats directly hinder Zenz's ability to continue his research and academic development of reporting in Xinjiang.

Interruption, Humiliation, and Intimidation

Cases of interruption by Chinese students and officials have become a slow-growing threat to academic freedom. Uyghurs, Tibetans, Falun Gong practitioners, and other marginalized groups with ties to China face intimidation, state surveillance, and threats to their family members in China when they speak out on international campuses about oppression by the Chinese government. Rukiya Turdush, a Uyghur-Canadian activist, was interrupted by a shouting Chinese student when speaking at McMaster University.[28] Turdush reported that a Chinese student in the audience was filming her speech as she displayed satellite photos and academic sources displaying the mass incarceration of Uyghurs in Xinjiang. Shortly after the event, the university's Chinese Students and Scholars Association (CSSA) issued a statement decrying the talk as separatist and promoting ethnic hatred.

Vicky Xu, a researcher and journalist working in Australia, faced immense harassment campaigned by Chinese authorities in the form of death threats and rape threats.[29] Xu is the lead author of the Australian Strategic Policy Institute report *Uyghurs for Sale*, and her work researches and condemns China's treatment of Uyghurs and its "reeducation" campaigns that have been known to engage in forced labor practices. After working with and attending conferences hosted by La Trobe University in Australia, Xu was verbally harassed and her work's credibility was publicly questioned by a pro-

28 Holmes Chan, "How Uighur Activist Rukiye Turdush Felt the Long Arm of the Chinese Communist Party, in Canada," *Hong Kong Free Press*, March 3, 2019, https://hongkongfp.com/2019/03/03/exclusive-uighur-activist-rukiye-turdush-felt-long-arm-chinese-communist-party-canada/. For other cases, see Bethany Allen-Ebrahimian, "Chinese Students at Cornell 'Taunt' Uyghur Classmate during Event," *Axios*, March 15, 2022; Sui-Lee Wee and Stephanie Nebehay, "At U.N., China Uses Intimidation Tactics to Silence Its Critics," *Reuters*, October 6, 2015, www.reuters.com/investigates/special-report/china-softpower-rights/.

29 Nick Bonyhady, "Outspoken Journalist in Australia and Father in China Harassed Online," *Sydney Morning Herald*, September 6, 2019, www.smh.com.au/politics/federal/outspoken-journalist-in-australia-and-father-in-china-harassed-online-20190905-p520au.html.

CCP attendant.[30] A 2021 report in the *Global Times*, a CCP mouthpiece, called her a "morally low person."[31] The level of harassment and intimidation these attendants commit toward prodemocracy activists in China seems to aim to make institutions across the world fear disruption and freedom of anti-CCP expression, making them hesitant to invite professors, journalists, researchers, and analysts like Vicky Xu and Anne-Marie Brady to speak.

Wu Xiaolei, a student at Berklee College of Music, sent a series of threatening messages to another student who posted fliers calling for freedom and democracy on social media. In one message, Wu wrote: "Post more, I will chop your bastard hands off." Wu threatened the victim and his family with information that Wu had been in contact with law enforcement in China about the fliers and that they would "greet" the victim's family there.[32]

A model statue went viral in early March 2023 on social media of American scholar Miles Yu kneeling in Cultural Revolution style with a sign on his neck stating that he is the modern Qin Hui and a traitor to his Chinese ancestors and his country of birth.[33] The name Qin Hui is synonymous with treason in China and therefore reference to his name encourages beatings and public humiliation of other dissidents. This image signals to Chinese historians worldwide that beating and public humiliation will be anticipated if any reference is made to the Cultural Revolution or opposes the Chinese government.

Hostage-Taking and Collective Punishment

The CCP's "hostage diplomacy" can be traced back to the 1960s.[34] Similarly, collective punishment—a means to inflict pain on the family, relatives,

30 Tom Canetti, "'Harassing, Targeting and Intimidating': Is Australia a Safe Place for Critics of the Chinese Government?" *SBS News*, August 24, 2022, www.sbs.com.au/news/article/deeply-unsettling-why-this-chinese-australian-feels-unsafe-after-speaking-out-about-chinas-treatment-of-uyghurs/7i7vl71w6.

31 Wee and Nebehay, "At U.N., China Uses Intimidation Tactics to Silence Its Critics."

32 Ross Cristantiello, "Berklee Student Indicted for Threatening Person over Their Support of Chinese Democracy," *Boston*, January 10, 2023, www.boston.com/news/crime/2023/01/10/berklee-student-indicted-threatening-support-chinese-democracy/.

33 Lei Shihong, "Burning Effigies: China Threatens American Academic Miles Yu," *Bitter Winter*, July 3, 2023, https://bitterwinter.org/burning-effigies-american-academic-miles-yu/.

34 Helen Davidson and Michael McGowan, "'Tit-for-Tat': China's Detention of Australian Cheng Lei Is Ringing Alarm Bells," *The Guardian*, September 5, 2020, www.theguardian.com/australia-news/2020/sep/06/tit-for-tat-chinas-detention-of-australian-cheng-lei-is-ringing-alarm-bells.

friends neighbors, etc, of targeted individuals—has a long history in China and has been used by the Chinese authorities to penalize or silence critics domestically and internationally.[35]

Li Taotao is a pseudonym for this scholar from northern China who was studying in the United States when he published remarks online, using his real name, that criticized Beijing. Shortly after these remarks were published, state security officials in China began harassing his parents, and later China's state police confiscated his parents' passports, barring them from leaving China.[36]

Dolkun Isa is an activist and scholar who fled China in 1994 and now heads the Munich-based World Uyghur Congress; he has been unable to contact family members inside China for years.[37] In 2019 he learned that his 79-year-old mother, Ayhan Memet, died in a "political reeducation" camp. He only learned about the death of his father, Isa Memet, eighty-six, when it was reported on China state media in 2022. In 2023, Isa learned that his brother, Hushtar Isa, who has been arbitrarily detained since 2017, is now serving a life sentence on terrorism-related charges. Family members of six Radio Free Asia Uyghur Service reporters in the United States who reported and documented atrocities in the Uyghur area committed by the CCP have been detained in concentration camps.[38]

Physical Attacks

A more extreme form of silencing academic discourse is through physical attack.

A recent Cornell graduate student, Kinen Kao, was attacked in June 2022 while putting up prodemocracy posters on campus. His post on social media read: "I was assaulted by a man in the Ithaca Commons, who tore down my Free Hong Kong and Free Uyghurs posters before pushing me to the floor,

35 Teng Biao, "Teng Biao: The CCP's Political Involvement," *Human Rights in China*, November 23, 2015, www.hrichina.org/en/node/15874.

36 Yu, "The State Security."

37 Shohret Hoshur, "Brother of World Uyghur Congress President Sentenced to Life in Prison in China's Xinjiang," *Radio Free Asia*, June 1, 2021, www.rfa.org/english/news/uyghur/hushtar-isa-06012021175745.html.

38 "The Families Left Behind: RFA's Uyghur Reporters Tell the Stories of Their Family Members' Detentions," *Radio Free Asia*, www.rfa.org/english/news/special/uyghurfamilies/.

leaving wounds on my left hand."[39] This case example directly references the danger Chinese students face when attempting to engage in free speech and academic discourse on college campuses. When students are unable to discuss current events and political issues on a college campus, the university violates its pledge to allow its students to freely pursue and engage in academic discourse.

Break-in/Theft

Professor Anne-Marie Brady at the University of Canterbury in New Zealand, after writing a prominent report on China's political interference, encountered theft of her computer from her home in February 2018 and her car tires deflated in November later that month.[40] Her work condemned the presence of Confucius Institutes in New Zealand universities, which have long been known to market the Chinese government's propaganda schemes. Her colleagues in China were taken in for questioning. Her family car was tampered with; she received a threatening letter ("You are the next") and answered numerous anonymous phone calls in the middle of the night, despite having an unlisted number. The latest came at 3 o'clock in the morning on the day her family returned home after a Christmas break.[41]

Abduction

The kidnapping of Gui Minhai symbolizes China's determination to smother criticism from abroad and encroach upon the fundamental freedom of academic study and free speech. Minhai was born in China in 1964 and was naturalized as a Swedish citizen in 1989. He is a poet, publisher, and distributor of books specializing in mainland Chinese politics and the lives

39 "Recent Cornell Graduate Allegedly Attacked While Putting Up Pro-democracy Posters," *Cornell Review*, June 8, 2022, www.thecornellreview.org/breaking-recent-cornell-graduate-attacked-while-putting-up-pro-democracy-posters/.

40 Leith Huffadine, "Professor Anne-Marie Brady, Who Warned about China Interference, Says Car Was Sabotaged," *Stuff*, November 16, 2018, www.stuff.co.nz/national/108649435/professor-annemarie-brady-who-warned-about-china-interference-says-car-was-sabotaged.

41 Eleanor Ainge Roy, "'I'm Being Watched': Anne-Marie Brady, the China Critic Living in Fear of Beijing," *The Guardian*, January 22, 2019, www.theguardian.com/world/2019/jan/23/im-being-watched-anne-marie-brady-the-china-critic-living-in-fear-of-beijing.

of Chinese politicians. On October 17, 2015, Gui was kidnapped from his own apartment in Pattaya, Thailand, by Chinese secret agents. The Chinese government had been silent about holding him in custody for three months, at which point a controversial video confession was broadcast on mainland media.[42]

On February 25, 2020, Gui was sentenced to ten years imprisonment and five years' deprivation of "political rights" by Ningbo Intermediate People's Court in Zhejiang Province.[43] It is reasonable to assume that Mighty Current Media was targeted as a warning to the entire Hong Kong publishing industry to stop selling books that Chinese authorities deemed "forbidden" in China. Sadly, Gui is not the only bookseller taken away by China. What is publicly known is that four other booksellers disappeared in 2015 in what is known as the "Causeway Bay Books Disappearances": Lui Por, Cheung Chi-ping, Lam Wing-kee, and Lee Bo.[44] China's abductions of the Causeway Bay booksellers demonstrate a blatant disregard for international law and human rights principles. Information about the circumstances of the booksellers' disappearances and their treatment while in detention is still incomplete and will be until the Chinese government provides an explanation. These disappearances highlight the far-reaching legal and political repercussions of China's decision to carry out extrajudicial and extraterritorial operations.

Torture

As described throughout the chapter thus far, the Chinese government has utilized various forms of torture. Within China, torture is rampant among various groups given the country's lack of judicial independence, party competition, and free press.[45] Torture is institutionalized, and torturers usually get impunity, especially in political cases. The abovementioned detained

42 Tom Phillips, "Missing Hong Kong Bookseller 'Confesses' on Chinese State TV," *The Guardian*, January 17, 2016, www.theguardian.com/world/2016/jan/17/missing-hong-kong-bookseller-gui-minhai-reappears-on-chinese-tv.

43 PEN America, *Writing on the Wall: Disappeared Booksellers and Free Expression in Hong Kong* (New York: PEN International, 2016).

44 PEN America, *Writing on the Wall.*

45 Margaret Lewis, "Freedom from Torture," in *Handbook on Human Rights in China*, ed. Sarah Biddulph and Joshua Rosenzweig (Cheltenham: Edward Elgar, 2019).

intellectuals all experienced torture to a different extent. Gui Minhai's torture was so brutal that he "refused" international support and "gave up" his Swedish citizenship.

Criminal Detention

In 1999, Song Yongyi, a librarian and researcher at University of California, Los Angeles (UCLA), went back to China to collect documents related to the Cultural Revolution, but when he arrived, he was detained for more than a hundred days by the Chinese government for "stealing state secrets" when in reality his goal was to pursue academic research.[46]

In July 2019, Luo Daiqing, a Chinese student at the University of Minnesota, was arrested in China and sentenced to six months in prison for tweets he posted while in the United States.[47] Luo tweeted an image of Lawrence Limburger, a cartoon villain superimposed with Chinese government slogans. The case not only represents a dramatic escalation of the Chinese government's attempts to shut down free speech abroad, but the arrest, by hindering Luo's ability to pursue his education and return to university, directly threatens his ability to engage in academic discourse and learning. The arrest further sends a message to Chinese students to remain silent in discussing or distributing images of Chinese government officials that may be deemed critical of the regime. Due to China's extreme and far-reaching surveillance measures, students are often even reluctant to attend prodemocracy campus events for fear of the Chinese government finding out.

Assassination and Murder

It is not rare that Chinese intellectuals, especially dissidents and activists, died in custody or soon after being released. The names of some intellectuals include Nobel laureate Liu Xiaobo, Cao Shunli, Peng Ming, Yang Tianshui, Tenzin Delek Rinpoche, prominent Uyghur religious scholars Muhammad

---

46 Doug Guthrie, "Detention and Release in Beijing: The Case of Yongyi Song," *Chronicle of Higher Education*, February 18, 2000, www.chronicle.com/article/detention-and-release-in-beijing-the-case-of-yongyi-song/.

47 Bethany Allen-Ebrahimian, "University of Minnesota Student Jailed in China over Tweets," *Axios*, January 22, 2020, www.axios.com/2020/01/23/china-arrests-university-minnesota-twitter.

Salih Hajim[48] and Abdulehed Mehsum,[49] among others. In a January 2019 update on interned, imprisoned, and disappeared intellectuals, Uyghur Human Rights Project (UHRP) reported that since 2017 five individuals are known to have died in custody or soon after their release. These individuals include religious scholars Muhammad Salih Hajim and Abdulnehed Mehsum and students Abdusalam Mamat, Yasinjan, and Mutellip Nurmehmet. A sixth intellectual, Erkinjan Abdukerim, a teacher from Awat Township near Kashgar, died on September 30, 2018, shortly after his release from an internment camp.[50] In addition, Mihriay Erkin died in 2021 while arbitrarily held in Kashgar Yanbulak prison. Mihriay was a Uyghur intellectual lured back to China during China's ongoing campaign to target prominent Uyghur scholars and activists in the diaspora who challenged their genocide.[51]

The Spectrum and Chinese Institutions That Threaten Academic Freedom

The spectrum[52] of the CCP's threat to global academic freedom and free speech falls into categories that include but are not limited to infiltration of media and disinformation, visa denial, protest against academic events or free speech, economic coercion, governmental sanctions, lawfare, frivolous lawsuits, collective punishment, defamation, harassment and intimidation, physical assault, criminal detention and conviction, and abductions. These activities are primarily performed by the Chinese government, but can also be threatened by Chinese media platforms, Confucius Institutes, CSSA, United Front Work Department (UFWD), and secret agents. The harm these activities pose to academic freedom can be measured on a 1–5 scale: 1 being a minimal threat and 5 being extreme. The most threatening activities to academic freedom and expression are harassment, physical assault, crimi-

48 Jilil Kashgary, "Xinjiang Authorities Detain Almost Every Family Member of Late Uyghur Muslim Scholar," *Radio Free Asia*, September 25, 2018, www.rfa.org/english/news/uyghur/scholar-09252018145144.html.

49 "WUC Confirms Death in Custody of Yet Another Uyghur Religious Scholar Abdulehed Mehsum," news release, May 29, 2018, www.uyghurcongress.org/en/press-release-wuc-confirms-death-in-custody-of-yet-another-uyghur-religious-scholar-abdulehed-mehsum/.

50 UHRP, "Detained and Disappeared: Intellectuals under Assault in the Uyghur Homeland," digital file.

51 "Campaign for Uyghurs Condemns the Death of Mihriay Erkin," news release, May 25, 2021, https://campaignforuyghurs.org/campaign-for-uyghurs-condemns-the-death-of-mihriay-erkin/.

52 Spectrum image created by Catherine Malanga.

China's Threats to Academic Freedom

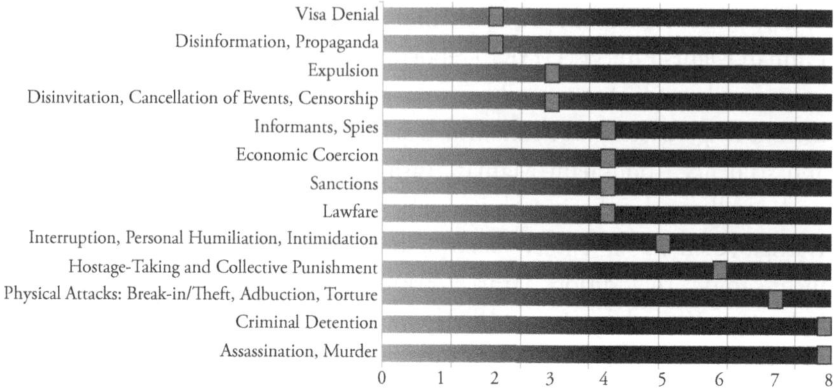

nal conviction, and forced abductions, but all actions performed by the CCP against free speech threaten global academic freedom.

Academic freedom is at risk from dubious party-state funding. The CCP operates Confucius Institutes, which are backed by "Hanban" or "Confucius Institutes Headquarters," funded by the Chinese government's Ministry of Education. Notably, these institutions are also funded by the CCP's Propaganda Department, an extension of the CCP's UFWD, which is a government agency dedicated to influence operations and propaganda campaigns both domestically and abroad.[53] The methods seek to influence overseas Chinese communities, foreign governments, and other actors to take action in support of CCP politics. Confucius Institutes have harmed academic freedom globally by selecting and training teachers, course materials, brainwashing lectures, and preventing sensitive speakers from being invited and sensitive topics from being discussed.[54] As of July 2, 2021, there are still more than a dozen Confucius Institutes operating in host schools and uni-

53 Government Accountability Office, "Agreements Establishing Confucius Institutes at U.S. Universities Are Similar, but Institute Operations Vary," GAO-19-278, February 27, 2019. www.uscc.gov/sites/default/files/Research/China's%20Overseas%20United%20Front%20Work%20-%20Backgr ound%20 and%20Implications%20for%20US_final_0.pdf.

54 Government Accountability Office, "Agreements Establishing Confucius Institutes at U.S. Universities Are Similar, but Institute Operations Vary."

versities across the United States.[55] Many Confucius Institutes have closed, but they maintain operations under new covers.

Rising self-censorship is also related to fears of nationalistic Chinese students recording and reporting on class discussions.[56] China's "Great Firewall" and The Golden Shield Project aim to monitor and censor what can and cannot be seen through an online network in China.[57] CSSA, which claim to be "student-run organizations," have formal links with the Chinese embassy and consulates, including funding support and organizing pro–Communist Party political gatherings on university campuses. UFWD, one of the major CCP departments, has been dedicated to influence operations and propaganda campaigns around the globe since the time of Mao Zedong. China has employed the UFWD and various organizations under its umbrella work to advance China's global propaganda schemes and smother criticism from abroad. The Chinese government has grown bolder in trying to shape global perceptions of the country on foreign university campuses, influence academic discussions, monitor students from China, censor scholarly inquiry, or otherwise interfere with academic freedom. Chaoyin International School in Richmond, BC, teachers were told to "tread lightly" on issues related to the CCP, Tiananmen Square, and the Dalai Lama. The school strictly follows the Chinese curriculum, which means the Chinese government funds and provides "culture and language training" using textbooks and other educational materials vetted by the CCP."[58] The website clearly states and encourages students "to develop an independent and confident attitude towards learning, as well as a positive and responsible attitude towards life"; learning in an environment that censors facts and spoon-feeds propaganda by the Chinese government leaves no room for a healthy learning environment nor fostering of

55 "Unraveling China's Attempts to Hinder Academic Freedom: Confucius Institutes," unsigned review by Zoe Gladstone, Joyce Ho, and Jenny Wang, *Human Rights Foundation*, August 4, 2021, https://hrf.org/unraveling-chinas-attempts-to-hinder-academic-freedom-confucius-institutes/.

56 "'They Don't Understand the Fear We Have': How China's Long Reach of Repression Undermines Academic Freedom at Australia's Universities," *Human Rights Watch*, June 30, 2021, www.hrw.org/report/2021/06/30/they-dont-understand-fear-we-have/how-chinas-long-reach-repression-undermines.

57 Stanford University, "Free speech vs Maintaining Social Cohesion: A Closer Look at Different Policies," https://cs.stanford.edu/people/eroberts/cs181/projects/2010-11/FreeExpressionVsSocialCohesion/china_policy.html

58 Maria Rantanen, "Teachers at New Richmond Private School Told to 'Tread Lightly,'" *Richmond News*, April 14, 2021, www.richmond-news.com/local-news/teachers-at-new-richmond-private-school-told-to-tread-lightly-3633608.

free discourse.[59] The CSSA prompted the UCSD to refrain from referring to the Dalai Lama as a "spiritual leader" or "in exile." After the Dalai Lama was told to deliver a commencement address to the university in 2017, Chinese students and members of UCSD's CSSA staged a demonstration to protest his attendance. The protesters' disapproval of the Dalai Lama, however, should have had no impact on his presence considering his widely influential role as a global leader in Buddhist teachings. The UCSD case illuminates the far-reaching measures Chinese government-funded organizations have on the international community's ability to engage in free speech and intellectual understanding. In short, their measures hinder global academic freedom.

Safeguard Defenders released an investigative report monitoring China's growing global transnational repression schemes. As of 2022, China has established fifty-four illegal policing stations across five continents.[60] Roughly 230,000 Chinese fugitives have been persuaded to return to China to face potential criminal charges for actions that go against the regime. Tools of persuasion include denying the target's children in China the fundamental right to education. These policing operations often use local "Chinese Overseas Home Associations" linked to the CCP's UFWD: "Abandoning any pretext of due process or the consideration of suspects' innocence until proven guilty, targeting suspects' children and relatives in China as 'guilty by association' or 'collateral damage,' and using threats and intimidation to target suspects abroad, is now becoming an endemic problem."

Countless scholars, authors, students, and family members have begun to practice self-censorship as a means to avoid potential troubles with the Chinese government. China Index found instances of self-censorship among German institutes and forms of pushback from the PRC side against research organizations and scholars whose work does not align with Beijing's efforts.[61] Even in Western countries that enjoy the freedoms of information and expression, individuals misunderstand China's influence operations and politics, and some do not realize the extent to which China has infiltrated not only their academic lives but in their every day.

---

59 Chaoyin International School, http://chaoyinschool.ca/.

60 "230,000 Chinese 'Persuaded to Return' from Abroad, China to Establish Extraterritoriality," *Safeguard Defenders*, September 12, 2022, https://safeguarddefenders.com/en/blog/230000-policing-expands.

61 "China's Influence in Germany: Academia and Media Are the Achilles Heel," *Friedrich Naumann Foundation*, July 7, 2022, www.freiheit.org/chinas-influence-germany-academia-and-media-are-achilles-heel.

Number	Activities	Actors	Threat level (0–8)	Frequency
1	Visa denial	Chinese government, Chinese embassy/ consulates	2	Sometimes
2	Disinformation, propaganda	Chinese companies, Chinese media, UFWD, Confucius Institute, CSSA	2	Always
3	Expulsion	Chinese government, Chinese embassy/ consulates	3	Sometimes
4	Disinvitation, cancelation of events, censorship	Confucius Institute, CSSA, Chinese embassy/consulates, UFWD	3	Often
5	Informants, spies	CCP, secret agents, pro-CCP students, UFWD, Confucius Institute, CSSA	4	Always
6	Economic coercion	Chinese government/ CCP	4	Often
7	Sanctions	Chinese government/ CCP	4	Sometimes
8	Lawfare	Chinese legislators, Chinese government	4	Sometimes
9	Interruption, personal humiliation, intimidation	Chinese media, UFWD, secret agents, pro-CCP students, Confucius Institute, CSSA	5	Often
10	Hostage-taking, collective punishment	CCP, secret agents, law enforcement officers	6	Sometimes

Continued

Number	Activities	Actors	Threat level (0–8)	Frequency
11	Physical attacks: –Break-in/Theft –Abduction –Torture	UFWD, secret agents, CCP-hired thugs, CCP, secret agents, law enforcement officers, CCP, secret agents, Chinese government, law enforcement officers, secret police	7	Sometimes–Often
12	Criminal detention	Chinese government, law enforcement officers	8	Sometimes
13	Assassination, murder	CCP, Chinese government, secret agents	8	Rarely

In terms of academic freedom, students studying in China and abroad have chosen to self-censor their voices in fear of the Chinese government. When college campuses invite speakers like the Dalai Lama or activists to speak of China's human rights violations, Chinese students are often reluctant to attend because of consternation that the Chinese government will revoke their visas. As articulated in the previous pages, scholars have become increasingly cautious about voice opposition, and undertaking research, and in some cases, Western scholars have become apologetic toward China and have been coerced into endorsing the party.

The classroom has become the most dangerous space for Chinese students: if professors discuss sensitive issues pertaining to China, the CCP, and Chinese politics, Chinese students retreat from the conversation due to a valid worry that a fellow Chinese student, university administration, or recent graduate will expose their stance on China. Western universities in China cannot guarantee academic freedom as claimed and as promised by the Chinese government. It is self-deceptive to believe that students, especially Chinese students, can join conversations freely when sensitive topics are discussed. In fact, two recent graduates from Duke Kunshan University and NYU Shanghai said not a single teacher mentioned sensitive topics for the whole four years of their time there.[62] In sum, China's push for self-censorship has harmed the education system in free countries across the globe.

US law enforcement agencies have struggled to respond because much of the censorship and harassment occurs in a legal gray area. Victims are often frightened or do not believe anyone can assist them. University administrators are not always eager to intercede because this would involve risking a lucrative financial stream. According to the Department of Education, since 2013 US universities have received more than $1 billion from mainland China from various individuals, companies, and government organizations. This number does not reflect the tuition Chinese students pay to attend US universities, of which roughly 370,000 Chinese students have come to attend their universities in 2019.[63] Moreover, the complexities of free speech and identity politics make administrators even more reluctant to confront Chinese state influence.

Beijing's manifold methods have created other harms in addition to self-censorship: personal reputation, career interruption, professional shift, financial loss, mental and physical pain, personal freedom, the suffering of family or relatives, deprivation of citizenship, and, in extreme cases, the loss of lives of the targets and/or their loved ones.

A Personal Message from Teng Biao

I taught in China between 2003 and 2013 and have been teaching Chinese law, human rights, and politics in the United States since 2018. In China, I was banned from teaching by the university for political reasons, and in the United States, I have witnessed and experienced how Beijing became an increasing threat to academic freedom.

In 2014, I was invited to be a visiting scholar at Harvard Law School, but my wife and daughter were blocked from leaving China. When asked why, the answer of the secret police was, "You know it yourselves." After several unsuccessful attempts to negotiate, my family reunion seemed to be a long

62 Interviews with anonymous students. See also Salvatore Babones, "It's Time for Western Universities to Cut Their Ties to China," *Foreign Policy*, August 19, 2020, https://foreignpolicy.com/2020/08/19/universities-confucius-institutes-china/.

63 Kaitlin Mulhere, "China and Academic Freedom," *Inside Higher Ed*, December 4, 2014, www.insidehighered.com/news/2014/12/05/lawmakers-look-chinese-influence-american-universities.

way off. I had no choice but to take the risk of smuggling my children across the border.

In December 2014, the American Bar Association (ABA) commissioned me to write a book entitled *Darkness before Dawn*, which aimed to convey Chinese politics and society through the raw and horrific stories of various human rights lawyers, including my personal experience of enforced disappearance and torture. On January 28, 2015, I received an email from ABA rescinding its offer due to a "risk of upsetting the Chinese government."[64] A scheduled talk between me and Chinese civil rights activist Chen Guangcheng was canceled at Harvard in 2015.[65] In 2019, I tried to organize a panel discussion at Columbia University titled "Panopticism with Chinese Characteristics: Human Rights Violations by the Chinese Communist Party and How They Affect the World," but the discussion was canceled after receiving threats from the CSSA to protest against the event.[66]

I co-led a seminar entitled *Human Rights in China* at the University of Chicago between 2021 and 2023 where students learned and engaged with material that revealed China's countless human rights violations. I was met with great concern from Chinese students in Chicago who informed me of their fear that their transcript with the course name would taint their reputation in China. As a result, students felt the urge to change their names for the sake of course discussion, and some even entirely transformed their research plans and dissertations after realizing the potential harm that writing on China's unjust politics would cause to their career and personal safety.[67] Some students told me they are supportive of my human rights work and research, but they dare not to take my course or ask questions in my public talks: many fear their job opportunities in China, their personal safety, or other potential trouble for themselves or their families.

64 Isaac Stone Fish, "Leaked Email: ABA Cancels Book for Fear of 'Upsetting the Chinese Government,'" *Foreign Policy*, April 15, 2016, https://foreignpolicy.com/2016/04/15/leaked-email-aba-cancels-book-for-fear-of-upsetting-the-chinese-government-american-bar-association-teng-biao/.

65 Matteo Wong, "The End of the Harvard Century," *Harvard Crimson*, April 23, 2020, www.thecrimson.com/article/2020/4/23/harvard-china-scrutiny/.

66 Jeremiah Poff, "Columbia U. Cancels Panel on Communist China's Human Rights Violations," *College Fix*, November 20, 2019, www.thecollegefix.com/columbia-u-cancels-panel-on-communist-chinas-human-rights-violations/.

67 Lloyd-Damnjanovic, "A Preliminary Study of PRC Political Influence."

Recommendations

It is imperative that international institutions are made aware of China's international human rights violations and prevent further complicity in China's overseas suppression. When human rights atrocities occur, the world must speak out publicly on behalf of the victims. All relevant stakeholders, including public and private donors, should redouble their efforts to protect and defend civil society and independent media from attempts by China and others to stifle and repress their important human rights monitoring work. In coordination with the UFWD, journalists and activists have routinely coordinated with the Chinese government to suppress free speech and harass, intimidate, and surveil Chinese student activists on university campuses (p. 10).[68] To effectively counter CCP influence operations on education, continued research and investigation is needed to further bring to light the activities of the UFWD, its role in the CCP, how it operates, and its links to other important CCP organs.

On March 21, 2019, Human Rights Watch published its Tweelve-Point Code of Conduct for colleges and universities worldwide to adopt to respond to Chinese government's threats to the academic freedom of students, scholars, and educational institutions:

All institutions of higher education should:

1. Speak out for academic freedom
2. Strengthen academic freedom on campus
3. Counter threats to academic freedom
4. Record incidents of Chinese government infringement of academic freedom
5. Join with other academic institutions to promote research
6. Offer flexibility for scholars and students working in China
7. Reject Confucius Institutes
8. Monitor Chinese government-linked organizations
9. Promote academic freedom of students and scholars from China

68 Alexander Bowe, "China's Overseas United Front Work Background and Implications for the United States," August 24, 2018, www.uscc.gov/sites/default/files/Research/China%27s%20Overseas%20United%20Front%20Work%20-%20Background%20and%20Implications%20for%20US_final_0.pdf.

10. Disclose all Chinese government funding
11. Ensure academic freedom in exchange programs and on satellite campuses
12. Monitor the impact of Chinese government interference in academic freedom.[69]

According to Education under Attack 2022, there have been over 320 attacks on higher education students, professors, and personnel.[70] The study found that at least one case of child recruitment at, or on the way to or from, the school was documented in four countries in 2020 and 2021. China was left out of the study.

According to Freedom House's Beijing Media Influence in 2022, Chinese state media have leveraged social media platforms by creating accounts that distribute content in national or regional languages.[71] The world has witnessed a rise in coercive tactics such as targeted intimidation of individual reporters, cyberbullying, and cyberattacks against new outlets that release content the Chinese government finds unfavorable.

The CCP's desire to interfere with global academic freedom is motivated by attempts to silence critics, cover up truths that harm the regime, shape a new international narrative, produce an environment that fosters safety for the regime, and avoid challenges to China's political legitimacy. China operates its sprawling system of transnational repression by working through the legal and political systems of foreign countries—including detentions, extraditions, and joint border patrols—and often using diplomatic staff at embassies and consulates run through China's Ministry of Foreign Affairs. Transnational repression exists as part of a wider trend of global authoritarianism that threatens to erode democratic norms worldwide. China's global campaign of repression and harassment—both physical and mental—of individuals living abroad has shifted from Central Asia to Southeast Asia, the Middle East, and the rest of the map. The numerous cases of forced

69 "China: Government Threats to Academic Freedom Abroad," *Human Rights Watch*, March 21, 2019, www.hrw.org/news/2019/03/21/china-government-threats-academic-freedom-abroad.

70 "Education under Attack 2022," https://eua2022.protectingeducation.org/#finding-one.

71 "Beijing's Global Media Influence," September 2022, https://freedomhouse.org/report/beijing-global-media-influence/2022/authoritarian-expansion-power-democratic-resilience?utm_source=HRIC+Updates&utm_campaign=aa0ef924ba-HRIC_DAILY_BRIEF_COPY_01&utm_medium=emai l&utm_term=0_b537d30fde-aa0ef924ba-259223237.

detention and threats to freedom of expression and safety breach fundamental rights and basic personal freedoms. Yet, China remains one of the world's most influential countries, and because of this, few on the international stage are willing to speak out about the PRC's repression and internment of individuals and communities around the world.

PART IV

Emerging Threats and Challenges

Chapter 17

Restricting Academic Freedom at Universities

How Corporations Contribute to the Problem

Hani Morgan

Introduction

Corporations can influence universities to restrict academic freedom in various ways. One of these ways involves the agreements they sometimes require researchers to sign to conduct studies about their products or services. These agreements frequently allow the funders the right to determine whether a study will be published. Although some scholars argue that industry funding is a valuable component of academic research because it contributes to scientific discoveries, critics argue that this trend has a corrupting effect on science.[1]

Industry-funded research can harm consumers because corporations frequently prevent researchers from publishing studies showing that their

1 Robert D. Atkinson, "Industry Funding of University Research: Which States Lead?" *Information Technology & Innovation Foundation*, January 2018, www2.itif.org/2018-industry-funding-university-research.pdf.

products or services are ineffective or harmful. If researchers break an agreement with a corporation, the corporation can sue them and their employers can fire them. Preventing researchers from publishing certain studies is incompatible with one of the main goals of many of today's universities. This goal is to encourage academic freedom to thrive. Allowing corporations to determine which studies get published prevents university researchers from achieving this goal because academic freedom includes the freedom to publish research results.[2]

Corporations can restrict academic freedom in other ways. For example, they can influence the design they want researchers to use to conduct a study. Corporations can also require researchers to sign agreements that allow the publication of only the findings showing that their products are beneficial.[3] This practice is detrimental because it contributes to misleading studies. Unfortunately, it is not uncommon for some corporations, like pharmaceutical companies, to fund research designed to yield deceptive findings. Examples of methods some companies use to get the desired results include designing research that compares their drugs to treatments known to be ineffective or to drugs given at doses too low to work well. Other methods include comparing a favored drug to one offered at a dose high enough to produce toxic effects, making the favored drug seem less toxic.[4]

Academic Freedom

Understanding how academic freedom protects researchers from practices that contribute to the corruption of science and other harmful outcomes can help universities avoid participating in misleading industry-funded research. Being aware of how academic freedom originated is important for understanding how this principle needs to be applied at academic institutions.

---

2 Donna R. Euben, "Academic Freedom of Professors and Institutions," *American Association of University Professors,* May 2002, www.aaup.org/issues/academic-freedom/professors-and-institutions.

3 Lisa Bero, "When Big Companies Fund Academic Research, The Truth Often Comes Last," *The Conversation*, October 2, 2019, https://theconversation.com/ when-big-companies-fund-academic-research-the-truth-often-comes-last-119164.

4 Susanna Every-Palmer and Jeremy Howick, "How Evidence-Based Medicine Is Failing Due to Biased Trials and Selective Publication," *Journal of Evaluation in Clinical Practice*, 20 (2014): 910, https://doi.org/10.1111/jep.12147.

Historical Background

Academic freedom in the United States originated over a hundred years ago when American academics made trips to notable German universities. When these academics compared the German universities to those in America, they started to feel that the mission of American universities needed to change in order to focus on advancing knowledge.[5] At the start of the nineteenth century, Wilhelm von Humboldt reformed German universities based on two concepts: freedom to teach and freedom to learn.[6]

In contrast to German universities, American universities were religious institutions during the first half of the nineteenth century and were designed to teach young men moral truths. In the twentieth century, however, a shift from a focus on religion to knowledge occurred. This change in the mission of universities was influenced by the academics who wanted institutions of higher learning to be more like German universities. The first American university to commit to the German model was Johns Hopkins, and others followed.[7]

The desire to make American universities similar to the German model was not the only factor that contributed to the development of academic freedom. In 1900, the firing of a professor for having unpopular views agitated the academic community. Jane Stanford, the widow of Stanford University's founder, requested Edward Ross, a professor of economics, to be fired for his views on labor, Asian immigration, and the gold standard. American professors began to wonder how they would be able to advance knowledge if a university member with more power but less expertise in their field could fire them.[8]

This concern was addressed in 1915 when a meeting was held to establish academic freedom for professors. John Dewey and Arthur Lovejoy organized this meeting, which resulted in the creation of the American Association of University Professors (AAUP). This meeting was crucial because it led to the formulation of the Declaration of Principles on Academic Freedom

5 Columbia Law School, "Free Speech and Academic Freedom," March 7, 2016, www.law.columbia.edu/news/archive/free-speech-and-academic-freedom.

6 Shannon Dea, "A Brief History of Academic Freedom," *University Affairs*, October 9, 2018, www.universityaffairs.ca/opinion/dispatches-academic-freedom/a-brief-history-of-academic-freedom/.

7 Columbia Law School, "Free Speech."

8 Columbia Law School, "Free Speech."

and Academic Tenure. Some of the statements of these principles indicate that once professors are appointed, the appointing authorities have no moral right to intervene and that the professors' responsibilities are mainly to the public and to their profession.[9]

Today, many universities rely on a statement developed in 1940 for information about academic freedom. This statement was created by the AAUP and the Association of American Colleges and Universities.[10] The statement created in 1940 was adapted from the one created in 1915. A conference was held in 1925 to shorten the 1915 statement. And in 1940, a restatement of the principles that were endorsed in 1925 was approved by the AAUP and the Association of American Colleges and Universities. The statement agreed upon in 1940 is known as the 1940 Statement of Principles on Academic Freedom and Tenure.[11]

Areas Academic Freedom Covers

The 1940 Statement provides instructors the freedom not only to publish the results of their research but also to discuss subjects related to the areas involving the content they are assigned to teach.[12] Academic freedom covers research, teaching, and public expression. In the area of research, it allows instructors to select the methodologies of their choice and to draw conclusions based on evidence. Instructors, however, are not protected from being critiqued for their claims. In teaching, academic freedom provides instructors the right to choose course content, create assignments, and evaluate students. Limitations related to teaching involve instructors who are incompetent, ignorant, or dishonest in their areas of expertise. Regarding freedom of expression, academic freedom allows instructors to share their areas of expertise through writing and speech.[13]

---

9 Columbia Law School, "Free Speech."

10 Euben, "Academic Freedom of Professors."

11 "1940 Statement of Principles on Academic Freedom and Tenure," *American Association of University Professors*, accessed December 19, 2022, www.aaup.org/report/1940-statement-principles-academic-freedom-and-tenure.

12 Euben, "Academic Freedom of Professors."

13 Organization of American Historians, "Academic Freedom Guidelines and Best Practices," accessed December 19, 2022, www.oah.org/about/governance/policies/academic-freedom-guidelines-and-best-practices.

In 2010, Cary Nelson, a former president of the AAUP, clarified aspects of what academic freedom allows faculty to do and the conduct it does not protect. In addition to the aforementioned ways it protects faculty, he indicated that academic freedom maintains integrity in the education system, thereby serving the public good. Nelson stated that it provides faculty members with the right to request a hearing if they feel they have been denied their rights and protects them from retaliation for disagreeing with policies. He also discussed that academic freedom provides faculty members with substantial leeway in determining how they can teach the courses to which they are assigned. Regarding serious charges against faculty members, academic freedom guarantees that such allegations will be heard before a committee of their peers. In these situations, faculty have the right to challenge their accusers with the assistance of an attorney.[14]

Although academic freedom allows faculty members to challenge views, it is often confused with an individual's right to free speech.[15] Free speech applies to all people and covers all forms of speech, but academic freedom applies to how educators communicate their discipline and involves teaching, research, and publication.[16] One difference between free speech and academic freedom is that free speech is an individual right, but academic freedom applies to an academic institution's commitment to creating and disseminating knowledge.[17] In other words, unlike individual rights, academic freedom involves the right of the discipline and can be judged only by the professionals within the discipline.[18]

For professionals within the discipline to have control of aspects involving research, teaching, and public expression, universities need to be autonomous. Institutional autonomy, however, has been increasingly under threat at institutions of higher education for various reasons, including pressure to accept funding that influences research priorities.[19]

14 Cary Nelson, "Defining Academic Freedom," *Inside Higher Ed*, December 21, 2010, www.insidehighered.com/views/2010/12/21/defining-academic-freedom.

15 Columbia Law School, "Free Speech."

16 Organization of American Historians, "Academic Freedom Guidelines and Best Practices,"

17 Columbia Law School, "Free Speech."

18 Columbia Law School, "Free Speech."

19 Judith Eaton and Stamenka Uvalic-Trumbic, "HE Institutional Autonomy Is under Siege across the World," *University World News*, June 26, 2021, www.universityworldnews.com/post.php?story=20210622133956498.

Harmful Effects of Corporate Influence

Since academic freedom involves freedom of expression and publication, any practice preventing university researchers from publishing their findings endangers this principle. Sadly, it is not uncommon for a corporation to fund a study and require researchers to sign agreements allowing the corporation to control the design of the research and to determine if the researchers can publish the results. When researchers break these agreements to reveal the dangers of a corporation's products, they may face repercussions, including the possibility of being dismissed.

Two Cases Involving the University of Toronto

Two cases that illustrate this problem occurred in Canada at the University of Toronto. The history of academic freedom in Canada is similar to that of the United States. For example, in the middle of the nineteenth century, the dominant approach in Canada was to protect religious orthodoxy.[20] Over a hundred years later, however, it became safer to express divergent views, although academics continued to be careful about expressing their beliefs about topics that might cause them to be perceived as troublemakers.[21]

One of the cases showing what can happen when someone reveals information that is threatening to a corporation involved Nancy Olivieri. Unfortunately, the poor administrative judgment associated with the Olivieri case may occur at institutions other than the one at which it happened. In addition to being fired, Olivieri's colleagues spread rumors that she slept with scientists who viewed her research favorably. Rumors that she stole money from her grants also spread.[22]

Olivieri held an academic appointment at the University of Toronto's Faculty of Medicine and worked at the Hospital for Sick Children (HSC) where she conducted clinical trials. In the 1990s, she started to suspect that deferiprone, a drug she was testing for the treatment of thalassemia, might

20 Michiel Horn, *Academic Freedom in Canada: A History* (Toronto: University of Toronto Press, 1999), 350.

21 Horn, *Academic Freedom in Canada*, 352.

22 Arthur Schafer, "Biomedical Conflicts of Interest: A Defence of the Sequestration Thesis—Learning from the Cases of Nancy Olivieri and David Healy," *Journal of Medical Ethics* 30 (February 2004): 8.

be ineffective and possibly toxic.[23] When she first became concerned about deferiprone, she contacted Apotex, the manufacturer of the drug sponsoring some of her research. But when she expressed concerns to Apotex and indicated that the existing consent forms would need to be amended, the company disputed her claims.[24] Olivieri then reported her concerns to the research ethics board at the hospital where she worked, and the board agreed with her evaluation. One of the reasons Olivieri expressed worries about the drug was her desire to inform the patients participating in the trial. After becoming aware of her concerns, the board authorized revising the consent form to inform the patients about the new fears associated with the drug.[25]

When Apotex found out the consent forms had been revised, it terminated Olivieri's trial. The conflict worsened after Olivieri decided to break a confidentiality agreement with Apotex by publishing her results in the *New England Journal of Medicine*. Both HSC and the University of Toronto declined to offer Olivieri legal support when Apotex threatened to take legal action after learning she intended to publish her results. The reason offered for refusing to provide legal support involved breaking the disclosure agreement. Although prominent academic scholars quickly became aware of the controversy and wrote letters requesting the University of Toronto to intervene, their efforts did not lead to a favorable outcome for Olivieri. On January 6, 1999, she was dismissed from her position at HSC.[26]

A report by the Canadian Association of University Teachers concluded that threatening to take legal action and stopping the trials was a violation of academic freedom. A representative from the university requested action to be taken to prevent researchers from having to worry that academic freedom and the ethical obligations they have would be undermined in this way again. Olivieri indicated that she experienced five years of harassment and vilification. She also felt the university and the hospital did not offer her support because they were expecting to receive substantial donations from Apotex.[27] Olivieri had a good reason for believing that the univer-

23 Francoise Baylis, "The Olivieri Debacle: Where Were the Heroes of Bioethics?" *Journal of Medical Ethics* 30 (February 2004): 44.

24 Baylis, "The Olivieri Debacle," 44.

25 Jennifer Washburn, *University, Inc.* (New York: Basic Books, 2005), 123.

26 Washburn, *University, Inc.*, 123–124.

27 David Spurgeon, "Report Clears Researcher Who Broke Drug Company Agreement," *BMJ* 323 (February 2004): 1085.

sity and the hospital did not treat her well because financial interests were involved in the controversy. Although representatives from the hospital and the university denied the way they handled the situation had to do with money, there was a potential conflict of interest. A story about the controversy in the *Canadian Medical Association Journal* revealed that both the university and the hospital were aspiring to benefit from sizable donations provided by Apotex. The story indicated that the director of communications at the university said her institution was hoping Apotex would make a large donation, perhaps as high as $20 million so that the medical school could expand. In addition to the chance of making this donation, Apotex had offered to make a $10 million donation to one of Toronto's teaching hospitals. Although the story indicated that there was insufficient evidence showing the negotiations involving the donations affected how Olivieri was treated, it stated that these are the kinds of situations that could potentially exert influence.[28]

Unlike Olivieri's case, another one at the University of Toronto did not involve breaking a disclosure agreement. At the same time the Olivieri controversy was receiving attention, David Healy was planning to leave his position in Wales to start a new one in Canada. In 2000, he accepted a position as the director of the University of Toronto's Mood and Anxiety Disorders Clinic.[29] Later that year, before his new position was scheduled to start, he gave a speech at the center and expressed criticism about the failure of drug companies to investigate the link between antidepressants, including Prozac, and suicide. Healy was then informed that the offer to work as director had been revoked.[30]

The email informing Healy about the rescindment indicated that members of the center felt he was not a good fit. Although a specific reason was not offered, it is easy to see how financial interests were involved. The center was receiving a considerable percentage of funding from corporate sources. Ely Lilly, the maker of Prozac, was providing $1.5 million to the center. The

28 Miriam Shuchman, "Legal Issues Surrounding Privately Funded Research Cause Furor in Toronto," *Canadian Medical Association Journal* 159 (October 1998): 986.

29 Schafer, "Biomedical Conflicts," 12.

30 Janice Paskey, "U. of Toronto Settles Dispute with Psychiatrist Whose Appointment Was Rescinded," *Chronicle of Higher Education*, May 1, 2002, www.chronicle.com/article/u-of-toronto-settles-dispute-with-psychiatrist-whose-appointment-was-rescinded/?cid2=gen_login_refresh&cid=gen_sign_in.

center was also getting 52 percent of its funding from corporate sources.[31] Healy sued the university for almost $6 million, charging it with a few unjust acts, including breach of academic freedom.[32]

Concealment of Research on Antidepressant Drugs

Healy had good reasons for being critical of the lack of effort to reveal the risks of antidepressant drugs. Investigations on the category of antidepressant drugs referred to as selective serotonin reuptake inhibitors (SSRIs) concluded that the makers of these drugs had concealed their dangers and ineffectiveness. In the 1990s, the number of young people being given antidepressant drugs rose considerably. Most of the published academic literature corroborated offering SSRIs to treat young people with depression. However, a 2004 FDA review of all pediatric studies, including those that had never been published, showed that the majority of studies found that taking an SSRI caused no more improvement than did a placebo or a sugar pill.[33]

In response to the suppression of this information, Eliot Spitzer sued GlaxoSmithKline (GSK), the maker of Paxil. Only one of the five studies GSK had funded on Paxil had been published. And the combined data from the studies indicated that taking Paxil increased children's risk of becoming suicidal more than taking a placebo. To make matters worse, other companies were withholding data revealing that antidepressants had caused the same outcomes.[34] Unfortunately, university scholars' names appeared in some of these studies. In fact, a large percentage of the authors of the Paxil studies were university scholars. One of the authors had received over a half million dollars from drug companies he endorsed at medical conferences and in journals. Although it was impossible to prove this case involved a causal relationship between distorted research and its funding sources, other scholars with ties to drug companies had published studies with distorted findings.[35]

---

31 Washburn, *University, Inc.*, 122–123.
32 Paskey, "U. of Toronto."
33 Washburn, *University, Inc.*, 113.
34 Washburn, *University, Inc.*, 113–114.
35 Washburn, *University, Inc.*, 114–115.

Ghostwriting

In addition to the chance an industry may try to suppress the publication of unfavorable results about its products is the possibility it may use the services of ghostwriters. Scientists sometimes accept money so that their names appear at the top of journal articles they do not write. In 2003, a story was published indicating that a high percentage of articles in medical journals are written by ghostwriters.[36] It is believed that there are even some cases involving scientists who are named as authors, although they have seen only the tables produced by a company without viewing the raw data.[37]

The ghostwriting process usually conceals the involvement of drug companies. And it can be a lucrative method for corporations because doctors decide on which drugs to use to a great extent based on what is printed in medical journals. The process often starts when drug companies pay agencies who employ writers to author content to promote a drug company's products. The names of these writers are not revealed, and the researchers whose names appear on top of a paper are paid well so that industries can use their reputations.[38]

Many journals and scholars have unfavorable views about ghostwriting because it can contribute to harmful consequences. One of the problems with this practice is that it conceals conflicts of interest. People who work for drug manufacturers may have participated in the design of a study, collected the data, performed the statistical analysis, and drafted an article without being listed as authors or mentioned in the acknowledgment sections. Such an approach can contribute to exaggerated results. It can also lead to the concealment of the risks associated with a product. Other deceptive practices, such as selective reporting, data manipulation, and inappropriate data analysis can occur.[39]

---

36 Antony Barnett, "Revealed: How Drug Firms 'Hoodwink' Medical Journals," *The Guardian*, December 7, 2003, www.theguardian.com/society/2003/dec/07/health.businessofresearch.

37 Sarah Boseley, "Scandal of Scientists Who Take Money for Papers Ghostwritten by Drug Companies," *The Guardian*, February 7, 2002, www.theguardian.com/uk/2002/feb/07/research.health1.

38 Barnett, "Revealed."

39 Bryan Dotson and Richard L. Slaughter, "Prevalence of Articles with Honorary and Ghost Authors in Three Pharmacy Journals," *American Journal of Health-System Pharmacy* 68 (2011): 1732–1733.

Ways to Prevent the Problem

Various methods can be implemented to prevent the harmful effects of corporate influence on university research. One of these involves supporting researchers who find problems with the drugs or other products of a corporation that funds a study. Other methods include increasing federal support for university research and implementing stronger disclosure requirements and a risk–benefit analysis.

More Support for Researchers to Conduct Trustworthy Research

Rather than threatening researchers with punitive consequences for breaking a confidentiality agreement, universities can support those who find a product to be ineffective or harmful. Such support was provided at the University of California at San Francisco (UCSF) when James Kahn made such a discovery. Kahn valued relationships between academic institutions and the private sector, believing these collaborations were complementary. However, in 1999, he found that his beliefs conflicted with those of the company funding his research after revealing his findings. Kahn concluded from his research that Remune, an AIDS drug, did not work. He wanted to publicize his findings so that patients could be aware of this problem. Although he had signed a confidentiality agreement, Kahn and the others he worked with submitted their findings to the *Journal of the American Medical Association*.[40]

One important difference between the Kahn case and other cases like his involved how UCSF responded. Rather than threaten Kahn with punitive outcomes for doing something that would harm a sponsor, UCSF defended him. Immune Response Corporation (IRC) funded the study Kahn led and disagreed with Kahn's interpretation of the data. IRC claimed that some of the data about their drug showed positive results. But Kahn said the data IRC wanted to include were not part of the study he led. In response to the dispute, IRC demanded $7–10 million in damages. A counterclaim was filed, asserting the data were wrongly withheld from the researchers. Fortunately

40 Washburn, *University, Inc.*, 103–107.

for Kahn and his colleagues, IRC settled without receiving any money for damages.[41]

More Federal Support for University Research

Since funding for independent research is not intended to serve the interests of corporations, this type of support would likely reduce the possibilities for biased studies. Increasing this type of funding is therefore an effective approach for dealing with corporate influence on university research. Allowing researchers to have more opportunities to conduct independent research appears to be the most effective strategy to prevent the negative outcomes associated with industry-funded research.[42]

In the United States, President Joe Biden is planning to implement such an approach. The budget he is proposing for 2024 includes an increase in funds for many federal science agencies. For example, the National Science Foundation, which provides a significant amount of funding for US academic research, would receive a 19 percent increase in funds.[43]

Another way to prevent the problem is by reducing the control corporations have over the research process. Universities can accept support from industries and still conduct authentic research that benefits consumers. For instance, the Massachusetts Institute of Technology (MIT) reduces possibilities for biased research by not accepting funding from corporations unless it has complete freedom to publish the results. This practice helps MIT maintain its reputation as one of the world's leading universities. Although such an approach should be praised, it has prevented this institution from benefiting from lucrative funding offers. Less prestigious universities may not be willing to accept such an approach.[44]

---

41 Susan Haack, "Scientific Secrecy and 'Spin': The Sad, Sleazy Saga of the Trials of Remune," *Law and Contemporary Problems* 69 (2006): 60–61.

42 Hani Morgan, "Reducing Corporate Influence on University Research in America," *Policy Futures in Education* (2022): 11.

43 Max Kozlov et al., "Biden Calls for Boosts in Science Spending to Keep US Competitive," *Nature*, March 23, 2023, 572–573.

44 Paul Basken, "How to Protect Your College's Research from Undue Corporate Influence," *Chronicle of Higher Education*, February 25, 2018, www.chronicle.com/article/how-to-protect-your-colleges-research-from-undue-corporate-influence/?cid2=gen_login_refresh&cid=gen_sign_in.

Stronger Disclosure Policies

For universities that need to rely on accepting funding opportunities requiring the funder the right to control the publication process, stronger disclosure policies can be implemented to determine the extent to which a study may be biased. In 2018, the majority of public health journals were found to have no requirements on the reporting of important information such as nonfinancial conflicts of interest and the role of the funder.[45]

In certain cases, university researchers conducting industry-funded research cannot disclose their conflicts of interest because of the nondisclosure agreements they sign with corporations. These agreements can prohibit researchers from disclosing the terms of the contract regarding their studies. Universities can take action to prevent researchers from signing such contracts, especially those with corporations likely to design misleading research. However, like the practice of accepting industry funding only if university researchers have the freedom to publish, refusing to sign agreements that ban researchers from revealing how a corporation may have influenced the research will likely lead to fewer partnerships with industries.

Implementation of a Risk–Benefit Analysis

Conducting a risk–benefit analysis is another approach that can be implemented. Such an analysis needs to focus on whether the influence of the sponsor may be harmful. This approach also needs to focus on whether a university's reputation may be harmed. In implementing this method, universities need to identify whether an industry's goals are replacing authentic commitments to advance science and avoid becoming involved if necessary. For example, some research institutions have banned accepting funds from tobacco companies.[46]

The tobacco industry has been blamed for using pseudoscience to participate in deceptive campaigns that have misled the public. In the 1950s and 1960s, this industry suggested that their products were safe and withheld

45 Karim N. Daou et al., "Public Health Journals' Requirements for Authors to Disclose Funding and Conflicts of Interest: A Cross-Sectional Study," *BMC Public Health* 18 (2018): 1.

46 Morgan, "Reducing Corporate," 11.

evidence showing they were harmful. In later years, the industry continued to deflect the science showing its products were detrimental.[47]

The guidelines the Canadian government recently released provide another example of how a risk–benefit analysis may be implemented. These guidelines are designed to prevent partnerships that could be harmful. Rather than protecting the reputation of individual universities from being harmed, however, these guidelines are designed to protect the entire nation. They were released in 2021, and universities are expected to follow them before submitting a grant application. The guidelines ask applicants to evaluate whether the companies or researchers they work with pose a security risk to the country. To ensure these new guidelines lead to the desired results, the government provided $25 million to Canadian research universities so that they could hire security officers to help faculty adhere to the new rules.[48]

In addition to the release of these guidelines, new rules were implemented requiring Canada's major research agencies to stop funding proposals viewed as problematic, such as those that benefit another nation's military. The United States, Australia, and other countries have also acted in ways to protect their national security.[49] In the United States, for instance, the Education Department requested some universities to supply records of their agreements and financial transactions with entities and governments in countries that frequently oppose American policies. This increased scrutiny resulted from new concerns about foreign influence consisting of economic espionage and interference in US elections.[50]

Conclusion

Corporations can restrict academic freedom by requiring researchers to sign agreements banning them from publishing their results without the corporation's consent. This practice is antithetical to the ideas on which academic freedom is based. Academic freedom not only allows researchers to pub-

47 Morgan, "Reducing Corporate," 11.

48 Jeffrey Mervis, "Canada Moves to Ban Funding for 'Risky' Foreign Collaborations," *Science*, February 25, 2018, www.science.org/content/article/canada-moves-ban-funding-risky-foreign-collaborations.

49 Mervis, "Canada Moves."

50 Erica L. Green, "Universities Face Federal Crackdown over Foreign Financial Influence," *New York Times*, August 30, 2019, www.nytimes.com/2019/08/30/us/politics/universities-foreign-donations.html.

lish research results but also offers them the right to select the methodologies of their choice, to choose course content, and to share areas of expertise through writing and speech.

By controlling the research process, corporations can participate in misleading practices that harm consumers. Fortunately, corporate influence on academic institutions can be controlled. Some of the ways to accomplish this goal include increasing funding for independent research and implementing stronger disclosure practices. Universities can also refrain from forming partnerships with companies interested in conducting deceptive research that can harm consumers. Such strategies will make it harder for industries to collaborate with university researchers to create studies that contribute to the corruption of science.

CHAPTER 18

Academic Freedom and Dark Money Donors

The Cases of Wisconsin, North Carolina, and Florida

ISAAC KAMOLA

American colleges and universities are no strangers to controversies over academic freedom, originating from all over the political spectrum. However, in recent years, academic institutions around the country have found themselves targeted by externally organized and well-funded right-wing efforts to reshape what gets taught in the classroom, the training and orientations students and faculty receive, the content of job posts, and even which faculty are hired and fired. These attacks on academic freedom are not isolated to specific campuses nor spontaneous, but rather part of a broader political strategy pushed by Republican governors and state legislatures—often in heavily gerrymandered states—who, along with their wealthy donors, have targeted academic freedom for political and partisan gain.

These state-level attacks on academic freedom are possible because state legislatures play a central role in shaping higher education policy. A long history of states' rights and skepticism of concentrated federal power has meant that the American higher education "system"—to the degree you can call it a system at all—is a highly heterogeneous patchwork of private and state institutions, ranging from massive state universities to community colleges, elite private research schools, regional public institutions, small liberal arts colleges, and even for-profit universities. And, as a result, the legal rights and responsibilities of faculty—including academic freedom—are not clearly codified into federal law. Instead, academic freedom is a right developed and enforced over decades through the work of professional associations, most notably the American Association of University Professors (AAUP). The AAUP has developed policy statements spelling out the best practices for protecting academic freedom, including language for institutional handbooks and collective bargaining agreements. However, these policies have proven insufficient to stem this most recent wave of right-wing attacks.

This is because AAUP policies concerning academic freedom and tenure were specifically created to protect faculty from retaliation by campus administrators and boards that disapproved of the content of a professor's teaching, research, or public speech. Writing in response to a string of firings and political retaliations during the early twentieth century, the AAUP's founding document, the 1915 Declaration of Principles on Academic Freedom and Academic Tenure, laid out the argument that academic freedom and tenure were necessary to ensure that teaching and research were free from external influence and, therefore, capable of contributing to "the common good."[1] These ideas were later crystalized in the 1940 Statement of Principles on Academic Freedom and Tenure, which laid out the institution of tenure as known today. According to AAUP guidelines, tenure is the practice whereby faculty members hired within an institution are reviewed throughout a seven-year probationary period, after which they receive a lifetime position. Once tenured, they cannot lose their job except in cases where "adequate cause" demonstrates severe misconduct, or a credible threat of financial insolvency necessitates that the institution cut tenured faculty positions. In both cases, dismissal should only take place after a transparent adjudication by a college or university's faculty committees, and through procedure that includes due process protections.[2]

1 AAUP, "1915 Declaration of Principles on Academic Freedom and Academic Tenure," in *American Association of University Professors: Policy Documents and Reports*, ed. H.-H. Tiede (Washington, DC: American Association of University Professors, 2015), 3.

2 AAUP, "1940 Statement of Principles on Academic Freedom and Tenure with 1970 Interpretive Comments," in *American Association of University Professors: Policy Documents and Reports*, ed. H.-H. Tiede (Washington, DC: American Association of University Professors, 2015), 13. See also Henry Reichman,

During the mid-twentieth century, the US professoriate expanded dramatically, alongside the norms of academic freedom and tenure. However, in recent decades, the growing reliance on contingent faculty and "non–tenure track" positions has substantially undermined the protections of academic freedom and tenure.[3]

However, more recently and within the broader context of funding austerity and mounting precarity, right-wing politicians and donors have seized upon culture war political tactics to pass a barrage of bills that actively undermine academic freedom.[4] Bills prohibiting the teaching of critical race theory (CRT) and so-called divisive concepts seek to shape the content of classroom teaching. Other bills have effectively ended tenure within state universities, empowering politically appointed presidents or governing boards to hire and fire faculty in disregard for AAUP protections. In these contexts, college lawyers and administrators have cautioned faculty against teaching certain topics for fear of running on the wrong side of vaguely worded legislation. These bills have created a chilling effect, leading many faculty to curtail their expression, especially in the classroom and in public speech such as social media. As a result, unlike previous campus controversies, the recent wave of legislative attacks on academic freedom are manufactured within a partisan infrastructure and designed to serve political interests.

Understanding Academic Freedom (Baltimore: The Johns Hopkins University Press, 2021); Matthew W. Finkin and Robert C. Post, *For the Common Good: Principles of American Academic Freedom* (New Haven: Yale University Press, 2009).

3 Note that the AAUP does not recognize a difference between tenure track and non–tenure track positions. The institution of tenure applies to all faculty who have been continuously renewed for seven consecutive years. However, it has become common for institutions to make an unprincipled distinction between "tenure track" and "non–tenure track" positions. See also Adrianna Kezar, Tom DePaola, and Daniel T. Scott, *The Gig Academy: Mapping Labor in the Neoliberal University* (Baltimore: The Johns Hopkins University Press, 2019).

4 For an overview of how antitax advocates harnessed the 1990s culture wars to justify defunding public higher education, see Christopher Newfield, *Unmaking the Public University: The Forty-Year Assault on the Middle Class* (Cambridge, MA: Harvard University Press, 2011). For a more recent example of the connections between Republican political gerrymandering and attacks on higher education in North Carolina, see Special Committee, *Governance, Academic Freedom, and Institutional Racism in the University of North Carolina System* (2022). See also Michael Bérubé and Jennifer Ruth, *It's Not Free Speech: Race, Democracy, and the Future of Academic Freedom* (Baltimore: The Johns Hopkins University Press, 2022); Ralph Wilson and Isaac Kamola, *Free Speech and Koch Money: Manufacturing a Campus Culture War* (London: Pluto Press, 2021); John K. Wilson, *The Myth of Political Correctness: The Conservative Attack on Higher Education* (Durham: Duke University Press, 2020).

These recent attacks on academic freedom dramatically increased after the Black Lives Matter protests during the summer of 2020. Partisan legislation targeting higher education and academic freedom, however, did not emerge out of some grave public concern. Rather, many of these legislative efforts are authored and supported by right-wing libertarian think tanks and advocacy organizations, which receive funding from dark money sources. Within the broader political context of extreme polarization and organized right-wing response to Black Lives Matter, the attacks on academic freedom have become a central tenant of a cynical plutocratic strategy for retaining political power, in the face of a mass demand for racial and economic justice.

This chapter examines three recent state-level attacks on academic freedom in the United States, namely Governor Walker's eradication of tenure in Wisconsin (2015); Art Pope's interference in the University of North Carolina (UNC) system; and the pummeling of Florida's public universities as part of Governor DeSantis's culture war agenda (2021–3). I demonstrate how, in all three examples, dark money organizations play an aggressive role in undermining academic freedom and tenure. Understanding how these organizations work is critical for pushing back against this these well-funded legislative attacks on academic freedom.

Wisconsin

The attack on tenure in Wisconsin set the stage for much of the legislation we are seeing now. Elected during the 2010 Tea Party mid-term wave, Scott Walker began his tenure as governor by taking aim at higher education. His first legislative battle was Act 10, or the Wisconsin Budget Repair Bill, which denied public employee unions—including those representing faculty and graduate students—the ability to negotiate contracts, required annual union recertification, and prevented public employee unions from requiring membership dues.[5] State legislators fled the state to prevent the passage of the bill and thousands of protestors occupied the Wisconsin state capitol between February and March 2011. Walker signed the bill over these objections and would go on to survive a recall and re-election, using his time in

5 Matthew Kearney, "Escalating Moral Obligation in the Wisconsin Uprising of 2011," *Social Forces* 96 (2017): 1574.

the governor's mansion to double down on conservative and libertarian legislative priorities such as curtailing early voting, promoting school vouchers, and continuing the assault on labor unions.[6]

This attack on academic unions, however, did not emerge spontaneously or from a widespread concern among Wisconsin voters. Rather, the effort was spearheaded by conservative libertarian activists and donors who had long sought to undermine public funding for social services, including higher education. As laid out in Hertel-Fernandez's book *State Capture*, a small number of partisan political organizations backed by considerable corporate donors coordinated the passage of Act 10.[7] The American Legislative Exchange Council (ALEC) wrote the model legislation that became Act 10. ALEC is a dark money–funded organization that brings together corporate interests ("private partners") to write bills—in this case, antiunion legislation—and hand them to "public partners" (state legislators) to enact into law. The Koch-funded Astroturf organization Americans for Prosperity led rallies in support of the legislation and spent $500,000 in TV advertising supporting the bill. And the State Policy Network (SPN)—an umbrella organization for free-market think tanks—along with the local SPN affiliate Wisconsin Policy Research Institute played an important role in pushing the legislation within Walker's inner circle and in the media more generally.[8]

In 2015, as part of the state budget negotiations, Scott pushed additional legislation that empowered the board of regents to rewrite tenure provisions, giving them the flexibility to fire tenured faculty "when such an action is deemed necessary due to a budget or program decision requiring program discontinuance, curtailment, modification or redirection."[9] This legislation, which Walker called "the Act 10 of higher education," allowed universi-

6 Monica Davey and Tamar Lewin, "Unions Subdued, Scott Walker Turns to Tenure at Wisconsin Colleges," *New York Times*, June 4, 2015, www.nytimes.com/2015/06/05/us/politics/unions-subdued-scott-walker-turns-to-tenure-at-wisconsin-colleges.html.

7 Alexander Hertel-Fernandez, *State Capture: How Conservative Activists, Big Businesses, and Wealthy Donors Reshaped the American States—And the Nation* (Oxford: Oxford University Press, 2019), 187–191.

8 Between 1998 and 2019 ALEC received $11.6 million from Koch family foundations, the right-wing Bradley Foundation, and two donor-advised funds—DonorsTrust and Donors Capital Fund—with close ties to Koch network. Likewise, AFP received $88.7 million between 2014 and 2019, and the SPN received $51.6 million between 2001 and 2019; see Wilson and Kamola, *Free Speech and Koch Money*, 166–167.

9 Davey and Lewin, "Unions Subdued, Scott Walker Turns to Tenure at Wisconsin Colleges." See also Colleen Flaherty, "Trying to Kill Tenure," *Inside HigherEd*, June 1, 2015; Colleen Flaherty, "Wisconsin Tenure Wars: Part Two," *Inside HigherEd*, November 3, 2015.

ties to terminate faculty without the usual due process protections and oversight, effectively ending tenure and undermining the possibility of shared governance.[10] In response to the board's revised tenure policies, the AAUP and American Federation of Teachers (AFT) noted that

> the University of Wisconsin system board of regents has adopted a policy that provides weaker protections of tenure, and thus of academic freedom ... What is not clear is why the regents have adopted such a policy. The policy appears to be only the latest step in an ongoing attack on the University of Wisconsin as a public good that exists for the benefit of all citizens of the state.[11]

This attack on tenure, and academic unions more generally, gutted Wisconsin's long tradition of treating public higher education as a public good. Since the mid-twentieth century, Wisconsin has been known for its strong state university system, with a deep commitment to public service—widely known as "the Wisconsin Idea." By attacking public employee unions and tenure, and relentlessly cutting university funding, Walker recast public universities as an economic drain on the state. His true contempt for higher education became public when the language of a revised mission statement leaked. The proposed revision "replace[d] the university system's public-service mission ... with language that emphasized higher education's role in meeting state work-force needs."[12] While Walker eventually retracted this language, calling it a "drafting error," his attacks on academic freedom and higher education would serve as a blueprint for Republican administrations and right-wing donors to emulate.

Walker's attacks on academic freedom, however, were justified using the libertarian language of balancing the budget and saving taxpayer money. More recent attacks on academic freedom, such as those in North Carolina and Florida, have increasingly embraced strident culture war language, even

10 Davey and Lewin, "Unions Subdued, Scott Walker Turns to Tenure at Wisconsin Colleges"; Valerie Strauss, "Is Gov. Scott Walker Putting the University of Wisconsin System in Jeopardy?" *Washington Post*, June 5, 2015, www.washingtonpost.com/news/answer-sheet/wp/2015/06/05/is-gov-scott-walker-putting-the-university-of-wisconsin-system-in-jeopardy/.

11 H.-J. Tiede, "Tenure and the University of Wisconsin System," *Academe* (May–June, 2016).

12 Karin Fischer, "A Playbook for Knocking Down Higher Ed," *Chronicle of Higher Education*, October 18, 2022, www.chronicle.com/article/a-playbook-for-knocking-down-higher-ed.

while being spearheaded by many of the same partisan organizations and funded by the same group of activist donors.

North Carolina

In 2022 the AAUP issued an unprecedented report on the state of academic freedom in the UNC system. The report documents the systemwide politicization of the UNC system and the long track record of political interference and violations of academic freedom. High-profile events, such as the revoking of tenure to Nikole Hannah-Jones, took place within a context of targeting for closure of academic centers run by scholars critical of the state's Republican political establishment. The AAUP's special committee "concluded that the statewide board of governors and the campus-level boards of trustees have repeatedly exercised their considerable power in a manner that violates AAUP-supported principles of academic governance ... plac[ing] academic freedom in 'growing jeopardy.'" And that these violations occur within the context of, and in relation to, "long-standing patterns of institutional racism to make the UNC system a particularly hostile environment for faculty, staff, and students of color."[13]

As with Wisconsin, the partisan attacks on academic freedom did not occur because of mass public concern over the UNC system. Rather, the politicization of the UNC system, and the systemic attack on academic freedom, was spearheaded by a well-funded political infrastructure. In North Carolina, Art Pope—a major political donor, many with ties to the Koch donor network—has funded not only the local politicians but also the think tanks and political institutions that have played a major role in politicizing North Carolina's higher education system. Pope served four terms in the North Carolina legislature and as the budget director in Republican governor Pat McCrory's administration (2013–15). But in addition to holding elected and appointed positions, Pope plays an even more significant role in pushing a right-wing libertarian agenda across the state. By 2014, the Pope Foundation had already spent $55 million building "a robust network of conservative think tanks and advocacy groups" in North Carolina.[14] And

13 Special Committee, *Governance, Academic Freedom, and Institutional Racism*, 6.

14 Matea Gold, "In N.C., Conservative Donor Art Pope Sits at Heart of Government He Helped Transform," *Washington Post*, July 19, 2014, www.washingtonpost.com/politics/in-nc-conservative-donor-

Pope established himself as "one of the most trusted members of the Koch's elite circle," and a regular attendee at Koch donor seminars.[15]

One of Pope's legislative priorities has been transforming the state's public higher education system. As early as 1995 Pope actively sought an appointment to the board of governors but was considered far too partisan for this nonpartisan position. In 2010, however, Pope funded the REDMAP project, pumping money into legislative races during the redistricting year, which allowed Republican majorities to gerrymander the state legislature.[16] In 2020 the Republican majority in the state legislature, which Art Pope helped create, appointed Pope to the board of governors, overseeing the entire UNC system.

Pope also funds several state-level think tanks, including The James G. Martin Center for Academic Renewal, John Locke Foundation, and Civitas. The Martin Center, in particular, targets higher education, focusing on right-wing culture war issues and claiming that free-market ideas are largely absent from the college curriculum. The Martin Center presents faculty as the primary opposition and therefore seeks to empower "parents, students, trustees, alumni, and administrators" in governance, with a focus on "encourag[ing] respect for the institutions that underlie economic prosperity" and "cost-effective administration and governance."[17]

In 2021 the gerrymandered state legislature continued its right-wing assault on higher education, appointing four new members to the board of governors and six new conservative members to the UNC-Chapel Hill's board of trustees.[18] In January 2023 the board of trustees at UNC-Chapel Hill passed a resolution instructing the administration to create a School of Civic Life and Leadership. Chairman David Boliek then went off Fox News

---

art-pope-sits-at-heart-of-government-he-helped-transform/2014/07/19/eece18ec-0d22-11e4-b8e5-d0de80767fc2_story.html.

15 Chris Kromm, "The Art Pope Empire: Media Outlets, Think Tanks and Election Machines," *Indy Week*, March 9, 2011, https://indyweek.com/news/art-pope-empire-media-outlets-think-tanks-election-machines/.

16 Sue Sturgis, "How Art Pope's Money Shaped UNC's Toxic Debate over Nikole Hannah-Jones," *Facing South*, July 16, 2021, www.facingsouth.org/2021/07/how-art-popes-money-shaped-uncs-toxic-debate-over-nikole-hannah-jones.

17 Martin Center, "About," www.jamesgmartin.center/about/.

18 Kate Murphy and Lucille Sherman, "Who Controls the Future of Higher Education in NC? Some New, Conservative Players," *News and Observer*, July 16, 2021, www.newsobserver.com/news/local/education/article252768763.html.

to boast that the new center would bring those with "right-of-center views" to campus to "provide equal opportunity for both views to be taught."[19] These efforts by political appointees to shape curriculum on campus were accelerated in 2023, when the North Carolina legislature introduced House Bill (HB) 715, which, if passed, would give university governing boards the ability to "ensure efficient use of institutional resources, including regularly evaluating and eliminating unnecessary or redundant expenses, personnel, and areas of study."[20] As in Wisconsin, this bill would make it possible for a politically appointed board of trustees to decide university curriculum using unsubstantiated budgeting claims to close academic departments and centers, and fire faculty, who expressed ideas that these politically appointees disagreed with.

Florida

In recent years, no state has exemplified the right-wing culture war attack on academic freedom more completely than Florida. Over the past few years, the Florida legislature and the DeSantis government have passed several bills explicitly designed to reshape the state's higher education system. In 2018, following a protest at the University of Florida that disrupted a talk by neo-Nazi Richard Spencer, the state legislature passed Senate Bill (SB) 4, the "Campus Free Expression Act." This bill gives campus speakers the right to sue a public college or university if their "expressive rights are violated" while curtailing the protest speech of the campus community. This bill was drawn from the Foundation for Individual Rights in Education (FIRE) model bill of the same name.[21] This bill was part of a national wave of campus free speech bills being advanced in statehouses across the country, with additional model bills written by other Koch-funded political organizations, including the Arizona libertarian think tank Goldwater Institute and

19 Ryan Quinn, "Confusion over a New Unit at Chapel Hill," *Inside Higher Ed*, February 7, 2023, www.insidehighered.com/news/2023/02/08/unc-chapel-hill-leaders-diverge-what-new-school-will-be.

20 For the text of HB 715, see LegiScan, "NC H715 | 2023-2024 | Regular Session," https://legiscan.com/NC/bill/H715/2023.

21 To compare the model bill to the passed legislation, see FIRE, "Campus Free Expression Act," www.thefire.org/research-learn/campus-free-expression-act; The Florida Senate, "CS/SB 4: Higher Education," March 5, 2018, lines 347–414, www.flsenate.gov/Session/Bill/2018/4/BillText/er/PDF. FIRE has been renamed the Foundation for Individual Rights in Expression.

ALEC.[22] Between 2000 and 2019 FIRE received more than $13.6 million from Koch family foundations, the Bradley Foundation, and DonorsTrust/ Donors Capital Fund.[23]

In 2021 the Florida legislature passed HB 233, which, amending SB 4, allows students to record their professors' lectures and use these recordings in litigation alleging that they have been "shielded" from controversial ideas. The bill also requires public universities to field a survey measuring so-called viewpoint diversity on campus. During the floor debate over HB 233, Democrats asked for evidence that a lack of viewpoint diversity existed in Florida's schools. The bill's cosponsor, Senator Rodrigues, admitted that while he talked to a few students who claimed that they experienced self-censorship, he could not point to any evidence of a lack of viewpoint diversity, but pointed to the survey provision was necessary to find out if the problem exists.[24] In other words, the unsubstantiated right-wing talking point that liberal bias and indoctrination run rampant on college campuses became the justification to deploy an actual survey, designed to prove these partisan assertions true.

In 2022 the Florida legislature passed HB 7—the "Stop Wrongs against Our Kids and Employees" (or "Stop W.O.K.E.") Act—that seeks to dictate classroom content itself. The first part of the bill offers a willful distortion of the scholarship and public discourse on race and racism in America, preventing students or employees from receiving trainings that address unconscious bias, or posits that a certain group "bears responsibility for ... actions committed in the past," or that certain groups should "receive adverse treatment to achieve diversity, equity, or inclusion." Intentionally vague and misleading, this bill effectively restricts discussions about structural racism and gender inequality from the classroom. In granting an injunction against the law, federal judge Mark Walker started his decision with a passage from Orwell's *1984* and called the bill "positively dystopian" and a fundamental violation of constitutional rights to free speech.[25]

22 Wilson and Kamola, *Free Speech and Koch Money*, 98–114.

23 Wilson and Kamola, *Free Speech and Koch Money*, 167.

24 Florida Senate, "Florida Senate Committee on Education January 26th, 2021 Audio Transcription," January 26, 2021, 56.

25 Andrew Atterbury, "'Positively Dystopian': Florida Judge Blocks DeSantis' Anti-Woke Law for Colleges," *Politico*, November 17, 2022, www.politico.com/news/2022/11/17/florida-anti-woke-law-block-colleges-education-00069252#:~:text=TALLAHASSEE%2C%20Fla.,taught%20in%20colleges%20

As with HB 233, HB 7 did not emerge from widespread concern among Floridians that "wokeness" is rampant in Florida's colleges and universities. Rather, it was, quite literally, as copy-paste bills cooked up within a partisan political and media ecosystem. The language from HB 7 is taken almost verbatim from the model legislation created by the right-wing think tank Center for Renewing America (CRA). The origin of this bill is closely tied to CRT moral panic, which exemplifies the considerable political infrastructure involved in undermining academic freedom. The story goes like this:

Christopher Rufo, a political operative based at the Manhattan Institute (a partisan think tank funded by a "who's who" of corporate libertarian donors), became interested in CRT during the fall of 2020, recognizing that existing attacks on "political correctness" and "wokeness" were not effectively pushing back against the demands for racial justice taking place in the street. He became interested in CRT not as a good faith participant in conversations about race and racism, but rather because he saw in it a perfect cudgel to swing at his political enemies.[26] By concocting a false caricature of CRT, which was then disseminated through right-wing think tanks and media institutions, Rufo created a weapon capable of scoring partisan political points. He presented this distorted version of CRT on Tucker Carlson's show,[27] where it was seen by President Trump when then contacted Rufo about the possibility of writing an executive order. In conversations with Rufo, Trump's director of the Office of Management and Budget (OMB), Russ Vought, wrote the 2020 "Combating Race and Sex Stereotyping" executive order, which prevented the federal government from funding trainings and workshops that examine issues of systemic racism in American society.[28] Vought left the White House in 2021 to form the CRA, under

---

and%20universities.The same year DeSantis passed HB 1557, dubbed by critics as the "Don't Say Gay" bill, outlawing most discussions about gender identity and sexual orientation in K-12 classrooms.

26 David Theo Goldberg, "The War on Critical Race Theory," *Boston Review*, May 7, 2021, www.bostonreview.net/articles/the-war-on-critical-race-theory/; Benjamin Wallace-Wells, "How a Conservative Activist Invented the Conflict over Critical Race Theory," *New Yorker*, June 18, 2021, www.newyorker.com/news/annals-of-inquiry/how-a-conservative-activist-invented-the-conflict-over-critical-race-theory.

27 "Critical Race Theory Has Infiltrated the Federal Government | Christopher Rufo on Fox News," *YouTube*, www.youtube.com/watch?v=rBXRdWflV7M.

28 White House, "Executive Order on Combating Race and Sex Stereotyping," September 22, 2020, https://trumpwhitehouse.archives.gov/presidential-actions/executive-order-combating-race-sex-stereotyping/.

the umbrella of the Conservative Partnership Institute (CPI), a 501(c)3 non-profit created in 2017 by former senator Jim DeMint.[29] This dark money entity has become the political infrastructure for Trump supporters and former staffers to advance an "America first" agenda and "fight for conservative principles" against the "D.C. Swamp."[30] Its current staff includes former Trump chief of staff Mark Meadows, Clete Mitchell (one of the lawyers who spearheaded efforts to overturn the 2020 election), and numerous other Trump political operatives and staffers.[31] Other organizations under the CPI umbrella include American Accountability Foundations, which attacks Biden's cabinet and judicial appointees, and America First Legal, run by Trump speechwriter Stephen Miller and focuses on litigation that "oppose[s] the radical left's anti-jobs, anti-freedom, anti-faith, anti-borders, anti-police, and anti-American crusade."[32] According to 990 tax documents from 2021, CPI had an annual budget of $17.1 million and revenues of $45.7 million. CRA's tax documents from the same year demonstrate $1,042,274 in financial contributions.

At CRA, Vought used the anti-CRT executive order he authored as the basis for a piece of model legislation banning CRT. Over the past two years, CRA pushed divisive concept bills in state houses across the country. For example, in just six months after its creation, CRA had initiated legislation based on its "false and manipulated explanation" of CRT in more than twenty states.[33] HB 7 is drawn directly from the CRA model legislation.[34]

---

29 SourceWatch, "Conservative Partnership Institute," *Center for Media and Democracy*, www.sourcewatch.org/index.php?title=Conservative_Partnership_Institute.

30 Conservative Partnership Institute, "We Provide the Support Conservatives Need," www.cpi.org/about/.

31 Nick Corasaniti and Alexandra Berzon, "Under the Radar, Right-Wing Push to Tighten Voting Laws Persists," *New York Times*, May 8, 2023, www.nytimes.com/2023/05/08/us/politics/voting-laws-restrictions-republicans.html.

32 America First Legal, "The Mission," https://aflegal.org/about/.

33 Chloe Simon, "A Former Trump Appointee Is Linked to 'Critical Race Theory' Legislation in over 20 States," *MediaMatters for America*, June 25, 2021, www.mediamatters.org/critical-race-theory/former-trump-appointee-linked-critical-race-theory-legislation-over-20-states.

34 To compare the Trump executive order, the CRA model legislation, and the text of HB 7, se: https://tinyurl.com/3hcv7y4j; "Model School Board Language to Prohibit Critical Race Theory," https://citizensrenewingamerica.com/issues/model-school-board-language-to-prohibit-critical-race-theory-2/; Florida Senate, "CS/HB 7: Individual Freedom," lines 65–108, www.flsenate.gov/Session/Bill/2022/7/BillText/er/PDF.

In addition to the STOP W.O.K.E. Act, Florida's 2023 legislative session is considering HB 999, which would also empower political appointees to directly interfere with the content of classroom instruction.[35] HB 999 allows the board of governors to prevent teaching that "utilizes pedagogical methodology associated with Critical Theory" and discontinue majors and minors in ethnic studies, feminist and gender theory, social justice, and intersectionality. The bill would also ban state colleges and universities from using state or federal funding to "advocate for diversity, equity, and inclusion."

As in North Carolina, HB 999 would also expand academic centers designed to promote teaching about Western civilization, offering an uncritical approach to American history and values and promoting a version of civic education that unquestionably celebrates the Founders. For example, HB 999 would empower the Florida State University's Florida Institute of Politics to develop K–12 and university curriculum celebrating "individual rights, constitutionalism, separation of powers, and federalism" and to host speakers that exemplify "exceptional individuals who have excelled in government, industry, or civic engagement to highlight the possibilities created by individual achievement, philanthropic ideals, and entrepreneurial vision." Centers such as the Adam Smith Center for Economic Freedom at Florida International University and the Hamilton Center at the University of Florida would have expanded capacity to hire and fire faculty, devise curriculum, and offer students majors and minors that promote these specific political agendas.

HB 999 also threatens the wholesale dismantling of university self-governance: placing faculty hiring, administrative appointments, and posttenure review of professors in the hands of the board of trustees and the university president, positions appointed by the governor. Faculty input will be eliminated in these hiring decisions. These provisions not only strip faculty of the freedom to determine the content of classroom instruction but also undermine the protections of academic freedom that come from tenure and shared governance.

The introduction of HB 999 was swiftly followed by DeSantis's appointment of anti-CRT crusader Christopher Rufo, and five other conservative

35 Florida Senate, "CS/CS/HB 999: Postsecondary Educational Institutions," www.flsenate.gov/Session/Bill/2023/999/?Tab=BillText.

activists, to the board of trustees at Florida's public liberal arts college. These appointees to the new college board have signaled their intention to transform the school into a training ground for political conservatives.

Conclusion

Wisconsin, North Carolina, and Florida are just three examples of the full-frontal attack on academic freedom coming from state legislatures in Republican-dominated states. In addition to Florida and North Carolina, state legislatures in Iowa, Texas, North Dakota, and elsewhere have also proposed legislation that would effectively end tenure. Alaska, Hawaii, Minnesota, Montana, Oklahoma, Oregon, and a half dozen other states have introduced bills targeting so-called divisive concepts. Legislators in Florida, Ohio, Tennessee, and Texas have proposed bills outlawing diversity, equity, and inclusion initiatives.[36] In addition to these bills targeting higher education, many states are seeing similar culture war attacks on K–12 instruction and public libraries.

On the one hand, it is important to understand these attacks on academic freedom as part of a broader political strategy, one funded by deep-pocket donors who want to discredit higher education. These donors have long advocated for defunding and privatizing public goods, including education, and therefore raising fears about political indoctrination and bias serve to delegitimize these institutions, making them increasingly prone to additional cuts. These donors also realize the significant role higher education plays in political, cultural, and social life. In recent years, and especially during the Black Lives Matter protests of 2020, many of the arguments and analyses about structural racism, gender identity, and the causes of economic inequality have gone mainstream, radically undermining the ideological underpinnings that justify plutocratic inequality and racialized poverty. Massive democratic protests in the streets, armed with ideas learned in classrooms across the country, frightened these plutocrats. The response was a well-organized and well-financed attack on academic freedom. Undermining academic freedom, and making faculty fearful for their livelihoods, gives plutocrats the

36 PEN America, "PEN America Index of Educational Gag Orders," https://pen.org/report/educational-gag-orders/.

tools to shape the knowledge that faculty produce, taking special aim at that which challenges economic, racialized, and gendered injustice.

By "following the money" it becomes possible to see the stakes of this latest attack on academic freedom. In such an analysis, the onslaught is seen as either the last violent spasm of a plutocratic elite fighting to justify itself, or the beginnings of a new era of virulent unfreedom within higher education. Determining which path we head down depends upon how militantly we defend academic freedom from the political interests of right-wing plutocrats and their political infrastructure. However, our ability to teach, research, and publicly speak about those issues that advance the common good requires nothing less than defending and expanding a robust understanding of academic freedom protections, including the end of academic precarity. There is much work to be done.

CHAPTER 19

Beyond Academic Freedom

Australian Universities and Post-Reform China

JOHN FITZGERALD

INTRODUCTION

In the mid-2010s, concerns began to surface in Australia about possible risks to academic freedom arising from a rapidly corporatizing Australian university sector linking up with counterparts in an increasingly authoritarian China.[1] At the time, those concerns were not widely shared by university executives, many of whom had been dealing with China without difficulty for decades. Nevertheless, continuing media revelations and occasional faculty confirmations alerted university executives to the importance of defending academic freedom for the maintenance of their universities' social license to operate. They were compelled to respond once the national conversation around threats to academic freedom broadened to embrace domestic sources in addition to foreign ones, including populist antiscience sentiment, domestic government intervention, demands from philanthropic

1 John Fitzgerald, "Academic Freedom and the Contemporary University: Lessons from China," *Australian Academy of the Humanities Lecture Series* (2016), www.humanities.org.au/wp-content/uploads/2017/09/AAH-Academy-Lect-Fitzgerald-2016.pdf.

donors, and the managerial practices of universities themselves.[2]

Amid this wider array of challenges to academic freedom, what came to distinguish the China challenge from others was not the risks to academic freedom alone but the challenges on other fronts exposed by violations of academic freedom in universities caught in China's embrace. These further challenges included risks to intellectual property, the conduct of research and teaching, and cyber security issues. Together, these wider challenges placed additional burdens on the practice of academic freedom in the liberal academy, particularly on the duty of faculty to speak out in defense of basic principles. In this chapter, we explore the connection between the protection of academic freedom on campuses and the broader defense of intellectual ethics, intellectual property, institutional integrity, and security in the Australian case.

Context

Australia's universities enjoy historically close relations with China. When Beijing first committed to "Reform and Opening" in the late 1970s, universities in many liberal democracies opened their doors to counterparts in China, along with international think tanks, research organizations, businesses, and governments. Revenues and resources followed. In the case of Australia, China came to account for more international students enrolled in universities and colleges than those from any other country, in an industry that contributed around A$37 billion annually to Australia's national economy before the COVID-19 lockdowns.[3] China was also a partner in hundreds of discrete research collaborations in the STEM disciplines across Australia and became the focus of ten specialist research centers and a dozen Confucius Institutes in Australian universities. China's Reform Era yielded a bountiful harvest for Australian higher education.

The dynamics driving university-to-university relations within China changed significantly once Xi Jinping drew the curtain on the Reform and

---

2 Miriam Bankovsky and Jacqui Hoepner, "We Need to Talk about the Actual Threats to Academic Freedom on Australian Campuses," *The Conversation*, December 17, 2018, https://theconversation.com/we-need-to-talk-about-the-actual-threats-to-academic-freedom-on-australian-campuses-108596.

3 Parliament of Australia, "Overseas Students in Australian Higher Education: A Quick Guide," April 22, 2021, www.aph.gov.au/About_Parliament/Parliamentary_Departments/Parliamentary_Library/pubs/rp/rp2021/Quick_Guides/OverseasStudents.

Opening Era. In its place, he announced the dawn of a "New Era," which involved halting and in some cases reversing reform measures and putting an end to open engagements with the liberal democracies of the world. The Chinese Communist Party (CCP) now aspired to command and control every institution in the country on a model of government aptly described as "CCP Inc."[4] Beyond China, the party embarked on a program of aggressive "wolf warrior" diplomacy and ramped up trade and other penalties targeting those liberal democracies that give offense to Beijing, including Norway, South Korea, Japan, Canada, and Australia. At the same time, Xi himself began speaking loudly and often about preparing his country for a protracted struggle while overseeing the greatest peacetime military buildup by any country in postwar history.[5] These exemplary punishments, and hints of pending war, were intended to teach other countries a lesson and compel their compliance with Beijing's geopolitical demands.

Not all have taken those lessons as intended. The message that Australian governments, people, and institutions took away from the harsh economic punishments and abusive diplomacy China's government directed at them was not that Canberra should comply with Beijing's demands but rather that Australian institutions should reassess the risks and benefits of engaging with China in Xi Jinping's New Era.[6]

For universities, the advent of China's New Era carried particular lessons. Along with other institutions, they entered relations in the Reform Era with the expectation that engagement with an opening and reforming China would benefit all concerned. As China's universities fell more directly under central party control, however, and surrendered what little freedom and autonomy they had begun to enjoy, the benefits of open and robust academic exchange diminished accordingly. Party authorities reduced universities to "carrying out orders from above," in the words of one of China's leading national academicians, Zi Zhongyun. "We can only wonder what other

4 Barry Naughton and Briana Boland, "CCP Inc.: Reshaping of China's State Capitalist System," *Center for Strategic and International Studies*, January 31, 2023, www.csis.org/analysis/ccp-inc-reshaping-chinas-state-capitalist-system.

5 John Pomfret and Matt Pottinger, "Xi Jinping Says He Is Preparing China for War: The World Should Take Him Seriously," *Foreign Affairs*, March 29, 2023, www.foreignaffairs.com/united-states/xi-jinping-says-he-preparing-china-war.

6 Euan Graham, *Australia's Security in China's Shadow* (London: International Institute for Strategic Studies, 2023).

depths they might be willing to plumb as they continue to debase higher education in China."[7] Those depths were plumbed in 2022 when China's five-year plan for cultural development directed scholars to "break out" and "decouple" from global mainstream work in the humanities and social sciences.[8] The new course charted for China's universities left little room for free and open critical inquiry in the human sciences and no room for the exercise of academic freedom.

The implications of these developments in China have proved troubling for foreign universities that engage closely with them. In Australia, concern has been expressed about the financial penalties borne by university partners that invested heavily in China or grew overly dependent on student revenues from China.[9] To be sure, significant sums are on the table, but so also are academic freedom, ethical standards, intellectual property, institutional integrity, and national security. For international university partners dealing with China, everything is on the line.

Universities in China Then and Now

In the Reform Era, higher education was one of China's many success stories. The national tertiary participation rate rose from under 1 percent to around 25 percent of the current age cohort toward the end of that period in a population that was one-third larger than at the start of the era. This remarkable achievement was a consequence not of international engagement alone but of China's domestic reengagement with an old East Asian Confucian model of education shared with Hong Kong, Taiwan, Singapore, Japan, Korea, and Vietnam. Four key elements characterize higher education in these national

7 Zi Zhongyun [資中筠], "Mourning Tsinghua," *China Heritage*, March 2019, http://chinaheritage.net/journal/my-tsinghua-lament/.

8 Australian analysts at *China Policy* read the PRC's five-year plan for cultural development (September 2022) as directing scholars to "break out" and "decouple" from global mainstream humanities and social sciences. See Australian Academy of the Humanities, *Australia's China Knowledge Capability: University Teaching, Research and Future Needs* (Canberra: Australian Academy of the Humanities, 2023).

9 See, e.g., Sian Powell, "Vice-Chancellors on Mission to Mend Fences with Beijing," *The Australian*, February 28, 2018, www.theaustralian.com.au/subscribe/news/1/?sourceCode=TAWEB_WRE170_a_GGL&dest=https%3A%2F%2Fwww.theaustralian.com.au%2Fhigher-education%2Finternational-students%2Fvcs-on-mission-to-mend-fences-with-beijing%2Fnews-story%2F34175521e4b10d51f4b31be3367fcb03&memtype=anonymous&mode=premium&v21=GROUPA-Segment-1-NOSCORE&V21spcbehaviour=append; Robert Bolton, "Unis Fear $12bn Hit as Chinese Students Stay Home," *Australian Financial Review*, April 28, 2020.

systems, including the role of the state in shaping the structures, funding, and priorities of national higher education systems; a trend toward universal participation driven by popular commitment embedded in cultural values; highly competitive national examination systems highlighting discipline and meritocracy; and a prestige market for attainment of world-class status.[10]

Within this transnational Confucian model, provision is made for academic freedom commensurable with the greater or lesser degrees of other civic freedoms tolerated in each of the countries that practice it, including freedoms of expression, of the press, of assembly, and of religion. Reform-era China eschewed all such civic freedoms, even while adopting the Confucian model of education, and showed commensurably less respect for the principles derived from those civic freedoms, including academic freedom. As a result, even in the Reform Era, the scope for free and open critical inquiry was constrained by the party's limits of tolerance, occasionally expanding but then contracting again in keeping with the political mood of the day.

In Xi Jinping's New Era, there has been a step change in the level of state control over higher education, involving a shift from the reactive model of the earlier Reform Era, toward proactive enforcement of strict ideological guidelines and efforts to draw universities into the party's broader strategy for confronting liberal ideology and liberal democracies globally.

Beijing's revised strategy for higher education is set out in formal state documents. The State Council's 2015 guidelines for higher education, for example, characterize the higher education sector as a "battlefield" for the struggle between China and its enemies in the liberal-democratic sphere. This has strategic implications: the guidelines call for "doing higher education propaganda and ideology work well and strengthening the construction of the higher education ideological battlefields [as] strategic projects."[11]

At the faculty level, individual academics are held accountable to this national battlefield strategy through their university's performance

10 Simon Marginson, "The Confucian Model of Higher Education in East Asia and Singapore: Strategic Responses to Globalisation," in *Higher Education in the Asia Pacific*, ed. Simon Marginson, Sarjit Kaur, and Erlenawati Sawir (Cham: Springer, 2011), 53.

11 State Council, "Opinions Concerning Further Strengthening and Improving Propaganda and Ideology Work in Higher Education under New Circumstances," *China Copyright and Media*, January 19, 2015, https://chinacopyrightandmedia.wordpress.com/2015/01/19/opinions-concerning-further-strengthening-and-improving-propaganda-and-ideology-work-in-higher-education-under-new-circumstances/.

appraisal systems, which operate under explicit direction from the Ministry of Education to measure compliance with communist party ideology and strategy. The ministry's guidelines on academic staff performance appraisal issued in August 2016 state, among other things, that "the illegal spread of harmful ideas and expressions in the classroom will be dealt with severely according to regulation and law."[12]

The "harmful ideas and expressions" banished from university classrooms were set out in an earlier party communiqué issued in April 2013 and forwarded to university presidents and party secretaries as a prescribed list of "Seven Prohibitions" governing university teaching and research. The seven banned areas all fall within the core curriculum of the humanities and social sciences in the liberal academy: constitutional democracy, civil society, economic liberalization, freedom of the press, historical critiques of the communist party, challenges to socialism with Chinese characteristics, and discussion of "universal values" (local code for human rights and freedoms, including academic freedom).[13] Faculty are deterred from raising these topics in the classroom and research publications for fear of being "dealt with severely" as law and regulations prescribe.

In December 2016 Xi Jinping placed his presidential seal of approval on the new strategic direction in higher education in a widely publicized speech about placing "ideological work" and "political work" at the heart of university education and management. Among other things, he proclaimed that all science was based on Marx's scientific socialism, which brooked no contradiction, and that it was the duty of university managers and academics to profess and inculcate the "scientific theory of Marxism."[14]

He also harnessed science and technology innovation in universities more explicitly to achieve all-round military goals under his signature "military–civil fusion strategy." This strategy, introduced during his first term

12 My translation of Ministry of Education guidelines issued in August 2016; see para. 10. Chinese original is available at: www.moe.gov.cn/srcsite/A10/s3735/201609/t20160920_281586.html.

13 General Office of the Central Committee of the Communist Party of China, "Communiqué on the Current State of the Ideological Sphere," April 2013, www.chinafile.com/document-9-chinafile-translation.

14 My translation of the Xi Jinping speech of December 2016; see Xi Jinping, "Ensure Ideological and Political Work Penetrate the Entire Process of Teaching and Learning (习近平：把思想政治工作贯穿教育教学全过程)," *Xinhua*, December 8, 2016, http://news.xinhuanet.com/politics/2016-12/08/c_1120082577.html.

as party general secretary, seeks to "leverage the research and development capabilities of universities to advance both the country's domestic economy and national defense apparatus."[15] Broadly speaking, this is not new to China, nor confined to China, as other governments also try to derive defense applications from university research. The difference lies in the deep fusion of civil and military resources under CCP Inc. to "strengthen and support its armed wing, the People's Liberation Army [PLA], Navy and Airforce."[16] International research collaboration is a key element of the new strategy. Hence universities, governments, and corporations outside China that collaborate or plan to cooperate with China's universities in the New Era need to "equip themselves with the knowledge and tools to inform their collaboration with and funding of Chinese research institutions."[17]

The Manifold Challenges of China's New Era

In view of their designated roles as battlefields for ideological confrontation with liberal democracies, and their intimate fusion with the party's military apparatus, China's universities present challenges for foreign partners that go beyond academic freedom to issues of intellectual property, research priorities, and institutional security. These new challenges place a burden on the practice of academic freedom that goes beyond defense of that freedom. In the liberal tradition, academic freedom carries a duty to speak truth to power and carries a moral sanction against remaining silent in the face of assaults on civic freedoms generally.[18] This duty and this sanction both come into play in managing security risks around university-to-university collaborations with Xi Jinping's China. Universities that fail to manage these challenges risk not just their revenues but their integrity, their intellectual property, their stand-

15 Audrey Fritz, "How China's Military–Civil Fusion Policy Ties into Its Push for World-Class Universities," *The Strategist*, May 19, 2021, www.aspistrategist.org.au/how-chinas-military-civil-fusion-policy-ties-into-its-push-for-world-class-universities/.

16 Peter Wood and Alex Stone, *China's Military-Civil Fusion Strategy: A View from Chinese Strategists* (Maxwell Airforce Base, AL: China Aerospace Studies Institute, 2020).

17 Fritz, "How China's Military–Civil Fusion Policy Ties into Its Push for World-Class Universities."

18 Ronald Dworkin, "We Need a New Interpretation of Academic Freedom," in *The Future of Academic Freedom*, ed. Louis Menand et al. (Chicago: University of Chicago Press, 1996), 181.

ing, and possibly their license to operate in a liberal democracy. To remain silent in the face of these threats is arguably a dereliction of duty.

Australian universities have acted to strengthen their public commitment to academic freedom and freedom of speech in response to mounting public concerns around university collaboration with China and parochial concerns about populist political attacks on universities generally. In 2018, for example, the Australian National University (ANU) convened a wide-ranging forum on the challenges to academic freedom in the current political and geopolitical environment.[19] The university subsequently issued extended guidelines for the defense of academic freedom on campus. Faculty at ANU proposed a charter of academic freedom, which was accepted by the University Council, and the university executive updated and strengthened its policy framework around academic freedom.[20] Beyond ANU, the federal government commissioned a review of the state of academic freedom in Australian higher education that served as a benchmark for universities nationwide.[21]

Other Australian reports showed that collaboration with Xi Jinping's China carried risks to intellectual property, national security, research priorities, and the values that lend the liberal university its distinctive character, including academic freedom. The *Australian Cyber Security Centre Annual Cyber Threat Report* for 2019–20 identified more than 120 cyberattacks against universities in the preceding twelve months. Cyber risks facing the sector are regarded as among the most challenging because cyber can serve as a vector for espionage, IP theft, and interference. In 2022 the Australia Security Intelligence Organisation (ASIO) told a parliamentary inquiry that it was aware of attempts to steal sensitive Australian IP through cyber compromises. In one case, malicious cyber actors attempted to steal IP data related to the COVID-19 vaccine.[22]

---

19 For a review of the ANU forum, see Bankovsky and Hoepner, "We Need to Talk about the Actual Threats to Academic Freedom on Australian Campuses."

20 Australian National University, "Academic Freedom and Freedom of Speech," https://policies.anu.edu.au/ppl/document/ANUP_6380896#IDC7Ehttps://policies.anu.edu.au/ppl/document/ANUP_6380896#IDC7E.

21 Hon. Robert French AC, "Report of the Independent Review of Freedom of Speech in Australian Higher Education Providers," March 2019, www.education.gov.au/higher-education-publications/resources/report-independent-review-freedom-speech-australian-higher-education-providers-march-2019.

22 Parliamentary Joint Committee on Intelligence and Security, *Inquiry into National Security Risks Affecting the Australian Higher Education and Research Sector* (Canberra: Parliament of the Commonwealth

Evidence of coercive pressure and espionage was not limited to the cyber domain. ASIO informed the 2022 parliamentary inquiry that it was aware of researchers and their families being threatened, coerced, and intimidated by actors seeking to have their sensitive research findings shared with a foreign state actor.[23] In other cases, universities themselves faced crude threats of financial coercion if they continued to support research regarded as critical of Beijing's policies.[24] In further cases again, co-option involved deception. The Australian Strategic Policy Institute (ASPI) reported in 2018 that top Australian university researchers were collaborating with PLA-linked institutions in defense-related research and research training, without knowing the true identities of those they were dealing with or appreciating the national security implications of their research. The report identified seventeen PLA university researchers who were traveling and working in Australia undercover whose work touched on national security.[25]

Through their research and policy engagement, universities are also involved in shaping public perceptions of social issues and geopolitics, a further site of potential vulnerability. In 2014 a prominent Chinese citizen made a significant donation to the University of Technology Sydney (UTS) to establish a new China institute focusing on Australia–China relations. The donor boasted publicly that he personally selected the institute director who would run the operation. The preferred director subsequently emerged as the most eminent and prominent university advocate in Australia supporting Xi Jinping's elevation to the leadership and promoting an "unabashedly positive and optimistic view of the Australia–China relationship" in the New Era. There was little covert about the operation. The director met with PRC propaganda chiefs; he publicly extolled Xi Jinping's "leadership for the world"; and, echoing Beijing, he condemned local critics of China's strategic ambitions and human rights record as engaging in "Cold War thinking."[26]

Another university vector of influence on public policy is the international network of Confucius Institutes, which in Australia serve as a bridge

of Australia, March 2022), ss 2.48–2.49.

23 Parliamentary Joint Committee on Intelligence and Security, *Inquiry into National Security Risks*, s 2.59.

24 Parliamentary Joint Committee on Intelligence and Security, *Inquiry into National Security Risks*, s 2.72.

25 Alex Joske, *Picking Flowers, Making Honey: The Chinese Military's Collaboration with Foreign Universities* (Canberra: Australian Strategic Policy Institute, 2018).

26 John Fitzgerald, "How Bob Carr became China's Pawn," *Australian Financial Review*, November 8, 2018, www.afr.com/policy/what-you-should-know-about-bob-carr-and-china-20181105-h17jic.

linking university executives and local PRC consular officials who are keen to silence public debate on sensitive policy matters. In October 2017, the Confucius Institute at the University of Queensland attempted to shut down a Taiwan historical documentary film festival on campus through internal appeals to the university and faculty executive, before its efforts were thwarted by a faculty member of the history program. The following year, a Confucius Institute at Victoria University in Melbourne successfully moved to prevent the screening of a critical film on the role of Confucius Institutes in higher education globally.[27]

Further reports showed that foreign interference presented challenges for universities committed to preserving their academic freedom and institutional autonomy. ASIO told the parliamentary inquiry that some countries covertly encourage their students in Australia "to counter certain things that are being said on campus as students go about their free speech" and to object to sensitive aspects of the university curriculum. In another case, the PRC consulate in Brisbane endorsed a group of pro-CCP students engaged in violent confrontations with other students demonstrating human rights violations in Hong Kong.[28] Human Rights Watch reported a case of academic censorship due to political pressure when a university withdrew from its website an interview with an academic, discussing Hong Kong's controversial National Security Law, following a barrage of protests against the published interview mounted by pro-CCP students.[29]

While these Australian reports highlighted risks attendant on university relations with counterparts in Xi Jinping's China, the responses they generated also illustrated what governments, universities, and think tanks could do to reduce or mitigate those risks. Responding to concerns around foreign interference generally, the federal government introduced a suite of legislation that gave it the instruments to counter foreign espionage and interference, including the National Security Legislation Amendment (Espionage

27 Richard Ferguson, "University Cancels Screening of Anti-Confucius Institute Film," *The Australian*, September 24, 2018. I witnessed this episode at the University of Queensland, which has not to my knowledge been publicly reported.

28 Ben Smee, "How a 20-Year-Old Student Put the Spotlight on Australian Universities' Cosy Relationship with China," *The Guardian*, May 24, 2020, www.theguardian.com/australia-news/2020/may/24/how-a-20-year-old-student-put-the-spotlight-on-australian-universities-cosy-relationship-with-china.

29 Parliamentary Joint Committee on Intelligence and Security, *Inquiry into National Security Risks*, ss 2.72, 2.76.

and Foreign Interference) Bill 2017[30] and Australia's Foreign Relations (State and Territory Arrangements) (Consequential Amendments) Bill 2020.[31] The former defined and established foreign interference as a criminal act, and the latter mandated federal notification of international agreements entered into by universities and state and territory governments while reserving the right of the federal government to cancel those it considered harmful.

Australia's federal government created a Counter Foreign Interference Taskforce (CFITF) to coordinate an all-of-government approach to foreign interference generally. For the university sector, CFITF launched a specialist University Foreign Interference Taskforce (UFIT) to work with universities on policy development around foreign interference in the education sector, placing particular emphasis on risk reduction, capability building, clarification and implementation of guidelines, and information sharing to raise awareness of foreign interference, data theft, and espionage, and to deepen universities' resilience against risks of this kind. CFIT in turn produced a set of UFIT guidelines that explicitly identify foreign interference as a threat to the sector through "efforts to alter or direct the research agenda; economic pressure; solicitation and recruitment of post-doctoral researchers and academic staff; and cyber intrusions."[32]

Some universities have followed the example of the government by establishing Foreign Influence Task Forces on their own account to identify and address risks on campus around foreign interference. Other universities are developing risk management tools of their own or incorporating countering foreign interference risk management into existing frameworks "to ensure a robust approach to reduce vulnerabilities and mitigating foreign interference threats to the University's people, information and assets." Australian university leaders generally support the UFIT initiative and point out that "no other Five Eyes Plus nation to [our] knowledge—certainly not the US, UK

30 Parliamentary Joint Committee on Intelligence and Security, *Official Hansard: National Security Legislation Amendment (Espionage and Foreign Interference) Bill 2017* (Canberra: Parliament of the Commonwealth of Australia, March 16, 2018).

31 Parliament of the Commonwealth of Australia, Australia's Foreign Relations (State and Territory Arrangements) Bill 2020.

32 Parliamentary Joint Committee on Intelligence and Security, *Inquiry into National Security Risks*, s 2.71.

or Canada—has yet achieved this trusted, collaborative approach between Government, agencies, and universities."[33]

Australia's houses of parliament have played a supplementary role in support of these federal government initiatives through public inquiries into the national security risks facing universities on specific issues, such as foreign interference, data theft, and espionage, and on national security more broadly. The Parliamentary Joint Committee on Intelligence and Security report, which is cited throughout this essay, is one outcome of such an inquiry. Beyond national security, governments and parliaments also assist universities in protecting the human rights of individuals subject to harassment or coercion by working to ensure that they are shielded from foreign government interference on university campuses.

Among think tanks, the ASPI produced a number of online tools and guides to assist universities manage security challenges without damage to legitimate research collaborations or harm to vulnerable faculty. These include the online China Defence Universities Tracker and online Critical Technologies Tracker.[34] ASPI also commissioned a guide to assist universities in managing research collaborations involving risks of cybercrime, intellectual property theft, espionage, or possible military and surveillance applications, without engaging in racial profiling or doing harm to individual researchers.[35]

Academic freedom remains an important underpinning of university responses to each of these challenges, and the prominence given to academic freedom remains a useful indicator of a university's commitment to meeting them. Universities could do more. They could for example refrain from participating in global rankings systems that place competitive per-

33 Parliamentary Joint Committee on Intelligence and Security, *Inquiry into National Security Risks*, ss 3.90, 3.101, 4.52.

34 Alex Joske, *The China Defence Universities Tracker* (Canberra: Australian Strategic Policy Institute, 2018).

35 From the guide: "Identifying possible breaches of research protocols by researchers' nationality or ethnicity risks stigmatising all researchers of Chinese descent and hence playing into CCP wedge politics. There are better ways to approach the problem. Identifying research risks through a research team's institutional affiliations, corporate ties, project focus, or real-world military and surveillance applications is a fairer and surer way of identifying research collaborations that may present risks. On the evidence, an institutional or project-based focus suffices for the purpose." John Fitzgerald, *Mind Your Tongue: Language, Public Diplomacy and Community Cohesion in Contemporary Australia–China Relations* (Canberra: Australian Strategic Policy Institute, 2019).

formance above demonstrated commitment to quality and values, as Chris Brink argues in this volume, without regard to academic freedom and further impeding its defense. They could limit their teaching and research collaborations to partner universities with stated commitments to academic freedom and institutional autonomy. Professional associations and national academies that value academic freedom and institutional autonomy could monitor the performance of universities on these indicators and hold them to account. Multilateral bodies could also play a role. UNESCO could establish clear and unequivocal reporting guidelines for member states to report on legal and other measures indicating their respect for freedom of inquiry and institutional autonomy in national jurisdictions. Member states could be asked to report annually on infringements and remedies, including available legal remedies.

Conclusion

For the avowedly liberal university, it matters that China's universities have come under the thumb of an all-embracing communist party that is avowedly hostile to academic freedom and institutional autonomy in Xi Jinping's New Era. The core currency of the liberal university is its values, including the value placed on academic freedom, and these values are incommensurable with those currently practiced in China's university system.

Australia's experience in the mid-2010s indicates that the first casualty of continuing university engagement with China in the New Era is likely to be academic freedom, but that this is only the first of many possible casualties for universities not alert to wider risks. The defense of academic freedom can serve as the leading edge of a broader defense of academic ethics, institutional integrity, and university security. A university's commitment to countering cyber security and espionage, upholding ethical research, preserving intellectual property, and maintaining institutional integrity is no less important than its commitment to the defense of academic freedom.

Media commentary on threats to academic freedom in Australia arising from overdependence on student recruitment from China and institutional connections with China drew attention to the social license under which universities operate. This too goes beyond questions of academic freedom. In the liberal tradition, universities operate in open-source environments where fundamental knowledge is discovered and shared. Public roles of this kind carry an obligation to protect the ethical foundations and collegial trust underpinning knowledge creation from corruption by state actors that do not share a liberal, principles-based, ethical framework.

Another feature of the liberal university's license to operate is its commitment to doing "good science" driven by curiosity and guided by ethics. China's universities are committed not to good science but to strategic science, guided by the party's science and technology priorities under its military–civil fusion strategy. Through collaboration, liberal universities committed to good science can find that their research ethics and priorities are unwittingly skewed toward the policy goals of CCP Inc. The risks are particularly high in collaboration with party-managed universities that enjoy deep ties to China's security arms and defense industries.

In China's Reform Era, these risks may have been negligible, but in Xi Jinping's New Era, they are less easily ignored. In this fraught setting, a university's commitment to upholding academic freedom now serves as a signal of its determination to avoid compromise on any front.

Chapter 20

Mining and Fossil Fuel Entanglements with the University in an Era of Climate Change

Impacts for Academic Freedom and Climate (In)action

Kristen Lyons

Introduction

Contemporary universities have been—and continue to be—reshaped by interrelated structural dynamics, including marketization, massification, and managerialism. This is now well documented, with outcomes including the commodification of research, the neoliberal capture of curricula, the dominance of precarious casual academic work, and declining levels of satisfaction among both staff and students.[1] While these conditions

1 Richard Hil, Kristen Lyons, and Fern Thompsett, *Transforming Universities in the Midst of Global Crisis: University for the Common Good* (London: Routledge, 2021).

all point to the contemporary university *in* crisis, it is also *of* the crisis.[2] Put differently, universities are not simply victims but also directly implicated as enablers of neoliberal and colonial power relations that are reimagining research, teaching, as well as the very fabric of the university. This has significant impacts for academic freedom, with pressures from both within—and without—the university reconfiguring broad understandings about the expectations of what academic freedom might mean, and what might be required for its defense.

In this chapter, I consider university alignment with the corporate sector to examine some of the challenges to, and impacts on, academic freedom. While a range of industries and sectors have invested substantially across the university sector, especially in Anglosphere countries—including pharmaceuticals, bio- and nanotechnologies, tobacco, and sugar—this chapter takes the case of the mining and fossil fuel industries. It is here that investments across universities have expanded in recent years, though the exact scale of investment is difficult to determine. Given that mining and fossil fuel industries are major contributors to rising greenhouse gas emissions and climate change, this raises questions and tensions for universities as public good institutions. How might mining and fossil fuel funding impact research agendas and teaching curricula at universities? And how might these entanglements with mining and fossil fuel interests curtail universities from engaging in the substantive work required to respond—rigorously and ethically—to the climate crisis?

In attending to these questions, this chapter begins with a brief outline of some of the key challenges posed by the climate crisis and considers some of the responsibilities of universities as public good institutions in responding to this crisis. It then describes some of the ways the mining and fossil fuel industries are shaping research, governance, and teaching across universities, thereby curtailing academic freedom across each of these core university domains. It concludes with some reflections on how such conditions constrain universities in responding effectively to the climate crisis.

2 Eli Meyerhoff, *Beyond Education: Radical Studying for Another World* (Minneapolis: University of Minnesota Press, 2019).

The Climate Crisis and Its Impacts

While the COVID-19 health pandemic has deepened socioeconomic and ecological inequalities across the globe, we were already facing an acute state of crisis. Before the onset of the pandemic, the climate crisis was already redefining life, work, mobilities, and learning, transforming both our individual and collective ways of being, relating, and knowing.[3]

The impacts of human-induced climate change—including rising sea levels, as well as increasing land surface heat and ocean temperatures—now threaten life and livelihoods around the world, including for those least responsible for global greenhouse gas emissions.[4] For critical Indigenous studies scholars such as Kyle Whyte,[5] this anthropogenic climate change is not altogether new; rather it represents the continuity of environmental disruptions that have occurred since European colonization of Africa, Asia, the Americas, and Australia. The expansion of colonial frontiers across Indigenous homelands continues up to today, enabled via the systemic assault on diverse ecologies and including more than human relatives, who are frequently reduced to "natural" resources for use in industrial growth and capital accumulation. These forces are driving an exponential increase in toxic emissions, environmental degradation, and catastrophic biodiversity loss—problems that now threaten the existence of all life on Earth.[6]

While there is growing consensus that urgent action is required to curb global greenhouse gas emissions to stabilize the Earth's atmosphere—

3 António Guterres, "The World Faces a Pandemic of Human Rights Abuses in the Wake of COVID-19," *The Guardian*, February 22, 2021, www.theguardian.com/global-development/2021/feb/22/world-faces-pandemic-human-rights-abuses-covid-19-antonio-guterres?CMP=share_btn; Kristen Lyons, Anthony Esposito, and Murrawah Johnson, "The Pangolin and the Coal Mine: Challenging the Forces of Extractivism, Human Rights Abuse and Planetary Calamity," *Antipode Online*, February 1, 2021, https://antipodeonline.org/2021/02/01/the-pangolin-and-the-coal-mine/; Sharon Stein et al., "Beyond Colonial Futurities in Climate Education," *Teaching in Higher Education* 28 (2023): 987–1004.

4 Irene Banos Ruiz, "Talanoa Dialogue: Giving Everyone a Voice in the Climate Conversation," *DW*, February 9, 2018, www.dw.com/en/talanoa-dialogue-giving-everyone-a-voice-in-the-climate-conversation/a-42479711.

5 Kyle Whyte, "Indigenous Climate Change Studies: Indigenising Futures, Decolonising the Anthropocene," *English Language Notes* 55 (2017): 153–162; Kyle Whyte, "Way beyond the Lifeboat: Allegory of Climate Justice," in *Climate Futures: Reimagining Global Climate Justice*, ed. Debashish Munshi et al. (Berkeley: University of California Press, 2020).

6 Naomi Klein, *This Changes Everything: Capitalism vs. the Climate* (New York: Simon & Schuster, 2014); David Attenborough, "Foreword," in *Our Planet*, ed. Alastair Fothergill and Keith Scholey (London: Bantam Press, 2019).

with most countries now signatories to a legally binding treaty on climate change, the Paris Agreement—there remain tensions about how to decarbonize.[7] Meanwhile, the already unfolding climate crisis has turned living ecosystems into "sacrifice zones," dispossessed and disappearing by rising sea levels, desertification, and the expansion of extreme resource extractivism.[8] Shalhoub-Kevorkian has described the growing number of Earth's lost places as "death zones," disappearing in the face of our climate crisis.[9]

In the continent now known as Australia, where the author of this chapter lives, the unprecedented 2019–20 summer bushfires were fueled by the hottest and driest conditions ever recorded. Climate scientists had long warned of such catastrophes, which are predicted to become more intense and frequent.[10] Australia's recent climate-fueled environmental catastrophes are, sadly, not unique. Recent bushfires in Brazil, North America, Indonesia, Russia, and Eastern Europe—including the heatwave-fueled fires that have ravaged Europe during the writing of this chapter—provide a snapshot of what we can expect as the new normal.[11] This enduring state of planetary precarity has both current as well as yet to be realized environmental and societal consequences.[12]

The convergence and intensification of the climate and health crises—for instance, cross-seasonal and zoonotically concurrent bushfires—has also generated a growing demand for emergency responders, care providers, and what United States-based correspondent Nathan Rott has called "apocalypse doctors": medics required to work at the frontlines of multiple crises.[13] Population movements, resource conflicts, and civil and political unrest are

---

7 Ove Hoegh-Guldberg et al., "The Human Imperative of Stabilising Global Climate Change at 1.5C," *Science* 365 (2019): 6459.

8 Klein, *This Changes Everything*; Damien Short, *Redefining Genocide: Settler Colonialism, Social Death and Ecocide* (London: Zed Books, 2016).

9 David Lloyd and Patrick Wolfe, "Settler Colonial Logics and the Neoliberal Regime," *Settler Colonial Studies* 6 (2016): 114.

10 Will Steffen, Annika Dean, and Martin Rice, *Weather Gone Wild: Climate Change Fuelled Extreme Weather* (Potts Point: Climate Council of Australia, 2019).

11 Alice Tidey, "Wildfire Season Has Started. Here's What Europe Is Doing Wrong," *EuroNews*, June 25, 2023, www.euronews.com/my-europe/2023/06/25/wildfire-season-has-started-heres-what-europes-doing-wrong.

12 Anna Tsing, *The Mushroom at the End of the World: On the Possibility of Life in Capitalist Ruins* (Princeton: Princeton University Press, 2015).

13 Nathan Rott, "Fire in California and Colorado Cover the West with Smoke," *NPR*, August 24, 2020, www.npr.org/2020/08/24/905536205/fires-in-california-and-colorado-cover-the-west-with-smoke.

also emerging as threats to nation-state and regional interests, as well as societal stability more generally.

An Expansionist Agenda Limits University Responses to the Climate Crisis

In the face of climate crisis, many observers have argued that universities have a particular responsibility to act, including to engage in deep and reflective consideration of what these institutions are for, whose interests they should serve, and the prospects they could hold for fostering the possibilities for ecological survival.[14] Stein and others also argue that universities have particular responsibilities in supporting students to foster the intellectual, affective, and relational capacities that may assist them in grappling with the challenges and uncertainties that lay ahead.[15]

In recent decades, universities have responded to the climate and broader environmental crises in ways that generally reflect those of other large institutions and organizations, including government departments and private sector corporations. They have, for example, introduced numerous "climate-smart" and "sustainability" initiatives, established sustainability committees and training programs, constructed green buildings and community gardens, as well as embedded "sustainability" topics across curricula.[16] The push to demonstrate performance "excellence" in this arena—itself a new opportunity for "green" marketing—has also given rise to new forms of instrumentality and institutional surveillance.[17] The UK's Green League Tables—

14 See, e.g., Lawrence Busch, *Knowledge for Sale: The Neoliberal Takeover of Higher Education* (Boston: MIT Press, 2017); John Lemons, "The Urgent Need for Universities to Comprehensively Address Global Climate Change across Disciplines and Programs," *Environmental Management* 48 (2011): 379–391; Petra Molthan-Hill, "Climate Change Education for Universities: A Conceptual Framework from an International Study," *Journal of Cleaner Production* 226 (2019): 1092–1101; Sharon Stein, "Reimagining Global Citizenship Education for a Volatile, Uncertain, Complex and Ambiguous (VUCA) World," *Globalisation, Societies and Education* 19 (2021): 482–495.

15 Stein et al., "Beyond Colonial Futurities in Climate Education."

16 David Rousell, "Dwelling in the Anthropocene: Reimagining University Learning Environments in Response to Social and Ecological Change," *Australian Journal of Environmental Education* 32 (2016): 137–153; Sharon Stein et al., "From 'Education for Sustainable Development' to 'Education for the End of the World as We Know It,'" *Educational Philosophy* 53 (2020): 274–287.

17 Stein et al., "From 'Education for Sustainable Development' to 'Education for the End of the World as We Know It.'"

which rank university environmental performance—reflect the rise of this "green audit" culture.[18]

But why do these kinds of neoliberal—including largely individualized and market-based—interventions tend to dominate university responses to these crises?[19] And are such interventions responsive to the enormity of the climate, and other environmental, challenges? Furthermore, might they align with students and staff, as well as broader community expectations, about the roles and responsibilities of universities in the face of the climate crisis?

At face value, the array of "greening" initiatives universities are engaged in—a few of which are named earlier—may seem impactful.[20] They may, for example, support changes in individual behaviors, including providing opportunities to recycle on university campuses, securely storing push bikes on campus, and thereby encouraging active transport, as well as supporting staff and student participation in food garden projects. They may also establish inspiring visual projects—such as living green walls or "carbon neutral" buildings—that can affirm institutional environmental values.

At the same time, however, these initiatives enable a form of "greenwashing" by providing piecemeal and nonbinding activities that may then be mobilized as part of university branding and marketing campaigns.[21] By investing in individualized—and often voluntary—activities in response to both environmental problems and the climate crisis, they may, at the same time, sideline collective action and structural transformations that will be required for effective and meaningful decarbonization.[22] They also frequently miss opportunities for fostering meaningful biocultural connections with the mostly unceded First Nations territories upon which universities are situated.[23]

---

18 Owen Jones, "Thatcherism Was a National Catastrophe That Still Poisons Us," *The Independent*, May 15, 2013, www.independent.co.uk/voices/comment/thatcherism-was-a-national-catastrophe-that-still-poisons-us-8564858.html.

19 See also Emily M. Eaton and Nick A. Day, "Petro-Pedagogy: Fossil Fuel Interests and the Obstruction of Climate Justice in Public Education," *Environmental Education Research* 26 (2020): 457.

20 See, e.g., Hil et al., *Transforming Universities in the Midst of Global Crisis.*

21 Laurie Adkin, "Petro-Universities and the Production of Knowledge for a Post-Carbon Future," in *Regime of Obstruction: How Corporate Power Blocks Energy Democracy*, ed. William K. Carroll (Athabasca: AU Press, 2021).

22 Eaton and Day, "Petro-Pedagogy."

23 Cathy Howlett, Jo-Anne Ferreira, and Jessica Blomfield, "Teaching Sustainable Development in Higher Education," *International Journal of Sustainability in Higher Education* 17 (2016): 305; Stein et al., "From 'Education for Sustainable Development' to 'Education for the End of the World as We Know It.'"

Stein explains the reluctance of university managers to attend to the complex historical antecedents of the climate crisis—including universities as implicated in this crisis—as tied to their expansionist agendas.[24] Universities' ongoing push to increase student numbers, expand campuses, and grow universities, for example, commits them to infrastructure developments, capital production, and endless accumulation.[25] As part of this expansionist agenda, they have also increasingly come to rely upon funding—as set out later—from the extractive industries, including mining and fossil fuels. These dynamics create significant challenges to academic freedom across research, governance, and teaching, as well as the broader culture of universities. As a result of these challenges, instead of taking a leading role in fostering transformative climate action, universities can be seen as engaging in initiatives that serve as a distraction or, as Carroll has described, part of a regime of obstruction, from the urgent need for decarbonization.[26]

University Entanglements with the Private Sector and Impacts on Academic Freedom

Increasing private sector investment across universities has coincided with the withdrawal—over many decades—of state funding for university research and teaching. This shift reflects part of a broader neoliberalization of universities; the conditions of which have facilitated an increasing presence by the private sector across universities worldwide.[27]

The increasing alignment of universities with private sector interests via funding arrangements—including the mining and fossil fuel industries, the focus of this chapter—poses challenges for universities as public good insti-

24 Stein, "Reimagining Global Citizenship Education for a Volatile, Uncertain, Complex and Ambiguous (VUCA) World."

25 Stein et al., "From 'Education for Sustainable Development' to 'Education for the End of the World as We Know It.'"

26 Damien Gayle and Anugraha Sundaravelu, "Students Accuse Cambridge University of 'Greenwashing' Ties with Oil Firms," *The Guardian*, November 23, 2019, www.theguardian.com/education/2019/nov/23/students-accuse-cambridge-university-of-greenwashing-ties-with-oil-firms?CMP=share_btn_link; William K. Carroll, ed., *Regime of Obstruction: How Corporate Power Blocks Energy Democracy* (Athabasca: AU Press, 2021).

27 Raewyn Connell, *The Good University: What Universities Actually Do and Why It's Time for Radical Change* (London: Zed Books, 2019); Adkin, "Petro-Universities and the Production of Knowledge for a Post-Carbon Future."

tutions. More specifically, the reimagining of both the ideological orientations and structural conditions of universities as a result of this increasingly privatized funding regime has impacts on academic freedom, with outcomes that significantly preclude them from engaging in the deep work that may support systemic transformation in the face of a changing climate.

The curtailment of academic freedom alongside financial investment in universities by an array of industries, including the pharmaceutical, tobacco, and other so-called health-harming industries (including alcohol, gambling, and ultraprocessed food and drink), is now widely documented.[28] In their research, for example, Harvard historian Allan Brandt exposed how the tobacco industry effectively "captured" academics by funding their research, and with the "added benefit of making academic institutions 'partners' with the tobacco industry in its moment of crisis."[29] Through their deployment of a public relations strategy that demanded more science, the tobacco industries' funding of science enabled them to engineer both knowledge production and public and policy debates.[30]

The pharmaceutical industry has also been widely exposed as curtailing academic freedom, including in those cases where their commercial imperatives don't align with health goals.[31] Bonnell has described, for example, the adverse impacts of a funding agreement (worth up to 150 million pounds by 2023) between the University of Mainz and the pharmaceutical company,\ Boehringer.[32] In this case, the Boehringer Foundation had a say over certain professorial appointments, as well as a right of veto over publications arising from funded research and "rights of oversight over operational matters."[33] There are countless other examples where academic freedom is impinged upon as a result of financial investments in university research by the pharmaceutical as well as other "health-harming" industries.[34]

---

28 Jeff Collin et al., "Conflicted and Confused? Health Harming Industries and Research Funding in Leading UK Universities," *BMJ* 374 (2021): 1657.

29 Paul D. Thacker, "Stealing from the Tobacco Playbook, Fossil Fuel Companies Pour Money into Elite American Universities," *BMJ* 378 (2022): 1.

30 See also Andrew G. Bonnell, "Corporate Power and Academic Freedom," *Australian Universities Review* 63 (2021): 19–25.

31 Collin et al., "Conflicted and Confused?"

32 Bonnell, "Corporate Power and Academic Freedom."

33 Bonnell, "Corporate Power and Academic Freedom," 19.

34 David A. Henry et al., "Medical Specialists and Pharmaceutical Industry-Sponsored Research: A Survey of the Australian Experience," *Medical Journal of Australia* 182 (2005): 557–560; Jane Mayer, *Dark*

This chapter now turns to the mining and fossil fuel industries' entanglements with universities and discusses some of the impacts of this on academic freedom and, as a direct result, (in)action on climate.

Mining and Fossil Fuel Industry Entanglements: Impacts on Academic Freedom

It would be useful to start here by setting out the size of mining and fossil fuel investments across universities. Unfortunately, this is virtually impossible to detail.

On the basis that universities often fail to publicly disclose this data, including at times refusing freedom of information requests, it is difficult to precisely know the scale of mining and fossil fuel investments.[35] Demonstrating this, in their research into several United States-based universities, Almond and others reported on the challenges in tracing the financial ties between academic institutions and corporations in general, including mining and fossil fuels in particular.[36] They also described corporate donations as being inconsistently reported, with less than a quarter of all financial reporting from energy research centers at some of the highest-ranking US universities—such as MIT, Columbia, and Stanford—including details of specific funders and their contributions.[37]

Despite opaque funding arrangements, mining and fossil fuel investments are significant—and growing—even in nation-states with heavy reliance on extractivist industries, such as Australia, the United States, Canada, and elsewhere.[38] This has complex and multifaceted impacts on academic

Money (Brunswick: Scribe, 2017); Marion Nestle, "Food Industry Funding of Nutrition Research: The Relevance of History for Current Debates," *JAMA Internal Medicine* 176 (2016): 1685–1686.

35 Collin et al., "Conflicted and Confused?"

36 Douglas Almond, Xinming Du, and Anna Papp, "Favourability towards Natural Gas Relates to Funding Source of University Energy Centres," *Nature Climate Change* 22 (2022): 1122–1128.

37 Almond et al., "Favourability towards Natural Gas Relates to Funding Source of University Energy Centres."

38 Adkin, "Petro-Universities and the Production of Knowledge for a Post-Carbon Future"; Thacker, "Stealing from the Tobacco Playbook, Fossil Fuel Companies Pour Money into Elite American Universities."

freedom, with Franta and Supran describing the fossil fuel industries' invisible colonization of academia.[39]

While levels of investment and other aspects of the mining and fossil fuel industries' incursion across universities may be invisible, some of their impacts—including for academic freedom—are rendered bare.

Demonstrating this, based on their investments in universities, mining and fossil fuel industries have and continue to reshape research programs, university governance, curriculum and teaching, as well as other aspects of university organization and culture. At the same time, the mining and fossil fuel industries can use their investments in university research to advance their branding as good corporate citizens. This is significant given many of these investors face reputational risks due to their climate, environmental, and human rights impacts—circumstances reflected in growing calls for universities, alongside banks and other institutions, to divest from fossil fuels.

Starting with research programs, Almond and others have described a "university-industrial complex," characterized by the mining and fossil fuel industries wielding undue—and often unaccountable—influence across universities.[40] Just as the tobacco industry was earlier effective in funding research as a strategy to obstruct action in the interests of public health, they describe mining and fossil fuel industries as harnessing research as a pathway to delay the just energy transition.[41] Demonstrating this, a recent investigation into the research outputs from university-based energy centers heavily funded by the fossil fuel industries found they were, on average, "more favorable in their reports towards natural gas than towards renewable energy."[42] This included research outputs from energy centers at Stanford, MIT, and Columbia, each a recipient of significant corporate funding, and each producing research outcomes that were "more positive towards natural gas than renewable energy sources, including solar and hydropower."[43] Tellingly, the

39 Benjamin Franta and Geoffrey Supran, "The Fossil Fuel Industry's Invisible Colonisation of Academia," *The Guardian*, March 13, 2017, www.theguardian.com/environment/climate-consensus-97-per-cent/2017/mar/13/the-fossil-fuel-industrys-invisible-colonization-of-academia.

40 Almond et al., "Favourability towards Natural Gas Relates to Funding Source of University Energy Centres."

41 Almond et al., "Favourability towards Natural Gas Relates to Funding Source of University Energy Centres."

42 Almond et al., "Favourability towards Natural Gas Relates to Funding Source of University Energy Centres," 1126.

43 Franta and Supran, "The Fossil Fuel Industry's Invisible Colonisation of Academia."

advocacy for gas as a current and future energy source from these institutions was found as "indistinguishable from that of the American Gas Foundation and the American Gas Association, whose explicit purpose is to promote the gas industry."[44]

As the analysis presented earlier demonstrates, the fossil fuel industries demonstrate their effectiveness in influencing the communication of research outcomes to ensure they align with gas industry interests. Funding research then supports a fossil fuel industry public relations strategy to neutralize and/or drive doubts about energy (and climate) science, as well as stifling actions that support decarbonization.[45] Similarly, Thacker has described how the fossil fuel industries' investment in carbon capture and storage—including championing it as a technological solution to the climate crisis—provides an additional strategy to delay decarbonization.[46]

In their analysis of United States-based energy and climate science and policy research centers, Frank and Supran reported that while some had stated commitments not to accept corporate donations—including the University of Chicago's Energy Policy Institute—others relied heavily on this funding stream.[47] They reported MIT's Energy Initiative as mostly industry-funded, including by Shell, ExxonMobil, and Chevron, as well as receiving $185 million from David Koch, a life member of the university's board, an oil billionaire and financer of climate denial. Similarly, funding for Harvard's energy and climate policy research was mostly provided by Shell, Chevron, and BP; Stanford's Global Climate and Energy Project was funded by ExxonMobil and Schlumberger; and UC Berkeley's Energy Biosciences Institute by a $500 million deal with BP.[48]

The entanglement of the mining and fossil fuel industries across universities is also reflected in university-based governance structures. Governance arrangements—including those that pertain to industry relationships—vary across universities. At MIT's Energy Initiative, for example, the external advisory board includes representatives from the oil and gas industry, such as Shell, Exxon Mobil, and Sweetwater Energy. It also includes representatives

44 Franta and Supran, "The Fossil Fuel Industry's Invisible Colonisation of Academia."

45 Franta and Supran, "The Fossil Fuel Industry's Invisible Colonisation of Academia."

46 Thacker, "Stealing from the Tobacco Playbook, Fossil Fuel Companies Pour Money into Elite American Universities."

47 Franta and Supran, "The Fossil Fuel Industry's Invisible Colonisation of Academia."

48 Franta and Supran, "The Fossil Fuel Industry's Invisible Colonisation of Academia."

from infrastructure, finance, and other mining-related industries, including the Grupo Ferrovial (with operations including mobility and energy infrastructure) and Sabanci Holding (including banking and financial services).[49] Meanwhile at Stanford's National Gas Initiative, members of its governance board—including ConocoPhillips, ExxonMobil, and Shell—have "help[ed] establish research priorities."[50]

Similar patterns related to mining and fossil fuel investment in university research and engagement in the governance and oversight of university operations are evident in Australia. Here, the Australian Coal Association Research Program, as an example, has provided over $145 million in funds for research projects across several of Australia's leading universities.[51] Mining and fossil fuel companies have also funded research chairs to lead research agendas. At the University of Western Australia, for example, BHP, Shell, and Chevron have each funded university research chairs to "carry out cutting edge research to address various constraints faced by industry."[52]

In various ways, the mining and fossil fuel industries have deployed funding as a way of orienting research agendas toward industry interests. Their participation in the governance of energy and related research centers at Australian universities has achieved similar outcomes. At one of Australia's highest-ranking universities, the University of Queensland's (UQ) Centre for Coal Seam Gas (now Centre for Natural Gas) provides an exemplary case. When it was first established, its membership model required a contribution of $500,000 for a seat on its strategic advising board. At that time, three coal seam gas companies committed to providing annual funding for at least the first five years of the center's operations: the Queensland Gas Company ($2 million), Arrow Energy, and Santos (each $500,000).[53] While the governance structure, alongside the research scope and agenda (including a name change), has occurred since its inception, this center provides compelling

49 Massachusetts Institute of Technology, "About the MIT Energy Initiative," https://energy.mit.edu/about/#leadership.

50 Franta and Supran, "The Fossil Fuel Industry's Invisible Colonisation of Academia"; Adkin, "Petro-Universities and the Production of Knowledge for a Post-Carbon Future."

51 Kristen Lyons and Carol Richards, "Mining the Integrity out of Australian Universities?" *Arena* 124 (2013): 7–9.

52 University of Western Australia, "Research Leaders Empower Industry Partnerships (2023)," www.uwa.edu.au/news/Article/2020/Uniview/Summer/Research-leaders-empower-industry-partnerships.

53 Lyons and Richards, "Mining the Integrity out of Australian Universities?"

insights into the normalization of investment as granting access to governance and decision-making.

Turning to curriculum, the Minerals Tertiary Education Council has invested more than $65 million since 2000 to support skills and education that enable advancements in the mining sector, including via the development of course materials, new microcredentials, and an undergraduate degree program.[54] Mining Education Australia has also established a venture between several universities to establish a National Mining Engineering School, with outcomes intended to "recast the way they teach" undergraduate programs.[55]

Eaton and Day have named the ways the oil and gas industries can shape the curriculum to maintain their hegemony as "petro pedagogy."[56] Through their involvement in the design of resources and curriculum, the coal, oil, and gas industries can entrench fossil fuels as normal energy sources. These petro pedagogic practices ensure energy transition, and, inter alia, imagining life without fossil fuels remains in the distant future. Through their research into public education practices in Canada, Eaton and Day documented petro pedagogy at work, including via the fossil fuel industries' insulation from criticism and young people being discouraged from "questioning or understanding the role of corporate power in the climate crisis."[57] Their research also revealed these pedagogical practices aligned with the promotion of neoliberal environmental subjectivities, including championing environment and climate "solutions" that were couched in individual, rather than collective, terms.

Despite the various ways petro pedagogic practices have effectively colonized the life worlds of universities, young people—including those enrolled in universities across many parts of the world—are at the forefront of global climate movements. University students' high-level engagement in the global school strikes, leading fossil fuel divestment campaigns at universities, as well as targeting banks and other financial institutions are each markers of this engagement.[58] Such movements—which are also being shaped by the

54 Minerals Council of Australia, "Minerals Tertiary Education Council (2023)," https://minerals.org.au/policies/workforce-innovation-and-skills/minerals-tertiary-education-council/.

55 Lyons and Richards, "Mining the Integrity out of Australian Universities?"

56 Eaton and Day, "Petro-Pedagogy."

57 Eaton and Day, "Petro-Pedagogy," 458.

58 Stein et al., "Beyond Colonial Futurities in Climate Education."

high levels of climate anxiety experienced by young people—will ensure universities remain contested sites of climate politics and pedagogic practices into the future.

Conclusions: The Mining and Fossil Fuel Industries Stifle Academic Freedom and University-Based Climate Action

This chapter has critically explored the convergence of private sector interests with universities, with a particular focus on the mining and fossil fuel industries. These entanglements, as demonstrated here, are directly tied to the marketization, massification, and managerialism that have come to define contemporary universities in an era of neoliberalism. As a result, universities face pressures from both within—and without—in regard to upholding academic freedom.

This chapter demonstrated how entanglements with the mining and fossil fuel industries have and continue to reconfigure research, governance, and teaching, as well as the broader culture of universities. These impacts are especially pronounced in nation-states dominated by extractive industries, including the United States, Australia, Canada, and elsewhere. The outcome of this curtails academic freedom, as well as the deployment of research and teaching activities that distract and/or obstruct urgent action on climate, including decarbonization and the transition to a low-carbon economy.

Universities are faced with the challenge of rendering visible their entanglements with the mining and fossil fuel industries, including the impacts on academic freedom arising from these entanglements. This will be a necessary first step in ensuring universities are able to act as public good institutions—including in ways that align with staff, student, and broader community expectations—in responding to the climate crisis.

Chapter 21

Academic Freedom in Online Learning

Katarzyna Kaczmarska and Corinne Lennox

Introduction

Distance learning, and in particular online learning, has made tertiary education more accessible globally.[1] Examples of "open universities" have proliferated around the world as ways of delivering higher education (HE) more flexibly, affordably, and with the aim to reach remote and marginalized groups.[2] Distance and online learning provision has been pursued both by Global South countries typically seeking to rapidly and efficiently scale up the availability of HE and by Global North countries seeking to extend access to their programs at the national level and to increase access and revenue at the international level, also through the provision of affiliated teaching centers in other countries. This latter form is often termed "transnational education" (TNE), which denotes circumstances where "the learners are located in a country different from the one where the awarding

---

1 For some examples of research, pedagogy, and policy in online learning, see specialized journals such as *Distance Education* (Taylor and Francis) and *Open Learning: The Journal of Open, Distance and e-Learning* (Taylor and Francis). Please note that in this chapter we use the terms tertiary and higher education interchangeably.

2 Gajaraj Dhanarajan, "Distance Education: Promise, Performance and Potential," *Open Learning: The Journal of Open, Distance and e-Learning* 16 (2001): 61–68.

institution is based"[3]; this includes branch campuses, "fly-in" faculty, and distance or online learning. Data for the UK shows that there are nearly 700,000 students registered in UK programs overseas.[4] This is part and parcel of a broader phenomenon called HE internationalization.[5]

Latterly, the use of digital platforms to deliver distance learning has predominated, enabled by the rapid expansion of internet technology and connectivity and facilitated by a new range of learning management systems for online learning. Teaching and learning strategies such as "flipped learning" have integrated more use of online teaching tools also in campus-based programs. There has been a proliferation of Massive Open Online Courses (MOOCs), which offer varying levels of certification and are often free of charge. There was also a hasty and mass shift to the provision of education through online learning formats during the COVID-19 pandemic, paralleling these existing initiatives.[6] Hybrid forms of learning continue even post-pandemic, with students more accustomed to this practice and HE institutions (HEIs) keen on the cost-saving measures. This includes "virtual mobility," which means offering students international (e.g., "junior year abroad") experiences that take place entirely online. According to a survey carried out by Universities UK, an organization uniting over a hundred universities across the UK, the COVID-19 pandemic prompted 63 percent of British universities to introduce or expand virtual mobility and many of those institutions plan to maintain this form of mobility long term.[7] All of these changes are overseen by new forms of digital educational governance,

3 UNESCO/Council of Europe Code of Good Practice in the Provision of Transnational Education (Riga, June 6, 2001), 2, www.ehea.info/media.ehea.info/file/BFUG_Seminar/21/3/TransnationalEducation-CodeGoodPractice_554213.pdf. Unless otherwise stated, all links last accessed August 9, 2023.

4 Universities UK, "Managing Risks in Internationalisation: Security Related Issues," 2020, 9, www.universitiesuk.ac.uk/what-we-do/policy-and-research/publications/managing-risks-internationalisation.

5 For a discussion of academic freedom and internationalization, see, for instance, the special issue on academic freedom and internationalization in the *International Journal of Human Rights* 26(10), 2022. For a review of challenges to academic freedom and various aspects of globalization, see Michael Ignatieff and Stefan Roch, eds., *Academic Freedom: The Global Challenge* (Budapest: CEU Press, 2018) and the *Free to Think* reports by the Scholars at Risk network.

6 Viktoriya Shevchenko, Nataliia Malysh, and Olena Tkachuk-Miroshnychenko, "Distance Learning in Ukraine in COVID-19 Emergency," *Open Learning: The Journal of Open, Distance and e-Learning* (2021).

7 UUK, "Student Mobility Data 2020–21: Foundations of Recovery," December 20, 2022, www.universitiesuk.ac.uk/universities-uk-international/insights-and-publications/uuki-blog/student-mobility-data-2020-21.

which enable monitoring of online teaching and learning in ways that can affect academic freedom.[8]

While market-related considerations have been an important driver of online learning, this mode of learning has become more prominent also in spaces where academic freedom is severely curtailed by the state or where conflict makes regular tertiary education more difficult or impossible. Technology allowed for connecting learners and educators based in multiple locations, mostly "under the radar" of authoritarian regimes. For example, following the Russian invasion of Ukraine, the Invisible University for Ukraine was established with a view to providing educational opportunities for students residing in Ukraine and in refuge.[9] Examples from Myanmar, Russia, and Turkey, which we will discuss in more detail later, show that technology made it possible to deliver education that—up to a point—is free from authoritarian state interference, with significant implications for how we understand academic freedom.

This brief introduction shows the wide range of contexts in which online learning can be applied. The sum effect is a proliferation of this mode of engagement with learners for reasons of accessibility, pedagogical innovation, marketization, and the need to circumvent political oppression, as well as extraordinary measures in times of crisis, such as war or pandemics.

In the context of academic freedom, online learning can present specific challenges. This chapter provides an overview of some key risks to academic staff and students in tertiary education. We will attempt to point to challenges across a range of contexts, from the use of online learning in HEIs that may be otherwise free, to specific threats that arise from the use of online learning in oppressive contexts. Given our focus on learning, we will also briefly outline what we see as the international norms that protect the right of students to academic freedom, which are not always clearly articulated. Finally, the chapter ends with a review of some practices that can be adopted in both democratic and authoritarian states to counter threats to academic freedom in online learning. While online learning presents new

8 See Karran and Kissoon, *this volume*.

9 For more detail, see the university's webpage: "Invisible University," www.ceu.edu/non-degree/Invisible-University.

ethical considerations regarding pedagogy, these go beyond the scope of the present study.[10]

Risks to Academic Freedom in Online Learning

Online learning may seem unrestrained because it takes place "from home" via the internet. And yet, it is affected by the varying sociopolitical contexts in which the learners, teachers, and education providers reside and are registered. For students living under authoritarian regimes, online learning offers opportunities for developing critical thinking skills, accessing a wider range of sources, and discussing themes that may be deemed taboo or outright banned in their home countries. Despite those important benefits, accessing the learning content online does not mean that the academic freedom of learners cannot be compromised.

When students undertake education offered outside of their home country, the risks arise most commonly at the intersection of two different political and regulatory systems—the system of the country that delivers education and provides certification, and that where a student is physically located. For example, UK-based home students and overseas students benefit from UK regulatory protections, inter alia, regarding data privacy and internet freedoms, but might still face threats to their academic freedom because of the topics they study or—in the case of overseas students—restrictions and threats stemming from the legal and political arrangements of their home countries. In authoritarian states, various forms of policing may include one or a combination of the following: surveillance of learners' communication, monitoring of their activities within a virtual classroom, or the censorship of resources available to them. Some of those practices—for instance, regular classroom surveillance—have been developed for in-person education and can be transposed into an online setting.[11] Even if the state does not always interfere with the learners' use of instruments that allow them to bypass local regulations, the very fact of their illegality puts learners at risk.

---

10 See, e.g., Bill Anderson and Mary Simpson, "Ethical Issues in Online Education," *Open Learning: The Journal of Open and Distance Learning* 22 (2007): 129–138.

11 Tim Pringle and Sophia Woodman, "Between a Rock and a Hard Place: Academic Freedom in Globalising Chinese Universities," *International Journal of Human Rights* 26 (2022): 1792–1793.

Students risk falling out with local legislation when participating in seminars or accessing recorded content online while being physically located in their home countries. For example, this concerns learners accessing material on subjects considered taboo, such as homosexuality or references to alcohol and drug use.[12] Students also could be prosecuted for violating national laws on sedition, blasphemy, or national security as a result of their written or oral expression. For instance, students who are physically located in Russia risk falling out with national law if they take part in an online seminar discussion concerning Russia's aggression on Ukraine or the Soviet Union's role in the outbreak of the Second World War. Any critical remark concerning the Russian military has been—since 2022—punishable under the Penal Code of the Russian Federation, as has been the undermining of the Soviet Union's contribution to the victory over Nazism.[13]

Accessing course material may constitute another challenge impacting academic freedom. Students who are physically located in countries that exercise online censorship may not be able to read specific course content as the governments may block access to selected articles or journals.[14] Certain activities or tasks may be impossible for students to engage with if social media channels, such as YouTube and Twitter, are banned. Teachers may not be aware of the specificities of their students' access to the learning material. On a related note, academic publishing experiences academic freedom constraints and challenges of its own.[15]

Another set of risks arises from covert or targeted monitoring of online learning spaces. In the early days of the move to online learning during the COVID-19 pandemic, the lack of security in online lecturing tools such as Zoom led to a rise of so-called Zoombombing, including in many dem-

12 For a broader discussion of these issues, see cases reported by the Scholars at Risk (SAR) network in *Free to Think 2019: Report of the Scholars at Risk Academic Freedom Monitoring Project* (New York: Scholars at Risk, 2020), 36; and *Free to Think 2015: Report of the Scholars at Risk Academic Freedom Monitoring Project* (New York: Scholars at Risk, 2016), 31.

13 Radio Free Europe/Radio Liberty, "'Discrediting' the Armed Forces: The Russians Caught Up in a Draconian Law," May 30, 2022, www.rferl.org/a/russia-ukraine-war-discrediting-armed-forces-law/31875273.html.

14 Catherine Owen, "The 'Internationalisation Agenda' and the Rise of the Chinese University: Towards the Inevitable Erosion of Academic Freedom?" *British Journal of Politics and International Relations* 22 (2020): 238–255.

15 For a broader discussion of the challenges at the intersection of academic freedom and academic publishing, see Jennifer Wright et al., "Supporting Academic Freedom as a Human Right: Challenges and Solutions in Academic Publishing," *International Journal of Human Rights* 26 (2022): 1741–1760.

ocratic states. This had a chilling effect on teachers and students facing unwanted forms of protest, hate, and harassment from coordinated groups intruding in online lecturing spaces, prompting some universities to issue specific guidelines.[16]

Academic freedom is also threatened when states engage in covert monitoring of their citizens' communications and activities in cyberspace, often in breach of their own legal regulations. Rather than conducting mass surveillance, those states monitor selected individuals, in particular those active in the social and political realms.[17] Even for students physically based outside their home countries, the possibility of being recorded during a seminar discussion and reported to the authorities creates risk and may hamper or impede engagement in an online class discussion. The following example, provided by Emory University researchers, illustrates this point vividly:

> It was the last day of class in a course about Chinese society at Emory University—by then, many Chinese international students had already returned home after the transition to online learning in mid-March. Students in the class, 85% of whom were from China, logged on via Zoom, excited to see their classmates and instructors one last time before the semester ended. But when the discussion turned to Chinese politics, the faces of some Chinese students were suddenly replaced by rows of blank avatars, pseudonyms, ceiling fans, and unidentifiable objects. "I was concerned about discussing sensitive topics in China, since the data [transmitted] through local VPN was under possible scrutiny," a student in the class later wrote.[18]

Similarly, the fear of surveillance and breaches in data protection may limit the topics that students choose to study for their coursework or disserta-

---

16 Tufts University, "How to Respond to a 'Zoombombing' in Real Time," https://diversity.tufts.edu/resources/how-to-respond-to-a-zoombombing-in-real-time/. See also Chen Ling et al., "A First Look at Zoombombing," *IEEE Security & Privacy* 20 (2022): 22–30; Scholars at Risk, *Free to Think 2021 Report*, 30.

17 Justin Sherman, "Russia's Internet Censor Is Also a Surveillance Machine," *Council on Foreign Relations*, September 28, 2022, www.cfr.org/blog/russias-internet-censor-also-surveillance-machine.

18 Hong Li, Levin Arnsperger, and Michael Cerny, "Censorship Fears and Vampire Hours: Chinese International Students, Zoom, and Remote Learning", *The China Project*, June 30, 2022, https://thechinaproject.com/2020/06/30/chinese-international-students-zoom-and-remote-learning/.

tions. Concerns about students' safety may also prompt mentors to discourage students from researching politically sensitive topics—be it for student dissertations or as part of research assistance work, especially if this research involves browsing material available online and if dissertation submission and marking takes place in a virtual setting.

Importantly, the fear of surveillance exists even if published examples of students getting in trouble for following courses online have so far been scarce. At times persecution may be applied for online extracurricular activities, as the following example from Purdue University in the United States shows:

> Kong [Zhihao Kong, a student at Purdue University in Indiana] who goes by the nickname Moody, had already accepted an invitation from an international group of dissidents to speak at a coming online commemoration of the Tiananmen massacre anniversary. Uncertain if he should go through with it, he joined in rehearsals for the event on Zoom. Within days, MSS [the Ministry of State Security in China] officers were at his family's door again. His parents implored him: No public speaking. No rallies. Moody realized it didn't matter where he was. The Chinese government was still watching, and it was still in charge. Just before the anniversary event, he reluctantly decided not to give his speech. "I think that the Zoom rehearsals were known by the Chinese Communist Party," he said. "I think some of the Chinese students in my school are CCP members. I can tell they are not simply students. They could be spies or informants."[19]

The two examples provided earlier show how home states may be monitoring students abroad; they also illustrate the extent of insecurity among the student body. This testifies to the effectiveness of authoritarian coercive tactics that do not need to be proven or visible on a grand scale to be effective in sowing distrust and fear. Similarly, the experience of Zoombombing tactics has exposed the vulnerability of freedom of expression and assembly in online learning spaces.

19 Sebastian Rotella, "Even on U.S. Campuses, China Cracks Down on Students Who Speak Out," *ProPublica*, November 30, 2021, www.propublica.org/article/even-on-us-campuses-china-cracks-down-on-students-who-speak-out.

A recent survey on academic freedom from a student perspective, conducted by the European Students' Union, did not foreground online learning but did nonetheless ask two—out of the total of thirty-eight—questions about the use of proctoring software and other surveillance measures. This suggests that tech security has become a serious concern to students. Research into the strategies adopted by students in response to cyber-related risks is scarce at best, but in conversations with educators, students usually identify several techniques they adopt to increase their security online while undertaking learning activities, including research for their dissertations.[20]

Online learning has also been offered from within nondemocratic states. One of the more recent examples is the Free University (also known as the Free Moscow University), an online tertiary education platform launched in 2020. The same risks described earlier apply but with a caveat that nondemocratic regimes have the means and resolve to clamp down on such initiatives when they are operating in their midst. The Free University was established in response to academic freedom violations and overbureaucratization of the state tertiary education sector. The university cooperated with a number of scholars who left or were made to leave the Higher School of Economics, an erstwhile stellar HEI, which gradually became more and more aligned with the goals of the government and the presidential administration.[21] The Free University Manifesto declared the enjoinment of academic freedom as its key tenet and offered a course on academic freedom.[22] In 2023, however, the Prosecutor General's Office of the Russian Federation declared the Free University an "undesirable organization." Since participation in the activities of such an organization can lead to prosecution, the university suspended its activities on the territory of the Russian Federation.[23]

20 Nascent research into why students turn their cameras off found that the main reasons were "anxiety/fear of being exposed/shame/shyness, desire to ensure privacy of the home/personal space, and chances that other people might walk into the background"; see Vasile Gherheș, Simona Șimon, and Iulia Para, "Analysing Students' Reasons for Keeping Their Webcams on or off during Online Classes," *Sustainability* 13 (2021).

21 Margarita Lyutova, "Dazhe V Sovetskoye Vremya Takogo Stesnyalis [Even in Soviet Times, They Were Embarrassed about This]," *Meduza*, April 17, 2023, https://meduza.io/feature/2023/04/17/dazhe-v-sovetskoe-vremya-takogo-stesnyalis.

22 The university's website available at https://freemoscow.university/#manifesto.

23 The Free University, "Statement of the Academic Council," https://the.freemoscow.university/en/university/statement-of-the-academic-council/.

Online learning is prominent in situations of exile. The more recent examples include Turkey, Myanmar, and Russia. The Off University was established in 2017 by academics from Turkey living in exile, mostly in Germany, many of whom faced persecution following the failed coup in July 2016 against President Erdogan's government, including some as signatories of the Peace Petition in January 2016.[24] The Off University serves as a hub for collaboration and online learning that now encompasses a very international community of scholars experiencing threats to academic freedom: "Where authoritarian regimes turn the university OFF, we turn it ONLINE again."[25] The invasion of Ukraine in February 2022 prompted or forced many scholars in Russia who opposed the war to leave the country. Some of them continued delivering their teaching online well into 2023. The Russian state, however, was quick to introduce economic measures aimed at limiting this activity, notably by increasing the rate of tax from 13 to 30 percent on income generated in Russia by nonresidents.[26] Income tax—even if at first glance does not look like a measure having anything to do with academic freedom—in effect limits Russian students' right to the type of education they want to pursue as their access to mostly liberally minded educators became curtailed. In Myanmar, after the military coup in February 2021, academic freedom was widely suppressed, particularly for members of the Civil Disobedience Movement (CDM), which included many from the academic community. Dozens of online education institutions have been established in parallel to state-controlled campus HEIs. One of the largest is Spring University, established in May 2021, which has seen rapid growth and now offers more than five hundred courses, employs two hundred CDM teaching staff and where over 15,000 students from across Myanmar have attended online courses.[27] Many of these online learning efforts are coordinated by the Ministry of Education under Myanmar's exiled National Unity Government (NUG).[28]

---

24 Zia Weise, "Turkey Loses Its Brains," *Politico*, January 17, 2017, www.politico.eu/article/turkey-failed-coup-purge-scholars-loses-its-brains/.

25 Off University, "Our Vision," https://off-university.com/en-US/page/about-us.

26 Article 224 of the Tax Code of the Russian Federation; for more details see https://stnkrf.ru/224.

27 See "Spring University Myanmar: Reimagining the Future," www.springuniversitymm.com/; Mizzima, "Spring University Fees to Be Paid Using NUG Pay," January 30, 2023, https://mizzima.com/article/spring-university-fees-be-paid-using-nug-pay.

28 Nilar Aung Myint, "Exiled Government Establishes Alternative HE Programmes," *World University News*, July 24, 2021, www.universityworldnews.com/post.php?story=20210721150221771.

The NUG is committed to the principle of institutional autonomy and has recognized independent Interim University Councils (IUCs).[29]

The surveillance risks described earlier apply to university teachers as well, in both democratic and authoritarian states. However, there are a few specificities worth a broader discussion. An important aspect is the location of the workplace and the modality of work, that is, whether the teacher is mainly campus-based or works—on a regular or intermittent basis—at an overseas teaching center. These "branch campuses" need to abide by local legislation, which in some places may impinge on a free discussion of topics such as gender, religion, or various aspects of politics, including the military and war.

In online settings, teachers' reactions vary and range from attaching a special clarification to the learning content to resorting to various levels of self-censorship. For instance, a professor at the University of Michigan decided to add a disclaimer to the course description informing the students that it contains content the Chinese government may consider sensitive and which therefore could pose a greater risk for students in China or of Chinese nationality.[30] Examples of self-censorship include deciding not to offer a course on a specific subject or cutting out a lecture dedicated to a theme deemed politically sensitive. Some teachers may be more careful with comments that might be seen as directly critical of countries where their students reside or in relation to contentious national issues. Comments made in online learning spaces can have more "permanence" than comments made orally in a physical classroom and are more easily monitored by third parties.[31] Self-censorship in an online setting may be variously motivated. Some academics may wish to remain "politically correct" or "under the radar," considering their risks of harassment or impaired job prospects, or other interests like entering a specific country in the future. At times the key motivation is the concern for the safety of the students undertaking a

29 Nora, "We Are Developing the Ability to Make Changes and Build the Future," *The Irrawaddy*, February 23, 2023, www.irrawaddy.com/in-person/interview/we-are-developing-the-ability-to-make-changes-and-build-the-future.html.

30 Tripti Lahiri and Jane Li, "Universities Teaching Chinese Students Remotely Need to Scale the Great Firewall," *Quartz*, August 23, 2020, https://qz.com/1888595/chinese-censorship-is-challenging-us-universities-online-classes.

31 Jonathan Poritz and Jonathan Rees, "Academic Freedom in Online Education: Bringing AAUP Principles Online," *Academe* 107 (2021).

learning activity; however, teachers have limited ability to assess the risks to student safety, which may result in excessive censoring of the teaching content. Self-censorship also may be dictated by the concern about one's reputation, in case an online lecture is recorded or written comments posted in online discussion forums are captured. A lecture recording can be obtained by malevolent actors and subsequently edited and/or manipulated. It can also be published on social media to shame the author.[32] Both genuine and manipulated recordings can be used to harass or discredit scholars and affect scholars' ability to conduct fieldwork or attend conferences in countries where their views are opposed or censored.

Existing Normative Protections for Academic Freedom of Students

There are two approaches to defining academic freedom. A credentials-based approach sees it as a guild right, that is, a right derived from professional competence. The second approach recognizes academic freedom as a human right, anchored in key human rights norms such as freedom of expression, the right to hold opinions without interference, freedom of association and assembly, the right to education, and the right to share in the benefits of scientific advancement.[33] With regard to online learning, the right to privacy also can be foregrounded here, given the increased scope for privacy breaches arising from online learning technology, some of which may pertain to academic freedom.[34] Under the first approach, students might more easily be excluded from protection if their "professional" status is disputed, whereas the latter approach enables them to claim academic freedom as human rights

32 Emma Pettit, "A Side Effect of Remote Teaching during COVID-19? Videos That Can Be Weaponized," *Chronicle of Higher Education*, March 24, 2022, www.chronicle.com/article/a-side-effect-of-remote-teaching-during-covid-19-videos-that-can-be-weaponized/.

33 See Klaus D. Beiter, Terence Karran, and Kwadwo Appiagyei-Atua, "Yearning to Belong: Finding a 'Home' for the Right to Academic Freedom in the U.N. Human Rights Covenants," *Intercultural Human Rights Law Review* 11 (2016): 107; Sejal Parmar, "Academic Freedom under Pressure," *EJIL Talk*, December 2, 2019.

34 See, e.g., Human Rights Watch, *How Dare They Peep into My Private Life? Children's Rights Violations by Governments that Endorsed Online Learning during the COVID-19 Pandemic* (New York: Human Rights Watch, 2022); Divya Singh and Mashamaite Peterlia Ramutsheli, "Student Data Protection in a South African Open Distance Learning University Context: Risks, Challenges and Lessons from Comparative Jurisdictions," *Distance Education* 37 (2016): 164–179; Poritz and Rees, "Academic Freedom in Online Education."

holders. The Universal Declaration of Human Rights (Article 27 on cultural and scientific advancement rights), the International Covenant on Civil and Political Rights (ICCPR) (Article 19 on freedom of opinion and expression, Article 21 on freedom of assembly, and Article 22 on freedom of association, in addition to Article 17 on the right to privacy as noted earlier), and the International Covenant on Economic, Social, and Cultural Rights (ICESCR) (Article 13 on education and Article 15 on the right to benefits of scientific progress) contain these core provisions. Notably, ICESCR Articles 15.3 and 15.4 further obligate states "to respect the freedom indispensable for scientific research" and to "recognize the benefits to be derived from the encouragement and development of *international* contacts and co-operation in the scientific and cultural fields" (emphasis added). Hence, the treaty contains provisions that could be cited in support of TNE. Yet despite the wide ratification of these treaties and the manifold additional instruments that have been created by states, HEIs, and student and faculty unions, there remains a gap between de jure and de facto protection of academic freedom.[35] Available data shows that half the world's population lives in countries in which academic freedom is in retreat.[36]

Academic freedom in online learning can be protected through laws and policies. For academics, the protection of academic freedom is widely embedded in international standards, national law, and university policies. In contrast, not all legislation will specifically name students as beneficiaries, nor will universities routinely include students within the purview of policy statements in support of academic freedom, creating lacunae. For example, the 1997 UNESCO Recommendation concerning the Status of Higher Education Teaching Personnel constitutes one of the first international attempts at comprehensively defining academic freedom but it does not include students as direct beneficiaries. In contrast, the Committee on Economic, Social, and Cultural Rights has put forward General Comment 13 on the right to education, in which the committee emphasizes "that

35 For a list of those instruments, see Robert Quinn, *From Words to Actions: A Call for International Guidelines on Implementing Academic Freedom* (Barcelona: Global University Network for Innovation, 2022), 143.

36 Katrin Kinzelbach et al., "2023 Academic Freedom Index 2023 Update," *FAU Erlangen-Nürnberg and V-Dem Institute*, 10.25593/opus4-fau-21630.

staff and students throughout the education sector are entitled to academic freedom."[37]

Taking one example at the national level, in England and Wales, there is national legislation that compels universities to protect academic freedom for staff, but provisions for students are limited to freedom of speech. For example, the Education (No. 2) Act 1986 requires education providers to "take such steps as are reasonably practicable to ensure that freedom of speech within the law is secured for members, students and employees of the establishment and for visiting speakers" (section 43). In contrast, the Higher Education Governance (Scotland) Act 2016 does not make an explicit mention of students, prescribing that "a post-16 education body must aim to—(a) uphold (so far as the body considers reasonable) the academic freedom" of persons engaged in the provision of learning and in research (section 23).[38] The UK government has also adopted the Higher Education (Freedom of Speech) Act that introduces several new measures regarding the protection of freedom of speech and academic freedom, although the Act only protects the freedom of speech of students, not their academic freedom per se, which is applied only to "academic staff." Students in the UK still need to rely on the human rights provisions of international law, including the European Convention on Human Rights and its articles on freedom of expression (Article 10) and freedom of assembly (Article 11), which are applied principally through the domestic law of the Human Rights Act (1998) governing the whole of the UK, to widen protection of their academic freedom. Students might also benefit from legal protections under criminal or civil law on unlawful speech that constitutes, inter alia, harassment, fear of violence, or hatred on the basis of protected characteristics.[39]

The challenge concerning online learning is that multiple jurisdictions can be triggered: for example, the jurisdiction of the host university, of the teaching center in another state, or of the state in which the independent learner is based. This raises challenges concerning wide variations in national legal protection for the academic freedom of academic staff and stu-

37 Committee on Economic, Social, and Cultural Rights, "General Comment No. 13 on the Right to Education (Article 13)," UN Doc E/C.12/1999/10 (1999), paras. 38–40.

38 The Act can be accessed here: www.legislation.gov.uk/asp/2016/15/pdfs/asp_20160015_en.pdf.

39 Equality and Human Rights Commission, *Freedom of Expression: A Guide for Higher Education Providers and Students' Unions in England and Wales* (Manchester: Equality and Human Rights Commission, 2019).

dents.[40] International law can provide some leveling out across jurisdictions, but the monitoring mechanisms are weak in most cases. There are also potential risks to students returning to their home countries after they study abroad, where national laws might be triggered to persecute them for activities undertaken during their studies. The absence of strong protection for the academic freedom of students in international standards and national law underscores their vulnerability when engaging in education of any kind, but may be exacerbated where their learning modality is TNE.

Practices to Support Academic Freedom in Online Learning

There are several options to put in place stronger protections for academic freedom in online learning. This volume has addressed many generally applicable policies, but, in this chapter, we will outline some specific considerations for this learning modality.

Universities can establish clear codes of conduct applicable to online learning. The authors of this chapter have worked with the Academic Freedom and Internationalisation Working Group to draft a "Model Code of Conduct on the Protection of Academic Freedom and the Academic Community in the Context of the Internationalisation of the UK Higher Education Sector."[41] It contains a specific recommendation regarding distance education, which advises UK HEIs to "take steps to protect the academic freedom of these members of the academic community engaged in distance education at a UK HE institution, including through safeguards for personal data, secure use of online discussion platforms, and safe access to online teaching and learn-

40 For examples of comparative European jurisdictions on academic freedom, many of which also do not expressly protect students in national law, see Monika Stachowiak-Kudła et al., "Academic Freedom as a Defensive Right," *Hague Journal on the Rule of Law* 15 (2023): 161–190. See also Klaus D. Beiter, Terence Karran, and Kwadwo Appiagyei-Atua, "Academic Freedom and Its Protection in the Law of European States: Measuring an International Human Right," *European Journal of Comparative Law and Governance* 3 (2016): 254.

41 The Academic Freedom and Internationalisation Working Group was established in 2019 and is composed of academic members, with support from some civil society organizations and the UK All-Party Parliamentary Human Rights Group. It aims to "uphold ... academic freedom in the context of internationalisation of UK higher education and promot[e] ... a collective and organised response by academic communities and HE institutions in the UK"; see School of Advanced Study, "Academic Freedom and Internationalisation Working Group," https://hrc.sas.ac.uk/networks/academic-freedom-and-internationalisation-working-group.

ing materials."[42] At the institutional level, the Open University in the UK, currently the largest provider focused on distance learning, has adopted a "Statement of Principles on Academic Freedom" (2019).[43] This is an example of a cross-cutting statement that applies to the whole academic community, including staff and students. Student charters can also include specific provisions for academic freedom.

The Model Code of Conduct also recommends improvements in monitoring and reporting on threats to academic freedom and the appointment of a specific contact point to assist any members of the academic community that are affected. This should include protections for independent learners and teachers who are participating in online learning from other countries. The monitoring practice should be supported by introducing academic freedom considerations into the ranking of HEIs.[44] International partnerships concerning TNE should assess risks to academic freedom from the outset, put in place mitigation strategies, and establish "red lines" on violations of academic freedom that would trigger the termination of cooperation agreements.

Another obvious starting point is to review protection measures within information and communication technology (ICT) used for online learning. During the pandemic, when there was a sharp and swift move to use of tools like Zoom to deliver teaching, it quickly became apparent that there were unforeseen security, harassment, and privacy risks with some software used for online learning.[45] General measures for cyber security are being increased in many universities,[46] for example, introducing multifactor authentication for logins, which can also safeguard against hacking into student accounts for covert monitoring of their studies.

---

42 School of Advanced Study, "Model Code of Conduct," https://hrc.sas.ac.uk/networks/academic-freedom-and-internationalisation-working-group/model-code-conduct.

43 The Open University, "Statement of Principles on Academic Freedom," https://help.open.ac.uk/documents/policies/academic-freedom-principles-statement/files/1/statement-of-principles-on-academic-freedom.pdf.

44 For a broader discussion of university rankings and academic freedom, see Katrin Kinzelbach, Ilyas Saliba, and Janika Spannagel, "Global Data on the Freedom Indispensable for Scientific Research: Towards a Reconciliation of Academic Reputation and Academic Freedom," *International Journal of Human Rights* 26 (2022): 1723–1740.

45 Thorsten Benner, *The "Zoomification" of Academia: Addressing Risks to Academic Freedom* (Berlin: Global Public Policy Institute, 2021).

46 Joachim Bjørge Ulven and Gaute Wangen, "A Systematic Review of Cybersecurity Risks in Higher Education," *Future Internet* 13 (2021): 39.

In high-risk security contexts, such as where distance and online learning are pursued in response to war or oppression, universities operating in an online environment can adopt both "high-tech" and "low-tech" strategies for safety in online learning. On the "low tech" side, students (and teachers) at risk may be advised to use a nickname/avatar or a nonpersonal email to participate in discussions without turning on their video camera, to access learning material from separate devices, and to refrain from communicating in parallel spaces with other students. This, however, has multiple downsides. It may pose assessment and certification challenges if learners cannot be legally identified. Avatars and switched-off cameras make it easier for trespassers to enter and participate in a class. They make teaching delivery difficult and introduce excessive anonymity that may prompt participants to share hateful remarks. This makes the establishment of ethical guidelines for online learning essential. In one online program offered to students in Myanmar, the courses begin with sessions specifically on how human rights education manifests itself in the virtual classroom through teaching core principles on academic freedom, freedom of expression, and mutual respect for differences of opinion.

On the "high-tech" side, careful consideration is needed of the pros and cons of different tools. To assist this, Off University provides learners with a detailed matrix on what kind of data is collected by different online learning tools, in order "to create awareness of how internet users can protect their data and defend themselves digitally."[47] At one virtual university operating in Myanmar, students are offered a four-hour training session specifically on security about online learning. The use of a "cloud" for storing learning materials and VPNs is widely advised. The use of VPNs, however, is not a failsafe option, and universities should carefully scrutinize potential security risks that might remain. In specific jurisdictions, VPNs may be illegal. In others, their use may be tolerated, despite constituting a legal offense. Students' use of VPNs may be negotiated between a university and the student's home country. Notably, an argument was made by concerned academics that an internet access agreement concluded by institutions representing UK universities still allowed Chinese government censorship in virtual

47 "Off-University," https://off-university.com/en-US/Blog/Detail/practicing-digital-self-defense.

classrooms.[48] Some universities provide advice "on bandwidth and firewalls" and on "accessing online learning in China."[49] This advice should be explicit about what it means that a VPN is state-approved. This type of information should also either direct students to resources concerning academic freedom or explain how firewalls and specific VPNs intersect with the academic freedom of learners.

The content management policies of the learning management systems, such as Moodle, Blackboard, or OpenEdX, constitute another important area for policy development. Software companies specializing in education technology may be vulnerable to pressure from authoritarian regimes to restrict access to certain materials for online learning within their jurisdiction, a procedure that is well known to international publishers.[50] Companies should review their policies and practices to determine what actions would potentially breach academic freedom. At the Off University, concerns over weaknesses of existing learning management systems prompted them to create an entirely new tool, Coworkingsquares, to provide enhanced security. Academics have also raised concerns about intellectual property rights that may be impinged by the user agreements of learning management systems as lectures, posts, or other teaching materials are uploaded online.[51]

Online learning modalities can be effective tools also to increase knowledge about academic freedom per se. Student inductions can include specific training on what academic freedom means for their studies. For example, Scholars at Risk (SAR) partnered with the University of Oslo to create a Future Learn MOOC on "Dangerous Questions: Why Academic Freedom Matters."[52] Learners are introduced to the concept of academic freedom and taught how to "identify challenges and threats to academic freedom in

---

48 See, e.g., the use of the Alibaba Cloud service by UK universities, which experts argue cannot adequately prevent monitoring and censorship by the Chinese government. Matthieu Burnay et al., "Internet Access Deal Allows Chinese Government Censorship in Our UK University (Virtual) Classrooms," *USS Briefs*, https://medium.com/ussbriefs/internet-access-deal-allows-chinese-government-censorship-in-our-uk-university-virtual-classrooms-4040a77df25d.

49 See, e.g., University of Edinburgh, "Delivering Teaching to Students Overseas: Advice on Bandwidth and Firewalls," www.ed.ac.uk/information-services/learning-technology/more/teaching-continuity/delivering-teaching-to-students-overseas; University of Bristol, "Accessing Online Learning in China," www.bristol.ac.uk/digital-education/guides/china/.

50 Owen, "The 'Internationalisation Agenda' and the Rise of the Chinese University."

51 Poritz and Rees, "Academic Freedom in Online Education."

52 Future Learn, www.futurelearn.com/courses/academic-freedom.

different contexts."[53] In the UK, an "edtech" company has been commissioned to create "a novel style of micro-courses to support student understanding about the vital importance and principles of freedom of speech and academic freedom" to be delivered via mobile phones in a video format.[54]

Another important step would be to place greater emphasis on academic freedom in online learning in policies and guidelines aimed at managing risks related to the internationalization of HE and crisis response. Universities UK is currently reviewing and updating the "Managing Risks in Internationalisation: Security Related Issues" guidelines.[55] It is important that the language in which such guidelines are constructed foregrounds academic freedom. At present, explicit references are somewhat lacking, with statements emphasizing primarily the security aspect.[56] The guidelines mention "protection from extraterritorial jurisdiction issues—consider carefully the risks faced by academics and students participating in online discussions about issues that some nation states might regard as sensitive and take steps to inform these individuals."[57] Academic freedom should be at the forefront of all crisis response activities undertaken by the HE sector in the future. UK universities supporting those in Ukraine have recognized the need to build "capabilities that will better position UK universities to respond to future crises," and online learning likely will form an important part of creating those capabilities.[58]

Data collection can inform this strategic planning. In the UK, the National Student Survey introduced a change that would allow for collecting data on students' experience of academic freedom.[59] The agreed ques-

---

53 Future Learn, www.futurelearn.com/courses/academic-freedom.

54 Advance HE, "Advance HE Partners with GoodCourse to Create Micro-courses on Freedom of Speech and Academic Freedom," February 7, 2023, www.advance-he.ac.uk/news-and-views/advance-he-partners-goodcourse-create-micro-courses-freedom-speech-and-academic.

55 Universities UK, "Managing Risks in Internationalisation: Security Related Issues," www.universitiesuk.ac.uk/what-we-do/policy-and-research/publications/managing-risks-internationalisation.

56 Universities UK, "Managing Risks in Internationalisation," 5.

57 Universities UK, "Managing Risks in Internationalisation," 36.

58 The quotation stems from the UK-Ukraine R&I twinning grants scheme webpage, see "Twinning Grants Scheme," www.universitiesuk.ac.uk/topics/international/international-research-collaboration/uk-ukraine-ri-twinning-grants-scheme.

59 The Office for Students undertook a lengthy consultation process on whether to include a new question. It was not uncontroversial; while some agreed it was necessary to monitor the freedom of expression, particularly given existing and emerging regulatory requirements, others felt it was a politicized issue and exaggerated the level of actual concern about these issues on UK campuses. See Office for Students, "Con-

tion is: "During your studies, how free did you feel to express your ideas, opinions, and beliefs?"[60] and will be directed at final-year students. Under this guidance, some universities may integrate a similar question into their surveys for their distance learning students. For example, the University of London Worldwide, which specializes in distance and online learning, will include this question in its biennial Student Experience Survey, which will also encompass independent learners and those learning out of teaching centers in other countries. The narrow focus on freedom of speech may, however, obscure other risks to academic freedom in online learning, such as essay topic selection, security concerns over data sharing on certain learning platforms, access to reading materials that may be locally proscribed, or course choices. One possible avenue of future research would be to compare responses by jurisdiction, home country, or learning modality (i.e., campus, hybrid, or fully online) of students.

Conclusion

Online learning has been on the rise for some time, but it was the COVID-19 pandemic that forced most of the HE sector across the world to switch to the virtual learning environment. Some institutions made the switch only temporarily, others incorporated online learning into specific areas long term, including introducing virtual international mobility for students and online dissertation supervision and marking. Various motivations are behind the preference for online settings, including accessibility, profitability, pedagogical innovation, and the need to circumvent oppression, surveillance, and harassment. There is little doubt that this mode of engagement with learners will continue proliferating. The guiding motivation behind this chapter was that precisely because of how widespread the practice becomes and how profoundly it will reshape the HE sector, it is crucial to discuss how the online mode of learning intersects with challenges to academic freedom.

sultation on Changes to the National Student Survey: Analysis of Responses and Decisions," October 28, 2022, www.officeforstudents.org.uk/media/c896af2e-f4b0-400d-a5db-76cdf6b0db86/consultation-on-changes-to-nss_analysis-of-responses-and-decisions.pdf.

60 The question will apply only to the survey in England. The funders of higher education in Scotland, Wales, and Northern Ireland "do not consider that the proposed question has value for providers in those countries"; see "Consultation on Changes to the National Student Survey," 27.

While online learning opens up a number of opportunities, it is not free from old risks and generates new challenges to academic freedom. Risks to academic freedom in online education stem from several principal sources: the technological tools and environment as well as the laws and policies of the country offering online learning and—in the case of online learning taking place transnationally—those laws of the home or resident countries of learners. Even if online learning is offered by HEIs registered in countries with robust de jure and de facto protection of academic freedom, learners and teachers can fall victim to gaps in the security of online learning platforms and are not impervious to practices employed by oppressive governments or hostile social groups.

In this chapter, we proposed several initial steps for strengthening academic freedom in online learning. These measures include the establishment of clear codes of conduct applicable to online learning; the review of protective measures employed by online learning platforms; the introduction of safeguards for personal data, secure use of online discussion platforms, and safe access to online learning materials; training for learners and teachers; and clearly articulated processes of lending support to affected learners and teachers. We also believe that it is vital to incorporate the assessment of academic freedom into the process of establishing international partnerships and to continue improving and extending the monitoring of academic freedom transgressions worldwide, with special emphasis on transgressions taking place in an online environment.[61]

We have not been able to touch on a number of issues related to academic freedom in online learning, for instance, other forms of support that can be offered to academics living under oppression through online networks, such as the Academics in Solidarity program.[62] We aimed to map out this dynamic field. Further research into the teacher and student experiences of online learning and their perceptions of academic freedom in virtual settings will give a more detailed picture of the distinct challenges to academic freedom.

---

61 For more information on the monitoring process currently in place, see the Scholars at Risk, "Academic Freedom Monitoring Project," www.scholarsatrisk.org/actions/academic-freedom-monitoring-project/.

62 For more information, see "Academics in Solidarity," www.fu-berlin.de/en/sites/academicsinsolidarity/index.html.

CHAPTER 22

Academic Freedom and University Rankings

CHRIS BRINK

INTRODUCTION

The promotion and defense of academic freedom is a Sisyphean labor. New threats, internal and external to academia, regularly arise and need to be countered. One suggestion that has recently been raised is that academic freedom would be advanced if it were to be incorporated as one of the parameters of university rankings. In this chapter, I caution against such a proposal. I argue that, on conceptual as well as pragmatic grounds, the proposed means would defeat the desired end, since rankings are themselves a threat to academic freedom. Moreover, a viable alternative is available.

THE "GOOD-AT" AND THE "GOOD-FOR"

By way of background, I distinguish two distinct themes in global higher education over the past few decades. One theme is our response to the question of what we are good at. In this theme, we focus mostly on our academic outputs, and we take as our guiding principle the notion of excellence. To measure excellence, we have developed a formidable array of quantitative indices, metrics, and rankings, which we use to compare academic performance on a linear scale and within a competitive paradigm. The other theme tries to respond in qualitative terms to the question of what we are good for. It speaks of our contribution to the common good, community engagement, sustainability, social justice, and societal impact. Its academic currency is a multidimensional notion of quality, rather than the one-dimensional notion of excellence.

There is a frequent oversimplification regarding these two themes that should be avoided. I refer namely to the view that a strong answer to the good-at question will suffice also as an answer to the good-for question. This view, prevalent for much of the second half of the twentieth century, considered our job as academics to consist of two and only two components: curiosity-driven knowledge generation, and teaching the value of knowledge "for its own sake." In other words, our job was to increase the supply of knowledge in the world. As long as we do that well (or so we thought), society will automatically benefit in the long run. Elsewhere, I have referred to this view, which sees academic work essentially as a supply-side activity, as the "invisible hand" argument. It is named after the famous metaphor of Adam Smith that in a free-market economy, supply will meet up with demand without the need for external regulation.[1] There is powerful inductive support for this argument, with many examples of how freely generated knowledge, created without any specific purpose in mind, turned out to be beneficial in various and often surprising ways. Still, even though the invisible hand argument may be true, it cannot be the whole truth, and although the free creation and dissemination of knowledge may gladly be acknowledged as necessary, it cannot be assumed to be sufficient. The invisible hand is slow in delivering results, and unpredictable in its effects. It is by definition not responsive to societal needs. In a world beset by societal challenges, it would be an abdication of moral responsibility not to try and generate knowledge with the specific purpose of addressing such challenges. For example, when the COVID-19 pandemic struck, it would have been irresponsible of the universities just to sit back and assume that the invisible hand would take care of it.

Even a strong response to the "good-at" question will not suffice, by itself, as a response to the "good-for" question. The latter needs to be responded to on its own terms. In fact, each of these two themes has a domain of discourse,

1 Chris Brink, *The Soul of the University: Why Excellence Is Not Enough* (Bristol: Bristol University Press, 2018).

a lexicon and a methodology particularly suited to it. This becomes evident when we consider the terms in which we evaluate each kind of activity.

For the good-at theme, by far the most commonly used evaluative term is excellence. It is worth understanding the preconceptions inherent in this notion. To "excel," according to the *Concise Oxford Dictionary*, is to be superior, preeminent, or outstanding. What that means is that excellence is a relational notion: when we claim that entity A is excellent, we do so in relation to other entities. The concept of excellence therefore rests on a key assumption, namely that of any two entities A and B (of whatever kind we are talking about), it makes sense to say that one of them is better than the other. This assumption then also applies iteratively to all the entities under consideration, at every stage pronouncing one of them to excel above the rest—in other words, to be excellent.

A mathematician would formulate the key assumption behind the notion of excellence by saying that the set of entities under consideration is assumed to be linearly ordered. It is, namely, the distinguishing characteristic of a linearly ordered set that of any two distinct elements A and B, it must be the case that either A > B or B > A. This is in fact a very strong assumption to make about any set of entities. It works well for numbers, but not always well in real life (and not well either for mathematical objects other than numbers, such as sets). Accepting the assumption of linearity means that we would be constrained to believe that if you have an apple and an orange, one of them must taste better than the other; if you have a rose and a lily, one of them must be more beautiful than the other, and if you compare Raphael to Rembrandt you must pronounce one of them the better artist.

It is exactly the assumption of linearity that lies at the bottom of university rankings. The defining purpose and main characteristic of such a ranking is that given any two universities—any two universities at all, anywhere in the world—it is assumed to make sense to rank one of them above the other. This is done no matter how these two universities might differ from each other. For example, University A might have an Engineering School and a School of Medicine, but neither a School of Agriculture nor a School of Law, whereas University B might have both Agriculture and Law but neither Engineering nor Medicine. One university might do an outstanding job of helping to uplift a local disadvantaged community, whereas the other might go about its business entirely divorced from its immediate surroundings.

One might be focused on responding to the UN Sustainable Development Goals, whereas the other is focused on pure mathematics, physics, and cosmology. No matter. On a ranking, one of A or B will be pronounced to be better than the other.

Constructing a Ranking

It is in fact not difficult to construct a university ranking. What is needed is not so much any technical skill as the blind self-confidence to make arbitrary choices between equally plausible alternatives. First, there is the choice of which categories of activities to evaluate. This choice is often driven by expediency because some activities (like research outputs) are easier to measure than others (like societal engagement). Naturally, the choice you make of what to evaluate will advantage some universities and disadvantage others. Second, you have to choose performance indicators in your chosen categories and how to measure them. Research performance, for example, has many plausible indicators, and whatever selection you make could easily have been different, with different outcomes. Also, when choosing performance indicators, you have to choose the manner and extent to which you use indicators of opinion vis-à-vis indicators of fact. "Reputational ranking," for example, is a matter of opinion, as is "student satisfaction." Third, for every performance indicator you have to come up with a number that represents your measurement of that indicator. The term "measurement" is a dubious suggestion of objectivity. In practice, the so-called measurement again requires a number of choices. You need to choose, for example, which data set(s) to use and what level of reliability of those data sets you will be content with. You also need to choose whether you will deal with gross numbers (which will favor larger institutions) or normalize the numbers according to the size of the institution (which tends to favor smaller institutions). Even normalizing your numbers "relative to size" involves a level of choice, because there is no generally agreed definition of what the size of a university is. (Is University A, with ten thousand students and two thousand academics, bigger or smaller than University B, with twenty thousand students and one thousand academics?) Fourth, having made many choices already to arrive at a number for each performance indicator, you still need to decide on a formula for combining those numbers into one number (which would then be your ranking). You could, for example, take the average—either mean or median. Or you could assign weights to each performance indicator—which can of course be done in infinitely many ways. There are many different ways of combining a set of numbers to yield one number, and, crucially, there is no strong reason, either mathematical or empirical, for choosing one method above any other.

To repeat: the construction of a ranking involves many choices, and there are no objective criteria for making one choice rather than another. Any ranking of universities therefore reflects the choices made by the ranker at least as much as it might be claimed to reflect an objective reality about those universities. It is hard to escape the suspicion that rankers make their choices according to their preconceived notion of which "the best" universities are. If a ranking did not fit their preconceptions, they would change their parameters rather than adjust their preconceptions. What this means is that rankings are normative, not just descriptive. They create a reality at least as much as they reflect a reality.

In short, university rankings are conceived in sin. Of course, criticism of rankings is nothing new—there are many discussions of their methodological shortcomings.[2] My summary here is however constructed to emphasize a particular point: any ranking suffers from the original sin of purporting to capture something which there is no reason to believe exists: a linear ordering of the set of all universities in the world.

The Rising Prominence of University Rankings

Despite these fundamental flaws, the phenomenon of university rankings has grown within two decades to become one of the defining features of global higher education. It is rare now to attend any meeting or seminar on any topic in higher education without the reality of rankings becoming part of the discussion. In the process, rankings have become big business. What the Times Higher Education started as a curiosity in London in the early 2000s, for example, has become an international commercial enterprise, endlessly but profitably recycling data, much of which comes from the univer-

2 See, e.g., Terence Karran and Lucy Mallinson, "Academic Freedom and World-Class Universities: A Virtuous Circle?" *Higher Education Policy* (2018).

sities themselves. Somehow the rankers have maneuvered themselves into the advantageous position of being both auditor and consultant, at the same time, for the same institutions. More to the point, however, rankings have grown in influence so much that they have global geopolitical consequences. This assessment has been convincingly demonstrated by the foremost expert in the field, Professor Ellen Hazelkorn. Tellingly, her groundbreaking work is titled *Rankings and the Reshaping of Higher Education: The Battle for World-Class Excellence.*[3] It gives copious references and has been updated by other publications. The final chapter summarizes how the reshaping of higher education has happened at three levels. First, rankings have changed higher education institutions. Many universities have turned themselves into ranking-chasing machines, narrowly defining their institutional mission in terms of the ambition to rise in one or more of the university rankings. Second, in many countries, rankings have been instrumental in the reshaping of national higher education systems. Politicians have come to regard university rankings as a measure of international competitiveness and have therefore restructured their national higher education systems, in various versions of an *Exzellenzinitiative*, with the declared intention of enabling a few "elite" universities to rise to the top of the rankings. Third, rankings have reshaped our understanding of knowledge itself. Hazelkorn speaks of rankings "reasserting the hierarchy of traditional knowledge production," with a focus on a narrow definition of knowledge, traditional outputs, and "impact" defined as something that occurs only between academic peers. There may well be people who honestly, though naively, believe that academic excellence is objectively represented by university rankings. The fact is, however, that the opposite is the case: the subjective and haphazard choices of the rankers have come to define what academic excellence is considered to be.

So the situation is this. There is a force, external to academia, run as a global money-making business, based on a false premise and implemented by ad hoc choices, which is influencing the career choices of countless young people, affecting the modus operandi of many academics, demonstrably shaping the way universities operate, influencing national higher

3 Ellen Hazelkorn, *Rankings and the Reshaping of Higher Education: The Battle for World-Class Excellence* (London: Palgrave Macmillan, 2011). See also Ellen Hazelkorn, ed., *Global Rankings and the Geopolitics of Higher Education: Understanding the Influence and Impact of Rankings on Higher Education, Policy and Society* (London: Routledge, 2017).

education policies, and fundamentally affecting our understanding of the nature and purpose of knowledge production. I would argue that any external force constraining higher education in such a manner must be considered as a threat to institutional autonomy and, therefore, also to academic freedom.

The situation is not improved by the fact that many universities and individual academics are complicit in this threat. Vanity is such a powerful motivating factor that those who do well on the rankings—even just momentarily—cannot resist the temptation to boast about it in public, even when simultaneously expressing private misgivings. Those who have done less well, on the other hand, feel that they cannot speak out against rankings lest they be accused of sour grapes. In this manner compliance follows in the wake of vanity, and the entire rankings-chasing exercise becomes self-perpetuating.

Academic Freedom and University Rankings: Proceed with Caution

It is time for us to take account of the fact that the global role of university rankings should be counted among the growing list of threats to academic freedom.

I would raise a caution, therefore, about any proposal, well-intentioned though it may be, that academic freedom should be included as a category of evaluation in university rankings. Recently, for example, a letter went out to all ranking organizations from the Global Public Policy Institute and the Scholars at Risk network, saying:

> Academic freedom is an integral part of quality academic research, teaching, and learning—yet so far none of the dominant university excellence rankings include measures of academic freedom in their assessments. University rankings are in a unique position to shape incentive structures for governments, universities, scholars, and students. The omission of academic freedom in existing rankings, on the other hand, negatively affects universities' and governments' impetus to improve academic freedom levels. With the creation of the Academic Freedom Index (AFi),

university rankings finally have a real opportunity to close this gap in their methodology.[4]

An article titled "Why University Rankings Must Include Academic Freedom" also appeared in *University World News* (one of the coauthors being the contact cited in the letter to ranking organizations),[5] while in the same time frame, the claim was made that "universities without academic freedom have no place in rankings."[6] The letter to ranking organizations is also featured on the website of the International Ranking Expert Group (IREG) Observatory on Academic Ranking and Excellence, an organization consisting of "ranking organizations, universities and other bodies interested in university rankings and academic excellence."[7]

To anyone committed to academic freedom, any proposal for its advancement deserves attention—but not uncritical acceptance. In this case, in particular, two areas of concern are apparent: conceptual and pragmatic.

Conceptual Concerns

My conceptual concern about adding academic freedom to ranking parameters is that, in principle, the proposal is self-defeating. In the letter quoted earlier, the writers themselves begin by acknowledging that "rankings are in a unique position to shape incentive structures for governments, universities, scholars and students." That is to acknowledge exactly what Ellen Hazelkorn argued, that in many countries rankings have been an external force instrumental in the reshaping of higher education systems, which is to say that rankings constrain free choice. Such a starting point can only offer the same advantages as surrendering before the battle begins. The very premise of the proposal is that by including academic freedom the rankings can be

4 Global Public Policy Institute and Scholars at Risk, *Accounting for Academic Freedom in University Excellence Rankings: An Invitation to Collaboration* (Berlin: Global Public Policy Institute and Scholars at Risk, 2021).

5 Robert Quinn, Janika Spannagel, and Ilyas Saliba, "Why University Rankings Must Include Academic Freedom," *University World News*, March 11, 2021, www.universityworldnews.com/post.php?story=20210311071016522.

6 Carsten A. Holz, "Universities without Academic Freedom Have No Place in Rankings," *International Higher Education* 106 (2021): 3–5.

7 IREG Observatory, "About Us," https://ireg-observatory.org/en/about-us/.

improved, and thus become even more influential—which means that they would become even more effective at restricting academic freedom. That is why I say the proposal is self-defeating: the proposed means would defeat the desired end.

The idea that rankings can and should be "improved" is very common, and proposals to this effect are often made. But improvement is in the eye of the proposer. Seldom does a specific proposal for "improvement" amount to anything other than offering a different set of choices from those already used, according to how the preferences of the proposer differ from those of the rankers. Thus, the current proposal offers academic freedom as an additional category of evaluation, and similar proposals have also been made for the inclusion, for example, of societal impact, sustainability, or ethics. Such proposals then also need to go further in suggesting some tweaks in the arithmetical formulae leading to the eventual ranking number. All of this is technically feasible and would not be hard to implement.

It has been claimed that "measuring and ranking universities is difficult."[8] I disagree. Technically, ranking universities is easy. Conceptually, however, if by ranking we mean objective ranking, it is not just difficult—it is impossible.

Let me motivate this bold claim of impossibility by returning to the distinction between what we are good at and what we are good for. I have already coupled the good-at theme with the notion of excellence, and hence with rankings. I would now argue that the good-for theme is coupled, not with excellence, but with the much richer notion of academic quality.

There are two fundamental differences between excellence and quality. The first is that whereas excellence, as mentioned, is a relational concept, quality is not. When we compare the apple and the orange, or the rose and the lily, we are interested in their various qualities, but we do not thereby relate one to the other as being better or worse. Quality inheres in an individual—it is part of what philosophers have long described as the essence of the individual. The second difference between excellence and quality begins with the tautological observation that quality is described in qualitative terms. To be a little less gnomic about it: quality has many aspects, and so it is a multidimensional concept, whereas excellence is a one-dimensional concept. As regards universities, then, under "academic quality" we would

8 Quinn et al., "Why University Rankings Must Include Academic Freedom."

include a richness of attributes, most of which are not relational. Under the quality of a university, we might incorporate its value system, for example, how it responds to societal challenges, or its contributions to issues of social justice, such as equality. In particular, and to the present point, it seems perfectly reasonable to consider academic freedom as one aspect of academic quality. Concepts such as values, social justice, or freedom, however, do not naturally lend themselves to ranking (although they can of course be forced into normative linearity by some process of quantification). Who is to say, for example, that the ethical basis of University A is better or worse than that of University B? When universities A and B each set out their value system via their vision and/or mission statement, we may be interested in asking each whether they practice what they preach, but we do not normally rank their value statements. We are back to the rose and the lily: while we can appreciate each on its merit, it makes no sense to rank one above the other.

All of this is to say—no more and no less than what philosophers have accepted ever since Aristotle—that Quantity and Quality are different categories. Neither can substitute for the other. That is why I argue that, in principle, rankings cannot capture quality.

Pragmatic Concerns

That still leaves what might be called the pragmatic argument. It goes like this: rankings are a reality that cannot be wished away, and therefore, whatever their conceptual shortcomings, it is better to join them than to try and beat them. That is, we should on pragmatic grounds accept excellence as a proxy for quality, and rankings as a popular assessment of excellence. In consequence, it would then be advantageous to incorporate academic freedom as a parameter of rankings so that it can ride on the coattails of their popularity.

In response, I would say: Consider the consequences. Imagine that the proposal is indeed implemented—that is, that some index of academic freedom is incorporated in the so-called university world rankings. Suddenly, then, the league table of the "top-200" universities in the world would look very different, according to whether or not the country within which a university is situated is judged to be free or unfree. Now consider the fallout. Inevitably, questions would be raised about the credibility of this move.[9] Two consequences appear to be likely. The first is that those universities that lost out will cry foul on the grounds that, whatever the level of unfreedom is in their country, it is not their fault. Along the same lines, those governments whose universities lost out would simply hold the entire exercise up to ridicule, arguing by the logic of excellence that the inclusion of academic freedom is a weak attempt to game the system and gain advantage by bringing extraneous factors into play. Academic freedom, they would say, has nothing to do with academic excellence—and for those committed only to the logic of "excellence," they would have a point. The second likely consequence is that whatever arithmetical wizardry was applied to factor in a freedom index could and would easily be reverse-engineered, leading back to whatever the original ranking would have been—and handing a propaganda coup to the "unfree" countries. Thus the pragmatic proposal fails, on pragmatic grounds, when we consider the consequences of its implementation. The game is not worth the candle.

In summary: we are dealing with two distinct domains of discourse. The discourse of rankings and excellence leads us to a one-dimensional league table. It is part of our response to the question "What are we good at?" The discourse of quality, on the other hand, is multidimensional and deals with concepts that are not by nature positioned on a linear scale. It is part of our response to the question "What are we good for?" As I argued earlier, the second question is not reducible to the first. Excellence by itself is not sufficient. The good-for question needs to be addressed on its own terms. The proposal to incorporate a qualitative concept like academic freedom into the quantitative game of rankings fails both on conceptual and pragmatic grounds, essentially because you cannot advance the case for quality by the logic of excellence, for the same reason as you cannot foster multidimensionality on a linear scale.

A Way Forward? Ratings and Rankings Distinguished

One question remains: for the concept of academic quality, is there an alternative to ranking? Is there a way of offering a comparison between variations of quality without forcing qualitative concepts onto a quantified linear scale?

9 I am of the view that any question raised about the credibility of rankings is welcome, but for the moment I am following the reasoning of the pragmatic argument.

Such an alternative is indeed available. It begins with distinguishing a rating from a ranking.

Rating qualitative concepts is very common. It consists of breaking down a qualitative concept into a number of categories, and then assigning a rating—which could be a word or a number—to each of these categories. Suppose for example a food critic decides to rate the quality of restaurants in a city. She might then break down "quality" into (say) five dimensions: the quality of the ingredients, the quality of the preparation, the quality of the presentation, the quality of the service, and the taste of the food. On each of these five dimensions she might further assign an evaluation, say "awful" or "mediocre" or "fair" or "good" or "wonderful." It makes no difference if she decides to use numbers as shorthand, say 0 for "awful" up to 4 for "wonderful." The point is that each restaurant gets an evaluation that consists of five ratings. So, following the order in which the five dimensions are listed, Restaurant A might get an evaluation that says "ingredients fair, preparation good, presentation good, service awful, taste good," or "2-3-3-0-3" for short. Restaurant B, on the other hand, might by the same method get an evaluation that says "1-4-0-2-4," which indicates a different kind of dining experience.

Following up on this little thought experiment, let me repeat by way of emphasis a number of points I have made before, and add some new ones. First, it would be perfectly possible (indeed, easy) for the food critic to turn each of these two sets of ratings into a single number, and thus get a ranking. Second, for this purpose, she could employ any one of a number of methods, all equally plausible but yielding different results. (Take the mean, then A=B; take the median, then A > B; take the mode, then A < B.) Third, no matter how she does it the ranking process would involve loss of information. Fourth (and this is a new point) whatever ranking method the critic uses the customer could use as well. The customer is perfectly capable of deciding for themself where to go and have dinner on the basis of the given ratings combined with their own individual preferences. Therefore, in conclusion, what is the point of doing the ranking at all? The ratings would suffice perfectly well—indeed, better than the ranking—for individual decision-making.

Now compare the thought experiment with the Academic Freedom Index—the flagship ranking of those who propose that academic freedom should be incorporated into university rankings.[10] At the outset, academic freedom is treated, very sensibly, as being multidimensional. There are five dimensions: freedom to research and teach, freedom to share research findings, institutional autonomy, freedom from surveillance and harassment, and freedom to express opinions. In each country, each of these dimensions of freedom is then rated on a five-point scale: 0 = completely restricted; 1 = severely restricted; 2 = moderately restricted; 3 = mostly free, and 4 = fully free. So far so good. What this means is that the method would assign to each country what might be called an academic freedom profile: a set of five ratings. However, like the restaurant critic, the Academic Freedom Index does not stop there. It employs a "state-of-the-art statistical model" to turn the five ratings into a single number and thereby produce a ranking. The same conclusions as earlier therefore apply. Above all: the ranking produced suffers from a grievous loss of information—so what is the point of doing it at all? Why not simply retain the multidimensionality, and present the rating results as they are, rather than arbitrarily compressing them into a single number? Why try to gild the lily?[11]

Such restraint is not impossible. The Research Excellence Framework in the UK, for example, is a major national exercise that evaluates research at each university and presents the results in terms of "quality profiles." Essentially, a quality profile is a picture that shows ratings under various headings.[12] What it is not is a single number. As ever, these quality profiles can indeed be turned into rankings (and again in various ways), and indeed the rankers lose no time in doing so. But the primary results—available in full on the internet—are quite deliberately given as sets of ratings, not as a ranking. As another example, even within the rankings world, there are examples of nonlinear presentations. There is, for example, a methodology called U-Multirank (an unfortunate misnomer for what could rather have been called U-Multirating) that presents its evaluation results in multidi-

10 V-Dem, "Academic Freedom," www.v-dem.net/our-work/research-programs/academic-freedom/.

11 The Academic Freedom Index is by no means the only example of an exercise that starts out as a multidimensional rating profile, but then at the last step gets compressed into a one-dimensional ranking. The Social Progress Index would be another such example, see Social Progress Imperative, "2024 Social Progress Index," www.socialprogress.org/2024-social-progress-index/.

12 See, e.g., REF 2021, "Understanding the REF 2021 Results," www.ref.ac.uk/guidance-on-results/guidance-on-ref-2021-results/.

mensional form, such as through a "sunburst chart."[13] It does not rank universities on a linear scale, but it does provide a facility for users to create their own rankings, according to their own preferences.

Almost all rankings begin with a system of ratings, which are in the final steps squashed together into linear form by some arbitrary arithmetic. It is a sad consequence of scientism that we seem unable to stop our quantifications until we have reduced multidimensional qualitative concepts to a single number. Yet such restraint is exactly what is required. A profile, or a picture, or a set of ratings, is far more informative than a single number and presents a viable alternative for purposes both of comparison and decision-making.

Conclusion

By way of conclusion, I repeat my caution against the idea that academic freedom would be advanced by incorporating it as a parameter in university rankings. The case for academic freedom must be made within the multidimensional paradigm of academic quality; it cannot be made within the one-dimensional discourse of excellence. For the defense of academic freedom, rankings are part of the problem, not part of the solution. Hence my recommendation: think again!

13 U-Multirank, www.umultirank.org/.

CHAPTER 23

Academic Freedom

Swimming against the Technological Tide

CHAVAN SHARMA KISSOON AND TERENCE KARRAN

INTRODUCTION

Over the past decade, a key trend in the UK higher education (HE) sector has been the embrace of digital transformation by UK HE institutions to make their operations leaner and more efficient and to expand the scope and reach of their teaching and research via digital technology-enabled efficiencies.[1] However, while these undoubted affordances of digital transformation for universities, researchers, and teachers are often what is accentuated in official institutional materials and research on digital transformation more generally, less attention has been given to how digital transformation shapes the individual autonomy of academics through the introduction of new digital education governance modes of technology-enhanced management.[2]

1 See, e.g., Oxford University, "Oxford's Digital Transformation," www.ox.ac.uk/students/news/2023-01-06-oxford-s-digital-transformation; University of Edinburgh, "Digital Transformation," www.ed.ac.uk/digital-transformation; University of Leeds, "Digital Transformation: University of Leeds Strategy 2020 to 2030," https://spotlight.leeds.ac.uk/strategy-digital-transformation/index.html.

2 Sascha Kraus et al., "Digital Transformation: An Overview of the Current State of the Art of Research," *SAGE Open* 11 (2021): 1; Swen Nadkarni and Reinhard Prügl, "Digital Transformation: A Review, Syn-

Within the context of the UK's highly marketized HE sector, where hyper-managerial approaches are normalized, working conditions are pressured, and work contracts are precarious, there has been an unacknowledged creep of technology-enabled management practices that are further eroding academic freedom.[3] Alongside this growth in technology-enabled management practices, there has been a corresponding culture change toward both university management and academic staff (the managers and the managed) coming to commonly perceive themselves through a quantified performance lens.[4] At the same time, while digital education governance management practices have taken root and are establishing themselves as part of the UK HE management toolkit and becoming part of the HE sector's everyday neoliberalism, less discussed are the precise ways in which digital education governance is shaping long-established academic freedom norms in the UK HE sector.[5] This, perhaps, is due to "the role of digital instruments in governing and guiding the conduct of diverse educational actors and institutions" being underappreciated due to the esoteric nature of digital technologies in terms both of how they work and of the logic that underpins their functioning.[6] A consequence of this is that organizational digital technology is rarely recognized as a variable that has the potential to significantly alter the ways in which academic freedom is operationalized in the modern UK university.

Academic freedom is explicitly recognized as a core value of the UK HE sector by Universities UK, the collective body representing 140 UK-based universities. Furthermore, a large number of universities have introduced

---

thesis and Opportunities for Future Research," *Management Review Quarterly* 71 (2021): 233; Ben Williamson, "Digital Education Governance: An Introduction," *European Educational Research Journal* 15 (2016): 3.

3 Morag Munro, "The Complicity of Digital Technologies in the Marketisation of UK Higher Education: Exploring the Implications of a Critical Discourse Analysis of Thirteen National Digital Teaching and Learning Strategies," *International Journal of Education Technology in Higher Education* 15 (2018); Mark Erickson, Paul Hanna, and Carl Walker, "The UK Higher Education Senior Management Survey: A Statactivist Response to Managerialist Governance," *Studies in Higher Education* 46 (2021): 2134; Chavan Kissoon and Terence Karran, *Academic Freedom in the Digital University* (London: University and College Union, forthcoming).

4 Björn Hammarfelt, Sarah de Rijcke, and Alexander D. Rushforth, "Quantified Academic Selves: The Gamification of Research through Social Networking Services," *Information Research* 21 (2016), http://InformationR.net/ir/21-2/SM1.html.

5 Williamson, "Digital Education Governance"; Fabian Cannizzo, "Tactical Evaluations: Everyday Neoliberalism in Academia," *Journal of Sociology* 54 (2018): 77.

6 Williamson, "Digital Education Governance," 11.

policies stating their appreciation of the value of academic freedom and their commitment to protecting it.[7] Within these institutional policy documents, academic freedom is variously framed. For the University of Nottingham, the framing is worker-centered and is focused on ensuring that academics have the "freedom within the law to question and test received wisdom and to put forward new ideas and controversial or unpopular opinions, without placing themselves in jeopardy of losing their jobs or privileges."[8] For the University of Exeter, their discursive framing focuses more on the institutional responsibility of the university to

> maintain and promote the academic freedom of all undertaking academic activities. That is to say freedom of education and discussion, freedom in carrying out research and disseminating and publishing the results thereof, freedom from institutional or other forms of censorship, and freedom to participate in professional or representative academic bodies.[9]

Within the context of how academic freedom is commonly constructed in UK university policies, academic freedom is not absolute and is often bounded by mediating factors. Taking the example of the University of Exeter, the operationalization of academic freedom within their institution is bounded by the university's corporate values and "the right of the University to make reasonable business decisions with regard to the provision of academic activities."[10] Additionally, UK HE institutions tend to bind the limits of academic freedom in relation to government legislation such as the Equality Act and the Public Sector Equality Duty and also bind the operationalizing of academic freedom in relation to institutional equality, dignity, and respect policies, which often take precedence over academic

7 See, e.g., University of Bath, "Academic Freedom," www.bath.ac.uk/corporate-information/academic-freedom; University of Exeter, "Agreement on Academic Freedom," www.exeter.ac.uk/staff/exeteracademic/yourdevelopment/citizenshipdevelopment/policies/academicfreedom; University of Nottingham, "Free Speech and Academic Freedom at the University of Nottingham," www.nottingham.ac.uk/governance/free-speech-and-academic-freedom.aspx.

8 University of Nottingham, "Free Speech and Academic Freedom."

9 University of Exeter, "Agreement on Academic Freedom."

10 University of Exeter, "Agreement on Academic Freedom."

freedom in situations where the policies may clash.[11] From these institutional policies, which to some extent relate to the 2023 Higher Education (Freedom of Speech) Bill, three factors ought to be noted. First, the ways in which these policies are formulated frame institutional understandings of what academic freedom entails in broad terms. Second, the policies, conversely, take a more specific approach to specifying which institutional (business) aims take priority over academic freedom. Thirdly, what these policies leave unaddressed is the recognition of how institutions are themselves engaging in the everyday erosion of academic freedom through the ways in which the surveillance affordances of institutional digital technologies are being used to govern staff (in the Foucauldian sense) through performance management monitoring, creating hyper-competition, and policing quality. This will be discussed later.

To facilitate a systematic analysis of the impact of digital education governance on academic freedom, this chapter utilizes the comprehensive definition of academic freedom set out by Karran, Beiter, and Mallinson, which pinpoints academic freedom as comprising two substantive elements and three supportive elements.[12] As will be shown, within this characterization, the constituent ingredients of freedom for teaching and freedom for research are identified in terms of a number of precise liberties. This chapter also outlines the ways in which the growing culture of digital education governance in the UK HE system is undermining academic freedom.[13] The chapter specifically focuses on the *freedom to teach*. It sets out the ways in which digitally enabled forms of worker governance constitute a new, hitherto unrecognized, and underappreciated variable shaping academic freedom for UK-employed academics. Drawing on the open-text dataset from a survey of over two thousand academics working in UK universities, this chapter sets out how one of the most pressing threats to academic freedom at the current time comes from the intersection of digital technologies, HE marketization, and HE managerialism, with digital governance being the umbrella within which these forces come together in tandem as a coherent force. The chap-

11 University of Bath, "Academic Freedom"; University of Exeter, "Agreement on Academic Freedom"; University of Nottingham, "Free Speech and Academic Freedom."

12 Terence Karran, Klaus D. Beiter, and Lucy Mallinson, "Academic Freedom in Contemporary Britain: A Cause for Concern?" *Higher Education Quarterly* 76 (2021): 563.

13 Williamson, "Digital Education Governance."

ter ends by highlighting the ways in which those who care about and value academic freedom can take proactive measures to protect academic freedom from the threats of digitally enabled managerialism. Next follows conceptual overviews of academic freedom and digital education governance.

Conceptualizing Academic Freedom

Most informed observers, both within academia and in the broader HE policy environment, would agree that academic freedom is important, on several levels. First, academic freedom is an essential prerequisite for individual academics, in their roles as creators and disseminators of new knowledge; second, it is crucial to the successful functioning of universities; and thirdly, it has an important role in ensuring democratic accountability. Hence, Bergan and others contend that academic freedom is "essential for universities to produce the research and teaching necessary to improve the human condition, which involves developing and maintaining a democratic society."[14] Moreover, based on this latter role, Machlup argues that "academic freedom is a right of the people, not a privilege of a few."[15] Consequently, it is surprising to find that, despite the apparent importance of academic freedom to three critical stakeholder groups, there is a lack of definitional clarity surrounding the concept.

In his book on versions of academic freedom, Fish makes the point that "academic freedom is a contested concept."[16] More helpfully, he sketches five distinct conceptualizations or "schools" of academic freedom, which he argues typify contemporary discourses about the topic. He labels these conceptualizations as follows: "It's Just a Job"; "For the Common Good"; "Academic Exceptionalism"; "It's for Critique"; and "Academic Freedom as Revolution." However, Menand's work suggests that such attempts by Fish (and others) rely on a "deeply misleading assumption ... of the university ... that there exists some unproblematic conception of academic freedom which

14 Sjur Bergan, Tony Gallagher, and Ira Harkavy, "A Word from the Editors," in *Academic Freedom, Institutional Autonomy and the Future of Democracy*, ed. Sjur Bergan, Tony Gallagher, and Ira Harkavy (Strasbourg: Council of Europe, 2020), 8.

15 Fritz Machlup, "On Some Misconceptions Concerning Academic Freedom," *Bulletin of the American Association of University Professors* 41 (1955): 753.

16 Stanley Fish, *Versions of Academic Freedom: From Professionalism to Revolution* (Chicago: University of Chicago Press, 2014), 142.

is philosophically coherent and that will conduce to outcomes in particular cases which all parties will feel to be just and equitable."[17] Moreover, as Matei points out: "There is no blueprint of any kind for academic freedom."[18]

In addition, the greater use of digital technologies (especially the new generation of technologies associated with the so-called Fourth Industrial Revolution, such as digital technologies that are underpinned by big data sets and make use of artificial intelligence and machine learning algorithms to aid data-informed decision-making), both within society at large and especially within the HE function (which is the focus of this chapter), has increased (rather than reduced) the degree of obscurity surrounding academic freedom. Indeed, Lackey notes that "the increasing role of the Internet in research, the rise of social media in both professional and extramural exchanges, and student demands for accommodations such as content warnings and safe spaces, the parameters of, and challenges to, academic freedom often leave us in uncharted territory."[19] Responding to such trends led the American Association of University Professors to assert that "faculty members must participate, preferably through representative institutions of shared governance, in the formulation and implementation of policies governing electronic communications technologies."[20]

However, for the purposes of this analysis, rather than attempting to address these definitional problems (that are important, but maybe intractable), we have followed the approach adopted by Karran such that "rather than trying to find a conclusive epistemological needle in a philosophical haystack, [our] concern is to provide a preliminary generic statement that is sharp enough with which to sew together the essential elements of the concept" of academic freedom with reference to the threat imposed by digital governance.[21] Despite differences in emphasis, all of the major defin-

17 Louis Menand, "The Limits of Academic Freedom," in *The Future of Academic Freedom*, ed. Louis Menand et al. (Chicago: Chicago University Press, 1996), 5.

18 Liviu Matei, "Academic Freedom, University Autonomy and Democracy's Future in Europe," in *Academic Freedom, Institutional Autonomy and the Future of Democracy*, ed. Sjur Bergan, Tony Gallagher, and Ira Harkavy (Strasbourg: Council of Europe, 2020), 35.

19 Jennifer Lackey, "Academic Freedom," in *Academic Freedom*, ed. Jennifer Lackey (Oxford: Oxford University Press, 2018), 19.

20 AAUP, "Academic Freedom and Electronic Communications," *Bulletin of the American Association of University Professors* 100 (2014): 33.

21 Terence Karran, "Academic Freedom in Europe: Time for a Magna Charta?" *Higher Education Policy* 22 (2009): 168.

ing international policy documents on academic freedom (e.g., AAUP's 1915 Declaration of Principles on Academic Freedom and Academic Tenure; CODESRIA's 1990 Dar es Salaam Declaration on Academic Freedom and Social Responsibility of Academics; Magna Charta Observatory's 1988 Magna Charta Universitatum; UNESCO's 1997 Recommendation on the Status of Higher Education Teaching Personnel; World University Service's 1988 Lima Declaration on Academic Freedom and the Autonomy of Institutions of Higher Education) identify the need for the substantive freedoms to teach and to undertake research. Similarly, analysis of the national constitutions and relevant legal instruments of the EU states demonstrates that the majority have some form of protection for academic freedom to teach or research.[22]

Drawing on both policy documents and constitutional and legislative instruments, Karran, Beiter, and Mallinson determined academic freedom to have five discrete constituent elements, two of which are substantive, and three of which are supportive.[23] The substantive elements are the freedom to teach and the freedom to research. The freedom to teach habitually includes the right to freely determine what shall be taught; how it shall be taught; who shall be allowed to study; who shall teach; how students' learning may be assessed and graded and who shall receive academic awards. The freedom to research normally includes the right to determine (without duress) what shall (or shall not) be researched; how it shall be researched; who shall research, with whom, and for what purpose research shall be pursued; the methods by which, and avenues through which, research findings shall be disseminated. The supportive elements are tenure, shared governance, and autonomy. Tenure takes the form of employment protection from dismissal awarded to academic staff following an independent and meticulous appraisal by their peers of their academic performance during a probationary period. To guarantee academic freedom, staff must have powers of governance including an equal right to voice their opinions on their institution's educational policies and priorities without the threat of punitive action and have a determinant voice and a prominent role in university decision-making processes along with

22 Karran et al., "Academic Freedom in Contemporary Britain," 566.

23 Karran et al., "Academic Freedom in Contemporary Britain."

the ability to appoint people into positions of managerial authority and hold them to periodic account by agreed democratic processes. Individual autonomy requires that academics can act as free agents in exercising their academic freedom rights, with respect to their professional activities of teaching, research, and shared governance without interference by internal or external individuals or bodies.

These three supportive elements acting in tandem are necessary for academic freedom, but each is individually insufficient for academic freedom to flourish. So, single elements are less individually important than the fact that they mesh together. Hence, where one supportive element falters, it undermines the other two, thereby weakening substantive academic freedom for research and teaching. Thus, if tenure is lacking (as is the case in the UK), academics may be unable to fully participate in shared governance and make objective decisions on, for example, subject teaching methods for fear of losing their jobs.

McCluskey and Winter demonstrate that "academic freedom is undergoing a great change ... colleges need to rethink academic freedom in light of these new technologies."[24] However, when looking at the integration and embedding of digital technologies in HE, it is evident that its impact has thus far been greater with respect to university teaching in terms of reach (i.e., all key aspects of teaching delivery and teaching content consumption are impacted) and scope (both faculty and students are affected), rather than research, not least because the research function does not impact as directly on students as that of teaching (and, therefore, research is subject to marketization and consumer logic in a different range of ways). In addition, governmental restrictions brought in to contain the COVID-19 global pandemic (stay-at-home orders, social distancing in classrooms, discouraging nonessential traveling) accelerated the adoption of open and distance learning approaches in universities and led to universities increasing their investment in educational technologies to maintain continuity of teaching delivery and student learning. The use of such learning technologies has been commonplace in national open universities (e.g., the UK O.U., the German Fernuniversität, and the Spanish Universidad Nacional de Educación a

24 Frank B. McCluskey and Melanie L. Winter, "Academic Freedom in the Digital Age," *On the Horizon* 22 (2014): 136.

Distancia) for many years, while "traditional" universities had only slowly been integrating some elements of technology-enhanced learning. The global pandemic forced a quantum leap in the scope, utilization, and sophistication of new technologically enhanced learning environments across the UK HE sector. Furthermore, the desire to ensure quality distance teaching during the pandemic engendered an interest in the use of these technologies to more closely monitor—for quality assurance purposes—the teaching activities of lecturers and the satisfaction levels of students. More recently, the 2023 Higher Education (Freedom of Speech) Act now requires HE providers to maintain a code of freedom of expression practices. Students are now able to make free speech complaints to the Office for Students (OfS—the UK HE regulatory body) if they believe they have suffered adverse consequences with respect to the revocation of their freedom of speech rights within the classroom. To guard against such legal actions by the OfS, and to ensure that the academic freedom of staff and freedom of expression of students are not undermined, may feasibly require universities to start taking a more proactive approach to digital monitoring, archiving, and analyzing the aspects of teaching and staff–student communications that are captured electronically.

Conceptualizing Digital Governance

The term digital education governance, coined by Williamson, seeks to characterize the complex multifaceted state of contemporary education systems and education institutions in the West, as the extended extract below details:

> Contemporary education is increasingly organized through a densely networked apparatus of computer code, algorithms, database infrastructures, architectures, servers, platforms, and packages; it is managed through new data analytics and other digital platforms that enable the collection, cleaning, and connection of data; it is mediated through websites, data visualizations and graphical forms of communication; it is peopled by new kinds of experts in digital data analysis, knowledge production, and presentation; and it is located in particular institutions, organizations and communities with their technical ways of doing things,

> scientific styles of thinking, professional subjectivities and objectives and aspirations.[25]

In essence, Williamson argues that "digital software technologies, data systems and the code and algorithms that enact them have become powerful yet largely hidden influences in the governing of education."[26] Using Williamson's definition, this chapter details how the practices of digital education governance shape the nature of work in the UK HE system, specifically in relation to how academic freedom is experienced, enabled, and eroded.

An important precursor to the concept of digital education governance was Dunleavey and others' concept of digital era governance.[27] In their conceptualization, following the decline of New Public Management as the "dominant set of managerial and governance ideas of the last two decades" in the UK public sector, a new form of governance emerged that took forward many of the core ideas of New Public Management (disaggregation, competition, and incentivization) but also departed from these via digital technology-enabled changes that brought the promise of productivity benefits at scale via accelerated digitally driven organizational transformation.[28]

A key feature of both digital education governance and digital era governance is the affordances that digital transformation brings in terms of what is in the literature called either digital monitoring or surveillance.[29] The two terms are often used interchangeably as there is no clear-cut distinction between the two terms among researchers and practitioners, although sometimes digital monitoring is used to refer to less exploitative forms of digital surveillance.[30] Here, as the focus is on working conditions, the term digital surveillance will be used. In the marketized UK HE sector, digital surveillance can be a powerful tool for improving the consumer (student) experi-

25 Williamson, "Digital Education Governance," 3.

26 Williamson, "Digital Education Governance," 4.

27 Patrick Dunleavy et al., "Public Management Is Dead—Long Live Digital-Era Governance," *Journal of Public Administration Research and Theory* 16 (2006): 467.

28 Dunleavy et al., "Public Management Is Dead," 478.

29 Sara Riso, "Monitoring and Surveillance of Workers in the digital Age," *European Foundation for the Improvement of Living and Working Conditions*, www.eurofound.europa.eu/data/digitalisation/research-digests/monitoring-and-surveillance-of-workers-in-the-digital-age.

30 Riso, "Monitoring and Surveillance of Workers in the Digital Age."

ence. For example, learning analytics systems can help universities identify students at risk of dropping out or students with learning behavior correlating with poor performance (poor attendance at class, low engagement with learning materials) and then prompt faculty to make interventions that can decrease the likelihood of student dropout or increase the likelihood of student success.[31] Learning analytics can also help universities and tutors measure the effectiveness of different learner engagement strategies, which can then feed into institutional approaches to teaching and learning going forward.[32] However, digital surveillance systems and processes are often designed along business-centric or consumer-centric lines, which can mean that the surveillance regimes that they produce can work against the interests of the worker and worsen working conditions through increased worker stress and lower worker autonomy.[33]

A third related concept is that of digital HE.[34] Castañeda and Selwyn see the infusion of digital into HE as something that is furthering the neoliberalization of HE through "the reconfiguration of educational practices and relations into forms that can be quantified and exchanged; governance practices are increasingly directed by market rationales, supported and fostered by principles of international ranking based competition."[35] For Selwyn, one of the most visible manifestations of this is the increased use of online metrics, measurements, and "analytics" by universities to monitor, assess, and profile academic performance on multiple levels (that of their faculty, that of their subject, and on the individual level).[36]

Without digital HE, it is not possible for digital governance to take root.[37] In the context of academic freedom, digital HE brings both threats and

31 Niall Sclater, Alice Peasgood, and Joel Mullan, "Learning Analytics in Higher Education: A Review of UK and International Practice," *JISC*, www.jisc.ac.uk/sites/default/files/learning-analytics-in-he-v2_0.pdf.

32 Sclater et al., "Learning Analytics in Higher Education."

33 Trade Union Congress, "Technology Managing People: The Worker Experience," www.tuc.org.uk/sites/default/files/2020-11/Technology_Managing_People_Report_2020_AW_Optimised.pdf.

34 Neil Selwyn, *Digital Technology and the Contemporary University: Degrees of Digitization* (London: Routledge, 2014).

35 Linda Castañeda and Neil Selwyn, "More Than Tools? Making Sense of the Ongoing Digitizations of Higher Education," *International Journal of Educational Technology in Higher Education* 15 (2018): 6.

36 Selwyn, *Digital Technology and the Contemporary University.*

37 Selwyn, *Digital Technology and the Contemporary University*; Williamson, "Digital Education Governance."

opportunities.[38] For example, new innovative digitally enabled research methods create opportunities to conduct new kinds of research not hitherto possible or feasible.[39] With this can come new expectations of academic worker skills, performance, and output and repositioning of the esteem in which certain disciplines are held (e.g., high-tech agri-robotics research can become more fashionable and institutionally prioritized compared to language research using traditional research methods). On the other hand, digital governance, concerned as it is with improving how universities govern academic staff performance, brings threats to the status quo of academic freedom through its focus on continually furthering the layers of academic worker surveillance.[40] After all, as Hare argues, technology is not neutral and should not be seen as neutral.[41] For Hare, technology is best understood as being ideologically representative of the political and historical systems from which they emerged and it is worth considering whose ends they serve the most (e.g., institutionally implemented technologies chosen by university management, while bringing benefits for all, may have particular employer–employee power relation benefits for university management).[42]

Research Methodology

This chapter draws on the open-text data gathered from a survey of the UK University and College Union (UCU) members into their views of how organizational digital technology has shaped their experiences of academic freedom. The survey comprised fifty-plus questions (mostly Likert-type questions) mapped to the key aspects of academic freedom detailed earlier. The UCU contributed to the survey design, in particular colleagues from the equality and policy teams. The survey comprised six sections. The first section sought demographic and employment information from respondents. The second section explored respondents' views on academic freedom and

38 Selwyn, *Digital Technology and the Contemporary University.*

39 For an overview of the University of Aberdeen's cutting-edge digital research case studies, see University of Aberdeen, "Enabling Discovery & Innovation | Digital Research," www.abdn.ac.uk/research/digital-research/index.php.

40 Williamson, "Digital Education Governance."

41 Stephanie Hare, *Technology Is Not Neutral: A Short Guide to Technology* (London: London Publishing Partnership, 2022).

42 Hare, *Technology Is Not Neutral.*

digital technology. The third section looked at digital governance and academic freedom in teaching, while the fourth section explored digital governance and academic freedom in research. The fifth section explored the trajectory of digital governance, and the closing section looked at freedom of speech and academic freedom in the context of recent government legislation. Each of those sections predominantly comprised Likert-type questions, but all also contained two or more open-text questions. This chapter solely focuses on and utilizes the open-text responses related to teaching.

The survey was distributed to all UCU members in May 2021 via dedicated email bulletins and featured in the UCU weekly newsletter. The survey received more than 2,100 responses over four weeks and generated over 242,000 words of open-text data. The open-text data was then thematically analyzed and the data was allocated to predetermined analytical themes based on the definition of academic freedom elaborated by Karran, Beiter, and Mallinson.[43] As discussed earlier, the Karran, Beiter, and Mallinson definition breaks down academic freedom into two substantive elements (which comprise multiple associated liberties) and three supportive elements.

Findings and Discussion

With the move in Western economies toward a digital society, there has been increasing digitalization of various aspects of life and a corresponding digitalization of work in general, including university academic work.[44] As a consequence of these changes, the variables that shape how academic freedom is operationalized, experienced, and takes form are also starting to take a digital turn and evolve.[45] For example, how universities direct, manage,

43 Virginia Braun and Victoria Clarke, *Thematic Analysis: A Practical Guide* (London: Sage, 2022); Karran et al., "Academic Freedom in Contemporary Britain."

44 Department for Digital, Culture, Media & Sport, "Policy Paper: UK Digital Strategy," www.gov.uk/government/publications/uks-digital-strategy/uk-digital-strategy; Jessamy Perriam, *Understanding Digital Societies* (London: Sage, 2021); Adi Kuntsman and Esperanza Miyake, *Paradoxes of Digital Disengagement: In Search of the Opt-Out Button* (London: University of Westminster Press, 2022); Deborah Lupton, *The Quantified Self: A Sociology of Self-Tracking* (Cambridge: Polity Press, 2016); Phoebe V. Moore, Pav Akhtar, and Martin Upchurch, "Digitalisation of Work and Resistance," in *Humans and Machines at Work: Dynamics of Virtual Work*, ed. Phoebe V. Moore, Martin Upchurch, and Xanthe Whittaker (Cham: Palgrave Macmillan, 2018), 17; Catherine Edelhard Tømte et al., "Digitalisation in Higher Education: Mapping Institutional Approaches for Teaching and Learning," *Quality in Higher Education* 25 (2019): 98.

45 Selwyn, *Digital Technology and the Contemporary University.*

and evaluate staff is taking a digital turn. In the UK, within an ideological framework that privileges the belief that academics must be accountable for every hour of their time, universities use digital workloading systems to allocate how much time academics spend on teaching, research, and administration.[46] In addition to deprofessionalizing academic work, as the data below shows, this links to the levels of academic freedom one has as the workload an academic is allocated structurally shapes that academic's realistic level of achievement. With these changes come both new opportunities *for* academic freedom (such as enabling new modes of teaching and research) but also new threats *to* academic freedom (such as greater surveillance and accountability).

While some of these threats from digital governance can be overt and are well known (such as the impact of research metrics and rankings on the *freedom to research*), some of these threats are less perceptible. This can be because these threats functioning as an invisible technology of power whereby adverse consequences are experienced, but the causes are difficult to identify; or, alternately, because these threats do not represent a tangible threat to academic freedom at the current time, but rather they contain the seeds of potential threats that may fruition in the future (e.g., the employee surveillance potential of Microsoft Office's 365 is only being realized now despite Microsoft's Office product having been in wide use in the UK HE for more than two decades and has long contained untapped digital surveillance potential).[47] As such, the challenges that digital governance brings to academic freedom can be conceptualized in a number of ways. The section that follows maps the threats that digital governance poses to one of Karran, Beiter, and Mallinson's substantive elements of academic freedom—the *freedom to teach*.[48]

Freedom to teach is one of academic freedom's two substantive *elements* and comprises six associated liberties.[49] These are the freedom to determine what shall be taught (i.e., the determining of course content), the freedom to determine how the content shall be taught (i.e., pedagogic approach), the

46 David Kernohan, "A Beginner's Guide to Academic Workload Modelling," *Wonkhe*, February 8, 2019, https://wonkhe.com/blogs/a-beginners-guide-to-academic-workload-modelling.

47 Byung-Chul Han, *Psychopolitics: Neoliberalism and New Technologies of Power* (London: Verso, 2017).

48 Karran et al., "Academic Freedom in Contemporary Britain."

49 Karran et al., "Academic Freedom in Contemporary Britain."

freedom to determine who shall teach (via transparent selection procedures), the freedom to determine whom shall be taught (the right to determine and enforce entry standards), the freedom to determine how students' progress shall be evaluated (assessment methods), and, finally, the freedom to determine whether students shall progress (via marking criteria and grade determination). Four of these associated liberties will be explored in depth: the determination of course content; the choice of pedagogical approach; the selection of assessment methods; and determining student grades based on expert academic judgment and disciplinary expertise.

Digital Education Governance: The Determination of Course Content and Pedagogic Approach

Recent years have seen an increase in more muscular quality assurance in the UK HE sector, with the launch of the Teaching Excellence Framework (TEF) in 2017, the creation of the OfS in 2018, and the impact that those two macro-changes have had within the meso-environments of universities (e.g., setting up of TEF teams, aligning institutional priorities to the new metrics) that faculty function in.[50] Furthermore, with the pandemic-induced move in UK universities to emergency remote learning and the postpandemic new normal of universities maintaining an enlarged digital teaching and learning provision, there has been an increased public debate about the need to assure the quality of education that universities provide to students.[51] While, in principle, the focus on quality assurance in the UK HE sector undoubtedly brings a large number of benefits to the student experience (the raising of standards, the eradication of variability in quality levels, the reduction of randomness in teaching delivery, and the providing of students with a clear set of expectations to navigate), the ways in which quality assurance is operationalized in the contemporary UK university can be problematic. UK universities tend to take a highly managerial approach focused on prioritizing student (consumer) views over academic staff views while taking advantage of one of the key affordances of digital transformation: digital technology's

50 Office for Students, "About," www.officeforstudents.org.uk/about/; Office for Students, "About the TEF," www.officeforstudents.org.uk/advice-and-guidance/teaching/about-the-tef/.

51 Sir Michael Barber, *Gravity Assist: Propelling Higher Education towards a Brighter Future: Digital Teaching and Learning Review* (Bristol: Office for Students, 2021).

ability to enable a certain form of digital governance through easy en-masse comparing of one discipline against another using standardized across-the-board metrics. The impact of this on academics was reflected by a survey respondent who commented:

> There has been a remarkable increase in Quality Assurance monitoring and reporting paperwork, in the past 10 years ... This work is time-consuming and not accounted for in workload planning, and it imposes a stultifying, bean-counting mentality on creative thought in teaching. Quality in teaching is driven by the ethical standards inherent to the disciplines and by the ethical standards we are raised with as social beings.

The same respondent further explained how the use of one-size-fits-all approaches facilitated by digital governance is leading to the inappropriate application of generic institution-wide quality standards:

> The University is implementing a one-size-fits-all approach that fails to recognize the differences in subject areas, their varied content, modes of teaching, resources, and the like. This is only possible because of the move to online systems. It is not the online systems per se, but the fact that now the efficiencies of e.g., life sciences, are evaluated against the efficiencies of philosophy, which they never used to be.

Additionally, survey respondents recognized both how quality processes are necessary in order to raise standards and also how, in order to meet their quality enhancement and quality assurance goals, university management can take an unnecessarily strong focus on enforcing standardization through increasing digital surveillance and monitoring. Another survey respondent stated:

> Academic freedom in teaching has diminished. Academics are no longer able to mark and deliver teaching exactly how they want to, but that's not necessarily always a bad thing. Some people have never cared about teaching and delivered very low-quality teaching. Being able to hold them accountable for poor performance is a good thing.

However, some survey respondents identified how one consequence of this increasingly forceful quality assurance monitoring has been to empower certain individuals who misuse their newly acquired power. For example, one respondent reported: "Some people can abuse power to make me work harder as a form of institutional bullying. Monitoring is healthy and necessary as long as it is used for good (learning, improvement, etc) and not bad (damaging probation, creating an intentionally bad reputation, etc)."

Furthermore, the data gathered by the survey showed that digital education governance impacts the "what shall be taught" element of academic freedom in a number of important ways. These can be conceptualized as university management exerting two types of pressure on staff, namely hard pressures and soft pressures. Hard pressures constitute institutional practices, such as staff with quality leadership responsibilities making use of their enhanced privileged access to digital systems to overtly and covertly inspect online course sites (i.e., Virtual Learning Environment [VLE] or Learning Management System [LMS] course sites on platforms such as Blackboard, Moodle, and Canvas) and to score VLE course sites against specific pedagogical criteria. One survey respondent reported:

> We've appointed an admin role to a colleague (pity them!) whose time is being wasted by checking everyone's [VLE] pages to make sure that they meet with the university-mandated template (photo on the front page of lecturers' webpages, with a welcome message, etc.). I can see a change not far off where this job is taken by someone who has a strong sense that every module (and not just their pages) should be uniform.

To understand why UK universities now closely monitor some of the perhaps more mundane aspects of academic work, it is important to understand the move toward standardization in UK universities and how this intersects with institutional spending on expensive technologies and the need for an institution to evidence a return on investment for their technology spend, as the same respondent elaborated:

> The university has regularized all assessment structures to a single template, and because this has led to student "dissatisfaction," now pressures academics to make "full use" of the potential to use the [VLE] for dis-

> cussions/quizzes, etc., however inappropriate to the content/learning outcomes. I think it's because they've invested so much money in the platform that they now need to prove to everyone that it's making a measurable "difference"; it's all very top-down, [with] edicts and memos from on high.

As the survey respondent's quote above demonstrates, part of the threat from digital surveillance comes from academics having the awareness that their VLE course may be inspected at any time and that they may get sanctioned as a result. This potential of being inspected at any time during the term can act as a deterrent (i.e., it can deter academics from noncompliant behaviors). This illustrates how the move toward digital transformation by universities has brought the affordances of surveillance capitalism to the HE sector, specifically to the micro-environment of a university workplace, and more specifically to university management.[52] Zuboff defines surveillance capitalism as a system that makes use of surveilled human experience for capitalistic ends (i.e., in the case of a university, to make use of surveilled data for more comprehensive employee performance management or to more closely monitor employee adherence to institutional goals).[53] A key feature of surveillance capitalism is what Zuboff labels *instrumentation power*, namely, the engineering of behavior through the act of surveillance and the use of surveillance data.[54] Instrumentation power allows certain managerial practices—such as the one detailed by this respondent below—to happen without staff having recourse to means with which to effectively push back or prevent:

> Up until recently, we have had the freedom to manage the curriculum and make use of the metrics that are taken to develop our teaching. However, during the pandemic (and possibly just before), these freedoms have been eroded and decisions are being made outside of our program that have a big impact on the content and teaching of the program.

52 Shoshana Zuboff, *The Age of Surveillance Capitalism: The Fight for a Human Future at the New Frontier of Power* (London: Profile Books, 2018).

53 Zuboff, *The Age of Surveillance Capitalism.*

54 Zuboff, *The Age of Surveillance Capitalism.*

The "freedom to determine pedagogy" aspect of academic freedom is also under threat from digital governance. Two specific aspects of the digital university pose threats to this freedom. The first threat comes from the move in the UK HE sector to the increased normalization of online or hybrid delivery.[55] This aspect will not be analyzed here, as on-campus teaching was the predominant focus of the research instrument. The second threat to the *freedom to "determine pedagogy"* comes from the omnipresence of lecture capture technology in the UK HE sector. As a consequence of the widespread adoption of lecture capture technology and the associated institutional policies governing its use, the university lecture is increasingly becoming less of a time-bound geographically located private experience between the teacher and those being taught (i.e., a lecture that takes place at a certain time in a specific building and that is experienced in real time by those present). Instead, through the use of lecture recording and hybrid delivery, a lecture is becoming an event that is often recorded and can be rewatched outside of its original context including by those not present, and the content covered can be used to discipline academic staff should hard evidence be needed to back up a student claim (e.g., around a microaggression or views given in relation to something politically sensitive).

In the UK HE sector, Panopto and Echo 360 are the two main lecture recording systems in use.[56] Panopto and Echo 360 both enable the normalization of lecture recording across a university by either allowing staff to manually record their sessions or for the institution to automate the recordings centrally (without staff needing to configure anything).[57] The recordings can then have captions either manually added or added via an AI caption service. Additionally, statistical records are kept of each lecturer's engagement with the system as well as student engagement with individual videos, and videos on a module and program level.[58] Whether academics choose to engage with lecture recording systems tends to be shaped by two factors. One is whether the institutional policy on lecture record-

55 Barber, *Gravity Assist.*

56 Panopto, "Remote Video Recording," www.panopto.com/features/video-recording/remote-recording/; Echo 360, "Learning, Inspired," https://echo360.com; UCISA, "Technology Enhanced Learning Pulse Survey," www.ucisa.ac.uk/News-and-Blogs/News/2022/November/~/link.aspx?_id=5326446515804E10A0E53E7B964115AD&_z=z.

57 Panopto, "Remote Video Recording"; Echo 360, "Learning, Inspired."

58 Panopto, "Remote Video Recording"; Echo 360, "Learning, Inspired."

ing specifies de facto mandatory recording. This tends to be done via the use of a lecturer "opt-out" policy framing, which is sometimes combined with automated recording of teaching sessions based on timetable system information.[59] When lecture recording is institutionally embedded in this way, it can become culturally difficult for academics to opt out. Two is whether the institutional policy specifies lecturer "opt-in." In opt-in systems, the use of lecture recording tends to be lower as use is not forced but rather an individual autonomy decision.

As organizational norms shift to teaching sessions being recorded as the cultural default through lecture capture technologies, a number of facets of how university teaching is delivered are changing. Firstly, the style of delivery is evolving. Being recorded without a lecturer's explicit opt-in can impact the freedom with which a lecturer delivers their lectures, and this reduced sense of autonomy can impact how much satisfaction a lecturer gets from their teaching, as this respondent details: "The recording of lectures is particularly problematic. Observed behavior changes behavior and adds another layer of emotional stress. It is impossible to be oneself when being recorded and sadly that has removed the sense of fun/enjoyment from my teaching interactions."

Compounding this, the very fact of a session being recorded can also impact students' engagement in class: "We now have compulsory lecture capture and this will severely limit the nature and atmosphere of the lecture, and the engagement of the students within this forum." In terms of power relations at work, the forcing of lecture recording can also shift some power away from the lecturer and to the student and lead to increased student-as-consumer behavior, as one respondent declared: "I feel constantly watched. In the past, if I made a mistake while explaining something during a live lecture it would either go noticed by students and have no impact on their learning (if the slide contains correct info). Now some students are constantly picking on tiny errors lecturers make because they can review a recording."

---

59 Manchester Metropolitan University, "Policy on Lecture Capture," www.mmu.ac.uk/media/mmuacuk/content/documents/information-systems/help-guides/DRAFT-Lecture-Capture-Policy.pdf; University of Edinburgh, "Lecture Recording Policy," www.ed.ac.uk/information-services/learning-technology/media-hopper-replay/help-and-support/frequently-asked-questions/lecture-recording-policy.

Furthermore, as well as empowering students in certain ways, mandatory lecture recording can also empower university management in new ways by providing them with additional sources of information (evidence) that can be (mis)used against staff years into the future, leading one respondent to comment:

> The recording and uploading of my lectures means that I have to approach with more caution in case what I am talking about is taken out of context as I am not there to clarify what I mean. This restricts the kinds of topics I am willing to cover because I'm anxious about how the recording will be read or received in the future.

As the respondent above shows, the use of lecture recording technology can be key in shaping how some aspects of academic freedom are operationalized. Lecturers can feel more self-conscious when teaching and fearful that any mistakes made in the normal course of delivering a lecture may be used against them in the future by either students or management. Hence teaching staff can feel pressured to deliver sessions in a more conservative way in order to reduce the risk of having a mistake that would otherwise be of little consequence captured on film. In addition, the use of lecture capture technology impacts where a lecturer stands during a lecture (e.g., the lecturer ought to stand closer to the podium in order for the microphone to capture their voice optimally), the lecturer's teaching style (more didactic as this mode of delivery lends itself better to lecture capture), and audience engagement (students may feel self-conscious about having their voice or questions captured on recordings and so reduce the kind of student engagement that would be captured in the recording).

The Impact of Digital Education Governance on Assessment and Grading

In a contemporary UK university, the use of centralized digital student information systems (SIS) and data warehouses has facilitated new forms of management practice based on institution-wide real-time surveillance of key student performance metrics, including student grades. While ostensibly the surveillance that SIS and university data warehouses provide is of student behavior (e.g., attendance at timetabled events, visits to the university library, engagement with support services), performance (grades), and outcomes, poor student performance is often seen as the responsibility of the teaching staff and solely as a consequence of bad teaching or poor support. Thus, one respondent declared: "I feel we are pressured to have particular pass rates irrespective of student performance and that poor student performance is viewed as a failing on our part rather than a joint failure." In this way, SIS and data warehouses also become tools with which university leaders create new layers of academic worker performance to manage.

One of the most popular SIS in the UK HE sector is Tribal's Strategic Information Technology Services (SITS: Vision) system.[60] Tribal Group's system provides universities with a sophisticated data infrastructure that connects their VLE (e.g., Blackboard, Moodle, Canvas) and other systems to Tribal Group's SIS, with the explicit aim to "transform the way staff collects, collate, analyze, share and act on information."[61] The system is able to map the contours of an individual student's experience at university via various data points, and the data gathered can be used in real time to identify at-risk students and determine interventions to shape student outcomes.

Many UK universities have now set up planning and business intelligence teams and maintain data warehouses to power institution-wide data-informed decision-making.[62] The University of St. Andrews' data warehouse "contains data taken from multiple source systems ... so that means it contains data about students, staff, accommodation, finance, our estate, etc."[63] The University of Edinburgh's data warehouse works similarly: "The Data Warehouse is a central repository of data for reports and dashboards that combine data from across the University and/or which show trends over time ... You can use the data from the Warehouse to write reports or create dashboards of strategic information."[64]

---

60 Tribal Group, "SITS-Vision," www.tribalgroup.com/solutions/student-information-systems/sits-vision.

61 Tribal Group, "SITS-Vision."

62 See, e.g., Glasgow Caledonian University, "Strategy, Planning and Business Intelligence," www.gcu.ac.uk/aboutgcu/supportservices/strategyplanningandbusinessintelligence; University of Manchester, "Business Intelligence," www.staffnet.manchester.ac.uk/planning/bi/; University of Bristol, "Strategic Planning," www.bristol.ac.uk/planning/strategicplanning/.

63 University of St Andrews, "Data Warehouse," www.st-andrews.ac.uk/staff/tech/datawarehouse/.

64 University of Edinburgh, "Data Warehouse," www.ed.ac.uk/information-services/enterprise-architecture/university-data/data-warehouse.

While these systems can provide rich business intelligence that enables better student support, improved student outcomes, and a richer student experience, as well as an institution-wide view of key metrics (mean grades, grade point average, number of fails, percentage of fails, etc.), they also usher in more data-driven ways of working and managing faculty. Specifically, they enable great managerial surveillance of academic work, which can encroach on academic autonomy with respect to the *academic freedom to determine student progression* (via the creation of marking criteria and determining grades) and *the freedom to determine how students' progress shall be evaluated* (through the selection of appropriate assessment methods). Universities, in particular, have dedicated significant attention to digital monitoring of student grade performance, partly due to pressure from the OfS to monitor grades more actively.[65]

The affordances of such tools can—in the context of the marketized UK HE sector and where student satisfaction has such great import and universities rely on student fees to stay solvent[66]—manifest in surveillance practices that lead to artificial grade inflation, as demonstrated in the two quotes below from respondents:

> I have noticed grade inflation in colleagues and a preponderance of passing students on the borderline of failing because it creates less hassle ultimately and the University will find a way to pass students. Also, because fee-paying students can now see pass rates, they will opt for higher ones this provides an external driver to pass more so courses are maintained rather than shut down. This is another form of monitoring interacting with students becoming fee-paying. Fees are one of the worst things to happen to universities.

> Since NSS and COVID-19, academic work is now about satisfying students and telling them what they need to learn ... the focus is on helping

65 Simon Baker, "Marking Boundaries and Algorithms Shift in Grade Inflation Row," *Times Higher Education*, February 3, 2021, www.timeshighereducation.com/news/marking-boundaries-and-algorithms-shift-gradeinflation-row.

66 University of Southampton, "Rankings and Reputation," www.southampton.ac.uk/about/rankings-reputation; Thomas Weston, "In Focus: Financial Pressures on Higher Education," *House of Lords Library*, March 21, 2023, https://lordslibrary.parliament.uk/financial-pressures-on-higher-education/.

> them to know what is being assessed ... It is about giving students high marks now and why grade inflation is the norm.

In essence, as the above quotes show, the combination of HE marketization, repositioning of students as consumers, and digital education governance intersects in a complex range of ways that impact various aspects of an academic's individual autonomy (e.g., marking student work is no longer just about marking student work; academics can feel a pressure to give higher marks and a need to consider the impact of their actions on future student recruitment numbers when simply trying to mark student work fairly).

Respondents attributed this erosion of academic freedom to the form of UK HE marketization that the current marriage of HE managerialism and digital technologies enables, as the below two respondents remarked:

> My employer seems to have lost interest in academic standards. My employer is very keen on grade inflation. My employer does not care about some forms of academic misconduct by students. My employer is focused on generating income by getting and retaining as many students as possible.

> Over a number of years, [my institution] has implemented different ways of uplifting marks, in a way that bears no relation to academic standards or the evaluation of work made by module teams. It has also resulted in grade inflation, ... and runs counter to the principles of academic freedom.

The data gathered also indicated that academics' abilities to assert their academic freedom and resist institutional pressure are dependent on a range of factors such as age, experience, and role seniority. As one respondent commented: "There are pressures for grade inflation and they will work through [the institution], so younger lecturers will award higher marks than more senior colleagues."

Grade inflation is indeed a significant problem in the UK HE sector and is a symptom of the dysfunctional behavior that a marketized HE sector incentivizes.[67] For example, the percentage of degrees classified as first-

67 Susan Lapworth, "Getting to Grips with Grade Inflation," *Office for Students*, July 11, 2019, www.officeforstudents.org.uk/news-blog-and-events/blog/getting-to-grips-with-grade-inflation.

class honor at the University of Surrey rose from 22.0 percent in 2010–11 to 50.1 percent in 2016–17.[68] The OfS has multiple times spoken out against grade inflation, warning that the UK HE sector needs to be more reliable in degree standards over time (and between institutions) and that the current situation of grade inflation risks devaluing UK university degrees in the eyes of employers.[69] The combination of digital surveillance practices, marketization incentives, and universities' customer orientation has led to the eroding of academic freedom in the area of student assessment, a poorer academic worker experience, and, in some respects, an inferior student experience as academic staff feel "pressure to grade higher ... trend towards blander feedback to students, pressure to adjust assessment in order to meet targets and workload allocations."

Greater institutional surveillance and monitoring have also led to institutions encouraging cultural conservatism in assessment design. As one respondent noted: "Currently the main issue with academic freedom in teaching is poorly thought out overriding institutional choices (by managers) especially restrictions on assessment types." To enforce these new regimes, as another respondent commented: "Managers use 'student voice' and spurious evidential claims to manipulate academics into complying with their demands."

Some respondents were clear in attributing these changes in their working conditions to broader societal evolutions and the ideology underpinning recent government reform: "Many of these changes are the result of the marketization of higher education and the pressures from government and the OfS. Monitoring and surveillance processes are a direct response to these pressures." The combination of this cultural drive to standardize assessment along with the UK HE sector's intense focus on specific forms of quality assurance has also led to the creation of new structures of bureaucracy for academics to navigate, the kind of bureaucracy that can be stifling for individual autonomy and discourage the assertation of academic freedom. One respondent commented: "There is very little leeway to change the module content and assessment. Any module review/change request has to

---

68 Sarah Harris, "Number of Students Getting First Class Degrees Sky-Rockets as Universities Are Accused of Grade Inflation: Making 'Desmond' (2.2 Awards) Almost Extinct," *Daily Mail*, December 18, 2018, www.dailymail.co.uk/news/article-6510157/Number-students-getting-class-degrees-sky-rockets.html.

69 Lapworth, "Getting to Grips with Grade Inflation."

go through a time-consuming bureaucratic process. Whatever the change, it could be rejected depending on who you are. It is all politics and nepotism to the core."

In the extended quote below, another respondent echoed these sentiments:

> Academic freedom in teaching has been declining as a result of increased centralized administrative control through so-called quality processes. Module design, including content, teaching methods, assessment structure, etc., goes through a lengthy process and approval by college committees—as does any subsequent change to a module. This stifles creativity in designing and delivering teaching and reduces tutors' ability to adapt and respond flexibly to the needs of students in an individual cohort. There is very little autonomy when it comes to setting assessments, for example, and none when it comes to the administration of marks.

As the quote above details, centralized quality teams are becoming increasingly forceful in shaping not just the broad work of academics but also increasingly pedagogic activities on the micro level. This, as respondent data shows, is an academic freedom issue as it is impacting institutional autonomy.

Although making changes to module assessment now requires the buy-in of a greater range of colleagues, this was not seen as stifling by all respondents. Respondent data indicated that the influence of some colleagues (such as those in their team or of fellow disciplinary academics) was welcomed more than that of certain categories of others (such as those from central teams or nonacademics).

> To me, academic freedom to make choices regarding course content, grading, assessment type, etc., means not absolute individual freedom, but freedom for decisions to be reached consensually by academics in the same Faculty/Department, prioritizing the benefit to students, without interference from administrators, and without pressure for conformity between different subjects. The pandemic has increased the workload and has increased opportunities for monitoring. The latter has both positive and negative aspects, depending on how it's used.

As the data above shows, the digital transformation of the UK HE sector has enabled greater institutional oversight and employee surveillance in a form that furthers the marketization of the UK HE sector, strengthens student (consumer) interests, and erodes academic autonomy in particular and highly specific ways.

Conclusion

Drawing on respondent data gathered from a survey of UCU members, this chapter has shown how the digital transformation of UK universities has led to significant changes in academic worker autonomy, and this chapter has detailed some of the ways in which employer-implemented technology has altered power relations across campuses and eroded academic freedom. One overt manifestation is in how digital technologies enable greater employee surveillance and better performance analytics potential. These combine to create new areas of knowledge asymmetry between university management and university workers and lead to new incentive and disincentive structures that can help align worker behavior with organizational objectives. Unsurprisingly, the two primary beneficiaries of digital transformation in the capitalist marketized UK HE system are university management and students (i.e., the consumers of the HE product provided by UK universities).

To prevent further erosion of academic freedom in teaching, there is a need in the UK academy for more muscular pushback and intelligent resistance against digital surveillance. A range of collective and individual tactics are required for this resistance to be effective. For individual academics, there is a foundational need to better appreciate digital technologies' role in shaping one's autonomy at work and one's role in power structures at work along the dimensions discussed in this chapter. For academic unions, there is a need to raise awareness among members of digital technology being a key variable in determining working conditions and for members to be actively aware of the nature of the threats to individual autonomy from digital technology. The UK is seen as a global leader in HE and is considered to have the second strongest education system in the world and the strongest in Europe, and the ways in which the UK HE sector develops tend to be reproduced in other countries (e.g., the Research Excellence Framework as a mechanism for distributing governmental research funds has been replicated in a number of other nations).[70] As such, while this chapter focuses only on the UK HE sector, much of the analysis may also be applicable to the HE system in other highly developed nations, especially those countries whose governments have sought to marketize their HE sector along UK lines and are now embracing the digitally driven transformation of the HE sector. There is a need for research exploring further the impact of institutionally implemented technology on managerial practices in universities as well as digitally enabled quality assurance processes and the relationship between these and academic freedom.

70 Quacquarelli Symonds, "The Strongest Higher Education Systems by Country," www.qs.com/the-strongest-higher-education-systems-by-country-overview/.

About the Contributors

Editors

Frédéric Mégret

Frédéric Mégret is Professor of Law and the holder of the Hans & Tamar Oppenheimer Chair in Public International Law. Previously he was a William Dawson scholar from 2015 to 2023 and the holder of the Canada Research Chair on the Law of Human Rights and Legal Pluralism from 2006 to 2015. In November 2022, he received an honorary doctorate from the University of Copenhagen in recognition of his work in international law. He was named to the Hans & Tamar Oppenheimer Chair in Public International Law for a seven-year term, starting September 1, 2023. He is currently coauthoring a book titled *Diasporas and International Law* with Larissa van den Herik (Leiden University). He is the coeditor with Philip Alston of *The United Nations and Human Rights: A Critical Appraisal* (Oxford University Press, 2020); with Immi Tallgren of *The Dawn of a Discipline: International Criminal Justice and Its Early Exponents* (Cambridge University Press, 2020), and with Kevin Jon Heller, Sarah Nouwen, Jens David Ohlin, and Darryl Robinson of *The Oxford Handbook of International Criminal Law* (Oxford University Press, 2020). He is also the author of *Le Tribunal pénal international pour le Rwanda* (Pedone, 2002). Prior to joining McGill University, he was an assistant professor at the Faculty of Law of the University of Toronto, a Boulton fellow at McGill University, and a research associate at the European University Institute in Florence. His scholarship has appeared in the *European Journal of International Law*, the *American Journal of International Law*, the *Modern Law Review*, the *Leiden Journal of International Law*, *International Criminal Justice*, *Human Rights Quarterly*, the *International Journal of Human Rights*, the *Human Rights Law Review*, the *Melbourne Journal of International Law*,

Transnational Legal Theory, *Global Constitutionalism*, the *Canadian Yearbook of International Law*, the *Revue Québécoise de droit international*, the *Revue belge de droit international*, *Global Governance*, the *Harvard Human Rights Law Journal*, and the *McGill Law Journal*, among others.

Nandini Ramanujam

Nandini Ramanujam is the Codirector and Director of Programs of the Center for Human Rights and Legal Pluralism at McGill University's Faculty of Law. She also directs the International Human Rights Internship Program as well as the Independent Human Rights Internships Program. She is the McGill representative for the Scholars at Risk Network and served on the Steering Committee of the Scholars at Risk Network, Canada section from 2016 to 2022. Her research and teaching interests include law and development, institutions and governance, economic justice, food security and food safety, the role of civil society and the fourth estate (media) in the promotion of the rule of law, as well as the exploration of interconnections between field-based human rights work and theoretical discourses. Before joining McGill's Faculty of Law, she was involved in the successful systemic reform of higher education in the former communist countries of Eastern Europe and the Soviet Union, including Aga Khan's Central Asian University and Smolny College in St. Petersburg. She served as the Director of the Higher Education Support Program of the Open Society Institute in Budapest and the Regional Director of the Baltic and Eurasian Programs of Civic Education Project. She received her doctorate in economics from Oxford University for her dissertation titled "Price Mechanism in Russia: Its Role in the Old Planning and the New Markets." She holds an MPhil and an MA in economics with first-class honors from Bhopal University.

Contributors

Jacob T. Levy

Jacob T. Levy is Tomlinson Professor of Political Theory, Chair of the Department of Political Science, and associated faculty in the Department of Philosophy at McGill University. He is the coordinator of McGill's Research Group on Constitutional Studies and was the founding director of McGill's Yan P. Lin Center for the Study of Freedom and Global Orders in the Ancient and Modern Worlds. He is a senior fellow at the Niskanen Center, a distinguished fellow for the study of liberalism and the free society of the Institute for Humane Studies, and a Templeton Adam Smith Tercentenary fellow at the University of Glasgow. He is the author of *The Multiculturalism of Fear* (Oxford University Press, 2000) and *Rationalism, Pluralism, and Freedom* (Oxford University Press, 2014), and editor or coeditor of *Colonialism and Its Legacies*; *Nomos LV: Federalism and Subsidiarity*; and *Interpreting Modernity: Essays on the Work of Charles Taylor.*

Sijbolt Noorda

Dr. Sijbolt Noorda is President Emeritus of the Universiteit van Amsterdam and former president of Universities of the Netherlands. Internationally, he was a board member of the European University Association, the Academic Cooperation Association, and the Magna Charta Observatory. His academic home is in the humanities (biblical studies, classics, cultural history, hermeneutics, and translation). Dr. Noorda writes and gives lectures on teaching and learning in higher education, on ideals and practices of internationalization, on open science, as well as on values and governance issues. He is an independent reviewer and consultant for individual universities and national systems in the European higher education area as well as an expert at the Global University Network for Innovation. In addition, he is and has been on various boards in the Dutch cultural sector and in professional training in the field of performing arts.

Jean-François Gaudreault-Desbiens

Jean-François Gaudreault-DesBiens, FRSC, AdE, is Professor of Law at the University of Montreal, where he was also Dean of Law from 2015 to 2019 and where he held the Canada Research Chair on Comparative and North American Juridical and Cultural Identities from 2006 to 2016. He is currently Vice President, Strategic Communications and Planning at the University of Montreal. Prior to joining the University of Montreal, he taught at the University of Toronto and McGill University. His research interests are constitutional law and federalism (domestic and comparative), fundamental freedoms, constitutional politics, and the anthropology of legal cultures. He has worked extensively on how legal systems grasp cultural identities or participate in their construction, which has led him to work on legal epistemology. He has published several books and more than a hundred scholarly articles in French, English, Spanish, Catalan, Portuguese, and Mandarin.

Zhidong Hao

Zhidong Hao is Emeritus Professor of Sociology at the University of Macau. He obtained his PhD in sociology from the City University of New York in 1995 and taught at both US and Chinese universities. He has researched in sociology of higher education, political sociology, historical sociology, sociology of religion, and sociology of intellectuals and published in journals such as *Higher Education, China Quarterly, Pacific Affairs, Issues and Studies,* the *Journal of Contemporary China, Chinese Sociological Review, China: An International Journal, Review of Religion and Chinese Society*, and so on. His most recent articles include "Totalitarianization and Democratization in Higher Education in China and Their Implication for the Nation's Political Development" (2024) and "What Kind of Nation-State Do They Want to Build: Chinese Intellectuals and Nationalism in Contemporary China" (2023). His most recent books include 《生死存亡十二年：平定縣的抗戰、內戰與土改》(2021) (*Twelve years of Life and Death in Pingding, Shanxi: The War of Resistance against Japan, Civil War, and Land Reform*); *Academic Freedom under Siege: Higher Education in East Asia, the U.S., and Australia* (2020), *Macau History and Society* (2nd ed., 2020); and 《十字路口的知識分子：中國知識工作者的政治變遷》(2019), a Chinese translation of his 2003 book *Intellectuals at a Crossroads: The Changing Politics of China's Knowledge Workers.*

Sejal Parmar

Sejal Parmar is an international human rights scholar and practitioner whose expertise and research interests lie broadly in the field of freedom of expression, such as issues of media freedom, digital rights, and harmful speech, including hate speech and disinformation. She is a senior lecturer in law at the School of Law and Politics at Cardiff University and ESRC/AHRC Academic Policy Fellow in Disinformation and Foreign Policy at the UK Foreign, Commonwealth, and Development Office. She has previously held a range of academic and policy roles, including as Director of the Human Rights Forum, Lecturer at the School of Law at the University of Sheffield, Assistant Professor of Law at the Central European University in Budapest and Vienna, Senior Adviser to the OSCE Representative on Freedom of the Media, and Senior Legal Officer at ARTICLE 19. She regularly acts as a consultant and expert for intergovernmental organizations, human rights NGOs, and technology companies. She was a Co-rapporteur of the Council of Europe Committee of Experts on Combating Hate Speech (ADI/MSI-DIS) and is a member of the academic constituency of the Global Network Initiative and an expert at global freedom of expression at Columbia University. Parmar has published broadly in the field of international human rights law on freedom of expression, including as a coeditor of the *Oxford Handbook on Hate Speech* (forthcoming).

Vincent Wong

Vincent Wong is an assistant professor at the University of Windsor Faculty of Law and a PhD candidate at Osgoode Hall Law School where he researches racial capitalism and status-excluded communities in Canada. Prior to academia, he was a research associate at the International Human Rights Program and African American Policy Forum, as well as a staff lawyer at the Chinese and Southeast Asian Legal Clinic in Toronto. He holds a Juris Doctor from the University of Toronto Faculty of Law as well as a Master of Laws from Columbia Law School, where he was a James Kent Scholar.

Kwadwo Appiagyei-Atua

Kwadwo Appiagyei-Atua is an associate professor at the School of Law, University of Ghana (UG), Legon, Accra, where he teaches public international law and international human rights law. He is a representative lecturer in the LLM Human Rights and Democratisation Programme, Centre for Human Rights, University of Pretoria, South Africa. Kwadwo is a member of the Ghana Bar. He completed his LLB at UG and his professional law degree at the Ghana School of Law. Thereafter, he proceeded to Dalhousie University and McGill University, both in Canada, for his LLM and DCL programs, respectively. He was a Bank of Ireland postdoctoral research fellow at the Irish Centre for Human Rights, National University of Ireland. Kwadwo held a Marie Curie International Incoming Fellowship at Lincoln University, UK, where he conducted research on "Building Academic Freedom and Democracy in Africa." Kwadwo has served as a consultant for various intergovernmental organizations and international civil society organizations such as the United Nations Office on Drugs and Crime (UNODC) on its Education for Justice (E4J) initiative, the Open Society Foundation's Global Program on Drug Policy (GPDP), and Open Society Initiative for West Africa (OSIWA). He is a member of the UN Working Group on Academic Freedom formed as a follow-up to the release of the 2020 report on academic freedom by the then UN Special Rapporteur on the Promotion and Protection of the Right to Freedom of Opinion and Expression. He is also a board member of the Global Observatory on Academic Freedom, Central European University, Vienna, Austria; an ambassador of the Magna Charta Observatory, University of Bologna, Bologna, Italy; and a member of the Academic Freedom Committee of the International Studies Association, University of Connecticut, Storrs, CT, USA. His research interests are in the postcolonial analysis of the historiography of international law, human rights, and academic freedom.

Tamara Thermitus

Ms. Tamara Thermitus, AdE, is *Boulton Senior Fellow* at the McGill University Faculty of Law. Called to the Quebec Bar in 1988, Tamara Thermitus holds a *Master of Laws from McGill University* (2013). Ms. Thermitus was Chair of the Federal Department of Justice's Advisory *Committee on Visible Minorities* (2004–2010) and Chair of the Quebec Bar's *Cultural Communities Committee*. In this capacity, she raised awareness of issues relating to racial discrimination in the profession and the justice system and created training on the social context of the law at the École du Barreau. It was under her leadership that *Développements récents en profilage racial* (2009) was published, the first book on the subject in Quebec. She negotiated the nature and scope of the mandate of the *Truth and Reconciliation Commission of Canada*. Her research focuses on race, feminist theory, restorative justice, racial justice, and the justice system. Recipient of the *Queen Elizabeth Golden Jubilee Medal* (2012), Ms. Thermitus has received numerous awards, including the *Mérite du Barreau du Québec* (2011), making her the first Black lawyer to receive such recognition. She has also received the *Employment Equity and Diversity Leadership Award* (Department of Justice, 2010 and 2016).

Sophie Bisping

Sophie Bisping is currently finishing her BCL/JD degrees at McGill University in Montreal, Canada. Prior to her legal studies, she completed a master's degree in transcultural studies and international public policy at Heidelberg University. Her thesis explored cultural diplomacy between countries that shared a colonial past, focusing on film coproductions. She then worked in public policy at the German Parliament as an international parliamentary fellow.

Angela Campbell

Angela Campbell is a full professor at McGill Faculty of Law and is also Associate Provost (Equity and Academic Policies) of McGill since 2015. Previously, she has served as Associate Dean of Graduate Studies in Law, as Director of the McGill Institute of Comparative Law, and as a convener of the McGill Research Group on Health and Law. She has researched and published in diverse domains, including family and successions law, sexual violence and criminal justice, and equity education.

Liviu Matei

Liviu Matei is a higher education scholar, educator, and policy entrepreneur. He is a professor of higher education and public policy and Head of the School of Education, Communication, and Society at King's College London. He has taught at universities in Europe and the US, consulted extensively in higher education, and conducted applied policy research projects for the Council of Europe, the European Commission, the World Bank, UNESCO, OSCE, other international intergovernmental and non-governmental organizations, and for public authorities and universities in Europe and Asia. He founded and directed the Yehuda Elkana Center for Higher Education, the Global Observatory on Academic Freedom, and the Global Teaching Fellowships Program. As Provost of Central European University, he played a central role in the efforts to safeguard academic freedom and institutional integrity at this university in the face of attacks from the illiberal regime of Viktor Orbán. Liviu Matei is a member of the Board of Trustees of the American University of Central Asia and the Governing Council of Magna Charta Universitaum Observatory. He serves on the editorial boards of *Internationalization of Higher Education: Policy and Practice* and the *European Journal of Higher Education*. His primary areas of expertise include university academic freedom and university autonomy, governance, funding, internationalization of higher education, quality assurance, and history and politics of higher education.

Stephanie Hennette Vauchez

Stephanie Hennette Vauchez is Professor of Public Law at Université Paris Nanterre (France) and a senior fellow at the Institut universitaire de France. She has served as the director of the research center on fundamental rights (CREDOF) at Université Paris Nanterre from 2015 to 2023. Her work focuses on human rights, through a focus on comparative human rights law's core concepts and theoretical underpinnings as well as on the logics that govern their evolution and the challenges it faces. She has published extensively in the fields of law and bioethics, religious freedom and secularism, emergency regimes, and antidiscrimination law. Her publications in English include (with Ruth Rubio Marin) *The Cambridge Companion to Gender and Law* (Cambridge University Press, 2022); "Can Religious Schools Discriminate on the Basis of Religion? A Comparative Law Approach," *Connecticut Journal of International Law*, forthcoming; "Taming the Exception? Lessons from the Routinization of States of Emergency in France," *International Journal of Constitutional Law*, 2022, vol. 5, pp. 1793–1819.

Andrey A. Shcherbovich

Andrey Shcherbovich was an O'Brien Fellow in Residence at McGill Centre for Human Rights and Legal Pluralism from 2021 to 2023. He graduated from the National Research University Higher School of Economics, Faculty of Law (Department of International Law), Moscow, in 2008. Between 2008 and 2010, he was a project coordinator in the NGO Inter-regional Library Cooperation Centre, a working body of the UNESCO Information For All Programme. Between 2011 and 2020 he has been a lecturer, then associate professor at the Department of the Constitutional and Administrative Law, Law Faculty of the National Research University Higher School of Economics in Moscow. In September 2013, he completed his PhD degree with a thesis entitled "Constitutional Guarantees of the Freedom of Speech and Right to Access the Information on the Internet." In 2019 he was a CyberBRICS research fellow and visiting professor at FGV, Rio de Janeiro, Brazil. His professional interests are related to Russian public law (constitutional and human rights law) with special regard to international principles of internet governance. Among others, he teaches a special course on the human rights of internet users. Since 2010, he has participated in the UN Internet Governance Forum. He writes scholarly monographs and articles on internet governance and human rights on the internet, and he researches current trends in internet regulation in Russia. Also, he translates international sources in that field from English into Russian, like the commented version of the Charter of the Rights and Principles for the Internet.

Nidhi S. Sabharwal

Nidhi S. Sabharwal is an honorary associate professor in the Department of Education Studies at the University of Warwick and an associate professor at the Centre for Policy Research in Higher Education (CPRHE), National Institute of Educational Planning and Administration, New Delhi, India. Previously, Dr. Sabharwal was in charge of the CPRHE and Director of the Indian Institute of Dalit Studies, New Delhi. Dr. Sabharwal has studied intergroup inequalities across human development indicators, focusing on the role of caste and gender in access to market and nonmarket institutions, as well as dimensions of academic freedom and academic corruption.

Nidhi's current research area lies in the access and equity in higher education, with a focus on issues of college readiness, diversity, social inclusion, and academic success of students from socially and economically disadvantaged groups. Her most recent research projects include a multistate study on student diversity and social inclusion, an evaluation study of publicly supported coaching programs in higher education, and modules to sensitize educational administrators and managers on issues related to student diversity and institutional strategies of inclusion in higher education institutions in India. Dr. Sabharwal is a key research partner in a University of Warwick five-year project on gender and higher education in Haryana, India; Co-PI in the University of Warwick-funded project on widening access to higher education in India; and a member of the Lancet Commission on Racism and Child Health. She has published widely on issues pertaining to her research area. Dr. Sabharwal is the coauthor of the Lancet Series on Racism, Xenophobia, Discrimination and Health (The Lancet, 2022), the coauthor of *Caste, Discrimination, and Exclusion in Modern India* (Sage, 2015), coeditor of *Bridging the Social Gap: Perspectives on Dalit Empowerment* (Sage, 2014), coeditor of *India Higher Education Report 2016: Equity in Higher Education* (Sage, 2018), coeditor of *India Higher Education Report 2022: Women in Higher Education* (Routledge, 2023), and coauthor of *Gendering the Massification Generation: Higher Education Access and Choice in India* (Routledge, 2024).

Brigid Freeman

Dr. Brigid Freeman is an academic fellow at the Australia India Institute, University of Melbourne, and recently a visiting professor at the Centre for Policy Research in Higher Education, National Institute of Educational Planning and Administration. Specializing in international comparative research, her focus is on higher education policies and systems, particularly in internationalization, governance, and the impacts of COVID-19. Dr. Freeman's research has extensively examined the educational bilateral relations between Australia and India and closely analyzed STEM policies to inform government policy development. She has also explored humanities research systems in Asia. Her international engagements have led to presentations in numerous countries including Australia, the US, the UK, Sweden,

Germany, Japan, China, India, New Zealand, Papua New Guinea, and Saudi Arabia. Her fieldwork extends to the US, India, Australasia, and Sweden. Her previous roles include faculty research positions at the University of Melbourne's Centre for the Study of Higher Education and visiting scholar positions at the University of Giessen in Germany and the Centre for Studies in Higher Education at the University of California, Berkeley. Dr. Freeman has also consulted for organizations including UNESCO, the Swedish Confederation of Enterprise, as well as Australasian and Middle Eastern universities. She has published widely including *Navigating the Future: A Comparative Analysis of Global STEM Policies and Directions for Sweden* (2024) and *Barriers to Higher Education Qualifications Recognition in India* (Australia India Institute, 2018). She coauthored *Ramifications of COVID-19 for Higher Education Systems and Institutions* (2022), coauthored *Australian-Asian Research Collaborations in the Humanities* (Australian Academy of the Humanities, 2020), and coedited *The Age of STEM: Educational Policy and Practice in STEM Across the World* (Routledge, 2015).

Teng Biao

Teng Biao is Hauser Human Rights Scholar at Hunter College and Deputy Editor-in-Chief of the *China Journal of Democracy*. He had been Pozen Visiting Professor at the University of Chicago and a lecturer at the China University of Politics and Law, Beijing. His research focuses on China's criminal justice, human rights, social movements, and political transition. He cofounded two human rights NGOs in Beijing —the Open Constitution Initiative and China Against the Death Penalty—in 2003 and 2010, respectively. Teng is one of the earliest promoters of the Rights Defense Movement and the New Citizens Movement in China and has received various international human rights awards, including the Human Rights Prize of the French Republic (2007) and the NED's Democracy Award (2008). He is completing a book on China's threat to global freedom and democracy.

Catherine Malanga

Catherine Malanga will receive her BA in Human Rights and Global Studies: Law, Borders, and Security from the University of Chicago in June

2024. While at the University of Chicago, Catherine has engaged in various research projects. She has studied China's transnational repression and global threats to academic freedom while serving as a research assistant to Teng Biao. She completed her BA thesis on Confucius Institutes and their role in US universities' pursuit of academic freedom. Her passion for human rights advocacy led her to intern at the University of Chicago Law School's Federal Criminal Justice Clinic, which engages in systemic reform of the federal criminal system to combat racial and economic inequities. Catherine is passionate about justice and human rights and strives to drive changes locally and globally.

Hani Morgan

Hani Morgan is a professor of education at the University of Southern Mississippi. He earned his doctorate in social and philosophical foundations of education from Rutgers University. Morgan is the author of *The World's Highest-Scoring Students* and the coeditor of *The World Leaders in Education*. He has also authored journal articles and book chapters. In addition to publishing his work, he has presented his research to international, national, and regional organizations, including the American Educational Research Association, the Comparative and International Education Society, and the National Council for Social Studies. Much of his research focuses on how various factors related to the learning environment affect students.

Issac Kamola

Isaac Kamola is an associate professor of political science at Trinity College, Hartford, CT, USA. He is author of *Free Speech and Koch Money: Manufacturing a Campus Culture War* (with Ralph Wilson, 2021) and *Making the World Global: US Universities and the Production of the Global Imaginary* (2019), along with dozens of journal articles and book chapters on the political economy of higher education, critical globalization studies, and African anticolonial theory. He is the creator of Faculty First Responders, a program that monitors right-wing attacks on academics and provides resources to help faculty members and administrators respond to manufactured outrage.

John Fitzgerald

John Fitzgerald is Emeritus Professor at Swinburne University in Melbourne, where he taught in the Asia Pacific philanthropy studies program from 2013 to 2017, and a nonresident senior fellow at the Australian Strategic Policy Institute in Canberra. He served as China Representative of the Ford Foundation in Beijing from 2008 to 2013 and as elected president of the Australian Academy of the Humanities from 2015 to 2017. He has served on the advisory board of the Australian government's Australia-China Council and its National Foundation for Australia-China Relations. His recent books include *Cadre Country: How China Became the Chinese Communist Party* (2022) and (ed.) *Taking the Low Road: China's Influence in Australian States and Territories* (2022). His earlier books include *Big White Lie: Chinese Australians in White Australia* (2007), awarded the Ernest Scott Prize of the Australian Historical Association, and *Awakening China: Politics Culture and Class in the Nationalist Revolution* (1997), awarded the Joseph Levenson Prize of the US-based Association for Asian Studies. He has a PhD from ANU and held a Fulbright postdoctoral fellowship at the University of Wisconsin-Madison. He is a graduate of the University of Sydney.

Kristen Lyons

Professor Kristen Lyons has over twenty-five years of experience in research, teaching, and service that delivers national and international impacts on issues that sit at the intersection of sustainability and development, as well as the future of higher education. Trained as a sociologist, Kristen's work is oriented toward climate and social justice, and in recent years her research has focused on Uganda, the Solomon Islands, India, and Australia. Kristen is also a senior research fellow with the Oakland Institute.

Katarzyna Kaczmarska

Katarzyna Kaczmarska is a senior lecturer in politics and international relations at the School of Social and Political Science, University of Edinburgh. Her research interests center on knowledge construction among scholars and practitioners of international politics and the ways in which the sociopolitical context influences academic knowledge-making and use. She is the author of *Making Global Knowledge in Local Contexts: The Politics of International Relations and Policy Advice in Russia* (Routledge, 2020). Her academic articles were published in *International Studies Review*, *International Relations*, the *Journal of International Relations and Development*, and Problems of Post-*Communism*. She coedited a special issue on academic freedom and internationalisation published in the *International Journal of Human Rights*. In 2021–22, as a Mellon/Scholars at Risk fellow, she researched the strategies of grassroots resistance to academic freedom violations in Russia. With her other project on academic freedom, Katarzyna aims to understand the challenges to academic freedom arising from the move to online teaching and research during the COVID-19 pandemic. Katarzyna is a member of the ISA Academic Freedom Committee, the European Coordinating Committee for Academic Freedom Advocacy, and the Academic Freedom and Internationalisation Working Group, AFIWG. Prior to joining the University of Edinburgh, she was a Marie-Skłodowska Curie fellow at Aberystwyth University and St Petersburg State University. At Edinburgh, she teaches courses on international relations theory, Russian foreign policy, and the politics of knowledge.

Corinne Lennox

Corinne Lennox is a senior lecturer in human rights and Codirector of the Human Rights Consortium at the Institute of Commonwealth Studies in the School of Advanced Study, University of London. Her research focuses on issues of minority and Indigenous peoples' rights, civil society mobilization for human rights, and global governance for human rights. She is Programme Director of the distance-learning MA in Human Rights, University of London, and was recognized as a senior fellow with Advance HE in 2024. She is the author of *Transnational Social Mobilisation and Minority Rights: Identity, Advocacy and Norms* (Routledge, 2020) and coeditor of the *Handbook on Indigenous Peoples' Rights* (Routledge, 2015). She is coeditor of the *Journal of Human Rights Practice* (Oxford University Press) and works closely with civil society organizations including the Dalit Solidarity Network UK, the Tom Lantos Institute, and the Global Centre for Pluralism. She holds a PhD and MSc in international relations from the

LSE, an MA in the theory and practice of human rights from the University of Essex, and a BA (hons.) in political science from McMaster University, Canada.

Christopher Brink

Professor Chris Brink is Emeritus Vice-Chancellor (President) of Newcastle University in England, former rector of Stellenbosch University in South Africa, and former pro vice-chancellor (research) of the University of Wollongong in Australia. Earlier he was Head of Mathematics and Coordinator for Strategic Planning at the University of Cape Town and a senior research fellow at the Australian National University. He was Convenor of the sectorwide Research Assessment Exercise 2020 in Hong Kong and currently convenes RAE 2026. Chris Brink is known as a champion of the idea of a civic university. His books include *The Soul of a University: Why Excellence Is Not Enough* and *The Responsive University and the Crisis in South Africa*. Before entering university management, he held the A rating of the National Research Foundation. He is a logician with a Cambridge PhD, an interdisciplinary DPhil, a master's degree in mathematics and philosophy, and a bachelor's degree in computer science. He has served in an advisory or assessment capacity for various universities and organizations and contributed to a number of international executive leadership programs in higher education.

Chavan Kissoon

Chavan Sharma Kissoon is a lecturer in digital education at the University of Lincoln. His research is on the sociology of higher education, technologies of governance, academic labor, academic freedom, and the future of work. Chavan's research interests revolve around the sociology of digital technologies, with a particular focus on how power is mediated through technological mechanisms in contemporary society. He has published on the impact of Industry 4.0 technologies on workplaces and the university curriculum. He has also published on the impact of worker management practices related to zero-hour contracts on how student-workers experience work. He is currently researching the relationship between learning metrics and student attainment outcomes. As a digital education specialist, Chavan has been involved in and led a range of innovative digital education projects, including the institutional rollout and evaluation of multiple learning technologies at the University of Lincoln.

Terence Karran

Terence Karran is Emeritus Professor of Higher Education Policy in the School of Education at the University of Lincoln, UK. He is also a docent professor in education technology at the Faculty of Education at Oulu University in Finland. From 2005 to 2007, he was a visiting professor of educational technology at the Autonomous University of Guadalajara in Mexico, where he undertook work with the World Bank Institute's Global Development Learning Network for Latin America and the Caribbean. His previous research publications focused on elearning and the European Credit Transfer System. His current research specialism is academic freedom in higher education, focusing on the de jure and de facto rights associated with academic freedom in the UK and the EU states and also in the US. In connection with his work on academic freedom, he recently undertook a nationwide survey on academic freedom for the University and College Union, the largest professional association in the UK representing higher education academic personnel. He is a member of the Executive Committee of the UK's Council for the Defence of the British Universities.

Index

J

K

N

O

P

Q

R

T